KEEPING MY HEAD

GW00472236

HARRY WICKS

KEEPING MY HEAD

THE MEMOIRS OF A BRITISH BOLSHEVIK

Socialist Platform Ltd

Published by Socialist Platform Ltd on behalf of Logie Barrow
Copyright © 1992 Logie Barrow

Typeset by voluntary labour
Printed and bound in Britain by BPCC Wheatons Ltd

ISBN 0 9508423 8 9

Socialist Platform Ltd, BCM 7646, London WC1N 3XX

Contents

Introduction

SINCE 1989, almost all 'Socialist' regimes have sagged and collapsed amid the contempt and joy of their peoples. Under this impact, many opinion-formers even on the 'left' have given Socialism up. 'Goodbye to all that' is their motto: Socialism of any kind was a world-wide mistake. Curiously, many such leave-takers had long prided themselves on having seen through Stalinism. Plainly, though, what they had not seen through was the elitism of which Stalinism was merely the most consistent version after Fascism.

Goodbye to all – what? Harry Wicks had spent nearly six decades answering this question from his own experience, that is, from a uniquely varied number of angles. So there is irony that he happened to die suddenly a mere six or so months before the hollowness of Europe's not-so-ex-Stalinist regimes became undeniable on all sides. Harry was a mainly self-taught worker who was not afraid to work among intellectuals and parties, but who never stopped learning to defend his independence. Hence the title I have given his book.

Some big chunks of this are certain to hook particular readerships. One of the most obvious candidates is his vivid account of the years 1927-30 which he spent at Moscow's International Lenin School, being supposedly moulded into a Stalinist super-cadre of international calibre. In Moscow and over much of the European part of the Soviet Union, his insights underlined suspicions that had struck him and a handful of his closest friends among the Young Communists of Battersea, South London, since the mid-1920s. Not least, he experienced the increasingly total party manipulation of the Soviet working class, and the inner disengagement or cynicism with which many workers responded. Back home, the CPGB's sectarianisation, in which most comrades had, willingly or not, been participating for two or more years, was concentrated for him into as many weeks. While at Comintern gatherings, Harry had witnessed the ratification of the Third Period line which had accelerated and ratified this process, and had been struck by the lowered level of debate at them. We are not being unhistorical in imagining that the collapse of 'Communism' would have shocked the Harry of 1931 fundamentally less than it has today's not-so-ex-Stalinists. For 1931 was the year in which he found himself among the founders of British Trotskyism, mainly for trying to warn British workers that Third Period policies were helping to bring Hitler to power. After January 1933, the threat of Nazism and, later, its defeat along with the tremendous sacrifices involved in achieving this, were to overwhelm generations of left intellectuals and others into taking the

Soviet Union not merely as a gigantic World Fact but, even more important, as an unquestionable one. This was never his mistake.

The crucial price of that kind of 'internationalism' which Trotskyists opposed was silence on the oppression and manipulation of countless working classes by Stalinism. During the 1930s, such 'internationalism' also isolated Harry and the handful of Trotskyists agitating forlornly against the Moscow Trials. To this day, the deafening silences of Stalinist 'internationalism' have helped guarantee that the one thing Socialist ideas do **not** mean to most working people anywhere is that the powerless seize power to reshape the world. From Leningrad to Daghestan, Harry observed some of the fruits of this disempowerment, miscalled empowerment. From then until now, the not-so-ex-Stalinist version of internationalism has aided regimes in what until 1989 were called East and West to play their working classes against each other. The ideological smog which most of us have grown up breathing is so obvious, that we forget how weird its chemistry has always been. It meant asking Lenin's fundamental question – **who** is oppressing **whom?** – about some parts of the globe, but not others. It meant condoning oppression under some regimes because they claimed to be liberatory, but jumping up and down about oppression elsewhere if it suited the interests of those regimes. You called a spade a flying saucer there, but a spade here. Understandably, nearly all victims of condoned oppressions are now keen to risk almost any other mistake – and some of them perhaps to commit almost any other crime.

Our generations are now tempted more than ever to respond to this world historic mess by ignoring its origins, saying 'goodbye' and walking away. This would be a rational response were there anywhere to walk to. If capitalism is **reformably** exploitative, sexist, genocidal and planet-ocidal, then by all decorous means let us tame this incontinent but sometimes cuddly old tiger claw by claw. After all, since the 1940s this system's flexibilities have surprised even most of its defenders. But we have only to look around us to see that these flexibilities have not changed its basic mode of operation. We must therefore work our utmost to undo the mess before too late. Lives such as Harry's prove we were anything but latecomers to the task. Even more important, they give us a few indications how to set about it.

But even this is not the only concern to which this book speaks loud and clear. Trotskyists and historians of their movement will be rivetted not only by Harry's chapters on 1927-30, and on his part in the Balham Group which founded it, but also by his full though of course briefer account of his meeting with Trotsky in Copenhagen of 1932. Unforgettably, he portrays the pressures brought on these Trotskyists, hurriedly gathered from all corners of Europe and further afield. Understandably, such pressures took their toll, occasionally inducing a paranoia which, with hindsight, was not so much unnecessary as merely premature. Nonetheless, crucial discussions were held. Harry was also Natalia Trotsky's bodyguard on the podium whilst Leon gave to the Social Democratic students of Copenhagen what was to be his last public speech.

For a mass of readers, Harry's book will be simply unputdownable for its sheer range of witness. One way of symbolising this is simply to list alphabetically some of those he heard speak: Belfort Bax, Bukharin, Charlotte Despard, CLR James, Kautsky, Lansbury, Larkin, Arthur MacManus, Tom Mann, Molotov, Sylvia Pankhurst, Shapurji Saklatvala, Henry Sara, Ernst Thälmann, Palmiro Togliatti, Bonar Thompson, Trotsky and many others will figure in this book.

Each of these aspects would by itself make Harry's book extremely rare. All of them together make it unique.

For me, though, its chief value lies in two qualities which Harry also possessed personally. From his teens, he was simultaneously a highly organised member of the manual (later, of the white collar) working class and, into his final week, he was a quietly but fiercely independent intellectual. Possibly, these two notes of his life were sometimes in tension but always, sooner or later, how fruitfully!

The very richness of his political activities around the interwar decades has yielded us an unequalled account of the labour movement in Battersea (a then overwhelmingly working class part of London) in all its strands. We can watch their interweavings and unravellings under the pressures of world war, depression, general strike and the sectarianism of the Labour right and of Third Period Communism. But this book is not a member of that irreplaceable genre, the 'what-I-did-in' type of autobiography, fascinating though Harry's part in major events often was. Far more important, Harry has somehow managed to give us a sense of how much people's room for manoeuvre varied from stage to stage in their struggles: a sense, for example, of how it felt to be a young working class man, open to a potentially muddling range of influences – feminist as well as Bolshevik, trade unionist as well as vegetarian, jazz-loving as well as SPGB.

Most fundamental of all, he gives us a past unusually like the present. By this, I do not mean that the world of, say, the Battersea of the late 1910s, the Caucasus of the late 1920s, or the isolated and near-starving British Trotskyists of the mid-1930s bears many or any direct similarity with our current problems. I mean something all too easily overlooked. There are always those for whom the present seems as clearly mapped as a system of tramlines, and the past as foggy as prehistory. Such people are obviously prone to lurch incoherently from dogma to dogma. There are others for whom the past possesses a clear simplicity which contrasts enviably with the present. On the left, such people often become labour historians (as I once did). But there are also some, of whom Harry is exemplary, who recognise the present as not essentially more muddling than the past once was, and who can yet show how movements and individuals developed amid everything.

Until his sudden death, Harry retained a priceless ability to relate the convictions and uncertainties of the present to those he had experienced up to 70 years earlier. Though he could also remember what old timers had related, over a cheap beer, about their and even their parents' experiences back into the middle nineteenth century, his was never a 'voice from the past'. Not only was he well aware that memory can play tricks, more important, he was always casting a critical eye at the very long present day of his, and sometimes earlier lives, and making them ours. For he devoted less energy than most of us do to gazing at the little pile of truths he had acquired, firmly though he defended it.

∴   ∴   ∴

As explained in my Editor's Note at the start of Chapter Seven, Harry had worked over and approved every word up to that point, that is, to the end of the Copenhagen episode. Readers will therefore be surprised that the pages after Copenhagen are so similar in style to the others. What blending of voices – his and mine – has occurred? I set out the history of the project in that note. When we began, I was Harry's transcriber: a hearing of our cassettes will surely confirm my memory that, however voluble or irrelevant my interruptions, he controlled the agenda of each session. Aware as I was that my ideas of grammar risked deforming his meaning, I tried to transcribe his words as literally as possible. It is for linguists to judge whether I was naive. What hurt both of us at the time, though, was his disclosure, some weeks after he had received my first batch of transcripts, that their literalness had intensified in him an old despair at what he called his 'bad language'. No doubt some historian of linguistic oppression is going to find something significant in so independent a self-taught man being so paralysed by such old wounds. But I am convinced that this is the reason why our project stalled during the late 1970s after the transcribing stage was virtually over.

A decade later, I tried to follow the transcribed words as faithfully as possible, whilst often filtering them through my own sentence structures. I also inserted some linking phrases or slightly longer passages. As detailed in the note, Harry was always closely in control of each paragraph, and was enthusiastic about the final version of each of the first six chapters. I am the last to be able to say how successful we have been. Readers with time are welcome to check the cassettes, transcripts and other documents which will be deposited, on publication of this book, at Warwick University's Modern Records Centre, as Harry had often suggested.

The pages after Copenhagen pose a more directly political problem. Although Harry had tens of pages of transcriptions dealing with the post-1932 years, he had never worked on them very much. I am convinced he would never have quoted as much as I have from publications and leaflets with which he had been associated. True, he had assembled all of these in connection with this chapter, but surely as no more than triggers for his memory. I am convinced all the more so because, more than once during the late 1980s, he mentioned to me that he now felt the position he and his comrades had taken on the Second World War had 'owed too much to the lessons of the First'. He always led me to expect a full explanation some time soon. Now it will never come. Frequently, I curse my patience.

I owe heartfelt thanks to Christine Weber for her tireless help via her word processor, to Sue and Reg Wicks for innumerable kinds of help, to Dietrich Beyrau for confirming that Harry's chapter on 1927-30 is indeed of major importance also to various species of specialist, and – last only in time – to the comrades of *Revolutionary History* for their wide-ranging editorial and biographical beaverings which are continuing as I write.

Logie Barrow
1 June 1992

Chapter 1
Growing up in Battersea

ACROSS the River Thames from Chelsea was the working class district of Battersea. Power stations, paint and candle factories, chemical and engineering works, railway engine sheds, flour mills, plumbago and gas works lined the three miles of riverside from Vauxhall to Wandsworth Bridge. Separated only by the width of a road were densely-populated streets of working class houses, where women, many of whom took in washing from across the river, battled daily against the grime belched from those riverside factories.

So Battersea was a densely populated working class borough, its eastern boundary less than three miles from Parliament Square. It was famed not only for its Dogs' Home, but also as a cradle of working class politics. In the 1860s Garibaldi, Italy's revolutionary democrat, had steamed, in a flag-bedecked train, into Nine Elms Station (which was then the terminus of the London and Southampton Railway) to be greeted by the rapturous welcome of 200 000 London workers, many of them behind union banners. In 1892 John Burns, known for his leadership of the London dock strike, three years previously, as 'The Man with the Red Flag', had become the MP for the constituency. He was to hold it till he retired in 1918. He used to claim that he put Battersea on the map. But, long after 1906 when he had renounced his Socialism for a place in the Liberal cabinet of Campbell Bannerman, the working people of Battersea continued to be in the forefront of advanced opinion. This borough was my home town, its streets my playground, its workers my teachers.

When I was five, in 1910, my father left the railway service and became employed by the Battersea Borough Council in their stables as a strapper. His job was to get to work at four o'clock in the morning to prepare the cart horses for their daily labour. What beautiful creatures they were; chestnut, white and black and some dapple grey, well groomed, even their hooves polished, all made ready for pulling the dust, water and sewerage carts round the streets of Battersea. My father was proud of those horses. Once a year there would be a horse show in Regents Park, an event we looked forward to as a family treat. For that occasion, my mother used to make rosettes, whilst my father busied himself polishing what seemed to us children an enormous heap of brassware.

On May Day the borough council, which had a 'progressive' majority – left wing Liberals really – let the carmen take the horses and carts on the May Day procession and meeting. The meeting was at Queen's Circus, near the Chelsea Bridge end of Battersea Park, and was addressed by trade union and Socialist speakers. All the men employed at the stables belonged to the London Carmen's Trade Union. I was considered too young to go to the meeting, but my brother, who was six years older, used to go with my father on the water cart.

We lived in Lombard Road, directly opposite the stables which backed on to the River Thames. As a boy, I knew those stables well, the farrier shop, where Mr Palmer used to hammer out the horseshoes on his anvil, fascinated me. Those stables were of a solid brick construction, and the horses were housed by means of a long ramp upstairs and downstairs. Crazy as it seems now, those stables served as our air raid shelter in the First World War. When the maroons at the local fire station sounded the air raid warning, the carmen's wives and children, whose husbands and fathers were away in the army, hurried to the stables for shelter in an empty horse box – an early lesson in the herd instinct.

My memories of the First World War are vivid, the constant interruptions in my schooling, taking my turn in the food queues, first for potatoes, then margarine, and the job I really detested most, pushing an old pram all the way to Falcon Wharf, Clapham Junction, in the hope of being able to buy 14 or 28 pounds of coal. With my father and brother away in the forces, my mother had to make do somehow on a niggardly army allowance, for herself, me, my adopted sister and my baby sister. (Curiously or not, she recalled later that my father's motivation for joining up in 1915 had been that the separation allowance would leave us better off than if he had stayed at his council job.) From the age of 11, I soon learnt the art of supplementing the family budget. I did a milk delivery round in the morning before school, and in the evenings and all day Saturday I worked in a shop.

In July 1918 the all too familiar telegraph boy delivered to our house the dreaded telegram – my father had died in a military hospital in Kantara, Egypt.

The last memory I have of my father is during his embarkation leave. We were all dressed in our Sunday best to go to the photographers for a family photograph. After that we were off to visit my grandfather (my mother's father) for tea. Grandfather lived in Doddington Grove, Battersea, which was a little street with cottages either side. Before his front door there was a porch with trellis work, plants growing and seats each side. Whilst my grandfather and dad sat talking in the front porch, I helped to feed the chickens in the back garden. A high tea marked the end of a happy day. But the eyes of my grandfather were moist as he said farewell. 'I'll look after them Fred', was the last thing he said, and I realised that this was a parting of two friends.

Often I sat in that same porch listening to the stories of my grandfather's life and work. He had been a navvy in the building trade (a labourer employed excavating the ground). Navvies were strong men, wearing corduroy trousers with straps at the knees where they kept their shovel scrapers. He had travelled widely and worked in America on railway excavation and construction. In his little parlour was a trunk that he had taken with him to the States. 'If that box could only talk', he used to say, and I knew he was about to spin another yarn about the fame of the British navvy. I learnt from him that there is a skill even in so-called unskilled labour. To be able by economy of movement and turn of the wrist to make the maximum impression with the minimum of effort on a cubic yard of soil was the test of a skilled labourer. Once he told me that he had worked on the foundations of the original Crystal Palace.

The navvy's enemy was seeping clay and water. Tons of earth could move without warning, a cave-in was an ever-present danger. He himself had been injured at work, which explained his shorter leg. He was a member of the navvies' union and had been compensated for his accident. He died within a year of my father.

When my dad went away to the war, he left us his two prize possessions. One was his service medal, received as a youth in the Royal Marines on HMS Philomel, for service in the Benin Expedition of 1897. A vague memory persists of him telling us of his early adventures on the West Coast of Africa. A white man's graveyard he called it. The aim, according to him, had been to destroy the last stronghold of the slave trade. Whether that was jingo propaganda of the time, I have yet to learn; what I do know for certain was that that medal was silver and could be pawned. I never failed to be intrigued by the pawnbroker, particularly by his gadget of a pen with two nibs, which enabled him to write two identical tickets at the same time. One ticket he would keep, and the other he would pass over the counter with the odd shilling. My father's other prize possession was his trade union sash, in blue velvet with silver embroidery and lettering which read: 'Presented to Bro FR Wicks by the Bros as a mark of respect for his past services to No 25 Branch of the London Carmens' Trade Union.' My brother had the medal, I still treasure that sash.

From the moment of that telegram, the desire foremost in my mind was to finish with school and get to work to help mum. Another whole year to wait. I was already in the top class, known at that time as ex-seventh, which meant another year of doing the same lessons or running the teachers' errands. I remember well my impatience to leave school and to start work.

At last the day came:

'All boys who will become 14 years of age before the commencement of the new school term in September are to report to the headmaster's study immediately after school assembly.'

We knew it: we were going to get our school 'character' or reference.

All smiles, feeling really happy, I hurried along to be given the sealed envelope to take to my mother. At that time, school references had something special about them, they were thought to be a passport to a good job. I ran all the way home, happy as a sandboy, as they used to say. Pleased to see me excited and so happy, my mother opened the envelope and started to read. I can only remember one sentence of the contents: 'His interest in the value of school was distracted by outside employment.' She was furious. A hurried bite to eat and back we went to school to await the headmaster's return from lunch. 'What sort of reference is that to take to his first employer?', she demanded to know. Reluctantly I witnessed her giving old Chaloner, the headmaster, a piece of her mind. As I learnt afterwards, it was a storm over nothing; school references, good or bad, did not provide any golden openings to a working boy of 14.

My formal education ended in stirring times. First, there were street peace parties and jollifications, and then other kinds of excitement took over. One of Battersea's main shopping streets, St John's Road, was blocked daily by discharged servicemen registering for employment. One old comrades' association held daily meetings and marches through the streets asking the same rhetorical question: 'Where is the land fit for heroes?' I was drawn to those meetings and marches as to a magnet. Those early unemployed speakers seemed to be expressing my innermost thoughts. The privation of the war years, our struggle for bare necessities, the loss of my father, the tireless efforts of my mother – all to what purpose?

In Battersea at least, the aftermath of the war soon brought a tremendous resentment against war itself and the losses and miseries it entailed. This atmosphere was intensified by fear associated with the influenza epidemic. As a child, one had got accustomed to funerals involving black coffins, black mourning and so on. But, in the epidemic, coffins were reduced to simple wooden affairs made from deal, and mourners clad themselves in almost any colour, mauve or whatever, other than the traditional black.

Another part of the horror – not too strong a word – was the rabies scare, which we associated with all those military animals coming home from France and elsewhere. In London during 1918, all dogs had to wear muzzles, it was an offence to have a dog on the street unmuzzled. As I mentioned, I used to work part time while still at school. One of my workplaces was RW Beard's leather goods shop in Falcon Road. Beard's stocked these wire muzzles for dogs. And when stocks ran out, I would be sent running around to different parts of London to try and find new stock. On one of these trips, I took the 19 bus to Hatton Garden where I had to pick up this consignment of muzzles. With my mind somewhat on this, I was dumbfounded to see, near that firm, men standing on the corners with paper tissues in their hands. They were holding up diamonds and trading them, something I had never before dreamt of.

At this time, I began to develop a consuming interest in social history. History became more intense and more understandable than it had ever been at school. The general atmosphere of horror added to a head of growing resentment which was to express itself in the general elections of 1922, 1923 and 1924. I remember the delight of old Mr Lavey, the dustman who lived next door to us, when the Labour Party captured control of the borough council in November 1919. 'That's rubbed out Mrs Despard's defeat', he shouted excitedly to my mother. Charlotte Despard had been the Labour candidate in the parliamentary election of 1918 just a year before. Her name seemed to recur constantly. The affection felt for her by so many registered in my mind.

I chanced to find out more about her via my job. Possibly because my father had been a railwayman, and two of his brothers still were, I was told by the Brighton railway company to go to London Bridge and have an eyetest. In September or October 1919, during the interval between that and my actually starting, the great railway strike occurred. At least one of my uncles had been heavily involved in the 1911 strike (when troops with busbies and bayonets were guarding Clapham North signalbox). They were involved now, I saw them in a railwaymen's procession that passed me to Clapham Common for a meeting. So, I was going into that! And, as soon as I did start work, my uncles took me down to the branch of the National Union of Railwaymen (NUR) and had me join. Since, during my initial period as a signalbox boy, I was earning a mere five shillings for a 48 hour week, they paid my sixpence a week subscription for me.

Now during my early years on the railway, I had the good fortune to work with a signalman, Harry Manning, in Victoria South signalbox. It was a busy box; three signalmen operating it in the morning and late shifts. But, during late evenings and especially on our Sunday turns, we had some quiet spells, and Harry would talk then about his Socialist convictions. He was a tall, bearded man, who always wore a red tie. He was known and respected by most of the railwaymen passing that signalbox. He had been Secretary of the Battersea branch of the Independent Labour Party as far back as 1910, the red tie had been a sort of mark of ILPers. His reminiscences about Battersea and its politics always fascinated me.

It was he who explained the popularity of Charlotte Despard. She was a member of his ILP branch and, in 1910, attended that party's eighteenth conference as the Battersea delegate. Her experience in the slums of Battersea had radicalised her totally from her Irish Protestant landowning background. (Her brother, Sir John French, became a top general.) She was already widely known for her propaganda on women's suffrage and for her abiding concern to end British domination in Ireland and in India. At that conference she was chosen to second the resolution on India moved by Keir Hardie. The struggle against British domination in Ireland and India was her consuming passion. At the height of the Independence War in Ireland, when the Black and Tan terror was so nakedly displayed, she stood in the Republican Connolly tradition, four square with the oppressed. Saklatvala, the Indian Communist MP for North Battersea in 1922 and 1924-29 was never to have a more devoted and influential supporter than Charlotte Despard.

The Irish struggle was an integral part of the politics of the Battersea labour movement. That was not surprising, since there was a large Irish population in the Nine Elms district of the borough. The area across the Dogs' Home bridge leading to Vauxhall was known as 'Irish Island'. In mean little streets of terraced houses sandwiched between the gasworks and railway engine sheds, a militant Irish working class had made their homes. It was there, in the very heart of the slums, that Mrs Despard established her house and built her base. Despite their Catholicism, the people of that district were always in the forefront of the labour struggles. When the police strikes occurred in 1918-19, it was the Nine Elms railwaymen, to the consternation of their union executive, who threatened sympathetic strike action. Ironically, seven years later, on the last day of the General Strike, in the synchronised police action against striking workers, it was these very Nine Elms railwaymen that were so savagely attacked by the Special Constabulary.

After the setting up of the Free State in 1921 and the crushing of the Republicans in the Four Courts, Mrs Despard returned from her vigils outside Mountjoy Prison to a heroine's welcome. Her triumphal homecoming procession through the streets of Battersea remains vivid in my memory. Wearing a long grey dress and a bonnet, she stood in an open car, waving to the cheering crowds lining the pavements. The marchers, headed by the St Joseph's school band, wound through the streets to Battersea Town Hall, where old George Lansbury addressed the crowd on the return of Battersea's Socialist warrior.

Earlier, the very first demonstration I took part in, shortly after my fifteenth birthday, was the protest march to Brixton Prison, where Terence MacSwiney was on hunger strike. MacSwiney was the Lord Mayor of Cork, an Irish Republican and member of the Dail, the illegal parliament. He was sentenced to two years' imprisonment for being in possession of a police cypher and of papers likely to cause disaffection. He began his fast at once on 12 August, a fast that lasted to his death in Brixton Prison on 25 October 1920. As those days and weeks passed, a flood of protest welled up.

At that time, I was working in Longhedge Junction signalbox, in the dip away from the main line, that directed goods traffic from the south to the Midland, North Western and Great Western railway systems. It was a vital railway link, on the very edge of Nine Elms. That box was a political forum. Platelayers, signalmen linesmen and railwaymen who had small allotments on the railway embankment used to meet there for a talk and a brew-up. No working class boy had a better university. With MacSwiney on hunger strike, what was happening in Ireland became the main topic of discussion. Those railwaymen belonged to different NUR branches, and exchanged opinions about a forthcoming demonstration and march to Brixton Prison. I decided to go.

On Clapham Common, behind the pond, there used to be a great cinderpatch. It was known widely as the meeting ground. Many generations of Socialist agitators have spoken there. This was the assembly point for the great march to Brixton Prison. Trade union and Socialist banners, Nine Elms NUR with a big contingent, the green, white and orange Republican flags that I saw for the first time, the lilt of Irish songs (*Wrap the green flag round me*), the vast numbers including so many young girls and women, all this stirred and enthused me. A nerve seemed to vibrate in my stomach.

Yet there was something about that exciting day that I did not understand. When the demonstration was halted, somewhere in the vicinity of the prison, the young girls and women knelt on the ground in prayer, fingering beads around their necks and hands. After such a great protest, such a wonderful feeling of unity and strength, it was beyond my comprehension to end on one's knees! I had a lot to learn. When MacSwiney finally died, all the papers, Tory and Liberal, expressed their shock and their respect for his courage. How bitterly scornful of such hypocrisy were the railwaymen in my signalbox.

I can't recall whether it was before or after MacSwiney's death that General Sir Henry Wilson was assassinated in Pimlico, but when the assassin was due to be hanged, I stood in the small crowd of sympathisers outside Wandsworth Prison on the morning of his execution. The gold hands of the prison clock moved inexorably to the appointed hour of execution. A minute or two before eight o'clock, an eerie silence, broken only by a muffled sob, fell on that prison forecourt. After a short interval, the heavy prison gates opened and a warder posted the notice stating that the hanging had been carried out and the prisoner had been certified dead.

Often my thoughts returned to those two separate experiences. The loneliness of one man's martyrdom in comparison with the other. Each in his own way was striking a blow for Irish independence, but MacSwiney's struggle stirred the labour movement and raised a banner for tens of thousands to see, whilst the individual act of terrorism produced not a ripple. There was no room for doubt, the road that wakened masses in a common experience of struggle produced more power and force than an assassin's bullet.

A year later, in the autumn of 1921, there was another march to

Brixton Prison, this time in a proud and defiant mood. The Labour Council of Poplar in the East End, led by George Lansbury, was imprisoned for contempt of court. They had refused to pay the county council precept as a protest against the saddling of local authorities with the burden of poor relief. Government policy was that the more impoverished councils, with the higher numbers of unemployed requiring poor relief, should be required to provide this relief out of their own resources. The message was clear, finance your own poverty, don't expect the royal and prosperous boroughs to share the burden.

Poplar's action was a challenge both to the government and to the Conservative London County Council. It roused working class London. Lansbury's plea at his court hearing, 'Guilty and proud of it!', echoed through the East End and beyond. Labour councils debated the issue. By a majority of one, Battersea Council voted against taking similar action, but recorded support for Poplar. This issue, particularly the imprisonment of the Poplar Labour councillors, brought thousands on the streets in nightly marches to Brixton Prison.

One such march stands out in my memory. We were a vast crowd, tightly packed in a street facing the prison walls. The leader on that occasion was an ex-police striker, sandy-haired, with an impressive physique and a deep stentorian voice. Some women brought out a kitchen table for him to stand on. He had no easy task to get that vast crowd perfectly quiet so that he could throw his voice high over those prison walls and converse with Lansbury and his comrades. There were no loudspeakers in that day. It was getting dark. In hushed stillness we heard the voice of Lansbury come over the night air. Following greetings of solidarity and relayed news of the mounting campaign outside, Lansbury's throaty voice could be heard leading the singing of the *Red Flag*. This inspiringly defiant ending contrasted so sharply with the earlier memory of the MacSwiney demonstration.

That exercise in political mobilisation brought a hasty government retreat. Not only were the Poplar councillors released from prison, but the government introduced a measure to even up the anomalies between rich and poor metropolitan boroughs. In the movement at the time, wherever unemployment and poverty lay heavy on the conscience, the campaign of the Poplar councillors was hailed as a victory. Not so in the upper leadership of the Labour Party. Poplarism, as it was termed, smelt too strongly of unconstitutional action.

Listening to speeches and discussions at such an early age sharpened my awareness of my own social environment. The childhood of my schoolmates, the worklife of our parents, the factories around us, the inadequacy of my education, all came clearly into focus. I noticed that my mates usually followed in their father's footsteps as bricklayers or railwaymen or whatever. But, in 1920-21, large numbers in Battersea were stepping out for the St John's Road Labour Exchange. Even for school leavers, work was difficult to come by. To struggle together for a better life made sense to me. Encouraged by the signalmen I worked with, I joined the Battersea Herald League. It was there that I met Jack Clancy and Raymond Postgate, both of whom influenced my life. They more than anyone else opened up the world of historical literature for me. And I became an avid reader.

But I am racing ahead. Inspiring though I found my own introduction into the labour movement (and there was much more to it yet), I must not now let it telescope my early years. No baby has yet come out of the womb spouting labour history.

My childhood had been a happy one. Ours was a home where children were welcomed, encouraged and played with. The only other home environment I experienced was when my mother would put a label round me, still a tiny kid, stick me in a guard's van at Clapham Junction, and, in this way, send me off to Frimley in Surrey to stay with her brothers and her grandmother. Frimley was like another world, not only from a child's point of view, but also from an adult's. I can remember one of my uncles using a scythe for harvesting.

But I did have more than my fair share of illness. At the age of eight, I fell ill with meningitis, and could not bear the light. So the room blinds were drawn all day. Whether meningitis was then notifiable and therefore subject to isolation puzzles me to this day, but what is remembered by my family is that I was nursed at home by my mother. At that time my eldest sister used to take a bowl all the way to Carlo and Gatti's ice factory near the Albert Bridge to buy ice for my waterproof pillow.

As I grew up hearing the family gossip about that illness, I could hardly fail to be interested in Carlo and Gatti's ice factory. The workers who were employed there were Italians. At that time, there was a small Italian colony living in Hyde Lane and Winstead Street. Big men in blue jerseys, they drove their carts round London to the hotels with great blocks of ice which they handled so expertly with large callipers. Those workers seemed a very closed community. In the early 1920s, days of great political excitement in North Battersea, they stood aloof, they were never attracted into the labour movement. Yet at that time we were great internationalists. We had an Indian member of parliament, a Liverpool-born Jamaican as a former mayor of the borough, a fistful of Irishmen as councillors, and in our socials could sing *Bandiera Rosa* (the Italian equivalent of the *Red Flag*). The only outstanding Italian we had in the borough was old Scala, the owner of the coffee shop opposite Battersea Park railway station, and he was outstanding because he had once won the Irish Sweepstake.

That illness of mine had lasted for some time, and there was no provision then for doctors except by paying. But there was a doctor in Falcon Road named Bean, and my mother really loved him. She depended on him coming to treat me, and although then there was no money to pay him, Dr Bean had never worried my parents for the money. But after that experience, my mother had joined what was known as the Battersea Dispensary. There, for the payment of some coppers weekly, you got medicine when you were ill. That Battersea People's Dispensary used to be situated at the corner of Battersea High Street and York Road, a Battersea landmark known as 'The Princes Head'.

The development of the railways into London in the second half of the nineteenth century had transformed Battersea from a riverside village into a compact industrial borough. In 1837 the streets had clustered round the parish church of St Mary's and the occupations of the inhabitants revealed a rural scene, cowherdsmen, blacksmiths, barge builders, millers, etc. But by the time of the 1891 census, the Battersea parish had 13 541 inhabited houses with a population of 97 204. That parish was roughly the same as what subsequently became the North Battersea parliamentary division. The main artery was the River Thames. But it was railway expansion that was dramatically to turn the tables on a rural scene. Connecting inner London with the south meant spanning the Thames from Battersea by two railway bridges; no less than 13 bridges were built to cross major roads. In the age of the private railway company, there were three locomotive depots, three goodsyards and a carriage marshalling yard. Miles of brick viaducts rose above the low-lying terrace houses.

By the early 1880s the local registrar of births and deaths was recording the occupations of fathers as engineers, gas stokers, bricklayers, railwaymen, factory hands and builders' labourers. A migration to London from Ireland and South and South West England supplied an expanding industry with their labour. The social and industrial pattern of Battersea had become established.

The skilled workers such as engineers, train drivers, railway signalmen, print and Post Office workers formed a sizeable segment of the growing population. But the most numerous were the factory hands and those employed in the building trades. Amongst the building trade operatives were the craftsmen, the bricklayers, carpenters and stonemasons, who, like their labourers, were periodically hit by the prevailing poverty. Those trades suffered acutely, both from the seasonal vagaries of the weather and recurrent commercial crisis. It was from those trades that the Battersea Social Democratic Federation (SDF) found their most consistent leaders and readiest audience.

Our home in Lombard Road backed on to Walls' sausage factory. My mother's friend used to live three doors away and used to do all the washing for the men who worked there. The way that woman had to work! All the men employed in the factory had white coats which got smothered in fat. Every week she washed those coats, dried and ironed them and then delivered them round the corner in Holman Road. They were boiled in the copper bath, but there was a problem with the drying. The backyard could not be used because, a few yards away, was the electric power station that was serviced by an overhead coal conveyor from the river wharf. On windy days it rained coal dust. Further along the road was Prices' candle factory, noted for its smell that impregnated everything. Poor Mrs Gilbert overcame the problem by drying everything indoors. Washing used to be strung along the passages right up the stairs and on the top landing. Coal fires were alight, winter and summer. She had three sons, all mates of mine, and when I went in her house her constant cry was: 'Mind the washing!'

But I also have gentler memories of Walls' sausage factory. I remember the slim brown horses which used to stand in Holman Road while the carts were loaded with sausages and pies to be delivered all over London and parts of Surrey. I took daily pleasure in watching those horses, but, one day during the First World War, I stood on the gantry by Lombard Road Cottages and watched while the army commandeered them all for the war. A second feature of that factory was a communal kitchen where broken pies were sold cheap. During the war, meat became scarcer and we used to be able to buy a jug of soup for a few pennies.

Dad's payday, to most of us, had meant a weekly treat, a visit to 'the pictures', or something special to eat. Friday nights' delight was fish and chips. The fishmonger in York Road used to cater for those days by selling halfpenny tailpieces for the children. A treat that stands in my mind was a visit to the Washington Picture House with my father. The picture we saw was *The Broken Coin* with Eddy Polo and Pearl White trapped in an underground cave full of skulls and skeletons. Did they escape? I still don't know, the film was a serial and finished at the most exciting moment. That was the only instalment of *The Broken Coin* I ever saw.

On pay days in the late afternoon, the carmen's wives used to wait outside the stables for their men to hand them money to get the evening meal. The main entrance had a wide-spanned arch, and, under it, a narrow kerb served to protect the horses from rubbing themselves against the brickwork. Halfway through was a little office window through which a man with a stiff collar used to hand all the carmen their wages. I had often stood there holding father's hand, enchanted by the scene. As each man received his wages, a golden sovereign and a half sovereign, he bent down to that narrow kerb before the window and bounced his coins, to make sure they were not counterfeits.

Further along Lombard Road, at the corner of Vicarage Crescent, was Odell's the barge builder. Adjoining was a small recreation ground, a quarter of an acre in size, originally reclaimed from the mud flats. It was constructed by the vestry, the forerunner of the borough council. A private contractor had started the project but went broke during the economic slump of the mid-1880s. Inspired by the Social Democratic Federation, the local unemployed had demonstrated to the vestry to let them complete the job. This became Battersea's first essay in direct labour (a department that was to last nearly 100 years).

As a youngster, I had known that recreation ground well, small lawns with their low iron railings, the 'Keep off the grass' sign, and the metal cup at the water fountain chained to the marble (as hygienic as a communal tooth brush!). But those asphalt paths and the stone parapet facing the river gave us a wonderful grandstand view of all that was happening on the Thames. From that wall I spent hours watching the barge builders repair and paint the barges with pitch. At high tide sometimes there was a special treat when we could watch the lightermen with their tugs manoeuvre those great barges into position, taking those repaired out into midstream, bringing others into position for repair. At the side of Odell's there was a bit of a dock, that is, a slope down to the river. The barges were anchored at the bottom of that dock. When the tide was up and the day warm, it served as the swimming bath for the neighbourhood children. The more adventurous of us would climb up the anchor ropes of the barges to dive off. We had no trunks or swimsuits, and we had dried our shirts in the sun. It was sheer enjoyment. Every now and again, a cop would arrive and we'd have to scatter. It was a dangerous sport, however. The danger had registered in our young minds when a boy had been sucked under the barges and drowned.

Next to the recreation ground was Rank's flour mill. Whether it was originally a place where the flour was ground I doubt. More likely it was a storage depot for the flour unloaded from the barges. The Rank family had long associations with industrial Battersea. (Years later, during the unemployed agitation of the 1930s, the Methodist influence in social work was quite outstanding.) What had attracted my attention, as a child, was the striking difference in appearance between those who worked at Rank's and those who worked a little further along the river at Morgan's, one lot white with flour, the others covered from head to toe in a grey-black lead. It was known at the time as the plumbago works. Plumbago was a form of black lead mixed with clay from which crucibles were made. In the evenings, those workers used to hurry along Lombard Road as black as any miner. How did they clean themselves? In that part of Battersea at the time, nobody had a bathroom. Once a year only, those workers were envied. It was when they used to hurry home through the streets with a little wooden box under their arm. That was Christmas Eve, when they took home to their families the Morgan Crucible Company Christmas Box, a chicken and some groceries.

In my youth when I became aware of social history, I found Charles Booth misleading for his view of Battersea as mainly home to the skilled artisan. That picture never conformed with my childhood memories. True, we never suffered the stark, brutal, unrelieved poverty of the East End. But the exemplary Shaftesbury and Burns housing estates, where many of the skilled workers lived in that day, were far from being typical. In North Battersea, huddled against the evil-smelling factories, lived workers' families that occupied one room only, in streets of tenement houses. Large numbers were employed in the notoriously seasonal building trade. When the rains came or the frost struck, they were sent home. In April 1914 their wage rates were then 11 pence per hour for craftsmen and eightpence per hour for labourers. The difference between the East End worker and those in Battersea was marginal.

I can remember there were about five pawnbrokers within about half a mile from where we lived. People used to visit them regularly, putting stuff in pawn on the Monday and taking it out on a Saturday. This was a part of working class life at that time. There were as many as 37 public houses strung along the main thoroughfares, Nine Elms Lane, Battersea Park Road and York Road. (I have a list of all of them.) Some were later destroyed by the bombing in the Second World War, others were demolished to make room for today's concrete jungle. So the working class scene which I grew familiar with during my childhood years was characterised by pubs and pawnshops. The Battersea artisans, living on the Shaftesbury estate, were not the only part of the story. Those who lived on Irish Island and in the crowded terraced houses that radiated almost from the river bank, they were the working class poor.

Board school education had suffered from wartime shortages, no woodwork class because there was no wood, biology and natural history were taught monotonously without experiments. The only specimen our classroom possessed was a species of snake in a bottle adorning the window shelf. The overriding stress was on the 'three Rs', with the daily scripture lessons having pride of place every morning. Leaving school, and coming into touch with a rich variety of books for the first time, made me wonder why we had not been introduced to them at school. I am positive that, had we had the opportunity as children, most of my school friends would have easily identified most warmly with many of the characters portrayed by Dickens.

My school reading had been dominated by the boys' papers of the time. I had been addicted to reading *Nelson Lee*, not a comic but a weekly story magazine. Thinking about such reading afterwards, it became clear to me that those writers of boys' stories reflected the real world around them at the time. The year could only have been 1917 or 1918 when *Nelson Lee* serialised the story of a strike by boys at a public school – the story of the organisation of the strike against repression, against the masters, and how the boys took over school, barricading themselves in, fighting the masters with flour bombs – that made an impression on me.

Like most children then and now, we had regarded school holidays as far too short. Together with my mates, I had spent days in the Natural History Museum at Kensington. It usually took us about an hour to walk there from Battersea. What pleasure that museum gave us! The spacious ground in front, with seats where we ate our lunch, vied with the attractions inside. There was great excitement in opening those little drawers of birds' eggs in a rich variety of colours and markings. Then we would draw and colour them in our drawing books to show our mothers. Always there was something new to see and draw. Some boys had been attracted to the Science Museum further along the road, where the models and push buttons were, but I preferred to stay where the animals and birds were so beautifully displayed.

Two of my friends, Harry and Ernie Osborne, shared my interest in drawing. One became a commercial artist. In the 1920s he painted a lovely banner for the Battersea Plebs League. The boys' mother was charlady for some well-to-do people who lived in the mansions. In the summer months, she used to travel to Hampton Court to clean her employers' houseboat. By now I was able to walk with my cousin to go and stay with my relations in Frimley, occasionally, for the walk was very long. But many a time, during the school holidays, I would walk with the Osbornes to Hampton Court and back. Down river from the old Hampton Court bridge on the Surrey side, stretches of the river were then lined with colourfully decorated houseboats – for those who could afford it, a pleasant retreat from the smoke and dirt of London. We would sit on the bank, opposite where Mrs Osborne worked, and try our hands at drawing and painting that scene. What a lovely feeling it would be, swimming in the river on our arrival at Hampton Court. I can see now the reeds at my feet as I swam in that clear water.

On summer holidays in the streets of Battersea, cricket flourished, interrupted only by the sight of a copper. Although we had two commons and a park within the borough boundaries, our games lacked club status and were restricted to the cinderfields. That was no real hardship because, in the streets near home, we learnt to hit the ball more accurately so as to avoid our friendly neighbours' windows. In our road, against two flank walls, we had a permanent pitch. A wicket painted on the end wall resisted the weather and bombing for 60 years, finally to be obliterated by the bulldozer preparing the ground for new houses.

Round the corner from my home, a matter of yards only, was the college settlement of Caius College Cambridge. There was nothing posh about it, though. Upstairs was the church. The stairs were high and so was the service, incense and all that were a feature whose arrival had prompted my mother, some years previously, not to take us to church any more. What we youngsters were now keenest on was the church hall, as it was there that the Caius Boxing Club met. At the time I joined, the club was a very rough and ready affair, although subsequently it made quite a name for itself in amateur boxing.

The equipment was most primitive, on a wood-block floor, posts were put up and a ring erected. We had two instructors, old labourers from Prices' candle factory, Ted Adams and Bill Lovell. In their day, both of them had fought in the famous Blackfriars Ring. They grunted and we panted in an effort to learn the 'noble art'. We hardly had a gym. There was a punchbag, skipping ropes and a long round canvas bag used to play a kind of indoor rugby. Against the alcove on the flank wall the top of a long trestle table was up-ended, and that was the goal. What we lacked in equipment we made up for in enthusiasm.

Training night was on Tuesday. The favourite run was across Battersea Bridge, along the Embankment to Chelsea Bridge, then down Prince of Wales Road back to the hall. We must have looked the oddest crowd of sportsmen. The lucky few had some semblance of a running kit, but most made do with bathing slips instead of shorts. These we acquired at the Latchmere Road swimming baths. (They had an odd rule there, if you went in the penny bath you could swim naked, if you went in the twopenny a bathing slip was compulsory.) They were as brief as the modern bikini, but, as we found on our training runs, most ill-fitting. Going round the three boxing clubs that we had in Battersea and coming into contact with boys my own weight but with far greater skills, I realised that I was no up-and-coming Joe Beckett. My active participation in sport lapsed when I started work on the railways, to be only briefly revived a few years later when Wally Tapsell and Jimmy Lane started the weightlifters' class of the Battersea Young Communist League.

I was fortunate, as a youngster of 14, to meet Jack Clancy, a stonemason by trade, of Irish descent and brought up on 'Irish Island'. In Jack's coat lapel, there was always the small blue badge with a bold white question mark. That Plebs League badge invariably provoked the curious to ask what the question mark stood for. No sooner asked, than Jack was off on his favourite theme, the need for independent working class education: 'We need an educational organisation to teach us the history of our class.'

'Why a question mark?'

'We need to question everything', he used to reply.

Daisy and Jack Clancy were, from my fourteenth year, the two people who exercised the main formative influence on me. They, more than anyone else, stimulated in me a lively interest in labour history and an enduring belief in a Socialist society. I was spending time with them, long before I could understand or assimilate a fraction of their wide interests. The Clancys were generous of their time with youngsters, taking them into their home, showing them their books, giving them a book to read as a taster.

Before 1914 Jack had been a building worker and a member of the Stockwell branch of the ILP. During the war, he held an internationalist position and became a conscientious objector (though, for medical reasons, he had not been called up). In the aftermath of the war he became active in both the Plebs League and the Battersea Socialist Society. As a delegate from the latter organisation, he attended the foundation conference of the Communist Party in 1920. Soon after, the Battersea Socialist Society and the Herald League joined forces to form the local branch of the Communist Party. At the time, we used to meet at the Latchmere Baths with Raymond Postgate in the chair, Jack as secretary and George White as treasurer. Those meetings were well attended.

Times were exciting, all efforts were devoted to propaganda meetings and to participating to the full in the local trades council and Labour Party, to which we were affiliated. The Herald League had a small library of Socialist books, and at every branch meeting we used to have a talk on some topical theme, mostly about the Russian Revolution or the unemployed. Stickers advertising the *Daily Herald* were handed out, to be put up at any vantage point – without being caught doing it.

Daisy Clancy (her original name had been Smith) never joined the Communist Party, but was keenly alive to all of Jack's activity. As a young woman, she had cycled with the Clarion Scouts and had played the piano at Battersea's Socialist Sunday School, nursery of so many second-generation Marxists and other Socialists. Both her parents were atheists and Socialists. Her father used to attend the Secular Society meetings in Henley Street. (These meetings went back prior to the formation of the Battersea SDF.) He was employed in the locomotive works of the London and Southampton Railway at Nine Elms, then moved to Eastleigh in Hampshire when the loco works went there. Did he, like John Burns, leave the Secular Society for the SDF? Of that I am uncertain. Without doubt his interests were there, my evidence for that is his marked copy, given to me by Daisy, of HM Hyndman's *Historical Basis of Socialism in England*, published in 1883.

Another pre-1914 organisation with influence on Socialist thought in Battersea, particularly in the building trade unions, was the Socialist Party of Great Britain. It was the Battersea branch of the SDF which had become the springboard for the attack on the Hyndman leadership that resulted in the SPGB being formed. From 1904-05 Sydney Hall in York Road became the centre of their activity and propaganda. It was from amongst the bricklayers that several powerful and erudite speakers and debaters came to the fore. The Irish bricklayer, Jack Fitzgerald, was one outstanding example, fearless in debate, he was so confident in his own party case that he would take on anyone, be they small fry or big cheese. His style as a debater was to treat his opponent, from whatever party – Tory, Liberal, Labour, ILP or Communist – as the exponent of the policy of their party. He invariably knew more about the programme and published material of his opponents' party than did his actual adversary. To get to grips, not with a brilliant speech but with the written word, was his method, the apt quotation to clinch an argument. If challenged, he would dive into his trunk of books to produce the evidence. His audience loved it. Undoubtedly 'Fitz' was the star, but there were others too, bricklayers and impressive SPGBers (Sloan, Cadman, Fenn and others). I believe each of them, in their day, taught their craft at the Ferndale School of Building, then sited in Brixton. Here, they pioneered or upheld extremely high standards of craftsmanship. Direct labour, too, was seen as upholding standards.

In the autumn of 1922 I met two young apprentice bricklayers, Jimmy Lane and Alf Loughton. Their union branch used to meet at the 'Swan' public house, by the river in Old Battersea, and I ran into them outside the pub. Through talking with Jim and Alf, I got to know of an SPGB class on Marx's *Capital*. The class was held in a little cottage in Hope Street, down York Road, inhabited (I think) by Cadman, one of the SPGB bricklayers. Open the front door, and you were in the little parlour where the class was held. Feeling self-conscious, because I was very young and not a building worker like the others, I concentrated as the sentences were read, trying to understand. It wasn't really a class, more a mere reading from *Capital*. The only interruption in the deep, monotonous voice of the reader came when the gas mantle flickered in the draught from the opening door, or when an old man started winding his large pocket watch, unthinkingly out of boredom. Only once did I go to that class.

With Alf and Jimmy I spent much of my time during my late teens. After evening meetings, we'd usually continue our discussions over coffee at Luno's cafe in the Polygon, at Clapham North. This closed at midnight. Afterwards, we'd carry on discussing all the way home, and, very often, we'd be so immersed in a discussion that, as we neared home, we'd decide to go round the common again. At weekends, we'd also go very often to Hyde Park's speakers' corner and would end up as part of the huddle, after the main meetings had petered out. Discussion was part of our lifeblood.

As a teenager along with Alf Loughton and Jimmy Lane, I also sat many evenings in the Labour Club drinking ginger beer, listening to old timers, members of the SDF, talk about early labour history. One old man, known for some reason as Donkey Morris, was an inimitable raconteur. He was a bricklayer who had been foreman on the Burns estate when it, too, had been built by direct labour in 1905. From him we learnt about Sydney Hall. What lived in his memory was not the dingy room and hard chairs that so upset Stephen Sanders, but the inspiration of Socialist debate. 'Everyone who mattered spoke there at some time or other', he used to say. Then he rattled off the names that 'mattered': John Burns, Tom Mann, Henry Champion, Joe Burgess, George Lansbury and Duncan Carmichael. Some he spoke of with warmth, others with a grimace as if his beer had gone sour.

According to him, the heyday of the SDF had been about 1885, when the trio of Mann, Burns and Harry Rogers, the blacksmith, had worked in close harmony, stirring up the people on the issue of unemployment. The trade depression had brought a liveliness and sparkle to their outdoor meetings. For both Burns and Mann, the dock strike of 1889 was the turning point. The tight corset of Hyndmans's SDF was no longer in accord with the possibilities of the rising movement. Both men left the SDF, Mann to become President of the Dockers' Union and to concentrate on his campaign for the eight hour day, and Burns to parliamentary politics, becoming a national figure, recognised as a serious contender for the leadership of the nascent labour movement.

Burns proceeded to fashion his own base by building the Battersea Labour League. At no time did it grow beyond the borough boundary but, as an organisation that advanced his political aspirations, it had wide support.

From then on, the forum of political debate switched to the Washington Music Hall, almost next door to Sydney Hall. There, Burns found not only a larger stage but also a wider audience. Sunday night became Burns night, whether it was a speech on the evils of beer and betting, or a report back from the Trades Union Congress, he often spoke to a packed house. When it was flush, the Labour League published his speeches as penny pamphlets. The ground was prepared for his election, first to the London County Council, then in 1892 as the Battersea member of parliament. With the passage of time his Socialist commitment, so clear in his first election address, became blurred. He had become yet another labour leader on the road to the Liberal camp. The defection of Burns from the SDF generated a rancour in Socialist circles in Battersea that had lasted up to the outbreak of war in 1914.

Across Lavender Hill, a matter of yards from Burns' home in 1892, George Potter had lived and died. His life had many similarities to that of Burns. If they met, each would surely have recognised the other for having travelled a similar road in his prime. Thirty years before, Potter had risen to prominence for his leadership in building trade strikes and lockouts. A fierce opponent of the established trade union leadership (later known as the Junta), he founded the trade union paper, *The Beehive*, and subsequently became the first chairman of the Trades Union Congress. Burns certainly possessed a file of *The Beehive*, he loaned it in 1934 to an exhibition celebrating the centenary of the

Tolpuddle Martyrs. But labour historians have not been too kind to Potter. The Webbs, in their history of trade unions, paid tribute to his remarkable energy, but, with the relish of a person tasting and spitting out a fine wine, damned him with a quotation from an obscure opponent. Potter 'had become the aider and abettor of strikes. He thought of nothing else; he followed no other business; strikes were his bread and cheese; in short, he was a strike jobber, and he made *The Beehive* newspaper his instrument for pushing his nose into every unfortunate dispute that sprang up.' Then as now, militancy had a bad press.

Shiftwork in the railway signalbox I found a great advantage. It made it possible for me to attend, either mornings or afternoons, the LCC Day Continuation School in Cedars Road and catch up on my schooling. Further, I was able, passively at first, to participate in the unemployed agitation of the early 1920s. But the big bonus was the wide ranging discussion on topical issues which took place at work.

From the signalbox window we looked down on the heavily laden goods trains moving to the scrapyards an enormous tonnage of First World War debris. As that traffic came to its end, we observed the heavy movement of coal stocks building up. The government and employers were making advanced preparations for the threatened coal lockout of 1921. The men in the box spoke bitterly about having to be a party to such preparations. At the time, the railway unions and the transport unions had a mutual pact with the miners, the Triple Alliance. Each successive NUR branch meeting became more crowded. For weeks, the topic of discussion was the forthcoming strike. This, unlike 1919, was bound to be short and sharp because the three most powerful unions, standing together, would bring the country to a standstill. Each past strike experience was relived. Some of those men had participated in the 1911 strike, and it was from them I heard more about my uncle, Ben Wicks, who was a platelayer at Clapham Junction. He evidently was held in esteem for his record not only in that strike but as union delegate to the annual conference of the old Amalgamated Society of Railway Servants.

I was on the two-to-ten late shift when the climax came. Old Bob Watts, the signalman I was working with, was impatient for the news and sent me to the union branch to find out what was happening. At that time, Battersea No 1 NUR branch used to meet in the basement of the Methodist chapel opposite Battersea Polytechnic, about 10 minutes' run from the signalbox. When I got there, I found the special meeting of the branch crowded to capacity with men standing on the stone stairway, crammed against the doorway and packed tight in on the smoke-filled hall. I wormed my way through, looking for a familiar face that could give me the news to take back. 'Tell Bob', said Sam Jessop, 'the strike is off. We are trying to get an explanation and shall see him as soon as this meeting finishes. You hop off back.' When I told

old Bob, he seemed neither puzzled nor surprised. He muttered something about double dealing and was quickly on the interphone relaying the news to other signalmen along the line.

Next day and the following weeks, dejection and bitterness spoilt our tea brew-ups. Not that any of those men were busting their braces to go on strike, far from it. For weeks there had been a sort of rehearsal of the hardship involved, when there'd be only union strike pay to live on. But all of them thought – and subsequent events proved them right – that a defeat for the miners spelt defeat for all workers. As each goods train passed, now loaded with Continental and American coal while the miners starved, it bred dismay and despair, but some, notably the old signalmen with white beards, clung to their faith in the ultimate unity of all workers.

Unemployed agitation in the years of 1918 and 1919 emphasised the indignation felt by the ex-servicemen at the conditions they met on their homecoming. The long dole queues and the paltry demobilisation payments never matched the politicians' promises. The old comrades' association was most vociferous in its demands for mass protest. When the short-lived postwar boom ended in September 1920 the unemployed agitation discarded its 'No charity, give us justice' image, and took on a more aggressive tone. From all over the country, local unemployed committees and associations met in conference and launched the National Unemployed Workers Movement with the demand for 'Work or Full Maintenance'. From the first, Battersea's NUWM became widely known, a constituent part of the local labour movement. Hunger marches from all parts of the country found shelter and sustenance ready for them at Latchmere Baths. A Battersea contingent were always marching in the London demonstrations, which in those days all too frequently ended with a police baton charge.

A host of speakers and agitators sustained the ceaseless campaign at the local guardians for outdoor relief. The memory of one or two is vivid to this day. Johnny Holmes was one such agitator. A short, rather tubby man with a sunshine face, he was on and off unemployed platforms for a decade. His early training as a speaker had been in the SPGB. In his pocket, he always carried a scrapbook of newspaper cuttings which functioned as his speaker's notes. Many still remember the meetings he addressed during the 1921 miners' lockout. Johnny talked on the income of the Duke of Northumberland, a big coal owner. Thirty bob a minute was his income, as much as a miner received for three days' work at the coalface. He had an infectious smile, as though he was laughing at his own speech:

'Imagine, 30 shillings each minute of the day. Whatever the Duke was doing, going to bed, eating his bread and cheese or sitting in his bathroom having a sh-sh-sh-shave.'

Each itemisation of the crowded minutes in the Duke's life brought fresh convulsions of laughter from the crowd.

Another speaker during this agitation was Jim Lane, a member of the Socialist Labour Party. (Later, after a long period of victimisation and unemployment, he was taken on by the council as a dustman or something similar.) At the culmination of one of those marches up to Wandsworth workhouse, I saw him standing on a beer crate, being listened to **intently** by a vast concourse of people as he gave them an impromptu open air lecture, entirely on industrial (that is, working class) history.

Another outstanding unemployment speaker in the 1920s was Tom Waller, affectionately known as Workhouse Waller. He too had got his Socialist education from the SPGB. Like his voice, his speeches were strong and rasping. Wage slavery and capitalism were his enemy, a Socialist society his objective. When the local board of guardians said that there was to be no more poor law relief without task work – which meant the workhouse – he was ready with the answer: 'We enter the workhouse all together.'

The march into Swaffield Road Workhouse in July 1921 fired the imagination of thousands in the Battersea labour movement. Coming, as it did, soon after the debacle of the Triple Alliance it helped to raise morale. Every night, meetings and marches to Swaffield Road brought the issues of outdoor relief, unemployment, poverty and the workhouse into public discussion. For generations the ageing poor working class man and woman had dreaded the day when poverty would force them 'to go up the hill' – the very word was taboo, spoken of only to one's life partner. It was the end of the road, the living death. Suddenly, through the unemployed agitation, the iniquity of this remnant of Victorian poor law was brought into public discussions by thousands. The occupation of the workhouse, and the raising of the red flag over it, was a tonic in class consciousness for employed and unemployed alike.

The 1922 general election saw a fierce political contest in North Battersea, where Saklatvala, the Indian Communist, was chosen, with national Labour Party approval, to be the Labour candidate. The national press focused on this battle, and tried to influence the electorate by calling up patriotic memories of John Bull's alleged glorious history. 'Sak', a short stocky lawyer with fiery eyes, was a magnificent orator. His speeches were lessons in economic geography and the history of imperialism. Hundreds attended his election meetings in different halls within the borough on the same night. His name in the 1920s became a household word in Battersea.

This brought my first election experience. Delivering leaflets, one day on the Burns estate, I chanced upon a friendly SPGBer I had met previously at the Marx class. He was short, somewhat bow-legged, always wore a bowler hat and sold the *Socialist Standard*. Maybe I was over-excited by the election, because in a kindly manner he set about deflating my high hopes. 'You are wasting your time and energy young man', he said, 'Socialism, not reforms, is what is necessary.' To complete the shock, he told me that he intended to write across his ballot paper in the election one word: 'Socialism.' I felt dispirited by that encounter, but the feeling was shortlived, Saklatvala was elected with a majority of 2000. That night we felt like storming heaven.

Ever since the November 1919 elections, the viewpoint of the local council had been Labour, and quite advanced for the times. Amongst the new councillors, a good number were influenced by the Socialist tradition of the borough and by the Russian Revolution. Other influences included the Plebs League and the Herald League, where I had been among the majority who had voted to join the Communist Party. Although, by the mid-1920s, those councillors who had been in the Herald League had recovered from their first flush of revolutionary fervour and moved to the right, nevertheless, at critical moments their Socialist consciousness asserted itself. I remember two such occasions. The first was when Lenin died, in January 1924. Horace Harling was then mayor of the borough and broke the mayoral convention by presiding at Battersea's Lenin memorial meeting. The second occasion was when the Baldwin government, on the eve of the General Strike in 1926, issued its secret circular to local authorities to organise the OMS (Organisation for the Maintenance of Supplies), the strikebreaking force. That circular was ignored by the Labour council in Battersea.

On the other hand, it was the Labour councillors, the dominant group at the town hall, many of whom had by now become trade union officials, whom Herbert Morrison was to use for effecting the split in the Battersea Trades and Labour Council in July 1926. No one fought the Labour splitters harder than Jack Clancy. His tenacity was rewarded, in the same year, by his election to the borough council, defeating both his Tory and right wing Labour opponents.

Another influence in the borough council was an outstanding group of Socialist women who were organised in the Cooperative Women's Guild. In the early 1920s, their ideas began to find expression. One area was cultural activities. Here, further backing came from Wally Okines, an old member of the Battersea Socialist Society. Okines had a fund of ideas on the cultural front. Through the amenities committee of the council, a municipal theatre was launched. Plays by such authors as Galsworthy and Ibsen were performed fortnightly by the Lena Ashwell players. Monthly, on Sunday evenings in the town hall, there were the Frederick Wodehouse Concerts, and on weekdays films for school children. At that time too, Battersea town hall became the mecca of ballroom dancing, especially on Saturday nights. The competition for booking the hall on those nights was heavy. Through the amenities committee, those lucrative bookings were allocated to organisations within the borough, instead of to outside commercial firms. Saturday night dances in the town hall thus became a means, small but helpful, of funding local organisations.

Fine drama, good music and extended welfare services, all efforts towards applied municipal Socialism, could not conceal the grim reality of the social conditions then existing. Marriage on the dole was not confined to Lancashire. Understanding the problem, a group of women Socialists advocated extending the welfare service to include advice on family planning. Such an initiative, proposed by the council, was immediately vetoed by none other than the solitary 'left-wing Socialist' in the first Labour government, John Wheatley, a Catholic who was Minister of Health.

All the efforts of those local Labour Party women had been directed to making birth control knowledge accessible to working people. Wheatley's threat to withdraw the Exchequer grant should local authorities persist in using the health and welfare services for that purpose, was a setback to their high hopes. To educate and influence the national labour movement on this issue now became a priority. The agendas of the London Labour Party conference, the women's and national party conference reflected widespread support. But the effort to commit the national Labour Party erupted at that moment when the party had tasted the fruits of government. Now, more than ever before, what was thought palatable for the electorate became the criterion of conference decisions.

Several of those women who were active on the local committee were familiar friends. There was Mrs Varran, whose taxi driver husband was the first secretary of the Church Ward of the Labour Party. Years later, I met her in Moscow when she arrived on a women's delegation. Another was Alice Loring, a most active and advanced woman. At one time, she had been a companion helper to Ellen Terry, the famous actress, and her daughter Iris had been trained for the stage. It was during the miners' lockout of 1921, at a meeting in the town hall, that I first saw her do a 'sketch' on a miner's child. The Lorings became great friends of Jimmy Lane, Alf Loughton and myself. Alice Loring's life was devoted to causes, animal or human. It was in her home that, as a youngster, I heard of the successes and failures, the enthusiasm and the indifference of local personalities on the birth control issue. She too, in her own way, remained a supporter to the last of left politics in Battersea. She died in Swaffield Road, the old workhouse again, then jazzed up as an old peoples' home.

Today, it is not easy to convey to a reader the constraints that existed in my adolescence against all open discussion on birth control and sex. Two memories of those times serve to illuminate that recent past. Clapham Common speakers' ground was the place on Sundays where almost any subject was debated. At that time, it was no tourist attraction or lark for the mindless, but a place where working men and women seriously discussed the problems of life. The *Daily Herald* was the first to report the arrest of Guy Aldred, a Glasgow-based Socialist, for publishing a booklet by Margaret Sanger on birth control. Aldred was no stranger to Clapham Common. His arrest, and the subject of birth control, rapidly found an echo in the Sunday debates.

It was around then that Bonar Thompson arrived on the common. He had a most pleasant face, a soft voice and a wonderfully rich vocabulary. At that time, he was a freelance speaker who depended on an appreciative audience not only to listen, but to walk afterwards to the roadway and part with the odd shilling. (The police forbad collecting or selling on the common itself.) He was widely known as the 'Hyde Park orator'. News of his arrival on the common quickly spread, denuding most other meetings of their audience. On this occasion, he did not use a platform. Walking in a wide arc, with his back to the roadway, smiling and talking almost to himself, he gathered the crowd before announcing the topic of his address: population. How beautifully, yet perforce euphemistically, he dealt with the contemporary issue of Margaret Sanger and birth control! He demolished the Malthusian theory and also the views then prevalent that war was nature's pruning knife to thin down a population. He contrasted the size of the families of the wealthy with those of the workers, lacking both the economic means and the knowledge to regulate the growth of the family. 'It was not', said Thompson, 'their superior morals, their chastity or abstinence that was the cause of the wealthy having fewer children, it was knowledge.' The issue was: should that knowledge be made available to working people? Margaret Sanger's pamphlet was an effort to provide just that. Thompson presented the Socialist case with all the care made necessary by the repressive opinion of that day: a remarkable speech. As the meeting dispersed, he moved to the roadway, where a companion quickly sold copies of Sanger's pamphlet from the poacher's pocket of his old raincoat.

Even in relatively advanced Battersea with its good library system, Marie Stopes' book *Wise Parenthood* was not allowed on open access, but made available only on request at the counter. Another example of how only those in the know could find out, was a barber's shop in Falcon Road, where I used to go during my early teens. That barber's shop had two chairs and two people to cut your hair, one of them was a young woman. The procedure, there, was for customers always to pay the old boy, who was obviously the governor of the shop. When he took the money, the regular thing was: 'Is there anything else you want, any cigarettes or anything?' The contraceptives weren't openly accessible like they are in shops now, but were in a drawer where he kept his money.

In relation to sexual liberation, I only understood later the full significance of some things. On one occasion, I went into town to see Elsa Lanchester dance at a social in aid of Russian Famine Relief. After the interventionist wars, Soviet Russia was swept by famine. In all countries where the October Revolution had struck a sympathetic chord, workers hastened to help. Not only money was gathered, on May Day in Hyde Park there was a cart with a banner announcing that workingmen's tools were being collected to aid reconstruction in Soviet Russia.

Elsa subsequently became a well known stage and film actress, and married Charles Laughton in 1929. She was a Battersea girl whose mother, Edith, had been a most committed Socialist in the local movement. Many years later, I learnt of the story of Edith Lanchester. She was a member of the Social Democratic Federation. She not only held, but made public, her view that the legal and religious ceremony of marriage made the woman a chattel, and she lived up to this by cohabiting with a working class member of the SDF. Shocked out of their tiny Victorian minds, her middle class family arranged for a medical specialist to see her. Predictably, he judged her to be a person of unsound mind. She was bundled more or less forcibly into what was then known as a madhouse. The local comrades campaigned outside, and eventually John Burns, by then an MP, intervened and, through efforts at top level, secured her release. Eleanor Marx, at this point, took Edith to convalesce at her house in Sydenham.

That story of the oppression of women, like those tales of the struggle for birth control and the experience of the workhouse occupation, lived on in the memories of Battersea Socialist women, and were passed on by them. Partly through their efforts, Battersea's infant mortality rate fell, despite many parents of the newly-born being on poor law relief or unemployed.

And Battersea's tradition on health did not stop at birth control or 'free love'. Most of the Labour women I've mentioned had been involved in or near struggles over vivisection and vaccination. In their image, these two often blurred. Before the First World War, Battersea Council had become famous for erecting a statue of a little brown dog which had been vivisected at a London hospital. A mob of medical students had come down and destroyed it. Battersea became the site of the Anti-Vivisection Hospital (which guaranteed to dissect no live animals). Those Labour women were important among the friends of that hospital. My mother was at least aware of all this. By chance, though, my direct experience of the Anti-Vivi was to be confined to paying two shillings in 1932 for having as many teeth extracted as could be while the gas lasted!

Battersea had also seen terrific opposition to compulsory vaccination. In or near the labour movement, it was a regular thing to refuse to have your children vaccinated. Certainly, when my sister was born in 1915, my mother, who was not the meeting-going type (she had left that to my father), decided to pay a solicitor the seven shillings and six pence he demanded for getting an exemption form signed. I remember how distraught she was over how to get the money together, what with my father in the army. But pay she did. After 1919, of course, when the Labour Party became able to nominate some JPs, a signature on the certificate became a costfree formality. Not that Battersea was in the least unusual in this, in the late 1920s, I knew a man from Aberdare in South Wales, a miner, who dumbfounded our hosts by refusing vaccination. This was at the International Lenin School, I'm racing ahead again.

Chapter Two

From Class to Socialist Consciousness

THE Battersea Herald League came into existence in the years of industrial strife of 1911-14. It made its mark as a working class united front in the builders' lockout of April 1914, when it had succeeded in breaking through the rancour of a divided political movement. It proclaimed its platform 'open to all and any thinkers, independent of this or that "ism", cult or party'.

Following the First World War, the Herald Leaguers were again in the forefront of political agitation throughout Battersea. They used to hold what at the time were called 'missions' – open air meetings – at a dozen different points, every night of the week. At those meetings, I heard a wide variety of Socialist speakers – students from the Central Labour College, industrial militants, old SDFers such as Walter Geard and Duncan Carmichael, British Socialist Party and Socialist Labour Party propagandists. They spoke about all the traditions, all those past struggles – marches, demonstrations, individual protests, collective agitation, unionism, solidarity. Into this stream I was swept, fascinated by the endless discussions, arguments; an ignorant kid, trying to grasp what it was all about, but knowing that I was part of something great that lifted me up.

Then, the issue seemed so clear. To stop the interventionist war against Russia, put an end to the colonial war in Ireland and get rid of the poverty and unemployment that were to be seen on the streets of Battersea. How delighted I was when the *Daily Herald* on its front page splashed the news that a special conference of the Trades Union Congress had decided:

'That if the government refuses to withdraw the troops and cease the production of munitions for use in Ireland and Russia, a general strike should be declared.'

Direct action by the workers was the theme of all the speeches at Herald League meetings.

Memories of that summer of 1920 remain. Two events, not unrelated, had a powerful effect on the labour movement locally and nationally. Early in July a big meeting at the Albert Hall greeted the return of the Labour Party delegation from Soviet Russia. This was the first opportunity (because of the Civil War and the Allied blockade) to learn what really was happening in Soviet Russia. For more than two and half years the newspapers, with the rare exception of the *Manchester Guardian* and *Daily Herald*, had reported Russian events through their Riga correspondents. At that time they were little more than propaganda despatches of interventionist governments. The report of this delegation seemed to reinforce the views of Labour's left wing on the social significance of the Russian revolution. The daily articles of AA Purcell in Lansbury's *Herald* on the aims and aspirations of the Soviet government provided a stimulus to the Hands Off Russia campaign.

Within weeks of the return of that delegation, the labour movement faced a critical test. The Russo-Polish war reached its decisive stage, the Red Army was within sight of the Polish capital. The possibility of a renewal by the British government of an interventionist war became once again both menacing and real. The Labour Party and trade unions met that threat with massive demonstrations against war, and a national network of Councils of Action. All the pacifist and anti-war sentiment that had accumulated since 1918 erupted in popular protest against the government. Clapham Common was the scene of vast crowds, larger than any I was to see till the eve of the General Strike.

The Herald League branch that I joined appeared to me, as a youngster, most forbidding. Not that its members were unsocial Socialists – far from it. The branch membership included men and women, councillors, secretaries and chairmen of Labour Party wards and local trade unions. Rather, their discussions and interests were so varied. At work in the signal box, I was used to hearing daily arguments about union organisation, grading, victimisation of Irish railwaymen for refusing to handle munitions. But these Herald League discussions were different. The new topics involved books and authors, Marx and the Labour leadership. This was a new experience. It was out of such a discussion of HG Wells' book *New Worlds for Old* that I was stimulated to read. New names registered in my mind: Wells, Marx, Lenin, Trotsky, Walt Whitman, Robert Blatchford and Jack London. Almost unawares, I had acquired a reading list for a lifetime.

For I was now in a reading culture. People talked to each other quite often about what they were reading or had read. One day, while cutting through the side streets near Clapham Junction on my way home from work, I saw a complete edition of Gibbon's *Decline and Fall* in the window of a secondhand bookshop. This I paid for in instalments, and had read by the time I was 18. In the Reference Library, I devoured JM Robertson's introductory book on what to read. These books reinforced my anti-religious instincts, as did my reading of the *Freethinker* during the mid-1920s. The more I read, the more my ignorance took my breath away. So one book led to a craving for many more. I also strengthened my (as we called it then) 'materialist conception of history' – as a social process, producing successive 'stages in the evolution of society' – by ploughing through, of all things, Macaulay's and TH Green's books on the history of England, and Frazer's *Golden Bough*. No wonder that, when the Hammonds' books on working class history began coming out during 1922-23, the pleasure they gave me was deeper than the most slap-up meal that anybody has ever eaten. So I didn't need to go to Moscow to learn my British labour history.

Our Herald League branch was one of three that sent delegates to the Communist Unity Convention. I was too young to understand the political meaning of that step, but the branch did. The letter sent out from the British Socialist Party head office over the name of Albert Inkpin, inviting organisations to appoint delegates to the Communist Unity Convention, made it quite clear what participation meant:

'Representation at the Convention will be held to imply that the branches, groups, societies, represented will accept its decisions and become branches of the Communist Party.'

There was nothing ambiguous about that. The basis of representation was one delegate for every 25 members. Our branch sent three. Following the Unity Convention, the Herald League, along with the Battersea Socialist Society that had sent two delegates, became the first Battersea branch of the Communist Party.

Now united, the revolutionary Socialists were favourably positioned in the Battersea labour movement. The newly-formed Communist Party became accepted as an integral and affiliated section of the local Labour Party. This undivided movement, including as it did the Communists, continued until February 1926. Large public meetings became the regular feature of Sunday evenings. All the most popular speakers of the left were attracted to Battersea Town Hall with its receptive audience. Colonel l'Estrange Malone MP – an ex-Tory who had become famous for envisaging 'a few Churchills' getting hung from lamp posts – Arthur McManus, chairman of the Communist Party, Jack Murphy of the shop stewards and TA Jackson. Jackson was the favourite. I remember the first time I saw him. I was standing in the vestibule of the Town Hall when he arrived with his first wife. They looked like tramps, such as were often to be seen making their way up the hill to the workhouse, TAJ, gaunt in features, with a big felt hat, thick lenses and long hair, a striking contrast to the well-dressed Malone. But what a command of language he possessed!

It was at the time of the Irish treaty that split the Republican forces. Jackson's speech was a history lesson on the civil war in Ireland, a biting denunciation of Lloyd George and the Black and Tan terror, followed by a reminder of the infamy of the shooting of the wounded James Connolly, and the dirty hands of the Labour leaders. That speech was received with rapture at a crowded Labour meeting. (Often, at those Sunday evening meetings, the Russian violinist Soermus would play

Russian revolutionary songs, early in the 1920s he was expelled from the country.)

Not that the left had everything its own way, but the right did manage to score one important own goal over the important question of who should have the Labour parliamentary candidacy. In November 1918, Charlotte Despard had it only after John Burns had refused it. He found that whole election, he said, 'sinister'. He was correct, the labour movement was ill prepared. By contrast, Lloyd George, as the head of the wartime coalition, held a commanding position. The euphoria resulting from the end of the war, he saw, was a favourable time to renew the coalition. In the spring of 1918 the government had already anticipated increased pressure for more democratic government with the end of the war. It had therefore passed a new Representation of the People Act. This gave a limited parliamentary vote to women, and a universal one to men; it also effected a more equitable distribution of parliamentary seats and created an absent voters' list for men on active service. In such circumstances, Charlotte Despard, standing for Battersea North, lost to the coalition candidate by 5597 votes.

But, by the time of the next general election in 1922, the local labour movement was in a better condition. In spite of the defeat of the miners in 1921, a high degree of class consciousness had found expression in Battersea politics. Significant Labour electoral successes were recorded. Control of the borough council was won in 1919 and a solid Labour opposition formed on the poor law board of guardians. Allied to those electoral gains there emerged, working closely with the trades council, a most militant unemployed workers' movement. From its early beginnings, the Battersea left had been inoculated against that rigid anti-parliamentarism that was such a feature of Scottish left wing politics. With us, the dominant philosophy was to use each and every platform to advance the interests of the workers.

And this was the moment – the eve of the 1922 Election – when the right proceeded to score its own goal, or rather, it laid the political ghost of John Burns, its old idol, and thereby helped raise up the Communist, Saklatvala. For years, Burns had hovered over Battersea; loved, hated, suspected, a permanent question mark. Would he come out of his retirement and again play a part in the reawakened movement?

The Battersea Labour League that Burns had formed in 1889, after he had left the SDF, had become the backbone of the radical Progressive Alliance. That situation changed with the end of the war. With the 1918 reorganisation, the Labour Party became a mass party with an individual membership which was grouped into local electoral wards. The Labour League became an affiliated section of the Labour Party. Most of the past organisers of Burns' electoral successes were now in the mainstream and were Labour councillors. On the eve of the 1922 election, it was they who made the final attempt to secure the Labour nomination for him. They convened a meeting to hear an address by him. It was a virtuoso performance, reviewing his lifelong role in the labour movement, puncturing Labour's current policies, inflating and exploding its leaders – some of them, to him, renegade Liberals – one by one and promising to put Battersea at the forefront of the national movement. (I am paraphrasing Bill Coltman's account in Kent's biography of Burns.)

But his earlier failures to utter a word in support of Charlotte Despard must have occupied the thoughts of many. Who would control this belated aspirant for leadership? In answer to the direct question, 'Would he accept the Labour whip?', he was most forthright: a blunt refusal to be bound in any way. With that answer, he cut the last of those slender ties that connected him to the labour movement. His sponsors – the organisation he had founded – withdrew his nomination. Instead, the local Labour Party chose Saklatvala to be its candidate.

Shapurji Saklatvala had come into the Communist Party via that group of ILP intellectuals which included Ellen Wilkinson, Marjorie and Walton Newbold, Helen Crawford, EH Brown, Rajani Palme Dutt, Emile Burns and Robin Page Arnot. This group had been pressing for the ILP to affiliate to the Third International. (Except for the last three, they mostly left the Communist Party after a few years.) 'Sak' had long shared platforms with Charlotte Despard, as co-fighter for the right to national self-determination of all colonial peoples, particularly the Irish and the Indians. His adoption as candidate was really something. He was an Indian and a Communist, and at that time you could count the numbers of so-called 'coloured' people in Battersea on one hand.

In the three general elections of 1922, 1923 and 1924, he won in all but the second. (One of his key supporters was John Archer, our black former mayor, also a comrade of Despard.) In the fiercely fought election of 1924, when the fraudulent Zinoviev letter was used, 'Sak' polled a higher vote than ever and regained his seat. As our MP, he introduced something that was unusual at that time – monthly meetings at which he reported his activities in parliament. I was then a delegate from my union branch to the Battersea Trades and Labour Council, and I remember him explaining that this is what they did in Russia – Soviet deputies there had regularly to give an account of their stewardship to the people. I can remember still those great crowds queuing up to get into the town hall to hear his reports. In addition to this, he circulated a large broadsheet containing an account of his parliamentary speeches and questions.

The post war boom ended during the autumn of 1920. The growing unemployment provided the employers with the opportunity to claw back the advances won by workers since the war ended. First, the miners were locked out in 1921 and defeated. Then came the turn of the engineers and the building workers. The trade union movement was on the defensive. Sliding scale agreements, which militants had initially been opposed to as a 'fodder basis', began a downward slide. Politicians and employers spoke of peace in industry, whilst, at the same time, introducing vast economies and rationalisation.

On the railway I was being moved about a bit from one signalbox to another. So my original box, my university, was abandoned. I was now what they called a relief signalbox boy, working in many boxes on the old Brighton line. In the end, I was moved up to Victoria South box, where, as I mentioned, I met Harry Manning, the old ILPer.

Far more important, during my time as a relief signalbox boy, I witnessed the economy drive on the railways. Work study teams logged the work of the signalmen. Every movement to progress the flow of traffic was recorded, be it moving the heavy levers or punching out the bell codes on Sykes signalling instruments. The physical exertion needed to move railway points and signals a distance from the box, and the responsibility of a congested time table, never entered their calculations. A deep sense of dejection, even humiliation, pervaded the signalbox as each motion was scrutinised and recorded. The lively and witty banter, the odd political disagreement, that was part of our working day, was lost. That mood, which had dominated our workplace all the time the economy team were with us, took a long time to go. It did pass, however, notably on Epsom race week. Then, we had a grandstand view of the royal train slowly pulling out of Victoria on its way to the Derby. What a magnificent sight that beautifully polished engine looked! Immediately the railway dignitaries left us after the passing of King George V on his way to the races, a lively conversation started. The old banter returned, social contrasts were made, and class inequalities came into focus.

One experience was widespread on the railways at that time. Railwaymen became more than ever preoccupied with sectional grade interests. Grade vigilance committees took on a fresh lease of life. In those years, the seed was being sown for a breakaway union of railway signalmen. To counter the growing apathy and mood of sectionalism, the idea of an all grades programme surfaced. What might well have been a kite launched by the union officials for their own reasons, became airborne when the National Minority Movement was organised in August 1924.

The trades council, in spite of the continued political agitation, sensed the changing mood amongst the employed workers. A decline in trade union membership and the falling off in attendance at branch and trades council meetings were warning signs. The militants, led by Jack Clancy, had the answer, a sustained effort should be made to develop a Socialist consciousness amongst the council's affiliated membership. With the aid of the local Plebs League, an ambitious programme of education classes was started. Students at the Central Labour College gave topical talks at union branches.

The Plebs League had a distinctive attitude, it sought to promote adult working class education completely independent of state aid, and untainted by the university curriculum. On the masthead of its monthly journal, *The Plebs*, was the declaration: 'I can promise to be candid but not impartial.' Each issue had a frontispiece drawing by Frank Horrabin. I still vividly remember three such illustrations. At the time when police baton charges of unemployed workers were not uncommon, *Plebs* illustrated the policeman, with baton upraised, with the caption: 'You can't prevent the spread of ideas with a baton.' As trade union leaders and employers spoke of the need to make each industry more competitive, *Plebs* depicted the boss with the caption: 'More production means more profit.' In 1924, when the Empire Exhibition opened, *Plebs* appeared with a drawing of a fine British lion with a magnificent mane in the symbol of pound notes.

This Plebs programme lasted from 1921 to the eve of the General Strike in 1926, and involved an extensive series of classes. How fortunate we were, because in those years the principal lecturers of the Plebs League came to Battersea. Bill Ryder, a foundation member of the Communist Party, introduced us to Marx's *Capital*. With chalk and blackboard, he opened our minds with his explanation of the Marxian category of surplus value. How that concept hit one – exploitation. I remember my mate, Alf Loughton (a bricklayer, and later mayor of Wandsworth), saying defiantly: 'Well, they won't get no surplus value out of me!'

Frank Horrabin, on economic geography, made use of maps to bring alive how continents were divided in the search for markets and raw materials. The concept of imperialism as a stage in the development of competitive capitalism enriched our understanding of the society we lived in. Raymond Postgate attracted a wide audience with his series of 12 lectures on revolution from 1789 to 1905. His class was held at the Lavender Hill Labour Club, and coincided with the attack by Herbert Morrison and Macdonald on the presence of Communists in the Labour Party. Its central issue – parliamentary road or revolutionary road? – was then live. The room was always crowded. The sharp formulations of the Communist International's 21 conditions of affiliation spilled over into the discussion in Postgate's class. At times, fierce debate was stirred. Maurice Dobb, so young and well dressed, introduced us to the economic theories of the leisure class, marginal utility and the anti-Marxist theories of value.

Those classes were widely attended and enjoyed by young and old – apprentices, skilled workers, Cooperative Guildswomen. From them there emerged a group of people who became the backbone of the left wing of the Labour Party. Historical materialism, industrial unionism and elements of Daniel De Leon constituted the Marxism in that period of Plebs education in the 1920s. The account of the development of society and the revolutionary part that the working class was destined to play in the social transformation lacked the vital answer of how the change was to be accomplished.

By contrast, the Marxism of Lenin and Trotsky was slow to penetrate the movement. It sought to harness the consciousness and daily struggles of the workers and direct them to the conquest of power. Here, the science of Socialism was seen as a dynamic class activity, led by a revolutionary party whose entire effort was concentrated on giving coherence to every facet of the workers' movement. Following the reorganisation of the Communist Party after its fifth conference in October 1924, an attempt was made to influence the Labour College and Plebs classes with these, for us, new Marxist concepts. This was the beginning of the rift within the Plebs movement. The idea of us Communists meeting separately before each branch, council or League meeting to decide the agenda or syllabus was anathema to many, even of our strongest supporters.

Due to the wide character of the movement for Independent Working Class Education (IWCE) and the party members' involvement in its leadership, the party acted with caution. Two separate problems had to be resolved:

1. The organisation and training of the party membership.

2. How the wider Labour College class movement could best be influenced to teach the more dynamic version of Marxism.

To this end, a conference of all party members involved in the Plebs League was convened under the chairmanship of an Executive Committee member. From that conference, a committee was established to promote the specific party training of each member for his varied work in all spheres of the labour movement. On the more controversial and divisive question of influencing the broader educational movement, it was decided to prepare a syllabus for general IWCE classes and to compile a list of party tutors to conduct the classes. Although the party members on the Plebs League Executive were involved in those decisions, a hostility was generated against the party organisation commission for having so slavishly applied the theses of the Third Congress of the Communist International (July 1921).

The differences between the Plebs and party leaderships deepened in 1924. More and more, the live issues of the conduct of the Labour government, its attitude to the Dawes Report and to the stabilisation of European capitalism occupied our Plebs classes. It was in the summer of 1924 that I went to my first Plebs League summer school at Cloughton, near Scarborough. Most of the outstanding personalities in the field of independent working class education were present at that school. Frank and Winfred Horrabin, Raymond and Daisy Postgate, Walton Newbold, Ellen Wilkinson, the Lawlers, Arthur Woodburn and Willie Paul.

The highlight of the school was to be M Philips Price (who had reported for the *Manchester Guardian* on both Russian and German revolutions) introducing a discussion on the foreign policy of the current Labour government. He was not able to attend, so his lecture was taken by W Paling MP. A most vigorous debate followed, lasting on into the evening. From the students nearest to Communist orthodoxy, there was bitter criticism of the Labour government's record. On the American Dawes plan for German stabilisation and on what a Socialist attitude should be to that, both Ellen Wilkinson and Newbold stressed the failure of the German working class to achieve what Zinoviev had so loudly prophesied would be the classic proletarian revolution.

In spite of the wide differences that were maturing, that school was a unique experience. Politically divided as that 1924 summer school was, it had many pleasant aspects, not least Willie Paul singing the Negro spirituals, long before they were popularised by Paul Robeson's visit to this country in the 1930s. Those social evenings usually ended with the singing of *The Internationale*; still vivid is the image of the theatrical Newbold standing to attention and saluting in his plus-fours.

To symbolise how the relations between Communists and the rest of the left were still at a richly ambiguous stage, I want to note an episode which occurred in 1924, the sixtieth anniversary year of the First International. Karl Kautsky came to London and spoke at the Horticultural Hall, near Westminster Cathedral. I was in the group from our economics class, along with Jack Clancy and Bill Ryder, that went to hear that arch anti-Bolshevist. The occasion was an ILP dance and social; the band stopped for some minutes and, from a raised dais, Kautsky spoke. He was an old man with a white beard, mumbling softly in an English which was very bad to my ears. All I recall was, he conveyed greetings for the International's anniversary. Bill Ryder never left the small coffee table even to listen, but, on our return, he was most critical. 'What was Kautsky doing on the fiftieth anniversary in 1914?', he asked. But the point is, his criticism and opinions were confined to our small circle. It shows how the movement was still one, you could have a group of CPers going along to hear that outstanding critic of the Bolshevik Revolution, without feeling bound to heckle. Long after his political demise as a Marxist thinker, Kautsky's books were still sought after by Marxist students. Three years later when I was told to prepare myself for entry into the Lenin School, his *Economic Doctrines of Karl Marx* was on the short list of compulsory reading.

This helps put a slightly earlier incident into perspective, a special expedition which, as so often, I made with the Clancys. One Sunday afternoon, we set out for the Central Labour College in Penywern Road, to hear Belfort Bax give a lecture. My expectations were high. Here was a name so often cropping up in conversations with SDFers – a link with the past, a founder member of the SDF and the co-author, with William Morris, of *Socialism: Its Growth and Outcome*. As we entered the hall, Bax was already seated at the table reading his paper. He had a heavy build, and stumbled in speech as he read, a great mind slowing down with age. Bax's reflections on the Socialist movement of 1922-24 could only have been controversial, yet I am sure that no discussion took place. Possibly, those young students regarded Bax as Jack did, with the deference due to his age and had great esteem for his pioneer contribution to Socialism in this country.

Plebs education in the 1920s was not the sophisticated Marxism of dialectical materialism that so captivated the left intelligentsia in the 1930s. Nor was it that type of many-sided education of a revolutionary that Lenin had written about. Essentially, it was a Marxism that relied heavily on America's Socialist Labour Party for its texts and, consequently, was thoroughly impregnated with Daniel De Leonist interpretations. It did, however, make us aware of the richness of the writings of Marx, and provided us with the answer to our question: what is the reason of class oppression?

This was the sort of atmosphere then: great activity. The Plebs League used to meet weekly, the Labour Party and the trades council used to hold big meetings, and the monthly meetings of the trades council had great representation from all the branches. That's the sort of movement I came into and was part of in those early days, as a kid.

And I was active, not only in Battersea, but also as a railwayman. This, too, helped accelerate my development as a Marxist.

After the Communist Party's October 1922 conference, the party was reorganised. Local party committees were built up. The South West (London) Local, as we used to call it, had premises in North Street, Clapham, and gathered the members in Clapham, Battersea and Wandsworth. Unlike a number of other people in the locality, I was involved in a vital industry, the railways, so I was brought along to meetings and paid attention to. I can remember going to party training classes where I was the only student, because they were catering for my shift. Similarly, I used to go by myself to R Page Arnot's flat, first in Mecklenburg Square and then in Broderick Street, Balham, to get my party training. This was part of the attention paid to comrades, not necessarily because of their abilities, but because of the nature of their employment. It was cadre material being built up. If you were in a basic industry such as railways – and in Battersea railways were the most important industry – you had an important, a strategic, position.

Thanks to the railway company, I also had a strategic position, from 1923, as an operator on the platform indicator at Victoria Station. **How** strategic will emerge in Chapter 3, but it also had a strategic effect on me intellectually. It brought me into personal contact with many of the left intellectuals whose writings influenced Marxist thought in the 1920s. For a few hundred yards outside the station, along Buckingham Palace Road, there was a beautiful Victorian corner house, No 162, which housed the Labour Research Department, the offices of the *Labour Monthly* and of *The Plebs*. Often I called there to collect the literature for our classes, and so became known to many who worked there. Daily, the personnel from those premises would cross the station en route for the Underground, and would often pause for a chat. At that time, the Labour Research Department was headed by the same R Page Arnot whose flat (as I mentioned) I used to attend for my party training.

The Labour Research Department and members of Arnot's team had earned great prestige in the trade union movement for the way they organised the publicity of the railwaymen's case in the 1919 strike. Now, in the mid-1920s with the miners under attack, they produced a wealth of material on the coal industry and on working conditions. This material exerted a vast influence. Members of that team were Harold Rathbone, Lydia Packman, JB Askew and Jane Tabritsky. Askew, an old member of the SDF who died in Moscow when I was there, was a delightful chap, with a beard and a very thin face. He was bilingual in German and did translation work for the LRD. He also did some translating of Marx. Jane later worked in the Marx and Engels Institute in Moscow under David Riazanov, and subsequently wrote those volumes on the Communist International under the name of Jane Degras.

In the basement of 162 (the Plebs office), I was always particularly welcome. Both Winfred Horrabin and Kathleen Starr were keenly interested in the growth of our NCLC classes in Battersea and the progress of our rank and file paper, the *Victoria Signal*. Many young workers like myself owed a lot to Frank Horrabin and Mark Starr. Frank stimulated so many of us to a wider reading. He always shared his own interest in books with you. From him we learned to enjoy *Jude the Obscure*, *Penguin Island*, *The Jungle*, *The Iron Heel* and *The Ragged Trousered Philanthropists*. He pioneered the idea of a sixpenny pamphlet, a guide to workers on *What to Read*. This was eventually published. Mark Starr's book, *A Worker Looks at History*, was a revelation in its day. It was written for an audience equipped with only a school board education. But they well understood its main thrust. Starr wrote:

'We study history not because of any love of the antique, but because, wishing to raise our class, we wish to learn how other classes found the road to power; looking backward to understand the present, and in order to march forward.'

Modern Marxists, with the benefit of the past 60 years of extended social history scholarship, dismiss Mark Starr's early essay as woefully inadequate. Suffice to reply – glance at the paucity of his bibliography and compare it with the vast libraries of social history that exist today. In addition to his interest in social history, he was an enthusiastic Esperantist. In one of his many articles in *Plebs*, he claimed that Zamenhof, the founder of Esperanto, was an uncle of Trotsky. Another person at No 162 was Arthur Reade. At the end of the First World War, he had been sent down from Oxford for publishing a paper called *Red* or *Free Oxford*. He was shortly to make us aware of Trotsky's ideas. At this time he was manager of *Labour Monthly*.

Also going backwards and forwards past my indicator on his way to No 162 was Walton Newbold. I had frequent impromptu discussions with him. And, calling once at the Plebs office, I chanced to step into a heated argument. Newbold was there, announcing that he had just come from the House of Commons (where he had in 1922 been a Communist MP) and had met JH Thomas, the right wing leader of the railwaymen, whom he had asked to write an introduction to his new book on railway finance. Several of those present were about to follow Newbold and Philips Price out of the Communist Party, but none shared Newbold's apostasy. The Plebs League leadership – Ellen Wilkinson, Ray Postgate and Frank and Winfred Horrabin – became prominent in the effort to regroup the left wing in the labour movement around *Lansbury's Labour Weekly*. In spite of my firm commitment to the Communist Party, I continued to have the deepest respect for those Plebs leaders who contributed so much to propagating Marxism, at a time when revolutionary theory in Britain was (as we now recognise) in its infancy.

Residence in Battersea brought further intellectual stimulus. Palme Dutt – whose internationalism had, like Reade's, got him into deep trouble at Oxford despite his academic brilliance – lived in York Mansions. We Battersea YCLers used to go there to have classes on Fascism and other things. It was there that I first saw a book on Italian Fascism. It was by a man called Odon Por. Dutt's mother was Swedish, with a very strong accent. His father was a huge fellow, part Indian, with a big beard. Palme Dutt, with his brother Clemens, a biologist, had no more than a limited involvement in the South West Local. He was also a member of the General and Municipal Workers Union, and this was even more a mere formality.

But involvement in the YCL was only to a minor extent a matter of intellectual training. At one time in the early mid-1920s, there was a slogan about 'going to the masses'. We wanted to break away from being a small group. In the streets of Battersea at that time – or in most of them – there was always a street cricket team and football team. We also used to go and play in Battersea Park. But the sportsfield there was made of ash cinder, you fell over and your knees were all grazed with ash. We had no equipment at all. The cricket ball we had wasn't leather, it was made of some sort of cork. Somebody had a bat or a couple of bats. It was primitive equipment.

From the slogan of 'going to the masses', we had the idea that it would be good to organise a broad youth movement which would get involved in all the sports activity, get the kids out of the streets, get them involved in politics. So, round the streets we went, got in touch with the teams and so on, and we invited them all to a meeting at the Labour premises at 445 Battersea Park Road. The Labour agent there was an old-time Burns supporter called Charlie Mason. That chap got scared stiff, so many kids turned up. It was just packed – doors, stairs, corridors, everywhere – you couldn't move. It was just what the kids wanted, to organise a pukka sports and get pukka equipment.

So, that's how the YCL started the Battersea Sports Club. It was like a British Workers' Sports Federation, only it was Battersea. In next to no time, they had scrounged and begged and borrowed the money, got hold of a piano, equipment for this and gear for that. And all this had been sparked off just by going round with the idea of pulling the youngsters' sporting activity together. Not surprisingly, many of them were pulled into the YCL from that. In the longest run, this fertilised another generation of Labour councillors. Later, in 1945-46 for example, there were a good number of people on that council who had been involved in that sports thing. Lots of respectable Labour councillors liked to boast later that they had been members. So did Ernie Perry, a Labour MP for very many years, although I never saw him around. He favoured the ILP Guild of Youth, at Bedford Road, Clapham, where they were more respectable, safe from the claws of the Communists. (Still one must admit the ILP did some good work, and had a formidable organisation then.)

The whole effort was a breakthrough for us, which had an impact in a dozen different directions. What made the whole thing possible was Arthur, we paid him for a room above his café. It was situated by the foot of Battersea Bridge, by the bus garage. Whenever the busmen needed to hold a meeting they used to fill that room too. We were obviously a sizeable organisation to be able to pay the rent. We had a library up there, and there was a piano. We held frequent Saturday dances and socials. Here, George White and Wally Tapsell made up our piano and drums 'band'. George was a real expert on the piano, and, with Wally as a drummer, they could keep it up for hours, improvising, syncopation, that jazz music with wonderful rhythms. It was music you just had to dance to. (Later, Wally Tapsell was on the Central Committee of the party, and got killed rather mysteriously in the Spanish Civil War.)

The Battersea YCL also used to run weightlifting classes, building ourselves up for the revolution. My close mates Alf Loughton and Jimmy Lane and I also tried to improve ourselves at about this time, by taking up vegetarianism. Perhaps we were influenced by our reading of Upton Sinclair's book *The Jungle* about the Chicago slaughter yards. Alice Loring also had an influence on us here, she was always on about the need for proper diet, the health foods angle. So when we had the money, we used to go to a vegetarian restaurant. There was one in Furnival Street and another in the Strand. It worried our mothers, though. They thought we were ruining our health, not eating meat. Anyway, it faded out eventually. And in the 1930s when we got un-employed, we couldn't afford to be choosey about food.

But the central activity of Young Communists was parallel to that of the adult comrades. Sport and fitness were hardly the main reason for our growth. The central one was that the postwar years swept large numbers of young people up into a great process of politicisation – a bad word, but I can't think of one better. The elections of 1922, 1923 and 1924 helped our YCL's expansion strikingly. During that of 1924 – which I remember as the fiercest of all – we YCLers had our own platform with our own speakers. We also had the capacity, not only to do normal election work, but also to chalk the pavements and walls with slogans. So much so, that the local press referred to the activity of us 'Boy Communists' and, afterwards, Sak came with his 12 or 13 year old son to our YCL meeting (held in the ladies' waiting room of Latchmere Baths, as we were now too big for our headquarters). He came to thank us for our activity.

The climax of that activity occurred at the end of polling day, when we assembled outside the Labour Party's headquarters at 455 Batter-sea Park Road and marched in a tremendous youth demonstration to Battersea town hall on Lavender Hill to hear the result. There were simply thousands of people right across the breadth of the road. Demonstrations on the actual day of an election were as unusual, in my experience, as they are today. And this, to my mind, illustrates the vitality and energy of us YCLers.

There were other important ways in which we interacted with the adult Communist Party. As I've explained, our industrial work and, even more, my political education were peculiarly boosted by the way in which the party reorganised and refocussed itself during the early 1920s. But this process was also to have negative effects which became clear as early as the mid-1920s, let alone later.

From the moment of the unification of the party in 1920, the Russian experience had an overpowering influence on the development of the Communist Party in this country. It couldn't have been otherwise, for the reason that the Marxism of the British working class movement was particularly weak. Prior to 1914, other than the Kerr translations from America (Marx's *Capital* and the old pamphlet, *Value, Price and*

Profit), the study of Marxism had been negligible. Lenin's, Trotsky's and Zinoviev's conception of Marxism as a science of the struggle for power penetrated the English movement only with the years 1918-20 – and then only in a fragmentary way. So, right from the word go, there was a heavy leaning on the Russian experience. And, with the degeneration of the Communist International which took place from 1923 onwards, the British Communist Party leadership's servility to the Russian Communist Party grew more and more pronounced.

With the 1922 'Bolshevising' reorganisation, there was a decline in the level of political discussion in the party. And that decline arose because the membership of the party (which only came to 3000) was preoccupied with organisational problems; that is, with building fractions and cells in different organisations, and with influencing factories and such bodies as trades councils. Where, previously, there had been all manner of political discussion, politics now took second place. That absence of political discussion in the party, of the clash of opinion, had an important influence on the history of the Communist Party.

It produced a situation, in the general election of December 1923, where the party can be seen to have moved completely to the right of the position that the International had formulated in its early Congresses of 1919, 1920 and 1921. True, the party produced quite a revolutionary manifesto for the election: nationalisation of the factories with workers' control commissions, full pay for unemployed workers, a whole series of demands for freeing the colonies and so on. But, when Labour emerged from the election the largest party, the possibility of a minority Labour government became the politics of the hour. The party now deviated so far to the right that it sent a telegram of congratulations to the Labour Party, and came out in favour of forming a minority Labour government with a programme so defensive as obviously to have been tailored to suit a minority situation. Now that, to my mind, was bending to the right, to suit the situation in the Labour Party.

For, within the Labour Party itself, there were three **other** positions on what should be done following the election. The first came from the group who met in Sidney Webb's house – made up of Ramsay Macdonald, Philip Snowden, Thomas and Webb himself – and decided for the formation of a minority government, if asked, to carry on the Government of the King. George Lansbury, with a few others in the Parliamentary Labour Party (that is, Labour MPs), came out with a second position. They argued against forming a minority Labour government, it would not have enough votes to carry out its programme. The third position was that of Maxton and the Clydeside MPs: a minority government should be formed, but should straight away advance a bold Socialist programme, on which to be defeated and go to the country in a snap election.

So, in that situation, there were two left wing tendencies in and around the Labour Party, taking two positions to the left of the Communist Party. Now that, to my mind, was the result of the over-concentration during the preceding two years on organisation the party had lost its way because politics had taken second place. So much so, that the party trimmed its pre-election programme to suit Macdonald.

Of course, that situation lasted for only three weeks at the most. On 4 February 1924 the Executive Committee of the Communist International came out with a pronouncement. While not explicitly criticising the British Communist Party, its conclusions were quite different. It drew attention to the fact that the minority Labour government had come about, not as a result of heightened class struggle, but as a result of a deal made with the Liberal Party, and that what was necessary was to win the workers to a revolutionary policy with a series of revolutionary demands. That demand of the ECCI was endorsed by the EC of the Communist Party of Great Britain – but without any comment! There was no explicit admission that this was an abrupt reversal of line.

To my mind, the policy which the Communist Party put forward during those three weeks was the first expression, in this country, of a bias towards what later came to be called Popular Frontism, something that inevitably involved trying to soft peddle the class struggle. Of course, if you look up this episode in James Klugmann's history of the Communist Party (which some still take as the last word), you will find that this trimming was done in the hope that a Labour government would give loans to the Soviet Union. But that is hardly the whole story. Still, in its distortive way, it does highlight the international aspect. This was crucial.

In 1923 the Communist International had regarded a revolution in Germany as a distinct possibility. In such a highly industrialised country, this was expected to be the classic proletarian revolution, in complete accord with Marxist theory. But as a result of a whole series of miscalculations, inadequate leadership and bad organisation, the German revolution did not materialise. An inquest was held, revealing sharp differences within the International and within the Russian party in particular. Out of this came the Trotskyist Opposition. Trotsky published a long article, *The Lessons of October*, in which he examined in great detail the problems of a revolutionary party on the eve of taking power. He analysed the Bolshevik experience in Petrograd and the German experience in 1923. Now this aroused a hornets' nest in the Russian party. Pages of history had been turned back, which some of the participants would rather had been left unturned. Ripples of the fierce controversy spread through the Communist movement.

Down on Victoria Station, one welcome visitor to my platform indicator was AE Reade. As well as being business manager of *Labour Monthly*, he was also a member of the London District Committee of the party. Tall, with a fine physique and ginger beard, he was admired by us members of the Young Communist League in Battersea for the talks he gave us on Marxism. He could read German, so it was from him that we first heard of the differences of Trotsky with the Russian party. To young Communists, Trotsky was the big hero. I remember, in the early days of the Young Communist League, one of our popular pamphlets that was published in Moscow by the Young Communist International, was *My Flight from Siberia* by Trotsky. Arthur Reade, to us youngsters, fitted into that pattern of the young revolutionary, audacious and committed to the cause.

On 30 November 1924 the Party Council, which included all members of the Central Committee plus representatives from the party districts, met to hear a report from Harry Pollitt on the Executive session of the Communist International which had discussed international trade union unity and the Trotsky controversy. That meeting condemned Trotsky for reopening the discussion in the Russian party. Trotsky had done this via a preface he had written to a book called *1917*. The English edition – from *Inprecorr*, the International's information outlet in Vienna – was not published till 26 February 1925. Nor had his *Lessons of October* come out in English yet. So, those present at that November 1924 extended plenum of the British Communist Party's central committee were condemning Trotsky without having read what he was being condemned for. And they did so without dissent.

But the matter now had to go to the districts for endorsement. And it was reported in our party local that AE Reade had succeeded in persuading London District Committee to oppose the blanket condemnation of Trotsky, and in getting an aggregate meeting of the London membership called to hear a spokesman from the Central Committee. Since our reorganisation, any discussion of international questions had become a rarity, so this added to the interest in the London aggregate of 16 January 1925 on the politics of the Russian party.

I went along to that meeting. JT Murphy and Andrew Rothstein, were the representatives of the Central Committee. Murphy had the aura of being our man in Moscow. That summer, the Communist International's Fifth Congress had elected him to the impressively named International Control Commission of the Communist International. He opened the debate by moving the following resolution:

'The Party Council of the Communist Party of Great Britain sees in the preface to Comrade Trotsky's book on 1917 an attempt not only to reopen the discussion closed by the decision of the Thirteenth Conference of the Russian Communist Party and the Fifth Congress of the Communist International. It is also an open attack upon the present leadership of the Communist International, which in the opinion of the

Communist Party of Great Britain will not only definitely encourage the British Imperialists, but will also encourage their lackeys of the Second International, and those other elements who stand for the liquidation of the Communist International and the Communist Party in this country...'

With arms flaying, he denounced those who criticised the Russian leadership as playing into the hands of our opponents. The baleful blending of inner party criticism with Labour and capitalist opposition to Russian party policy became hereby increasingly a standard method of debate.

Murphy's resolution was supported by Andrew Rothstein. Well groomed, in gold rimmed glasses, with the dignity of a party cover name ('Roebuck') and close links to the Russian party, and with his service as a translator to the recent Russian trade union delegation well known, he too radiated authority. He concentrated his attack on those who pleaded a lack of information as an excuse for not condemning Trotsky. To my astonishment, he appeared to convey that it was un-Bolshevik to require all the information before making a decision. In other words, when members were trying to influence the party line, all they needed to know was – what was the party line? The discussion was lengthy, many speaking. When another motion was put to adjourn the meeting until documentary materials were available, a sizable minority of the 200 present supported it. (Oddly enough, the *Workers' Weekly* experienced difficulty in reporting what it described as a 'Keen Discussion of Trotsky' accurately; its underestimate of the numbers present and particularly of the size of the minority led to protests which produced a two column correction in the next issue – something which LJ Macfarlane, in his *History of the Communist Party* has apparently failed to read.)

So, when Reade rose to move his amendment to Murphy's resolution, he had an attentive audience. His speech widened the issue to one of overall support of the positions of the Left Opposition within the Communist International on questions that few knew anything about. His amendment read:

'This aggregate meeting of the London District membership of the Communist Party of Great Britain joins with the District Party Committee in regretting the hasty vote of the Party Council in condemning Comrade Trotsky without full information, and this meeting at the same time takes the opportunity to express the London membership's most emphatic support both of the left wing's minority fight in the Russian party against bureaucracy, and equally of the Comintern's struggle against right wing divergences from Leninism in the French, German, Bulgarian and other sections of the International.'

When this amendment was finally voted on, it was overwhelmingly defeated. I was one of the 15 who supported Reade – or were we 13?

All this sparked me off to find out more about Trotsky. I managed to get hold of some copies of *Inprecorr*. This wasn't easy, particularly with a Labour government and JR Clynes as Home Secretary, there were often missing numbers. Trotsky's *Lessons of October* was first published in English in *Inprecorr*. Then the British party published it in *The Errors of Trotskyism*, a heavily subsidised tome of nearly 400 pages, more than three-quarters of it devoted to attacking Trotsky.

But a big difference from later on was that no one thought very strongly on the issue. There was disagreement, but among comrades. Trotsky's reputation and prestige remained high. The names Lenin and Trotsky were still inseparable. I remember that the posters advertising one of our Battersea town hall meetings nicknamed one of the speakers, Bert Joy – carpenter, member of the Central Committee, powerful agitational speaker and a leading light in the Minority Movement – as 'the Tooting Trotsky'. Nobody gave this a second thought. What strikes one now, at this distance in time, is the indifference displayed on an issue of this magnitude. Under the guidance of Rothstein and the Comintern representative (known under the name of Bennett), the British party played safe. So the party congress of mid-1925 could, without any debate or discussion of any kind, pass a resolution condemning Trotskyism. As far as the British party was concerned it was a non-issue, and the leadership was happy to keep it that way.

That was the last the party heard about Trotskyism until 1932. It was also the last it heard of Reade, too. The statement was made at that congress that there was no evidence of 'Trotskyism' in the party, but that one person in London had raised the issue and been 'dealt with'. What this meant was that Reade was expelled from the party but in a secret sort of way. He quickly left the country for Greece (where he stayed some years, till forced back to Britain by getting accused of libelling the Greek king, I was to bump into him again during the 1930s). As it chanced, I was working at my platform indicator when he dropped by and said he was going to be off on the boat train. He did not tell me why. He merely said he was out of the party and off to Greece. Given my sympathy with his politics, this raises the question of why I was not spurred to find out more about why he was out of the party. I can only say that my image of left intellectuals – so soon after so many of my Labour Research Department friends had left the party – was that they moved around, whereas we workers did not move around. Intellectuals, I assumed, were birds of passage as far as organisational allegiance was concerned.

Chapter 3

To the Masses – The General Strike

AT the age of 18, in 1923, after four years of recording the passing of trains from a signalbox window, my encyclopedic knowledge of the Victoria-Brighton line timetable had been rewarded by promotion to the indicator on Victoria Station. That train indicator was completely hand operated. It had two dozen clocks, which showed the time, platform and destination of departing trains. A phone connected me with the signalboxes and the guards' lobbies, so that both the travelling public and the traffic staff could be informed of any unscheduled changes.

Under that indicator there were cupboards. These I was able to use for keeping those publications I was selling. And I was always dodging around the station, because things would go wrong, trains used to come in at the wrong platform. So that gave me one excuse. And, in addition to that, I was a seller on the station of the *Railway Review*, an excellent paper which the NUR used to publish weekly. There used to be a sort of competition as to how many you could sell. That too increased the legitimacy of my dodging around. Thus, I built up contacts. The disadvantage was in my being so young. But it was a fruitful period – seeing how to operate as an individual in a workplace. And I did have quite a degree of support on that station. They were nearly all members of the three or four Battersea branches of the NUR, by and large, the workforce at Victoria all lived in Battersea. Later, I initiated the duplicated Communist paper, the *Victoria Signal*, which I was in a position to distribute at the same time as the *Railway Review*.

The reorganisation of the party introduced great changes in the activity of its members. In place of the weekly branch meeting where opinions were exchanged, the membership was divided into working groups directed to a specific function, either in their union, Labour Party, trades council or workplace. The purpose was to weld the party membership to the working class and to its organisations, and so be able to give leadership and coherence to the daily struggle. This, we were taught, was 'Bolshevising' the party.

When I began to build a workplace branch of the party on Victoria Station, I was the only member. But I was not without supporters, most of the railwaymen living in Battersea were influenced by its advanced tradition. In the guards' and shunters' lobbies could be found pre-1914 Herald League and ILP members, many of whom were committed supporters of Battersea Labour Party's left wing politics. Outside the station, I had the help and expertise of Claude Healey, the Westminster Communist Party organiser. He was secretary of the typewriter mechanics' trade union and had an office in Fleet Street, above Jack Hobbs' cricket shop. It was from there that we produced the two page *Victoria Signal* fortnightly, though its actual content was prepared by regularly calling supporters to meetings in the lavatory attendants' lobby at Victoria itself.

That paper won extraordinary support. It circulated up and down the Brighton line and was looked for. If it arrived anywhere late, you were soon made aware of this. Even the platform inspectors paid their halfpenny. The reason for its popularity lay in its agitational treatment of simple issues and its lead on how to remedy a wrong. It brought into prominence the ordinary grievances of railwaymen and carried their discontent into the union branches. In that way, the hope was to build solid support for Communist politics in the union branch.

One such agitational issue, highlighted by the paper, was the condition of the shunters' lobby. At the end of the old No 7 platform, beneath the connecting stairs, was a mean little lobby that was used by the shunters. In the days of the steam train, railway shunters had the dirtiest and most dangerous job, uncoupling railway carriages and engines and coaches. Manually breaking the Westinghouse coupling required much strength, and resulted in them being smothered in filthy black grease. Their lobby, where their worksheets were pinned up, was sparsely furnished. There was a bare table in the centre, a naked electric bulb, a gas ring for a brew up and a few hooks to hang coats and mackintoshes on. To clean their hands, the shunters were supplied with rag shoddy and a tin of soft soap. Such conditions were a recipe for discontent.

Another reflection of working conditions in the 1920s on Victoria Station was the employment of outside porters **for no wages**. Those men used to stand in front of the station with a trolley and take luggage from the incoming taxis. Then they would see the passengers onto the train. These men depended exclusively on tips for their pay. But the railway company controlled the numbers of outside porters employed. Each man had to deposit his insurance card in the station superintendent's office and was issued with an enamel armband with a registered number – 'Outside Porter No XYZ' – and a peak cap. Even the term 'outside' was a misnomer because, when important trains arrived (such as the Dover boat train with passengers from the Continent, or the 'Brighton Belle'), those outside porters were expected to meet them so as to handle the passengers' luggage. It was a precarious living, even if it could not strictly be termed casual labour.

In the months preceding the General Strike, the *Victoria Signal* campaigned for 100 per cent trade union membership – as did CPers and others up and down the country. To that end, we were successful in persuading the union branch to organise a trade union 'showcard' day. By that method, we learnt our union strength and weakness on the station. It was that effort to unionise the station that had brought to light the plight of the outside porters. Many were ready – even anxious – to join, in the hope of stabilising their position. This agitation also had repercussions within my branch of the National Union of Railwaymen – Battersea No 1 – which was normally right wing and pro-Jimmy Thomas. At that time, the branch members had the utmost difficulty in resisting my proposal for a showcard day. I also used to be on the Southern District Council of the NUR as a deputy delegate, and I can remember the embarrassment my proposal caused there too. So with that campaign, we were hitting the nail on the head. We were putting ourselves – Communists and sympathisers – in the factories or in the railway depots in good standing with other workers who were interested in strengthening the union. We organised those outside porters. I took a deputation of them to the Battersea No 1 branch to try and get them into the union; the branch appealed to national headquarters. But the leadership resolutely refused to organise them.

At one stage, we tried to organise the outside porters to boycott the incoming boat trains. The idea was that instead of the outside porters moving with their trolleys to meet them, they should remain at the front of the station. We had planned for that day and tried to organise supportive action from the other station staff. But, on the vital day, it only needed one porter to move his trolley in the direction of the arrival platform for that token strike to collapse. This happened. Such action was expecting too much from men whose sole means of livelihood were the tips, the generosity of the public. True, some months later, in the massive May Day demonstration to Hyde Park which, in London, formed the prologue to the General Strike, some of those outside porters could be seen marching under the banner of the *Victoria Signal*. But, once the strike had begun, some of them were to scab, despite our bringing out a special edition, specifically urging them not to.

A popular feature of our station paper was the profile of a railway company director. Applying the technique developed by Walton Newbold, we illustrated – by using *The Directory of Directors* – the multiplicity of directorships a given railway company director held. When listed, that information reinforced the image of the wealthy employer who dismisses the railway workers' just claims, as embodied in the *All Grades Programme*. This agitational series was greatly appreciated and warmly discussed.

But the *Victoria Signal* was merely one of three such efforts I was involved with. In Dorman and Long's steel works, just along by Battersea Power Station, near what used to be the Great Western goods depot of Nine Elms Lane, we had a YCL factory cell, which produced a duplicated paper called the *Iron Fighter*. And at Nine Elms – which was not only a marshalling yard but also had engine sheds – we had contacts or party members, and so the *Nine Elms Spark*, a factory paper, was produced there. So, what with the *Victoria Signal*, there were two Communist Party workplace papers connected with the South West Local, while the YCL produced the *Iron Fighter*.

The railway depot papers, of which the *Victoria Signal* and the *Nine Elms Spark* were examples in the period of 1924-26, reached a wide audience. They initiated a new form of working class journalism that came into full bloom in the days of the General Strike. What made them a success was the extraordinary regularity with which they appeared, and their close ties with their readers. In the effort of the Communist Party and Minority Movement to rebuild a militant spirit on the railways – to halt the retreat, to campaign aggressively against sectionalism – they made an important contribution. Nationally, such factory papers took off about the period of 1925-26, and were really an expression of local talent coming forward for the first time.

In December 1925 the Railway Wages Board – a representative tribunal with an 'impartial' chairman – published its findings against the railway unions' claim for a wage increase. That wages board award produced a stir all through the railway system. A special general meeting of the NUR was convened to consider the situation, and decided by a narrow majority to accept the award. At the time, it seemed to me that the *Victoria Signal* and my speeches in the union branch were really in tune with the thoughts of all railwaymen.

The front page symbol of the *Victoria Signal* – what today is called its logo – was based on the Beecham's pills advert which had a signal in it, this we copied onto the stencil. Now, about this time, JH Thomas, the NUR's right wing leader and, by now, an ex-cabinet minister, came to Battersea. I went to that crowded railwaymen's meeting in Battersea town hall, expecting the seething anger that existed to erupt. I came away thoroughly dejected. Jimmy Thomas – butt of the cartoonist, idol of the Establishment and persuasive leader of the railwaymen – rose to speak to what I thought would be a highly critical audience.

He commenced by reminding us all of his long, dedicated service to the union and of the conditions of service that we then enjoyed, compared to the time when he had been on the footplate. Then he attacked the *Victoria Signal*, not for its politics, but as an example of outside interference in our union affairs. Taking the current issue of the paper with its masthead illustrating a railway signal at danger, he asked: 'Has any railwaymen ever seen a signal pointing towards the railway track?' That crowded meeting rocked with laughter as he ridiculed those ignorant outsiders who sought to instruct us railwaymen what to do. Our simple little mistake – we hadn't given it a thought – had them all laughing. Particularly when you're young there's nothing more wounding than ridicule. A protest from me at that point resulted in a notice of a motion in my own branch to remove me from the branch committee.

That Thomas meeting was presided over by Tom Pocock who was also my branch chairman. He was a signalman at Victoria North box, a pre-1914 member of the Independent Labour Party, an executive member of the union and a governor of the Central Labour College. He was respected as an able negotiator. From the time when I joined the union – introduced by my uncle Ben Wicks – Pocock had encouraged and assisted me. His supportiveness had been despite his surely knowing one of my early mentors to have been his fellow signalman, Harry Manning, he and Harry had been at great odds, politically and personally, for decades. Often, he made it possible for me to act as deputy delegate to the union's Southern District Council, of which he was secretary. Now he was sponsoring the resolution to remove me from the branch committee. Not that there was anything personal in this. It was very much part of a national pattern, as the coming pages will show.

August 1924 had seen the inaugural conference of the National Minority Movement, the organised opposition within the union movement. The hope was that militant minorities would one day become the majority. After all I have said about Battersea, no one will be surprised to read that our town hall should have been the venue for the NMM's founding conference. This was during the one summer of Labour's first government – born, and soon to be buried, by grace of much of the Liberal Party. This government was currently providing a salutary lesson in parliamentary politics. The repeated threats by that government to use troops and emergency powers against strikers was more of an eye-opener than any number of photos of His Majesty's Labour ministers decked out in top hats, knee breeches and dangling swords. To the exasperation of industrial activists, unions seemed riddled with sectionalism. This had been aggravating the industrial retreat, ever since the immediate postwar boom had collapsed into slump.

Presiding in Battersea town hall over the NMM's founding conference was Tom Mann. He had been an inspiration to workers since the London dock strike of 1889. We now numbered miners and metal workers, women from London's rag trade, unemployed and employed, railwaymen regardless of sectional and craft divisions. What inspiration he gave us! It was time to stop the rot, time to break barriers down, time for industrial unionism to come into its own. And for him the purpose of industrial unionism was not only to obtain another penny in the wage packet, but to fashion a more efficient weapon in the hands of the workers in their battle to change society. As he emphasised, stepping to the front of the platform, pushing up his shirt cuffs, 'kicking capitalism off the face of this planet', he demonstrated the kick like a footballer taking a penalty.

Big Jim Larkin was there. What a giant of a man, demanding to know what the movement was going to do about 'poor little Ireland'. From the South Wales coalfield Arthur Horner, then checkweighman at Maerdy, outlined the grim condition of his miners since their betrayal by Thomas and the transport workers' leaders on Black Friday of 1921. Horner brought the message that the Miners' Minority Movement was stirring the valleys, and the prophetic warning that cheap reparation coal extracted from defeated Germany would, once the Ruhr mines were back in full operation again, result in fresh attacks on the miners by the coalowners in this country.

In the town hall vestibule was a man with a friendly face, a big hat and wide girth. It was George Hicks, a rising star among the left wing trade union leaders. He was no stranger to the Battersea movement. In fact the bricklayers' branch in Battersea had been for years his base. Yet to push open the door leading from the vestibule to the conference and identify himself with the Minority Movement was something he never did. Both he and AA Purcell, who were destined to dominate the industrial scene in the years 1924-26, had since the engineering lockout in 1922 advocated a more effective centralisation of the Trade Union Congress General Council.

But to become committed to an organised effort to fight the more conservative trade union leadership was not their cup of tea. They chose to remain on the sidelines, to fraternise at embassy receptions, to sign a few ghosted articles for left papers and, in May 1926, when the hour of decision struck, to capitulate to the right wing of the trade union movement.

During the course of 1924, it became clear to anyone in the Communist Party (and outside) that the Labour government was, at most, carrying out Liberal policies. This realisation brought very widespread working class disillusionment – often with 'politics' as such – which found expression in a switch to a more aggressive attitude within the industrial arena. And this too helped nurture the rank and file efforts that came together and formed the Minority Movement during July-August 1924. This development was spontaneous, and not simply Communist Party instigated. It was the return of the base movement to old syndicalist ideas which had existed continuously in Britain since around 1910. In this country, there has always been a tendency for trade union consciousness to boil up without necessarily any broader political conclusions being drawn; as I see it, a recurrent contradiction in the rhythms of the British movement, going back to 1832 at least. We were about to see all too much of this during 1926.

Some weeks after the NMM's launching, the TUC convened for its 1924 congress. Millions of workers, aching for an economic revival, were sympathetic to the Labour government's efforts to reopen trade links with Russia. And here at Hull, as fraternal delegate from the Russian unions, was Mikhail Tomsky. He received an enthusiastic welcome. Tomsky, a 'worker-diplomat' as he now described himself, was involved in the tortuous negotiations with the Labour government and the financiers to obtain credits. It was during these negotiations that he established relations with the TUC General Council. Purcell was its current president. Less than three years previously, Purcell had been involved in the launching, in Moscow, of the Red International of Labour Unions. Now at Hull the seed was sown which, months later, was to blossom ambiguously into an Anglo-Russian Trade Union Committee.

But these tendencies served only to aggravate the Labour government's problems to its right. Dependent on toleration from Liberal MPs, it initiated the prosecution of 12 leaders of the Communist Party. When this attempt flopped, the government fell. The main issue in the ensuing general election was Labour's alleged softness on Communism. Almost on the eve of election day, the media – abetted as we now know by circles in or near the Foreign Office – splashed a forged letter from Zinoviev, the head of the Communist International, whose terms underlined Labour's role as a witting or unwitting Trojan horse for Moscow. In Battersea, this scare did not stop Sak recovering the seat he had lost in 1923. Nationally, too, the main panic was among Liberal voters, not Labour. But the Liberal rout was shared by Labour's right wing leaders. Kicked out of Downing Street, Macdonald and his friends drew a simple lesson – never again must they be even misrepresentable as stooges of Bolshevism. Their bruised resolve was to affect us in Battersea sharply.

The return of the Tories to power signalled a renewed attack on working class living standards, underpinned when Churchill, eager to be the chancellor who raised the pound sterling to its former glory, put it back on the gold standard at a rate punishingly high for British industry. As in 1921, all eyes were on the miners. The owners were clamouring for miners' wages and hours to be worsened. The miners stood firm. During the summer of 1925, tension climaxed as they appealed to the General Council. Locally, meetings became larger, louder and more frequent. (Incidentally, when Rodney Mace and other 1970s historians say our area was quiet during this period, they forget the limitations of their sources; most of our greatest meetings took place on Sunday evenings when, not surprisingly, local journalists took time off!) When the General Council stood firm, the government appeared to back down. On Friday, 31 July 1925, it offered yet another official enquiry and, to keep production running smoothly in the meantime, a subsidy which was due to end on 1 May 1926. The day of this offer was quickly dubbed Red Friday among trade unionists. Amid the rejoicing, left wingers and militants were quickly aware that the government was beating no more than a tactical retreat.

But I said 'quickly', not 'immediately', I must not oversimplify this awareness. For, coincidentally, I acquired a unique insight into the lack of perspective among at least some important left wingers immediately after that Red Friday 'victory'. This was also the first time I went abroad – and tasted champagne. That summer, thanks partly to the overvalued pound, French francs were cheap. The National Council of Labour Colleges organised a one week summer school at Wimereux, a tiny place situated a mere tramride along the coast from Boulogne. From my Victoria indicator, I was of course still in contact with my Communist Party and ex-Communist Party friends who worked at the Labour Research Department. Raymond Postgate suggested I come along: why not? This was not the big school of the kind I've mentioned at Cloughton the previous year. Indeed it turned out to be hardly a school at all. There were only 12 or 15 of us, all told.

We were a fascinating mixture. On the one hand, we numbered some left wing members of the General Council such as George Hicks, and Alonzo Swales plus his wife, who, like him, was a pleasant and highly political Yorkshire ILPer. On the other, there was more than one type of intellectual: the Horrabins, the Postgates, Ellen Wilkinson and her sister, and Willie Paul and his wife. Paul was a self-taught theorist of workers' power, a former SLPer and a very independent mind. We convened only a week or so after Red Friday. I can remember everyone's concern at how utterly exhausted Ellen Wilkinson looked, physically, from the punishing amount of public speaking she had been doing – giving her all – up and down the country during the previous month or two.

Willie Paul and I hit it off particularly well. For one thing, we both loved swimming. We used to go splashing along the coast, and the lifeguard would blow a cow horn for 'danger' and call us in. The term 'summer school' in respect of Wimereux, 1925, was thus a misnomer. In contrast to other Plebs schools, there were no structured lectures or debates. We were merely an intimate gathering of left wing union and political personalities. They, it seemed to me, were prone to off-the-cuff exchanges of opinion. So the looming crisis between unions and government expressed in the ominous speeches of Baldwin (the PM), was not discussed.

I found myself simply on holiday with Pleb Leaguers whom I had a great respect for. We swam, and lazed on the sandy beach. Ellen Wilkinson took us on rambles around the French countryside, generally relaxed. In the evenings Frank Horrabin would spark off a conversation about books. French authors that were of social significance, Emile Zola, Anatole France, Henri Barbusse and Georges Duhamel. Ray Postgate would enthuse over a new history of French Socialism recently published. The 'school' ended with a convivial social evening. With few exceptions, the party left next morning for Paris. Postgate told me it was their intention to visit, in Pére-Lachaise cemetery, the Wall of the Communards (a memorial place where, following the fall of the Commune of 1871, the Communards were shot). But my annual week's holiday was now over. So, reluctantly, I had to return to my indicator at Victoria.

Looking back, one can all too easily expect or imagine these people to have energised each other in all sorts of ways. But some of us were desperate for a pleasant break. And it was to be only a short one. Immediately following Red Friday, the Communist Party recognised the situation as one of truce, not victory. To generalise the struggle was from the very beginning the keynote of our strategy. Via Battersea Trades Council, two conferences were convened of all affiliated organisations and union branches. Particularly at the second, on 13 September, I remember the mood as euphoric and vibrant. Even the more right wing branches seemed to be responding to the militant mood. This was best expressed by my own Battersea NUR No 1, which sent a resolution on the need for unity arising from Red Friday, and by the Battersea branch of the National Unemployed Workers Committee Movement with which I had links. Our NUWCM submitted six 'suggestions', ranging from 'the need for more coordination between itself and union branches', to 'the advisability of a rotary scheme [job sharing] being put into operation by the borough council on all council work', and to a minimum wage for all, including particularly the armed forces. The list ended challengingly with 'Was the miners' victory a fiasco?'

At the national level, though, developments were brewing which were to wreck this unity. Admittedly, Lon Swales might make a militant presidential speech at the Trades Union Congress in Scarborough, calling on the whole movement to rally against further wage cuts. Superficially indeed, this Scarborough meeting might seem a triumph for the left. Never before had a TUC been so outspoken on international politics. Resolutions were passed condemning the Dawes plan on Germany and against imperialism in India, Egypt and China. It was as if all the insularity of the British movement had been swept away by the North Sea breezes blowing on the seafront. But this was only part of the story. On the crucial question – what were we to do here, on the home front – those same delegates who had applauded any speeches on the colonies, retreated to their parochial and craft positions. How else can we explain that the issue of granting more power to the General Council was referred back for further consideration?

Indeed it was the right who were already setting the pace. During the intervening weeks, Macdonald – self-consciously now a former PM – declared that, on Red Friday, the government had 'handed over the appearance, at any rate, of victory to the very forces that sane, well considered, thoroughly well examined Socialism feels probably its greatest enemy'. He thus lined up beside his Tory successor. Of course, he covered himself in his customary woolly way, industrial muscle was 'unethical'. But his meaning was clear enough. And at Scarborough the voting to the General Council produced a right wing recovery with Jimmy Thomas and JR Clynes making a comeback.

No less important, in October a few weeks later, the right wing persuaded the Labour Party conference at Liverpool to make a complete break with Communists. The conference not only, once again, threw out the Communist Party's application for affiliation, but now added that no individual Communists were either to be members of the Labour Party, or to attend as delegates of unions or of other affiliated organisations. In Battersea, Tom Pocock became a linchpin of the effort to break the local influence of Communism, his motion to remove me from the branch committee was merely a tiny part of that.

Temporarily, the government came to the rescue of the left. A fortnight or so after Liverpool, police raided the headquarters of the Communist Party and NMM as well as the homes of leading Communists. Twelve leaders were arrested and indicted under the 1797 act against incitement to mutiny. This immediately sparked a campaign which affected all parts of the labour movement for some months. Even Macdonald felt impelled to rise to his feet in the Commons and criticise the government's action.

As the 12 were housed at Wandsworth Prison, the main march there gathered on Clapham Common meeting ground. It was the largest sea of people I had seen since the MacSwiney demonstration, possibly even larger. They were milling around seven or eight platforms, the Communist Party had one, so did the ILP's paper the *New Leader*, so did Lansbury's *Labour Weekly* where Lansbury himself spoke. Once the march had set off, it was accompanied not only – as often then and now – by a thin line of policemen but also, for the first time, by stewards who had responded to a call in the *Labour Weekly* – a paper in which Raymond Postgate too was heavily involved – for a worker's defence corps. On the way to the prison, both sides behaved themselves, though one steward (whom I knew) complained to me afterwards that policemen had been kicking his feet and heels whenever this could be done unobtrusively.

Wandsworth prison proved to be no Brixton, though. We could not shout or sing to each other over the wall. Facing Wandsworth Prison, at that time, was a small road. Into this area, the police shepherded the demonstration; meantime, immediately in front of the prison, a heavy police cordon was placed. Following further speeches and singing of revolutionary songs, the main demonstration broke up. Not so the East End contingent, they resolved to march all the way home.

As I was obviously with the Battersea lot, I didn't witness what followed. Lansbury claimed later to have advised against marching, but to have gone along with the majority decision. The route intended was

Windmill Road, straight up Battersea Rise, past the north side of Clapham Common and on to Stockwell. But when they got to the corner of Battersea Rise with Windmill Road and Vardens Road, they were charged at by mounted police. Despite this, most of them re-grouped and proceeded to the East End. There was no further attacks by the police.

A narrower experience had also recently confirmed the attitude of us Communists towards the police. During one of our London District conferences in 1924 or 1925, a noise or rustling was heard from under the platform. And – yes – there were two men underneath who had been taking notes. And the extraordinary thing is, that these police agents beat it – got clean away – but left their notes behind. The Communist Party's *Workers' Weekly* published these and challenged the government to prosecute it – which the government never did. As will be relevant later, we normally assumed that all Communist Party premises were under some sort of surveillance.

The demonstration to Wandsworth Prison, let alone its violent aftermath, seemed to symbolise a solidifying of the whole labour movement – and around the left. But in February 1926, the Labour Party's national executive instructed all Constituency Labour Parties to implement the ban, proclaimed at the Liverpool conference, on Communist members. The leader of Labour's right wing in London, Herbert Morrison, picked out as the most dangerous the trades council in Bethnal Green and the Labour Party and trades council in Battersea.

Immediately, at the moment that edict was received in Battersea, the reaction was: 'We're not standing for this nonsense.' Our Labour MP was a popular and widely respected Communist who had regained his seat at the last election, against the national trend, even though he had not been endorsed nationally by the Labour Party. We were doing fine together. All our wards, along with the Women's Section and the Coop Women's Guild, were for carrying on as if the edict had never come. Not that there was unanimity, but this was the overwhelming mood. Furthermore, Sak no longer had as his agent the old Burnsite, Charlie Mason; instead, he had Jack Clancy. And yet, despite all this, the movement started coming apart – to the extent that, by the begin-ning of May when the General Strike began, we had in embryo a situation in which there were rival ward organisations, one of these affiliated nationally and the other not, and also virtually two trades councils. True, with something like a General Strike looming more and more obviously, old friendships and loyalties simply carried on, so as to see the strike through.

Tragically, in the year after the General Strike, the disaffiliated party – which began with majority support – went down to defeat. Those who left it for the affiliated organisation were not necessarily right wingers. Far from it. Many of them simply could not bear disaffiliation. These were the generation who had made such an impact in municipal politics and municipal enterprise around 1920 as Herald Leaguers, or as members of the Battersea Socialist Society or ILP. So they still retained some class consciousness. When the government started asking local authorities to register volunteers for the special constabulary and for the official strikebreaking organisation (the Organisation for the Maintenance of Supplies), this Battersea Labour establishment was one of the few which refused to play along. This contrasted with the situation across the borough boundary in Wandsworth, where all libraries and public offices were thrown wide open for such recruiting. But when Battersea's establishment complied with Morrison's circular even while ignoring the government's, an underlying factor was that, as individuals, many of them had become full time organisers for various unions – particularly in the building industry and among the general workers. In order to see the strike through and, subsequently, so as to survive its aftermath, they found they had more in common with those to their right than with those to their left. Even during the strike itself, this process was helping to muffle our impact.

Not that the months leading up to May 1926 found Communists politically isolated. The *Sunday Worker* appeared under the editorship of Willie Paul in 1925, so as to organise the left current that was growing within the unions and Labour Party, and soon had a circulation of 100 000. The Communist Party had the *Workers' Weekly*, whose 1925 circulation of approximately 60 000 had risen to 100 000 by May 1926. Under HN Brailsford's editorship, the ILP's *New Leader* was often left wing too. And 1925 also saw the start of Lansbury's *Labour Weekly* with the aim of building ginger groups within the movement so as to get back to the task of changing society. It was soon reputed to have a circulation of 150 000. Here, both Postgate and Horrabin were involved. For some time the Communist Party had been warning about the various old colonels and suchlike who were hoping to imitate Mussolini's Fascists. But our idea of forming a workers' defence corps against them and against the authorities was taken up loudly in the *Labour Weekly* – and taken up not casually but directly, at article length.

And another thing in which *Labour Weekly* was clearly ahead, during the run up to the General Strike, was over the need for workers' control of information. Its editorial for May Day 1926 called on 'the printers and organised journalists' to 'combat the lies which the ruling classes are telling the people... to act as a workers' censorship on the capitalist press'. It reminded them of how, 'during the railway dispute of 1919 the compositors had shown their loyalty and their power' in this way. To 'write and print lies designed to mislead the workers' was, it pointed out, 'a form of blacklegging, and one of its worst forms'. As we know, when a day or two later the printworkers on the *Daily Mail* refused to run a particularly provocative editorial, Stanley Baldwin and his government used this incident to break off negotiations, call the TUC's bluff and get the strike started at a good moment. I have always imagined that some of those printworkers must have read or heard of that *Labour Weekly* editorial.

By the spring of 1926, the long propaganda campaign to swing the whole labour movement behind the miners was bearing fruit. In March Lansbury's paper reported that 1.5 million workers had declared their union's support for the proposed Workers Industrial Alliance. The engineers had voted for it two to one – a constitution was in the making. The organised left wing in the trade union movement, the NMM, called a special conference of action on 21 March in Latchmere Baths, Battersea.

The response indicated the depth of feeling flowing through the movement: delegates assembled from 547 organisations representing 957 000, no less than 52 trades councils sent delegates. One measure of its impact was that Hicks, Turner and Findlay, three members of the TUC General Council, sent messages to the conference, although each letter confined itself to expressions of protest at the arrest of the imprisoned Communists.

The conference opened under the presidency of Tom Mann. But the official welcome was given by Jack Clancy, as chairman of the Battersea Trades and Labour Council. He brought the conference alive by relaying the news of the disaffiliation of Battersea and Bethnal Green Trades Councils for their refusal to operate the Liverpool Labour Party Conference decision on the expulsion of the Communists. Tom Mann, in a memorable analytical speech, examined the issues facing the class. The prime minister, Baldwin, had asserted that the wages of all workers must come down. The purpose of the Coal Commission was to divide the movement. On all sides could be seen the growing preparations of the employers and government to impose their solutions to the crisis. Extreme right wing strikebreaking organisations were mushrooming. The British Fascist organisations were appearing at workers' meetings. No worker could be indifferent. He went on:

'Therefore prepare at once. Let us perfect our relations with each other; let us have our industrial machinery ready for action. The real central body through which we must function is the General Council of the Trades Union Congress. All unions should be loyal thereto and cooperate therewith.'

This was the clearest possible expression of Communist and Minority Movement opinion in the days preceding the General Strike.

It would be false to present either Mann or the Conference of Action leadership as passively directing all their efforts to official channels. The great positive programme for the immediate days ahead, a programme that served the class in the nine days of May, was its call for:

1. Each trades council to constitute itself a Council of Action that embraced all the workers' organisations in the locality.

2. To establish under the auspices of the trades council a Workers' Defence Force against Fascism.

3. To organise the workers on the job into factory and pit committees.

4. To demand the right of soldiers and naval ratings to refuse strike service.

We had little more than a month in which to begin implementing this. During the ensuing weeks, hardly a trades council existed that was not compelled to consider the implications of becoming a Council of Action. The cleavage with the right wing in the movement, who had been content to go along with a general agitation for the justice of the miners' claim, now asserted itself. It was on the issue of preparation that the left found the greatest response. Only weeks now separated the workers from the actual struggle. In those weeks the revolutionary left, the Communists and Minority Movement, struggled against the right wing in the movement.

As the General Strike approached, the organisational situation in and around Battersea could hardly have been more complex. The simplest part was our own. The South West Local of the Communist Party had its own premises in North Street, Clapham. Throughout the strike, its committee (of which I was a member) was responsible for the whole of South West London. We prepared for the eventuality that some of us might be arrested. John Mahon was supposed to be renting a flat in Brixton, along with a woman who was posing as an artist. From this flat, we hoped to give continuity to our communications and to the editing of our strike bulletin, should any of our other premises be raided or any of us get lifted. Further, since 1922, we had continually been told how vital it was to report to party organisers all relevant information as to what was happening. We were even encouraged to scribble these reports down. Through our habit of reporting, our leadership was not to be left operating in a vacuum. And indeed, during the strike, our South West Local party committee was well abreast of developments in the area.

We also knew we could draw on our links and our experience with Battersea's NUWCM For some years, this had been able to get a demonstration together any day of the week. And again, as YCLers, we had long been accumulating our own experience of putting up a platform at street corners and speaking for hours and hours, sometimes far into the night. So this was certainly the type of activity which came naturally to people like me, here, we expected we could set our own pace. We felt we had made all possible preparations.

1 May 1926 dawned with the miners already locked out. It was the greatest May Day in living memory. In every town and city, from hundreds of meetings and demonstrations the workers asserted their solidarity with the cause of the miners. In Birmingham, the conservative base of the Chamberlains, more people were on the streets than had been seen at a recent royal visit; thousands marched.

London's May Day was the crowning achievement. From the 29 metropolitan boroughs, from mid-morning to late afternoon, the streets were alive with demonstrators. Trade union banners that had not been aired for years floated in the breeze; across all the Thames bridges, marchers stepped out for Hyde Park. Those contingents whose line of march was to pass Memorial Hall, where the conference of trade union executives was in session, were told by the excited delegates that the General Strike had been called for midnight of 3 May. To the rank and file trade unionists, it seemed that at last the fruitless negotiations were over and now the movement was being made ready for action.

In Hyde Park, from a dozen platforms, a militant mood swept that vast crowd of people. This was the real measure of the workers' feelings. Deep down, in whatever industry or job, each felt that a defeat this time for the miners would be but a prelude to an all-round attack on the whole of the working class.

The conference of the trade union executives, which for three days had been in session, appeared to be entirely uncritical of the General Council's negotiating team. At that time, no-one knew, least of all the rank and file, that Arthur Pugh, the TUC president, had only a few days before been alone with Baldwin at Chequers. Even the absence of a miners' representative on the negotiating committee, and the last-minute inclusion of MacDonald and Henderson went unchallenged. Like the masses, the lay union representatives at that conference, with their virginal illusions, thought that the General Council, by its decision to call for a General Strike, was by that act identifying with the hopes and aspirations of the whole movement.

The leading core of General Council negotiators had other plans. No sooner was power passed to them than they sought to utilise the remaining days, not to perfect the organisation for the strike itself, but to find a formula to prevent it happening.

Anxious to secure a compromise, begging for a settlement, they finally approached Baldwin with a formula calculated to break the deadlock, behind the backs of the miners' leaders. In essence, they agreed to urge on the miners a cut in wages, subject to the mineowners and government accepting the proposals of the Royal Commission on the miners. But the government with all its preparations in an advanced stage, its proclamation of the state of emergency off the printing presses, the armed forces mobilised for despatch to the main industrial centres, the OMS and special constabulary at the ready, broke off all negotiations with the TUC.

All that was then known throughout the movement was the General Council's strike call. And it was to that call that the workers responded with undreamed-of enthusiasm – a response so overwhelming that both the government and the union leadership were staggered by its magnitude.

But even in Battersea the situation was not as ideal as I have so far painted it. As I have mentioned, the General Strike came upon a split trades council, or rather a two-headed one in embryo. This creature formed itself into a Battersea Council of Action. Its main official purpose was to issue permits for the movement of goods. It was in almost continuous session, day and night throughout the strike, and produced its own bulletin whose content reflected the timidity of the TUC's *British Worker*. Now, on this body, the older left wingers such as Clancy had known the right wingers for years and years, and could get on with them. But youngsters like us were outside this field of relationships. Of course, during the strike itself, I dropped in on meetings of that Council of Action almost daily. My friends and the party fraction were operating within it. But when youngsters like me spoke, they were no more than listened to. The right paid no attention and the non-Communist Party left felt uneasy – as did even some of the older Communists.

Worse, something that flabbergasted me from those meetings of the Battersea Council of Action was the absence of linkage. They didn't seem to know what was happening next door in Lambeth or Clapham. And as for further afield within London, there was Frank Smith, Battersea Trades Council's delegate to the London Trades Council. He was a highly political person. An engineering worker and former SLPer, he had been a shop steward during the war (alongside JT Murphy) and had met Lenin in Moscow during 1920. But now it was as if his delegacy to the London Trades Council meant absolutely nothing, as far as the area was concerned. This wasn't his fault. Though the LTC did meet, it was still dominated by right wingers who actively blocked ideas for interconnecting the trades councils. Indeed I remember that a former SDFer called Duncan Carmichael underwent so much strain from the effort of motorcycling around London, trying to act as a link, that he died shortly after the strike ended.

As if all this confusion were not enough, each union anyway took charge of its own members, information and instructions were relayed from union head offices down to branches. So branch meetings became for most members a vital source of news, even more than usual. Worse still, some branches scented dangerous novelty in any Council of Action, even of the Battersea type. For example, my own NUR branch viewed affiliation to such a body as against union regulations, and so stayed aloof from it. Of course, when I came off duty at 10.00pm on the eve of the strike, I reported to that branch, down at Unity Hall. But I found that it had already organised its share of the picketing. So, early the next morning, I was out with the Young Communist League.

For the opening day of the strike, the first thing we and the NUWCM had decided to do – and Jack Tierney, our local fulltimer, was kept fully informed of this – was to start a march around the factories and bring people out on strike. The first factory we came to was Morgan Crucibles. This was partially organised and came out at once – led, incidentally, by Bill Savage, an old Wobbly (who was subsequently victimised). And then along Lombard Road there was Carson's Paint factory. They were not unionised. But as soon as we approached along the road we could see them, too, coming out, and putting their coats on to join us. And similar things happened as the march got bigger and bigger. People were obviously wanting or expecting to come out. At that time there used to be a generating station in Lombard Road, owned by the council. Here I can remember their ETU steward, George Mott, coming out to wonder what the position of his men was; for some reason, they had not been called out.

Outside each workplace, the demonstration would stop, hold a meeting, explain the General Strike and get a response. Not surprisingly, the Council of Action endorsed our initiative afterwards.

Battersea is cut in two by this vast expanse of railway. This obviously made the strike particularly noticeable. Not a train was to be seen or heard. Nor was there any movement of buses or trams. Such transport as did move had orange and black labels – 'By permission of the TUC' – on their windscreens. Also, there were very few special constables in evidence – though this was to change radically later on.

Apart from the quiet, the main feeling among most people was of being absolutely starved for news. Copies of the TUC's *British Worker* or even of Churchill's *British Gazette* or of the Paris edition of the *Daily Mail* were soon being passed from hand to hand, often till they fell apart. So were our cyclostyled Communist Party *Workers' Bulletins*. For information, people depended otherwise on two things. One was the wireless. We know now from historians that hardline Tory ministers like Churchill thought the BBC dangerously soft. But strikers could see it was outrageously dependent on right wing sources for its information, it amounted in effect to a strikebreaking device. So, in our *Bulletins* and on our platforms, we spoke about how one could, in effect, jam such broadcasts. And our speaking was the second thing. The street outside the Prince's Head had been a meeting place for decades. Not that we had always attracted large crowds over the years. But now, right from the word 'go', we kept our platform there. The corner of Winders Road was where we pitched it, and I can remember how the vastness of the crowds forced us to take it deeper and deeper into Winders Road. Day after day and night after night, we were speaking to one continuous open air gathering.

The workplaces on which we had been concentrating our agitation, during the previous two or more years, were now on strike. So their workers were now all dispersed. Thus, general speaking had to become our main focus, our YCL elocution classes certainly paid off. You spoke as far as your voice would carry. The crowds seemed colossal, though I remember recognising some of my old schoolmates there. As there was now no public transport in our area, there was seldom any interruption. People were aching for information, encouragement, ideas. Towards the end of the first week of the strike, the Council of Action took over these meetings and supplied the speakers. Following the arrest there of a noted left wing councillor the police closed the meetings down.

One effort that the organised unemployed made during those days was to march to Bow Street, where Saklatvala was up on trial for words he had spoken in Hyde Park on May Day. I don't know whether the organisers had done the normal thing and informed the authorities of the intended route. But all I do know is that when we got to Albert Bridge to cross the river, we were blocked by lines of police. We were not going to be allowed to proceed. So, on my own initiative, I walked along the river and over Chelsea Bridge, and made my way to Bow Street. I did get there, though I was unable to find the trial. The point is I needed to walk no further than Sloane Square to know I was almost in a different world. In contrast to the stillness on the south side of the river, here you saw buses. Each was being driven by a university student, with a policeman sitting beside him in case of trouble. Two sides – there was no more than the Thames between us.

The only other time I ventured north of the river was when someone on the Battersea Council of Action told some of us YCLers that, in Townmead Road, Fulham, there was a Union Jack petrol depot operating for the OMS. So Alf Loughton and I got on our bikes and went over to find out. We found there were also some soldiers involved there. But the main work of filling the petrol tanks of the OMS vehicles was done by girls. Now, I remember cycling there, observing the activity and speaking to many of those girls opposite the depot. They were very friendly, brought out two chairs and a cup of tea. Alf remembers me persuading them to promise to come out the next day (which apparently they did) and also our shooting off on our bikes when mounted police were rumoured to be approaching. But here my memory is vaguer.

The point is, though, that there was so little coordination between Battersea and Fulham, that someone in Battersea felt a need to send two lads over to Fulham to do an important and apparently easy thing which Fulham should surely have attempted for themselves as early as possible. And even on our side of the river, the Battersea Council of

Action did not know what was happening as nearby as Clapham tram depot. Here, the closing stage of the strike saw friction between police and strikers; as YCLers, we heard of this soon enough.

Now, I've already mentioned the vacuum of news, the confusion of organisation and, overall, the general atmosphere of not knowing what to do next, all of which characterised most people's experience of at least the first week of the strike. These weaknesses were related to far deeper problems within the union movement and throughout the left.

One problem was a very wide one indeed. Continuously for at least a generation (and intermittently since Thomas Spence around 1800), many working class militants had assumed that their class as a whole had only to strike, and power would flow to the workers. Into the 1920s, the phrase 'war of folded arms' had become a cliché, deep in the minds of a whole generation of activists, at every level, who still viewed themselves as left wing. I remember Tom Mann standing on a public platform and demonstrating how you had only to fold your arms and you'd be **there**. These 'syndicalist' views on the final confrontation with capitalism were particularly strong during the 1910s. Some of those militants who had come to the fore during the strike waves of 1910-14 and around 1919 had become influential locally or nationally. The Labour College movement had organised from 1909 as part of that surge and, into 1926, kept it very much alive. Politically, it could be very left, the group around Lansbury's *Labour Weekly* had raised slogans for the replacement of parliament. The Communist Party leadership denounced this as 'revolutionary phrase-mongering', but was quite happy to echo it very soon after and to claim that it had 'found a wide response amongst the workers'. This obvious little switch by our leaders underlines that the people around Lansbury were capable of tuning into the thoughts of large sections of advanced workers.

Two prominent examples of this 'folded arms' perspective occurred in Battersea during the strike. One was Noah Ablett. A South Wales miner, one of the pre-1914 syndicalists, now a Labour MP – and sitting for a South Wales constituency. After Red Friday, his prominent position hardly made him vocal against the line of the Labour leadership that, now that the government had set up a Royal Commission on the coal industry, everyone should pipe down so as to give these wise men a chance to deliberate undisturbed. But, all right, now that the strike had begun, what contribution did this admired rebel, after all his years of class war education, have to make? Deliberately to court arrest!

As I've mentioned, May Day had seen Saklatvala being quietly detained after making some allegedly 'seditious' remarks in Hyde Park. The next day was a Sunday, and palpably the eve of the strike. Ablett chanced to be the speaker in Battersea town hall that evening: 'I shall repeat the words of Saklatvala, which he got arrested for yesterday...' So **he** was arrested – quietly, after the meeting, just as Sak had been.

Unlike Sak, though, he was released very quickly. I remember Jack Clancy telling me that the great man had been drunk. True, Jack saw drink as lying at the root of many a left leader's decline. But, politically speaking, Ablett was, without doubt, hung over.

A second and astonishingly sadder instance was George Coppock, secretary of the Building Workers' Federation. He was second in his industry only to Hicks. Because of the way in which the recent amalgamation of many building unions was working out, Coppock was not on the General Council of the TUC, but nonetheless he was well known at the TUC's headquarters in Ecclestone Square, over the river. As he happened to live in Battersea and had a local reputation for his links with Ecclestone Square, it was easy for the Council of Action to call a meeting with him as principal speaker. Given the general hunger for news, it was more than easy, the town hall was packed from floor to ceiling, with more crowds trying to get in. And what did Coppock have for feeding their hunger? Throughout that meeting, he did nothing but make jokes, had them rolling in the aisles almost. As a comedy act, it was an unsurpassable one man show. But as for strategy, guidance or even hard news, he was bankrupt. We had all ached for him to give us some perspective on what was happening nationally. I was **shattered**. And so, I remember, was Clancy.

Nor was this passive view of general strikes confined to leading members of that syndicalist-influenced generation. I can still remember meeting with it in conversations with all sorts of people in the movement. Take Jack Tierney. Originally from Tyneside and only a few years older than me, we've already met him as a fulltime organiser for the Communist Party in our part of London. Shortly before May 1926, the party issued a compilation of writings by Lenin and others and called it *On the Road to Insurrection*. Tierney had an extremely sharp mind, and had certainly been a founder member of the party in a more mature way than me. But I remember him devouring this pamphlet in our HQ at Morris Hall, very much as if he believed that its title described the situation literally.

Similarly, Jimmy Lane believed in a Leninist way what older people like his father believed in a syndicalist or at least industrial unionist way; that this was **it**, and that the wonderful thing about the General Strike was – that it was there at last. (Strictly, of course, it wasn't even general, the General Council had pedantically called out no more than its 'first line'.) Personally, I did not believe we were necessarily very far along that 'road'. But I was convinced we ought to make great strides along it. I didn't think we were near revolution yet, but I thought we were at a crucial moment in the class struggle and that the party had a marvellous chance to develop.

Some vital factors in our final disappointment were within the party itself. I recall even some party members – very much part of the mood during the strike's first week – saying: 'Jimmy Thomas isn't so bad!' Even those *Workers' Bulletins* – which, as I shall show, we were distributing at increasing risk of arrest – only started criticising union leaders during the second week; and even then, they made a specific point of having one criticism for the right wing and a different criticism for the left. We can certainly see, with hindsight, that the left wing union leaders were more or less as bad as the right. And what the right were up to was abundantly clear from the start of the strike. The Communist Party's own leadership had little appreciation of what was taking place at the top level in the unions. Or, if there was such an appreciation, it was not communicated at all clearly to ordinary party members such as ourselves.

It is not that Britain was in, by Leninist definitions, a revolutionary situation in May 1926. You only have to read Lenin on thoroughly revolutionary situations to see the obvious difference from our reality. During these last few decades, Trotsky has often been said – both by Stalinists and many Trotskyists – to have argued that May 1926 actually did see Britain already in such a situation. But both sides need to use selective quotation to prove he ever said so much. The point, rather, is that the British labour movement of 1926 had not only been sapped by years of unemployment and employers' offensives, but was also betrayed by the right with the confused connivance of the union and Labour lefts. What Trotsky, at the time, was correct to emphasise were the opportunities which the strike opened for the Communist Party to take political initiative, provided it was clear in its own mind as to what was happening. Instead, the Communist Party became part of the confusions, sometimes praising the left leaders, and sometimes warning about their unreliability. Thus its members shared all too much in the experience of the rest of the class for whom, as Dutt well put it, the 1926 betrayal came as 'a thunderclap'.

Our party's share in these confusions was also partly to do with its interest in the Anglo-Russian Trade Union Committee. Originally, the Communist Party had seen this body, quite correctly, as helping to legitimise the position of the Bolshevik state and as providing a possible conduit for Bolshevik influence via the very top of the British movement. But some Trotskyists have argued, in recent decades, that Stalin and his supporters (who were, of course, increasingly dominant in Russia and thus in the Comintern) were so interested in gaining credits from Western bankers for Russia's industrialisation, that they turned the Committee into a device for hitching British revolutionaries to the vagaries of unreliable left union leaders. Now, I am self-evidently no friend of Stalinism. Yet the truth is that (as we saw in relation to the start of the first Labour government during 1924) the British Communist Party needed no manipulation from anywhere outside itself, in order to go too far to the right.

And the fate of the Anglo-Russian Committee provides a good example of this. The autumn 1926 Trades Union Congress was obviously going to be haunted by the debacle of May. Faced with this prospect, the General Council took Arthur Pugh's line that any postmortem on the General Strike should be held over, as the miners were still on strike themselves. To his disgrace, the miners' own leader, the left winger and former Communist AJ Cook, supported this stance. And one major voice against it was Tomsky's. Unlike in 1924, the British government refused Tomsky permission to come to Britain for the Congress. So instead, he sent an extraordinarily long telegram – one of those telegraphed manifestos – which went into some of the important lessons. Now, Tomsky's name underneath these vituperations was obviously a sign that his was also the view of the Russian Politbureau and of the Comintern. But the British party's leaders were very definitely against the line taken in that telegram. Supporting it directly would have ruined all their hopes of being able to lean on the left leaders. A few years later, JR Campbell and other leading Communists were to admit this much – but then only as part of their turn to the sectarian and even more disastrous line of the 'Third Period'.

So I'm racing ahead, though not surprisingly. The point was the thunderclap: everything seemingly growing in solidarity and then, all of a sudden, an apparently astonishing betrayal. For us, this thunderclap came in Battersea town hall. Jack Clancy, as chairman of the Council of Action, was sent to Ecclestone Square to clarify what were thought to be nasty rumours. Once again, the town hall on Lavender Hill was packed to the rafters and surrounded by a dense throng of people. Poor Jack had a shattering experience – of coming back as bearer of news that was totally against his convictions. And as soon as he started announcing that the strike had been called off but that the miners were still out – he could say no more, the loudest boo that I've ever yet heard went up from those masses of people and was echoed down Lavender Hill. The mood was angry in the extreme. Indescribably.

Given this anger – which almost every history and memoir and memory confirms from up and down Britain – we can hardly be surprised that the next day saw more people out on strike than ever before. This was of course strengthened by the growing actuality of victimisation. So now, the union leaders as well as the employers had a problem: how to get everyone back. This was where the prime minister, Stanley Baldwin, came in with his guarantee (purely verbal, of course) of no victimisation.

By this time, in Battersea at least, our enemies were also bringing other pressures to bear. Here, the police had been almost quiet during the strike's early days. The short term reasons for this are perhaps only divinable within a wider perspective. But at the time – starved as ever for news – we knew only that we were not being molested. However,

Saturday the 8th saw two arrests. Councillor Andrews, a left wing member of the Council of Action, was taken from his bed that evening and charged with making a speech likely to cause disaffection. And a busman called Cousins was also lifted. He had been speaking at the 'Prince's Head' for months past. The next morning, representatives of the Council of Action – which had decided to take over the 'Prince's Head' meetings – arranged their platform, began the meeting and were then surrounded by a squad of police, headed by two inspectors, who ordered them to stop, stating that no more meetings were to be held there.

However, we YCLers had further outlets. We were involved in producing and distributing our *Workers' Bulletin*. Unlike the trades council's bulletin, this was a party publication. The editorial matter plus the national news items were fed out from the party HQ at King Street, Covent Garden, but we put the local news items in for ourselves. Now, during the strike's closing stages, we reported in our *Bulletin* a rumour that some soldiers in a Guards regiment stationed across the bridge in Chelsea barracks, had disobeyed orders. From that instant on, open distribution of our *Bulletins* was impossible, we had constantly to try and melt into those enormous crowds so as to circulate our copies from within them.

This was how Alf Loughton was caught out. On the last day of the strike, the YCL were holding a meeting outside the railwaymen's headquarters on Falcon Road. As a railwayman I was inside, my branch was meeting to consider the terms on which, we were being informed, the strike was to end. I knew Alf was outside on the platform, speaking. Some railwaymen rushed in and told me he had been arrested – in fact one or two were amazed to see me inside, as they thought it had been me. (Not that they had tried to prevent the arrest.) I rushed out. Jimmy Lane and I went straight along to Battersea Bridge Road police station. As we approached, we could see that the policeman who had been standing at the top of the steps up to the entrance went in, as if to warn of our arrival. As we came in, the doors were shut and blocked behind us. We were immediately searched for leaflets. By pure chance, neither of us had any in evidence (though in fact, the sergeant was put off going deeper into one of Jimmy's pockets when Jimmy joked that the pipe in it was a revolver!). Not so Alf, and we could not reach any understanding with the police about bailing him out. In fact, they threw us out. Later Jimmy's father – as a former Mayor of Battersea – was allowed to offer sureties of £50, and so was Alf (not that he, at least, had remotely this kind of money).

But, shortly before Alf was lifted, another railwaymen's premises had been the scene of a much more serious incident. Throughout the strike, members of two other NUR branches as well as of the locomotive engineers would hang around outside their headquarters in

Wandsworth Road, opposite Larkhall Rise, waiting for news. When rumours and then information of the surrender began to spread, these crowds became larger than ever. At this moment, they were, without any shadow of provocation, assaulted by carloads of special constables, who simply appeared and waded in with batons. Only slightly further afield, the trouble outside Clapham tram depot also occurred at about this time.

On the eve of the General Council's surrender, the party's *Workers' Bulletin* abandoned its diplomacy towards the trade union leadership. The right wing were now accused of 'betrayal' and the left leaders, who had been assiduously courted so long by both the party and Moscow were accused of 'cowardly silence'. This was an abrupt switch from the policy of 'all power to the General Council', and it was made at the moment of the greatest confusion. This message was coupled with the slogan, 'refuse to return to work'. This was on the leaflets which we YCLers distributed round the railway depots from five o'clock in the morning of the day when the movement was due to surrender unconditionally. Such leaflets became a ticket to prison for hundreds of party members.

These developments coloured the days around the betrayal. We saw them in the context of the declarations by the Attorney General and by Mr Justice Astbury that the strike was illegal. In the Battersea area at least, the toughening of police tactics felt like part of a crackdown on a suddenly confused and demoralised working class.

But demoralisation can take place at many different speeds even within the same person. Nothing, for example, could have been less demoralised than the way in which we Victoria railwaymen returned to work. **Despite** the surrender 'thunderclap', my branch (right wing though it was) decided that, along with all other Battersea railwaymen working at Victoria, we should **march** back to work.

My branch decided this; and there was nothing Bolshevik in singling oneself out for needless victimisation. Given that the railway companies had already, like so many other employers, posted notices up, warning that the strike had been a breach of contract and that employees would be taken back 'subject to the exigencies of the service', the élan of even this right wing branch was remarkable. We marched as one body from Battersea to Victoria, a magnificent gesture, given that probably none of the 200 or so of us knew who might find they still had a job when we arrived. And when we did turn from Buckingham Palace Road into the entrance of the station, we could see Old Hopper – the station superintendent who was regularly so resplendent in his shiny top hat, which was always so new for seeing King George and Queen Mary off to somewhere or other – was standing there to observe us. The horror on his face was a sight to see. But of course, he had the last laugh. We all had to line up and be told our individual fate. His office had a long table, a line of interviewers was waiting for us all. The railway companies now sorted individuals out and shuffled them around.

As it turned out, I was indeed one of those subjected 'to the exigencies of the service'. In fact, the defeat had a personal impact on all three of us – Alf Loughton, Jimmy Lane and myself – which would have to be multiplied by at least tens of thousands to measure its disorienting effects on the labour movement.

Soon after the strike ended, Alf appeared in court, charged with the heinous offence of being in possession of Communist literature. Along with many other Battersea YCLers, I took the day off in order to attend his trial. But we were not allowed into the building. Alf served three months in Wormwood Scrubs prison. Of course, he was hardly the first Communist to land there, and fresh batches seemed to be arriving all the time. Luckily, Alf had for some time been studying Pitman's shorthand. So he asked and got permission to have a pencil and paper. This was the start of the *Wormwood Scrubber*, produced on toilet paper and circulated during church service. Edited by Tommy Jackson, it helped keep up morale among the political prisoners – who by now included Dave Springhall and Sak. (Years later, Harry Pollitt was to laud Jackson's role, but to forget Alf's.)

Jimmy and I met Alf on his release in July. But by then, our trio was being dispersed. For Jimmy had an untypical stroke of luck. Some rich Communist or sympathiser was having a house built in or near Monte Carlo. So Jimmy and another victimised building worker, Bert Joy (our famous 'Tooting Trotsky') went down to lay bricks in the sun for many months. Not that I blame them. Through the decades, I was never able to find out from Jimmy what was involved. But, given that a more prominent comrade whom I later met in Moscow also turned out to know about this, I assume it had been arranged via some party grapevine.

My fate was in between. The railway company transferred me from the strategic heights of my Victoria Station indicator to Deal, a place I at first viewed as lying on the outermost rim of Kent. There, I was given 'general porterage' duties. Much of the time, I seemed to be cleaning out cattle trucks and sheep pens, not a very pleasant job.

At first I was alone. But when I heard that Alf was at least temporarily without a job in London, I went down to the local Labour Exchange and asked if there were any jobs for bricklayers. They said there were, and gave me a green card which I sent to him. So Alf and I lived together in Deal for some months. We made a little contact with the local trades council, though we were obviously unversed on the main issues in the area.

Luckily, the autumn saw the end of our time in Deal. At this time, Jimmy Lane's father was full time organiser in the south-east for the bricklayers' union. When his organising duties brought him down to

Deal, he inquired after me at the booking office. He told me that people in the Battersea labour movement and Labour Party were aware of the difficulties my mother was currently in, my elder brother had recently married, so she was partly dependent on my income to top up her war widow's pension. Old man Lane's words to me now were: 'Keep your nose clean, and I'll see what I can do.' And here he mentioned that he knew the stationmaster at Deal, a Mr Hunter. Anyway, he seems to have impelled him to set the wheels in motion to get me transferred back to London. What strengthens this impression in my mind is that, the moment after Alf and I had got into the carriage for the actual journey home, this Mr Hunter came along the platform and most warmly wished me the best of luck. (As an apprenticed bricklayer, Alf no longer anticipated any difficulty getting a job in London.)

Back in South London, I became a porter at a number of places on the inner parts of the Brighton line. But more important was the deepening involvement of Alf and myself in the YCL. On that, was to hang my going to Moscow in October 1927. (Luckily my mother remarried while I was in Moscow.)

Through Berlin to Moscow

MY selection for the International Lenin School ran counter to the previous rhythms of my life. I have **never** enjoyed national or wider set-ups. I have always been happier taking part in practical work, rooted in a local class movement. Into the summer of 1926, this had increasingly been the main richness of my life. And my preferences still remain this way. This is nothing to do with whatever degree of modesty I may have. It is simply that I feel more secure in such surroundings.

My selection also happened against the grain of many important developments on the national and international level. In the autumn of 1926, the YCL held its congress in Sheffield. I was not a delegate. But when the time came to elect the YCL's Executive Committee, an upset occurred. The party leadership presented the congress with a panel or slate, a list of candidates to be endorsed or rejected as one whole. This panel had been drawn up by Willie Rust (the YCL's secretary) with the help of two international comrades; Richard Schuller (an Austrian who attended as official representative of the Young Communist International) and a Czechoslovak whom we knew as Percy (and who later worked on *Rote Fahne*). This slate consisted almost entirely of people working full time for the Russian trading agencies in London. At this, Alf, who **was** one of the London delegates, created an uproar: 'Why all these office wallahs, and what about some industrial workers?' And the other London delegates backed him. The question then became: have you any alternative nominations? And Alf nominated me. As an industrial worker, known among London YCLers, I was elected to the Executive. The first I knew about this was a telegram from Rust, to attend the meeting of the Executive Committee at its Great Ormond Street offices. So I went up there and learned of my election.

The Executive used to meet every Wednesday night. At that time we were doing quite a lot of industrial work, not least with the miners. We were also plugging away to get a delegation sent from the Labour League of Youth and the ILP Guild of Youth to Russia for the tenth anniversary of the revolution in October 1927. This was the period of work for a united front with the youth organisations. I was part of both efforts and was sent around to speak a bit, including to Barnsley and Hemsworth in the South Yorkshire coalfield.

On the Executive Committee of the YCL, we were thrown rather deeply into internal Communist politics. Andrew Rothstein represented the Communist Party's Politbureau at our meetings. Not only did he supervise our work generally. He also gave weekly reports on how things were going at party headquarters in King Street. Because of my industrial background and activity, I was looked on in a very favourable light.

In particular, Schuller, whom we had nicknamed Bonzo, had a respect for this. Although there were at least 10 years between us, there was also a rapport. Of course, we didn't mix socially. I knew that Comintern functionaries lived a life that was simultaneously risky and bureaucratic. Not that they were necessarily under constant surveillance at this time, but they could always have been deported. And their drinking, for example, was out of the range of us ginger beer YCLers. Indeed, it distinctly disgusted us. Some time earlier, Jimmy Lane, who had been coopted onto the YCL executive, resigned after experiencing a social night out with the International's representative. I remember him saying angrily that all that extravagance had been paid for by the Russian workers.

But in 1925, when I **had** been to the YCL's conference, Schuller and I travelled overnight from Manchester back to London, and spent virtually the whole seven or so hours of the train journey talking about books and particularly about working class history. He was obviously interested in a young railwayman who had read deeply in labour history. Subsequently, as the YCI representative, he must have heard, in some way, that my work among the railwaymen involved a lot of self reliance. These two aspects must have impressed him, and must be the reasons why I was nominated for the International Lenin School.

When the school had opened during early 1926 for an 18 months course, its first intake had been mainly party functionaries. For recruiting the second batch, the Comintern gave instructions to try and draw students from a broader layer, from districts and so on. As a result of problems which were becoming clear during the first course, the second was lengthened to three years. The Communist Party of Great Britain was told to nominate 12 students, and it asked the YCL to contribute one of these. For the YCL, Rust nominated me. I was the last of the 12 to be selected. (When I arrived at the school, I turned out to be the youngest there.)

I was told to go along to King Street to find out what it was all about. There, I was briefed by Tom Bell and by a man called Joss who were on Agitprop work at the time. And they explained that, on arrival in Moscow, potential students would have to do a written exam on the basis of a number of books. Kautsky's *Economic Doctrines of Karl Marx* was the only one I didn't know. It had only recently been translated. It was a treatment of Volume One of *Capital*. From Dobb and others, I already knew a bit about Marxist economics. The other books were the *Communist Manifesto*, Lenin's *State and Revolution* and *Left Wing Communism*.

So then, the thing was laid on. The delay, the delay, the delay. When on earth was I finally going to leave? The summer of 1927 was dragging into autumn. For the Comintern, let alone for the Communist Party, the year's most spectacular development had occurred during May. Police raided the Russian trading company in London, Arcos, and the British government broke off all relations with Russia. Both the International and Communist Party press were convinced that war was in the offing. To get a Russian visa, I would have to go via Berlin (and similarly, to get there, I had to get a visa for Germany from the German embassy in London).

Unlike the other 11 new students, who went in groups, I was to travel entirely alone. This was probably because I was also given some letters to deliver personally to officials at the Karl Liebknechthaus (the German Communist headquarters) in Berlin. I was also – much more important – given one of those silken Comintern passports, stamped by the Communist Party of Great Britain; obviously, I was to tell no-one of this till I reached the Russian border.

The journey was via Harwich and the Hook of Holland. On arrival in Berlin, I went to the address I had been told about: evidently a secret address for the British party. A lady there put me up, gave me a nice bed in a room to myself, and told me where I could find the Russian embassy, on Unter den Linden. So the next morning, I went there and walked up to the man at the desk. And at this moment, I suddenly learnt something of the effects of the Arcos raid! The moment he saw me, the man became rather hysterical, frantic to get me out of the building at once. Apparently, I had come in via the tradesman's entrance. He must have feared some provocation. Such was obviously the state of nervous tension in Russian diplomatic circles during those months at least. Well, I didn't know any German and had made precious little progress with a Russian grammar before leaving London. (to make things trickier, this book used the old lettering!) But, via a mixture of my English and his gestures, he gave me directions to the Alexanderplatz, where the Karl Liebknechthaus was situated. He was obviously relieved to see the back of me. When I got to the Alexanderplatz, I found that the Karl Liebknechthaus was built like a fortress, you had to peer through an entrance window and be let in. This time, I was obviously using the front entrance, but here too I had a bit of trouble at first. Fortunately, though, one chap there spoke English. I told him whom I wanted to give the letters to. When I had handed them over, I was told to stay in Berlin, report daily and await further instructions.

After a few days at the flat, I experienced another instance of the jumpiness of Communist officials in the aftermath of Arcos. To my surprise, a member of the Communist Party's Central Committee called Bob Stewart turned up. And he was utterly furious that that address had been given to me. He obviously saw it as a place exclusively for Central Committee members plus regular couriers. So he turfed me off the bed and I went and slept on the couch. Not that this bothered me in the slightest. But the pettiness has stuck in my mind.

I stayed in Berlin for two or three weeks. The local Young Communist comrades were very good to me. They took me round the town and to their party meetings in Neukölln and Wedding, working class areas whose long rows of tenements reminded me of Battersea Park Road. They also took me along to a congress, held in the Landtag building, of the Berlin district KPD (German Communist Party). This, a mere district meeting, involved a huge hall, with delegates sitting at desks, just as if it were a city council session. The issue under discussion was the Fischer-Urbahns Trotskyite Left Opposition group. What struck me, as someone still unfamiliar with the German language, was how aggressively guttural, almost savage, the debate sounded to me. More important was the liveliness – and length – of the speeches and the large number of people who spoke. In the room adjoining the hall, an enormous buffet had been laid on; loads of grub, beer galore. Outside the hall there was an electric signboard, flashing the names of the speakers. There we were, eating and drinking, but when the name of Thälmann came up on this indicator, everyone flocked back into the conference hall. It was my first experience of a conference on such a scale.

My time in Berlin came to an end when I was given another batch of letters, this time to take to Albert Inkpin, Secretary of the Communist Party of Great Britain, who was in Moscow. At last I was on a train from Berlin to the Soviet border at Negoreloye. On this train, I got chatting with a small man, an American Jew and Communist who was visiting his family in Minsk. He must have had a lot of money to spend, on the rack and in the luggage compartment he had a wealth of cigarettes and much else. When we reached the German-Polish border, we had to get out and go through the crisp snow over to a big hut where our passports were stamped and where our luggage was checked by Polish customs. My new friend unloaded a section of his cigarettes on to me.

Eventually, we resumed our progress towards Negoreloye and he stood me a meal in the restaurant car, never before had I seen such grub, much less eaten it. And when at last we reached Negoreloye, my feelings were indescribable. I was coming to the Fatherland, something we had read, thought, talked about ever since leaving school. I felt exalted, walking on air. Anyway, we got out of the train to go over to the broad gauge Russian train. In between, though, we had to pass through another long wooden hall, this time full of Red Army officers. As I have mentioned, I knew this was the moment to show them this silk Comintern passport, which had since been countersigned in Berlin. So I did, and this officer immediately put me on the Russian train –

though not before giving me some bread with a bit of meat fried in breadcrumbs plus a bottle of beer to see me to Moscow.

Shortly before the train started, this American rejoined me. He of course did not know about my Comintern pass. But he knew that he had been charged – skinned alive, he said – for everything he had brought in. He was most indignant with me and I didn't understand why. He'd bought me a meal, hadn't he? But I didn't know what it was all about: innocent. He said he now had a bill for so many thousand dollars and in Poland he could have exchanged money at an infinitely better rate than here in Russia; but he'd been honest about it and had been charged the earth for all he had brought in. This was the cause of his indignation. He thought I could've done something about it. And I suppose I could've. But at the time, it just never entered my mind. Of course, I had nothing to declare. All I had was what I stood up in, plus a toothbrush, vest, pair of pants and a couple of shirts or so, a tiny attaché case.

After changing trains in Minsk, I reached Moscow. And who should be there on the platform but Albert Inkpin himself. He was extremely friendly. I had met him once or twice at King Street when I had been the YCL representative on the commission set up after the General Strike to enquire into the performance of the party press. He now took me in a car to Mokhovaya, the headquarters of the Comintern. Across the Red Square and just at the extremity, stood a great big building. That was where all the Comintern cars were, Inkpin said, in an enormous underground car park. We stopped at a red building. We went through the same business here as in Berlin: show your credentials. Inkpin had a CI pass and he took me in and we went up to the top floor. A man was sitting outside the door with a revolver. This was OMSK – organisation department – and I delivered those letters I had got in Berlin.

As the YCI was headquartered in the same building, Inkpin took me downstairs to see them. They included some people I knew, such as Kathleen Rust (wife of Bill) who was working there as a referencer. One's memory can be strangely selective, on her table were cuttings from *The Times* she was assembling, and on her window sill were the internal phone numbers of various people. I remember reading names such as Bukharin, Stalin, Tomsky.

We had a bite to eat, and then Inkpin and I were driven to the Lenin School on Ulitsa Voroskova, off the Arbat. Possibly because this street had a number of embassies on it, it had been named after Vorovsky, a Soviet diplomat who had been assassinated in Switzerland. The building housing the school had previously been a girl's boarding school. It had a forecourt. At the front of this, we again had to negotiate the security precautions. Into the school building we went. It was rather old and beautiful, but to one side of it a great granite structure in the new-style 'architecture' was in the course of completion. I was given a room with two Chinese lads. Nice room. All amenities laid on. Then I met the English students. There were Bert Williams and another chap from Wales (from Aberdare) whose name I don't remember, and there was Olive Budden, who later married R Page Arnot. They were the first three students of the first intake; they made me feel at home, showed me around a bit, sort of initiated me.

Not that I was likely to learn many more names – real names. Immediately you joined the school, before you met the other students, you surrendered your ordinary passport, and you surrendered your name and exchanged it for a cover name. Thus during the 10 or so years around 1950, I was to recognise former contemporaries of mine from newspaper photos. Anna Pauker was unmistakeable (she was Romania's foreign minister, purged in 1952); another was Chervenkov (Bulgaria's prime minister for some time); the woman whom I sometimes met when I went to his room and who married him was also a Lenin School student (and turned out to be Dimitrov's daughter – not that Dimitrov was a big name yet); and another future prime minister or rather party leader was Bierut, from Poland. Even from the 11 British contemporaries in my intake, I still don't know all the real identities.

Obviously, all this would have had less point, had we already known most of each other by name. But in the 1920s, as far as most Communist Party members were concerned, you figured in your locality. Even those members whose names got into print, did so via local factory papers. Nationally, the party's press was overwhelmingly filled by its intellectuals, essentially those around Buckingham Palace Road and King Street. And as for demonstrations, there was no such thing as a national one. Thus, few of us had seen or heard of each other before. Admittedly, party names had little meaning for people from Britain. But they were vital for most other students, who were due to return to countries where party work was illegal.

The cover name I was allotted was 'Jack Tanner'. This was surely a strange choice, as a very real Jack Tanner had been a leading shop steward and founding party member. Worse, he even visited Moscow during my final winter there and had the ill luck to ring for someone at the school just as I happened to pass its only phone. In Russia, you gave your name when picking up phones. 'Hallo', I said, 'Jack Tanner speaking.' The real Jack Tanner was at the other end. What he imagined was going on, I don't know. And it was a bit odd for me too; by this time, I had been functioning for two years as 'Jack Tanner' and had started thinking of myself as 'Jack Tanner'. Another British student at the school took the name 'Maxton'. Luckily the real James Maxton never phoned!

Though they greeted me warmly, the three British students from the early intake were in the throes of finishing their course. Inevitably, they could only devote a limited amount of time to me. Also, they may possibly have regarded me as extremely young. As the other 11 British students in my intake were due to arrive a week or two after me, there was a short interim period during which I was left to my own devices.

Very soon, I felt an urge to go out and see more and more of the city. Seeing was not easy, though. The public transport system, such as it was, was an adventure in itself. After getting onto a tram, you literally had to fight your way to the other end to get off. Not that you had a clue about where you had got to, as ice had frosted the windows up completely. But it wasn't only the thick ice and snow that gave Moscow an unusual sort of beauty for me. Many or most of the buildings were dilapidated. (When I arrived, granite monstrosities, such as the big, black Lenin Library and Institute which glowered so mercilessly across at the beautiful old headquarters of the Moscow city soviet on Sverdlovsk Square, were few and far between.) Most buildings had a dignified yellow ochre colour and often lovely roofs.

There were also heartening little details, like the brackets in the outside walls where red flags were placed for May Day and other holidays. Very roughly speaking, much of the city was built on concentric circles, each of these being a wide boulevard. We could come out of the school, turn left, walk down to the crossing and then on to a boulevard. After an hour or two of walking along – or slithering, depending on the season – we would still be on that boulevard, because we would gradually be circling the centre.

And it was along this particular boulevard that, to my astonishment, I stumbled across the famous NEP market. During that winter, the New Economic Policy (of limited concessions to private enterprise) was in its last 12 or so months. I was familiar with London street markets, Club Row, Petticoat Lane and of course Battersea High Street. But Sukharevka felt like a different world. Most of those involved seemed to be either peasants or old people, and what they had on offer seemed little more than pathetic scraps. Anything seemed up for sale, and almost nothing. It struck me as rather poverty stricken. Against the cold, the women and men of any age seemed to be dressed in ragged clothing which they had padded up; poverty stricken again. Nearby, I came across workers standing around with their tools. One tool which intrigued me was a bow saw of a very primitive type. I concluded that these men were unemployed and were in some stage of trying to find work.

This was my very first walk in the capital of the homeland of Socialism. It didn't quite register as I had dreamt or even thought of it. My prevailing feeling was that my ideas were being confronted by reality, which was at a lower level.

During my first few months or even weeks, some of these feelings were mitigated somewhat by visits to the Bolshoi and soon to cinemas. (Films, being of course silent, were linguistically almost as much of a holiday as the ballet.) In particular, I went out of my way to get tickets for *Krasny Mak* at the Bolshoi. This portrayed events in China and the oppression of Chinese workers in the extra-territorial concessions which the imperialist powers had within China's major ports. Russian cinemas, for a young revolutionary, were very exciting places. There were no foreign films available and the fare consisted almost exclusively of aspects of the Russian civil war: entertaining stuff, however present day film historians may evaluate it. This was before the advent of productions on agricultural advance, such as *The Good Earth*.

An impression which I got only a little later was of what was known at the time as the Chinese Wall, very near Red Square. Along this very lengthy wall was an enormous secondhand book market, barrowloads of old books. Even though my Russian was still no more than rudimentary, I began browsing here, and even buying one or two. I distinctly remember being told, during those early months, that the Oppositionists, who were being exiled from Moscow, were bringing their books here to be sold.

For us in the school, pay day came once a month. I can't remember the exact sum I received, but we had adequate. For me, the day meant two things, a visit to the international bookshop and a meal out. Until the summer of 1928, there were innumerable restaurants dotted around Moscow – NEP restaurants, presumably. With our pay from the School, we could go to one of these, share a bottle of wine and have a good yarn over our meal. Almost next to the Lux Hotel, there was a huge place where you could get something cheaper; a mug of beer and a few crusts of chopped, dried salty bread. Here you could sit and listen to a Gypsy orchestra.

The same street, Tverskaya, also boasted a palatial cooperative store. This place had only one problem; it had practically nothing to sell. Worse, Tverskaya exhibited regular evidence of prostitution. On the corner by the Pushkin statue, there was a line of drozhkys (horse drawn carriages). Here, you could see men picking up women and driving off with them.

But it was the besprizornye who staggered me most. These orphan children from the period of war and civil war were surviving in conditions that are difficult to describe. They roamed the streets, living in any shelter they could find. From time to time they would be rounded up and put into children's homes. But they would break out and return to the streets. These youngsters (some of tender age, but some only about six years younger than myself) were astonishingly able – as thieves and survivors. I have three clear memories of this. One is of the number of delegates to the Sixth World Congress of the Communist International in 1928 who arrived at the Hall of Columns minus their fountain pens and similar possessions. During the short walk from the corner of Tverskaya to the hall, besprizornye had been doing overtime on them. My second incident took place in Rostov, near the Black Sea, during our journey to the Caucasus in 1929. We got out onto the platform for the usual purpose of filling up with hot water (for brewing tea) and to try and get hold of some chicken – and there, climbing out from **under** the train, were some besprizornye. They were completely smothered in filthiest dirt. But there they were, and that was how they had travelled all that way – underneath. The third eye opener occurred later, on one of my journeys back to Moscow from the South. The train was just easing out of Kharkov station when, all of sudden, a clatter. Some of the luggage that had been on the top racks was no longer there. With breathtaking ingenuity, some besprizornye had poked a very long pole in through the open window, and had flicked some hand luggage out of the window. Though the stuff happened not to be mine, I can well remember the consternation of this working class family who had so instantly lost many of their slight belongings.

Some other memories I have of Moscow itself are to do with religion. Into 1927 at least, something that still struck visitors was the sheer number of churches. Almost every street seemed to have one, and some had more than one. Now and then, I would have a look inside. After my vaguely Protestant early childhood and thoroughly rationalist teens, I always had violently mixed feelings at the sumptuousness of the decorations and vestments. The congregation never sat down, but always seemed to be standing, in a huddled sort of way. Our own life in Russia was impregnated with the consciousness of those Russians we moved among most; the Pioneer-YCL-party type of consciousness with which we moved around factories and discussions and socials. This naturally strengthened our assumption that the needs of anyone of our generation were being attentively catered for. But here, amid the **masses** of people in the churches and cathedrals, I could see not just old people, whose presence I had half expected, but also many persons of my own age. That rather shook me.

By the Chinese Wall in the middle of a narrow entrance to Red Square, there stood a beautiful little stone shrine, hardly bigger than a phone kiosk. This shrine seemed always to have a priest officiating in it. Passers-by crossed themselves, beggars occupied the pavements. This was in the very heart of Moscow around the tenth anniversary of the revolution, such was the influence of religion. Overlooking that shrine, high up on a wall, was an official slogan: 'Religion is the Opium of the People.'

And religion became increasingly controversial during these very years. As the situation turned towards forced collectivisation and as the International was swung towards the sectarian line of 'Class against Class' which was to have such dire effects in Germany and so many countries – so, there was instituted what was called the Campaign against God. It was led by Emilian Yaroslavsky, Stalin's hatchetman whom we shall meet soon – mainly in connection with his wife, who ran the Lenin School. He presided over a Society of the Godless which flourished during these years. Churches now became targets for demolition. One in particular, that I passed almost every day, jutted out into the road. Not only did many people cross themselves while it was being demolished, but they carried on crossing themselves after it was no longer there. Clearly, the religious influence on these Muscovites was deep.

Indeed this brought me another little surprise. After a strenuously academic day at the school, I would usually go for a walk. One day in 1929, I stumbled upon a knot of people having an argument outside St Isaac's cathedral. At once, I imagined I had at last found something like Battersea's speakers' corner. The discussion turned out to be about religion. But by no means all the participants were anti-religious!

Even by the late 1920s, people on shorter visits to Moscow were protected from most of the shocks such as I experienced from reality. I discovered this, in practice, during the same year, 1929. A Communist called Kathleen Duncan led a delegation of British working women from the Cooperative Women's Guild and so on to see Moscow. One of those elected onto this group was Mrs Varren, whom I have mentioned near the end of Chapter One. My mother mentioned this in a letter to me. I asked her to take this chance to send some underclothes, which she did. More important, Mrs Varren got my address from my mother, and wrote and asked me to take her round myself, show her the 'real' Moscow. She was obviously fully alive to the rigging and manipulation that was going on, even at this time.

The bee in her bonnet was to see how the workers lived; she didn't care for façades. At that time, three generations of a family frequently lived in one small room. One gathered from one's contemporaries that this made their sex lives rather tricky to arrange. (This problem was less acute if you went out with someone involved in the Comintern, who at least had a room to themselves.) Amid such overcrowding, cleanliness suffered too. A word that you picked up pretty quickly was klop: bug!

I was delighted at the prospect of showing Moscow to someone who had been so important to me. By showing a friend, you somehow get more pleasure yourself. But from the very moment her group arrived at the station till the moment they left, despite my making all the time I could, their schedule was so tight that, even though I knew Kath Duncan and other members and had no problem in gaining entry to their hotel, I managed to snatch no more than a short trip with Mrs Varren one evening before her supper. I took her to see some area beyond the Arbat on the road to the Zoo. Here she could see the log structures where the workers lived, and could observe the clothing. There also chanced to be some sports parade or Spartakiade. While we were watching these tens of thousands of youngsters march through Red Square, I was able to chat with her for a time. But that was all.

In a peculiar way, I could, had I wanted, have spent a lot of time in hotels, or in two particularly. One was the Bristol, which was for foreign comrades on short visits. The other was the Lux, for longer-stay comrades. The Lux has rightly become famous – and often infamous. It housed the foreign personnel of the Comintern and of organisations such as the YCI. Personally, I never set foot in the restaurant; I had not only the life of the school but was also (like all its students) a member of the Russian party. This gave access to factories, socials and meetings of all kinds. As a young person, I was also a Komsomol, or member of the Young Communists. But unlike me, the Comintern people were isolated. The Lux and its restaurant became a sort of home to them. Their main contact was with visitors from their country, there was a continual to and fro from abroad. As I was involved with the little circle of YCI people in particular, there was hardly a week when I could not have had access to two or three parties in the Lux to welcome this or that delegation. Not that I often did, my academic work was not easy and I usually needed time for quiet concentration.

But some of these parties I did go to. I remember one given by the British Communist Party delegation to the Comintern's Ninth Plenum in 1928. The British had come to Moscow determined to fight the left turn. As soon as they had accepted it, they threw a party to celebrate their switch. Vodka has never been my cup of tea, to me, it feels like pointing a blowlamp down one's throat. But, amid all the liquor that was flowing on that night (which was also the eve of this delegation's return to Britain), Willie Gallacher stood out. True to his Scottish teetotal Socialist background, he insisted doggedly on getting his Narzan, his mineral water. He always made a thing about his Narzan. I must say, as someone whose drinking went nowhere beyond a little 'four ale' (the cheapest of beers in London), I liked him more for the fuss he made.

The Lux had many fascinating individuals flitting around it. The old Wobbly, 'Big Bill' Haywood, died there during the spring of 1928. You could bump into Sen Katayama, the Japanese comrade who had embraced Plekhanov at a meeting of the Second International during the Russo-Japanese war; an old man, padding around. For some time there were also Heinrich Brandler – though he returned to Germany after his views turned out to be heretical – and the leading CPGBer, Tom Bell. All these people were more or less exiles, whether or not they could go home without being instantly arrested, they had (unlike us) no party political life on their doorstep. Their politics and their life depended on their reading 'from afar' the newspapers from home, and on contact with visitors. So isolated, their thinking might become impoverished. Tom Bell was the person who most gave me the impression of being mentally stale.

We now know that the coming decade was to bring the biggest purges. We can easily understand how, for those with so few close friends to share the tensions, every corridor in that hotel must have expressed menace.

This was the country and these were some of the circles where I was to spend three of the most important years of my life. We now need to be clear about the Lenin School itself.

The International Lenin School

The place to start is the Comintern's Fifth Congress in 1924. In a number of Communist parties during and after this, the alliance or 'troika' of Zinoviev, Stalin and Bukharin was beset by Oppositions, basically pro-Trotsky: the Fischer-Urbahns group in the KPD, the majority of the Polish Communist Party; much of the Belgian, the successors of Gorter and Pannekoek in Holland, and so on. In Russia itself, the troika had been able to contain this opposition and push it back. But internationally they needed further weapons. Thus was conceived the aim of raising a new cadre for all the non-Russian parties. This cadre was to be, first of all, politically safe. The 'Lenin Levy' (mass recruitment) had helped Stalinise the Russian Party on Lenin's death. Zinoviev and Co hoped the same could be done internationally – only now by means of a smaller, more strategic number of people; some hundreds of new cadres whose manifestly superior training would hold them in key leadership positions – and who would be reliably anti-Trotsky. To avoid any danger of Trotskyite contamination from within the Comintern, this training was to come under the supervision, not of the Comintern, but directly of the Russian party. The course was planned to last two years. With my intake, it was lengthened to three, as I have mentioned.

Prototype courses, of shorter duration, began from 1925-26. A pyramid was built up, with the International Lenin School as its top. There was the Sun Yat Sen University with literally hundreds and hundreds of Chinese students. Till 1927, its principal was Radek. Then there was the University of the Toilers of the East for Mongolians, Middle Easterners, Africans, Lascars and Indians and American Blacks. Then there was the Western University, for Europeans, mostly from Eastern Europe plus a few Italians. This structure was such a pyramid that even the living standards were graded. I experienced this via an Italian woman who for some reason (possibly academic) did not fit at the Lenin School and therefore transferred to the Western University in 1929. She certainly felt a drop in living standards. In a sense, it was also felt by a sitar (owned by an Indian student whose small get-together I dropped by at, one evening). I sat on it by mistake, such was the crush. And I happened occasionally to visit the Eastern University to pass the time with a black American friend, Otto Hall (half-brother of my own colleague Harry Haywood), who later became quite a figure in the Communist Party of the USA; the physical provision was self-evidently inferior to ours. Our fare can only be called lavish. The school had a chef; its restaurant (self-service) had three full meals a day, with a menu for each meal. Relatively, it was **luxury**. True, we began sleeping four to a room. But later, when the annexe building was completed, we moved to two to a room; nice beds, nice rooms with a desk for studying at. There were also excellent facilities for recreation. The older of our two buildings – beside our brand new granite monstrosity – had been a school for ladies, and therefore comprised a riding school which was universally used – as we shall see. In fact, it was there rather than at the Lux that I met Heinrich Brandler who used it particularly.

Again, unlike the three other international universities in the Communist pyramid, the International Lenin School was situated in one of Moscow's main thoroughfares. The embassies there included the Afghan, Lithuanian and Polish, and the British consulate. I was thus able, from the roof of the school, to have a vantage point for the first visit by a monarch to the Soviet Union, King Amanullah of Afghanistan processing in and out of his embassy. Similarly for the funeral of Mayakovsky; the school was directly opposite the Writers' and Artists' Union, where Mayakovsky lay in state after his suicide, and from where his funeral procession started. We were in the hub of the capital city.

What all this underlines is that the key to the International Lenin School was its extra high priority in the eyes of the dominant Russian leadership. A tiny but clear symbol was that, every winter, an area of ground behind the school would deliberately be flooded so as to give us, a mere 140 or 150 students, the chance to skate.

Politically, too, we were privileged. Via the Lenin School's party nucleus, we were involved in the political life of the Russian Communist Party at almost the highest level. No other students had this facility. We also received, not just internal passports (necessary for movement within Russia), but also special Central Committee passes. These gave entry to, among other things, the Lenin Institute, the Marx and Engels Institute, and of course to the Comintern, where we were expected to participate in the geographically appropriate section.

Once all the students had arrived, we were put through the most searching medical examination I was ever to have till the 1980s. They measured not only our bodies but our heads. They gave us psychological tests, in which we had to say what we thought when confronted with various blobs and blotches. The doctors were all Russians and needed an interpreter. Ours was a Yugoslav whom we knew as 'Vuk'. Somehow, he had picked up some English while working on the railways in Mexico. But not enough, the questioning became more and more intimate, and reduced him to gestures. It got to my sexual experience. In those days, anyone of my age was very lucky if they had any at all. But I was closely pressed as to how often I masturbated. (Vuk's gestures became more embarrassed than ever.) Afterwards, sitting on our beds (which were temporarily four to a room), we British students had a loud laugh at this and at the lies we had told. Significant about our generation, though, we later trimmed our talk in such areas for the ears of one of us, Maggie Smith or 'Jordan', simply because she was a woman. ('Vuk', funnily enough, ended up as a respected historian in the Yugoslav party; I hope he found trustworthier sources!)

What puzzles me is that, after all this solemn farce, I know of nobody – at least among the English-speaking students (the 'English Land Sector', as we were designated) – who was rejected on medical grounds. So, what was it all about?

I sometimes wonder, too, what all the secrecy was about. It might lead to nonsensical situations, such as the one which so mystified the real Jack Tanner, but it wasn't always consistently applied. And inconsistent secrecy is itself consistent nonsense. Two examples here.

The first involves the riding school. I'll explain later how seriously we were supposed to take this. For most of us, it wasn't easy. And with the pressures of academic work piling up, few of us really wanted to make an early morning thing of it. So, one winter, a reward was held up to us; come the spring, we would all go out into the countryside for a real ride around. Well, eventually, the spring came, the snows melted and here was this conspiratorial Lenin School. All the horses in that stable, and it was quite a lot, were all mounted by students. There were Blacks, Chinese, Indians, Irish, Letts, British – all up that street with all those embassies. Obviously, such a striking spectacle made mere rigmarole of the school's conspiratorial side.

And my other example involves a Polish comrade who had a room next to mine. She always seemed to be suffering (despite, presumably, that medical screening) from some internal complaint. Whether it was ulcers, I don't know; but she was always on a diet. One day, she ended her sufferings by shooting herself. Naturally, she was given a Red Funeral, but directly from the school. We all lined up in one big group, and marched across Moscow to the crematorium; again, anything but unobtrusive.

What ordinary Muscovites must have made of these processions, I don't know. But I do remember how, very early on, we were clearly instructed that, if any asked how our studies in their city were being financed, we were to explain that the funding came from our own Communist parties and not from the Russian, as was really the case.

So the official estimate of ordinary people's internationalism was obviously that it was less than the difference between our living standards and theirs.

After the written exam and the medical formalities, we were put through a six week induction course. This was almost entirely about the errors of Trotsky. And here the personality at the top of the school becomes relevant. Until 1929, the nominal head was Bukharin. But under him was the real head. Kirsanova was the wife of Emilian Yaroslavsky. Yaroslavsky had been on the Orgbureau with Stalin since 1923 and worked as Stalin's main ideological hack, penning most of *Pravda*'s big editorial onslaughts on Trotsky. Kirsanova, too, could at least speak very fluently. Not that I can remember her ever speaking any language other than Russian. But she had the ability to mix well within the school while somehow standing on one side. Humanly, if not ideologically, she seemed reassuringly independent. On one occasion, I happened to be standing in the hallway of the school with one of its 'Red Professors' (or heads of department), Ivan Mints. Someone came in and asked for Kirsanova, who happened to be visible in a room off this hallway, talking with one of the secretaries or translators. 'There's your contemporary Soviet woman', Mints said, pointing to her. Yet he was referring, not only to her independence, but also – tongue in cheek – to the fact that she was always much better dressed than most working women. She wore a different dress every day, of well chosen and beautiful material. Not that she was flashy.

Kirsanova was responsible for the school directly to the Russian party's Central Committee. Hence our induction course. She herself briefly addressed our first students' General Meeting on recent events near and at the top of the Russian Party. The party was moving towards its Fifteenth Congress, where the Oppositionists were expelled. She gave details that were available only to the highest party members: about Trotsky's exile to Alma Ata and the demonstrations at his departure, the exiling of other Trotskyists, their arrivals at their various places of exile, and even the details of their private correspondence with each other. I also remember Joffe's suicide being reported, along with various capitulations by individuals. It was the power of the party that was being expressed; the omniscience of the great leader, Stalin.

During the next three years of the course, Kirsanova would address the whole school body two or three times a week, on average. There was no discussion. The form these meetings took was like this. We would all – 140, possibly 150 students – meet in the biggest assembly hall. Kirsanova would enter and come on to the podium. And around her, the four 'Land Sectors' would group themselves separately. One person from each would stand up with his back to her, so as to translate instantaneously into the language of that sector. These translators could be students at the school, whoever was available. As mentioned, there were professional translators in the school turning out stuff for us. But these were not used for the meetings.

The Land Sectors were the Russian, French, German and English. You could take the full course in any of these languages. There were lavish facilities for translation between these, and into them from other languages. Texts were constantly being translated into one's language of instruction and duplicated as study material – money no obstacle. Our Land Sector included anyone who was more at home in English than in any of the other three languages. After a time, you picked up enough political Russian to be able to do without translations. After some months, I could read a news item in *Pravda*, and by the end of my stay I could address a workers' meeting; we had learnt enough of the language to be able to **flow**. But, try as I sometimes did, I was never able to read in Russian even those works of literature that I already knew in English translation, whether Maupassant or Chekhov. Nonetheless, whenever there was a discussion, the Slav students enjoyed a linguistic advantage and, as they were politically docile (indeed extremely subservient), they used this advantage to lay down the law.

After Kirsanova's initial warm-up, our induction course proper was taken, for the English Land Sector, by Stewart Smith, a Canadian of partly Ukrainian background who was a year ahead of us within the school. The Russian party had recently published what were known as the *Six Volumes*, a compilation of quotations from and about Trotsky, edited so as to put him in the worst possible light. At this level of argument, Smith was in his element. One could sense this immediately. Two years later, when he became editor of the Canadian Communist Party's paper, it filled with quotes from the big names, most of them still about Trotsky; unreadably stodgy. So, from him, the Lenin School got even more than it bargained for! But not everyone was satisfied with this level. In particular, I soon became aware how cynically Mints viewed it. He seemed to work 23 hours a day, and so hard that at times he appeared to be walking in his sleep. He believed in studying anything in depth; potted quotes were, in his eyes, beneath contempt. (Interestingly, though he was to be one of those attacked in 1930 by none other than Stalin for 'bourgeois objectivity' and 'rotten liberalism', he survived, to end as an Academician.)

After the induction course, we embarked on the full course. The overall structure, within each of what turned out to be our three years, was academic work at school from the autumn into the early summer; then, during the summer, the so-called 'practical' work. This, as we shall see, might involve travelling very far afield.

Academically, the curriculum included the following: Russian revolutionary politics back to the Decembrists of the 1820s; Marxian economics, based on the three volumes of *Capital* which we were taken through; philosophy, particularly from Locke and Hume, through Hegel to dialectics and dialectical materialism; the history of the European labour movements. Obviously, the British students concentrated particularly on the British labour movement – in fact we studied the British radical tradition back to the seventeenth century; the Levellers and Diggers.

The main rhythm of study would be that one would be given themes for three week projects (for example, on Chartism). Study groups would divide the topic into individual assignments, and each person would have to report back on what he or she had found out. The day was an intensive pattern of lectures and report back discussions. There was also provision for discussing problems individually with instructors, or in the 'study cabinet' of the relevant 'Red Professor'. These people would also want to consult with you if they discerned problems in your own intellectual political line! Mints, a historian by training, was Head of Leninism. The Head of History was L Rudas, a philosopher and an outstanding man. A Hungarian, he had been educated at Heidelberg. He had taken part in the 1919 Budapest Commune. He taught philosophy and British labour history to the English Land Sector students, and was also one of the outstanding political directors. During the early 1930s, a series of his articles on dialectical materialism was published as a pamphlet by the *Labour Monthly*. Some years later – or so we are now told in Roy Medvedev's *Let History Judge* – he became a victim of Stalin's purges.

If you showed aptitude, you were encouraged – though never forced – to go off on byways. When doing so, any weakness you might develop within some other part of the same area – of, say, labour history – would be excused. Given my earlier readings within that very area, I grabbed with both hands the opportunity to dig deeper wherever material was available. That was when I studied whatever there was in English about the Owenite communities, for instance.

So, in this way, whenever a student insisted on introducing a subject, it got a discussion. An instance concerns one of the Irish students whom big Jim Larkin had picked for the school. This lad was no recluse. He seemed to get on all right with a crowd of women school teachers; used to circulate in some girls' college and seemed rather successful in that way! But intellectually he seemed a loner, even among the other Irish students. One day, in a Rudas seminar on dialectical materialism, this chap suddenly became vocal. He introduced the topic of spiritualism: he was convinced that 'materialisations' did take place and that spiritualism was therefore materialistic and thus all right. An extraordinary discussion ensued. At its end, Rudas took him into his office. At that time, the new edition of Marx and Engels' *Collected Works* was being published; so Rudas promised this lad an English translation of a piece by Engels on spiritualism.

The system was flexible also from the point of view of the individual Red Professor. Rudas, as a philosopher, was fascinated by the latest developments in physics. He once showed a group of us a photo of (he said) an atom splitting. On another occasion, he gave us an assignment to read some extracts from Marx's early writings on Hegel and the left wing Young Hegelians. This stuff was just being translated into English. Normally, after preparing the assigned text, we would each express ourselves on what we had got from it. But, with this piece, we found the language more than difficult; we had never experienced anything like it. As is clear, I had been reading works such as *Capital* (though only Volume One) long before entering the school. But this was something new. Rudas very soon realised he had drawn a complete blank here. So he read it to us, explaining it sentence by sentence. It was so thrilling that I remember saying to myself how I must at all costs remember it for Jimmy Lane and Alf Loughton to enrich our philosophical discussions, the next time we walked round and round Clapham Common together. But of course, I soon forgot many of the details.

Not only was there all this heavy philosophy plus the second book of *Capital*. There was also the sheer volume. When I started home at the end of the course, even a small selection of the duplicated study guides and specially translated materials was to fill a huge crate, as we shall see. And these were merely in addition to the many books available in the school's library. Further, apart from one's political work outside the school, there was also the party nucleus and trade union branch within the School to be attended to. So, the load was tremendous. I couldn't keep pace.

At first, I imagined the problem was peculiar to me. But very soon we realised we all shared it. Luckily here, the school sought to involve students in its day-to-day running. Even its financial statement was circulated to everyone and passed back. The school also had a journal, open for anyone within the student body to express themselves on school organisation, on the study programmes or on internal party work. The formal mechanism for consultation was also clear; each Land Sector elected its representatives to the party nucleus bureau, to which each sector organiser was directly responsible and where anything was discussed. So the school authorities were made well aware of the overload, and brought a specialist along to give us ideas on how to study. We were all ears. But, grill him as we did, all we learnt was the importance of keeping the room at the right temperature, of keeping the desk tidy and of taking notes in a scannable, retrievable way. Following this visit, the school even printed special forms for note taking, with space for the source, the material itself and one's remarks on that material. All this underlines again how high a priority we were.

Despite the load which the authorities must have known was coming our way, I know of no-one who was rejected on academic grounds at the time of the entrance exam. However, a few of us did drop out during the three years, and were sent to study lower down the hierarchy of foreigners' universities. Those I was closest to were two or three of Jim Larkin's students. Presumably they were good militants. But they had no Communist background and were therefore not up to the academic side of the course. One of the Irish contingent who did survive the full three years, though, was Jim Larkin junior whom I swam and travelled with and knew very well. (He subsequently became a Labour member of the Dáil.) Within the British group, too, there were some who were academically stronger or weaker.

Beside these academic requirements, we were all expected to take part in Osoaviakhim (war preparedness training). We began with basic weapons. A fine uniformed Red Army officer came in with an assortment of Russian and other small arms and sub-machine guns, modern and old. He would take them apart, jumble up the parts and get us to reassemble them. Later – and of course this bit was special to the International Lenin School – we progressed to the study of insurrections. We used wargames and simulations; our recent examples included Russia, the Hamburg rising, Estonia, Ireland of 1916 and so on. In this context I met Erich Wollenberg who was one of the authors of 'Anatole Neuberg's' book on techniques of insurrection.

Another activity that was seen in the context of military training was the riding school. It wasn't there simply for our recreation or to teach us to trot daintily around. It was run by this old Cossack – you know, I can see the little sod now. He was a short, bandy-legged fellow with a long whip which he seemed to relish slashing, to make the horse do what he wanted and to get us novices to do gymnastics on horseback: to stand on the saddle, to ride backwards facing the horse's tail, to stand still, to jump onto a running horse. This led to a funny incident which still concusses me. One of the tricks he made us learn was to run alongside the horse, holding its mane, and to **leap** on while the animal was in motion. One week, we had had a gutful of trying and failing to bring this off. So, one morning, I got up extra early with the resolve to master this before breakfast. If I went there first thing, I might get a smaller animal, surely a bright idea. This part turned out to be the easiest. And now, this was going to be **it**. Here I was, and here was this horse cantering down the side of this riding stable. At the old sod's command to 'leap on', I did. Oh I gave such a leap, finished up bang! against the woodwork. Whether I had leapt **over**, or whether the horse had accelerated, I still don't know.

But this shows the level of professionalism we were supposed to reach, to become thoroughly trained and versatile personnel. One of the outstanding instances comes from my second year. By this time, I was party organiser for the English Land Group. This meant I had to make sure that all its students – whether the British, the Americans, the Irish, the Indians, the Chinese, the Mexicans, the Icelandic woman or whoever – attended their courses and party meetings. Now, we were given the task of learning to drive a train. For this purpose, we were taken to a station siding and given a locomotive with one carriage. We all piled in, and took it in turns to go forward to the engine and discover how to open the valve, shut it, feed the boiler and apply the brakes.

We were soon out in the beautiful countryside, and at first the atmosphere was like that on an excursion. But our carriage was 'hard', we were sitting on nothing but wood. It soon seemed all the harder as each inexperienced student opened and shut the valve. Somehow, our enjoyment faded! But nevertheless, this was only the first 'session' of an official course. For the second, fewer turned up, and for the third, fewer still. The party nucleus committee (which I was on, as sector organiser) took a dim view of what it saw as the apathy of my sector's students.

So I was told to reason with them; to try and motivate my co-students to attend further sessions. In carrying out this task, I made what turned out to be a fateful mistake (or so I thought for a time). For the sake of argument, I gave my friends (as I believed) my own view, which was at least as negative as theirs. I spoke as a railwayman, son of a sometime railwayman, with railwaymen uncles, one of whom drove the Victoria-Eastbourne express. After these journeys, while taking empty gas cylinders a few miles down the line to be dumped at Eardley Junction, he had sometimes picked me up at my signalbox to give me a ride on the footplate (where I would sit on an upturned bucket). To me now, in 1929, this business of teaching successive carriage loads of amateurs to do the work of drivers and firemen was laughable; in a revolutionary situation, in the highly unlikely event of your not getting a sympathetic train crew, you could at worst point a pistol in the right direction and convince someone to take you. So I remarked, in passing, that, to me, the whole exercise smacked of 'Blanquism' (that is, of making revolutionaries into a professional elite).

Purges and Stalinisation

That was the thought I uttered. Nearly a year later, during the autumn of 1929, the chistka reached the school. This was a special purge of the party's membership, organised as soon as Stalin had managed to oust the 'Right' (Bukharin, Tomsky and others) from the Politbureau. In fact, the chistka reached the school rather early. Of course, the whole process was as broad as it possibly could have been; with forced collectivisation grinding on, there could be no compromising with any 'Bukharinites' who might dare to try and alleviate it. Compromise was seen officially as sabotage. Not that the school was seen as Bukharinite – nor should it have been. But Bukharin was still our nominal head.

Soon after the chistka and the changes in the Comintern, Kirsanova called a school assembly and with relish – or so it seemed to me – announced to us that Bukharin was no longer school principal: no questions, no discussion, not a murmur of dissent.

Each of us was 'cleansed' in turn. For each, we would all gather in the main auditorium. The chistka went on and on, from morning till night, for weeks. All school work was suspended. Each of us had to stand alone, up on the platform in front of a row of Red Army colonels and generals and other high dignitaries; our Cleansing Commission which was under the jurisdiction of the Central Committee of the party. And they or anyone in the school could ask you questions about your social origins, your biography, your politics – about anything which might smell or be made smelly. You did at least have the right to reply in your own language. But as soon as any gap was found in your biography, the questions would come surging through that gap. Everyone had to be cleansed, from Kirsanova down, including of course every student. When the discussion on each person had been closed, there was no vote. But the chistka commission would immediately make its decision, which would be communicated to the party nucleus bureau in the school.

My turn came to stand at that lectern and, lo and behold, one of those Bulgarians who had acted as interpreter during the engine driving sessions brought up my remark on Blanquism. And to my horror, not one of the English Land Sector people spoke in favour of me. They all sat there and apparently enjoyed me being **toasted**. As a consequence of that, I had my Russian party card endorsed – which was a censure by the Russian Party. I felt it could land me in a hell of a mess. This turned out to be pessimistic. I remained the youngest in the school, and I suppose they made allowances for that. But, reflecting on it afterwards, I thought: what a lot! These were party members; I had been giving expression to their own beliefs and thoughts about that. None of them had had anything found against them. And they just sat there and laughed it off. Later, some of them happened to be standing around when I was summoned to the nucleus bureau to have my card endorsed. They tried to say: 'Ah well, it's nothing, Harry.' But to me it was serious.

Still it wasn't the end of the world. I didn't even lose any of my party functions. There were deep reasons for this. Within the Russian and Communist context, I simply was not an oppositionist, whether of the left or right. It was not merely that I was young and keenly enjoying my Russian experience. Within the British context, I had long been critical of the then party leadership for trailing the left union leaders, as my chapter on the general strike has made clear. This was the main bone of internal contention. On this, I was seen as a good left winger (and, as we will see later, not as a Trotskyist).

This perception was correct. Late in 1929, a contingent of cadres from the British Communist Party came to the school for the so-called 'short course' which lasted nine months. These people included Marjorie Pollitt, Allen Hutt, Percy Glading (whom the real Tanner tried phoning) and Maurice Ferguson. Like me, they were mostly on the left within the party, thoroughly dissatisfied with what they saw as the right wing actions of its Central Committee. The party was due to hold its conference in Leeds towards the close of that year, and its students at the School were to send two delegates to that. These two were expected to plug the Comintern's 'left' line as against the 'right' one represented by the British Central Committee. For these two delegacies, there were three nominations. One was Séan Murray, an Irishman with long experience of the British party, and who had been on the London District Committee before coming to Moscow. The second was Bob MacIlhone, a particular friend of mine. And I was the third – and the one who was defeated, though narrowly. The important thing is that those on the sidelines of this tiny election – the American comrades plus the Russians and people of any nationality within the party nucleus – very much regretted I had been defeated. They looked on me as being more sharply left. 'Left' meant the line of the Comintern, as against the right within the Russian, British or any other party. The British party leadership was seen as a classic example of a right wing one. Every opportunity was taken to push that party leftwards.

Many opportunities were created; the Executive Committee of the Communist International (the ECCI for short) held its Ninth and Tenth Plenums in February 1928 and July 1929, and in between there was the Sixth World Congress.

Around this time, any number of parties were undergoing internal upheavals with more or less assistance from the Comintern. In the school, one heard echoes of some of these. The struggles among the German comrades had become explosive (my Berlin experience suggested this!). And after the chistka, several German 'Rightists' were sent packing, back to Germany. (This was when Brandler stopped turning up at the riding school.) No Americans were sent home; rather, their tensions within the school were contained when Stalin gave the leadership of the whole US party to Foster. There had even been two Cannonites (supporter of the left faction) among the American students, though these two separated themselves from Cannon after 1928. And as for the Hungarian party! When Béla Kun, for long its leader, was arrested in Vienna, Rudas remarked that Kun's being stuck in a capitalist jail was 'no concern of mine', or words to that effect. Intellectually, I still admired old Rudas so much. But this only increased my disgust; in the British party, we at least expected to stick together and support each other personally. The sudden absence of this was what so upset me while I was standing up in front of the Chistka Commission.

Observance of the party line – subservience, as I was beginning to see it – was setting in, but unevenly. In fact, Stalinism had set in before the chistka. The Red Professors were the main, if not almost the sole, contributors to the Russian party's most deeply theoretical journal, the *Bolshevik*. Now and then, they also held semi-private discussions on theoretical matters; some of us school students were sometimes allowed to sit in on these. Their high level and cool tone contrasted all too much, for me, with the untidy discussions I had been used to in Britain. (Something else which rather intrigued me, though, was that the participants included some exceptionally beautiful women whom I never saw elsewhere.) The Red Professoriate was regarded as Bukharin's baby, and as the most coherent theorists in the Russian party. Yet, when Bukharin's party position had clearly begun to crumble – a full year before the chistka – some Stalinist intellectuals (plus Stalin himself on at least one occasion) went into the school and held some heavy discussions with these professors. The discussions had the effect of sorting sheep from goats. The sheep were then given what was called a Komandirovka, the party took them out of all school activity for a period of six or eight weeks, and gave them the assignment of digging up as much dirt about Bukharin as possible. Out of this came volumes with titles such as *Bukharin's Difference with Lenin*, reams of quotations, just as we had earlier been given about Trotsky during our induction. In the ensuing struggle against the 'Right', Stalin laced these quotes into his speeches. So a sufficient number of Red Professors fell for Stalin's line, and furthered it.

In form, the chistka was no respecter of persons. I can remember Kirsanova, during her chistka, telling how she had done anti-militarist work for the party before the war and even explaining, with a smile, how for a period she had not been active, which of course was when she had been having children. But in practice, the questioning seems sometimes to have been more sparing to those who were reliably Stalinist. Only later did I realise that no-one had tried to explore her position at the time of the Brest-Litovsk treaty with imperial Germany, even though her husband, Yaroslavsky, had been in the faction around Bukharin (along with virtually the entire Moscow party organisation) against signing. Of course, given that the ideal biography had by now come to include unswerving loyalty to both Lenin and Stalin (even when, as often, the two had disagreed), there was no less silence on Kirsanova's position during 1919 when Yaroslavsky and Stalin had disagreed with Trotsky and Lenin over the need to use Tsarist officers.

Not that every chistka went through without explosions. One of the German students had earlier been editor of a provincial party paper. He was grilled on some criticisms he had voiced of Thälmann's leadership. At the time of the chistka, Thälmann was in a tight corner within the German party, and these internal differences could be heard among the 12 or 15 German students at the school. So, objections from the Brandlerites – or at least from so-called 'conciliators of the Brandlerite tendency' – were voiced loudly during the chistka.

But the chistka became most serious among the Slav students. The Czechoslovak contingent at the School was rather large, reflecting the size of the early Czechoslovak party which had a history of recalcitrance to the Moscow line. Thus, there was quite a factional struggle going on among the Czechoslovak students. So, when it came to many of them, the chistka went out of its way to establish whether any had had anything to do with the Czech Legion which had fought for the Allies and against the Bolsheviks during the Russian civil war.

Luckily for any Czech or Slovak, nothing like this could be proved. But there was one Yugoslav whose chistka concentrated increasingly on his participation in the First World War and on his activity afterwards. Immediately after this, he was never seen again. When we enquired, his room mate simply remarked: 'Oh, he was taken during the night.' And that was the end of him, as far as we were concerned. So we were fully aware of what lay in store, if only for the very worst offenders.

The chistka unfolded right across Russia and soon erupted within the Comintern. We were able to go along to the Comintern chistka – if we wanted. I did not. These political destructions were not my cup of tea, even then I was distinctly conscious of being a little disgusted with the whole business. But I heard about the 'cleansing' of a number of people whom I knew in the YCI's secretariat. One of these was an American who had been in charge of the YCI's Eastern department and with whom I shared an interest in India. Another, and in the end even more negative chistka which I very quickly heard about, was that of David Petrovsky.

Under his alias of AJ Bennett, Petrovsky had been in and out of Britain during the mid-1920s as the Comintern's representative. I heard from friends who did attend his chistka how he had been really ground in. From that moment, he was arrested. He went to the camps and, as I gather, was subsequently shot. He was no anti-Communist, by any stretch of the imagination. As I'll show soon, he made himself particularly unpopular with Stalin by the clarity of his support for a heretical analysis which was held by most of the leadership of the British party.

His wife was Rose Cohen, who had been one of the group working at the Labour Research Department in Buckingham Palace Road. She went to Moscow, married Bennett, worked in the Comintern, and had a child. Now the thing I remember, vividly, about Rose Cohen was, when she was about to have her baby, Gallacher, who used to come to Moscow, would bring her baby clothes. At that time such things were very difficult to come by in Moscow. So the relationship of the British leadership with Rose Cohen and Bennett remained that close. Well, she too was arrested, during the 1930s, like Bennett. She disappeared. And the British party never did anything to save her – or if it did this has never been told. Rose Cohen was not the only one. There was Len Wincott, a sailor who was in the Invergordon Mutiny of 1931. He went to Russia, took Russian nationality, got picked up in the purges and sent to the labour camps. And the next piece of news to come out about him was in the 1950s. A German who got back to the West reported that prisoners in one of the camps had gone on strike. And what stuck in his mind was that, one of the leaders was a British sailor. So now, **that** started up a campaign in this country about Len Wincott: what's the party doing about it? And when Khrushchev and Bulganin came to this country in the mid-1950s, the Trotskyist movement did quite a bit of work in connection with that. And then, lo and behold, the *Daily Worker*, as it was then, published a letter from Moscow, from Wincott in which he announced that he was all right – and that the past was past. So obviously he had made his peace about the business.

Now, from the 1930s, the leaders of the British party were as vocal as anyone in their support of the purges. Gallacher, and Harry Pollitt even more, used to boast about the scores of times they had been back and forth to Moscow. So they must have been aware of what was happening, at the very least to someone like Rose Cohen. They never came clean. There is a logical possibility that they tried to pull strings behind the scenes. But if so, it obviously didn't work; and anyway, we're still waiting to hear about it.

Certainly, conformism and silence did not grow within the British party alone. Two examples. In the summer of 1928, I spent a very pleasant month at a party rest home on the Black Sea coast; countryside, swimming and a good social life. One of our group was a Lascar seaman whose school name was 'Ochkov'. He noticeably never hit it off with the other two Indians in the school, who were definitely better manicured. I found him a very interesting person and got on well with him. He used to receive the Indian newspapers regularly, via Paris. Inside these papers, letters would be folded which he used to deliver to the Comintern. So he was frequently going back and forth to the Comintern's Eastern Secretariat which was in contact with the Indian party. Now, while we were on holiday, he for some reason urgently wanted to stay in touch with these things. And he had heard that Gregory Safarov, who had played quite a role in the Comintern during its Zinoviev years, was staying in a Central Committee rest home near Kastropol, where we were. Safarov had been exiled for supporting Zinoviev, but he had capitulated, and so was able to work (for, as it turned out, another year or two) back at the Comintern as a specialist on Indian and British affairs.

Our only way of reaching the rest home was on foot. It was a beautiful but very long walk along the cliffs and the day was very hot. Our Lenin School pass gained us access to the grounds. We asked for Safarov. Out he came, saw Ochkov – and instantly turned on his heels, back into the building. We had walked all that way for absolutely nothing. Ochkov had no pretensions to being a grand theoretician, but his verdict was precise: 'None are prepared to commit themselves.'

My other example is presumably from early 1930. Ralph Fox, the novelist who was to be killed in the Spanish Civil War, occasionally dropped in on the British students at the school during these years. He mentioned a big event that was about to take place at the Communist Academy. Not only was Raskolnikov, the sometime ambassador in Kabul, going to read a paper on India, but Radek was going to participate in the discussion. Raskolnikov had been quite a figure in 1917 and was therefore interesting in his own right. But, in addition, his paper was going to be about the recent upsurge of Indian nationalism; and as we shall see, there had recently been some massive switches in the Comintern line on the question, in a sectarian direction. Thus, any discussion seemed bound to be most interesting. Half-a-dozen of us went along. These included Ochkov and one of the other two Indians in the school, a well-to-do bourgeois called 'Magharab' who had been one of our group who travelled to Daghestan. (The third Indian, who always seemed politically out of place, was a nephew of Tagore, the Bengali philosopher.) We were all looking forward to a political treat; Radek, who had been exiled in 1927 but had since made his peace with the party, was going to intervene. It was a small seminar room, Radek was sitting a few yards away. Raskolnikov gave his paper. Radek never tried to say a word. During subsequent days, we asked around, and were informed he had been warned not to do so.

Another aspect of this growing brittleness and lack of discussion, was the mounting hysteria against Trotsky. Already at the end of our induction course, Stewart Smith (our instructor on it) had proposed a resolution which included the phrase 'Trotsky, objectively counter-revolutionary'. This was the first time we had heard that word coupled with Trotsky's name. One American student, Joseph 'Cass' (real name Zack) moved an amendment to delete the phrase. I seconded. But we were the only students in the whole English Land Sector to take umbrage at those words.

It would be completely false to paint me as at any time, during my stay in Russia, an outspoken protagonist of Trotsky's. I did not feel myself to be opposed to the regime, or even necessarily to Stalin. To understand oneself is notoriously hard. But what made me more open to Trotsky's ideas than many another also more or less self-taught working class Leninist? Possibly, some role was played by the multiplicity of currents in Battersea at the time I was politically growing up. But was Battersea so unique? And anyway, I was not the norm there either. More likely, the Reade controversy of 1925 sowed some seeds. As mentioned too, I had always been excited by Trotsky as a personality. And I was aware, by the time I arrived in Moscow, that the Russian party had conflicting wings. That induction course alerted me, at the very start, to how the victors in this type of conflict were using the situation to paint the losers in the worst light imaginable. So I remained little more than interested in Trotsky, not a supporter as such. What fascinated me most was the wider canvas of Comintern politics. Still, my earlier experiences rounded my desire to learn more. Thus I collected, listened and discussed.

Discussion was still possible. Thus, when our study of Russian party history reached the 1905 Revolution, I came out, in an academic way, in favour of Trotsky in his controversy with Lenin. In this debate, Trotsky arrived at the kernel of his theory of Permanent Revolution as against Lenin's then theory of the democratic revolution of the proletariat and peasantry. Our teacher was of course, Mints. He was not merely a Red Professor but also the editor, jointly with Yaroslavsky, of a four volume history of the Russian party. I became excited about Trotsky's idea, here in 1905, that the revolution needed to go beyond a bourgeois-democratic content and to pose the question of the transition to workers' power. As a result of this intervention of mine, Mints took me into his office and questioned me closely. He was not hostile, this was no interrogation. We merely went over the different points which had emerged during our discussions. And he gave me additional material to read, including a translation of that extremely rare pamphlet which Trotsky had written from Geneva during 1904, *Our Political Tasks*. (Later on in the course, we were each anyway issued with a copy of this.) Possibly, my intervention during that session might have been less forgettable had I not been making it during the tail end of the academic term, when we were preparing to leave Moscow for our 'practical' work.

Similarly, it was still possible for us to argue against the abolition of the 'party maximum' (that is, of the limit, calibrated to the wages of a skilled worker, on the income of party members). Its abolition late in 1928 went to the root of the egalitarianism of the old Communist movement. We can now see it as sealing Stalin's alliance with the party functionaries. I raised the issue during one of Rudas' seminars. In response, Rudas behaved towards me, as Zack put it, 'like a roughneck'. Perhaps symbolically, among those gorgeous women I have mentioned seeing at the Red Professors' seminar, I remember one who was wearing strikingly expensive-looking silver furs.

Of course, none of us had an inkling of what the future held in store for Zack. I discovered this only around 1960 when, in Battersea library, I came across a book co-authored by him. It was virulently hostile to any kind of Socialism. Like many of the Americans at the school, he had his wife with him in Moscow. After the three years of the course, his Comintern work kept him mainly there (though he also went as an emissary to Venezuela during 1932 or '33). So his wife and, soon, child stayed on. Then, after some disagreement with the Comintern, he returned to the USA. But he was unable to get his family out of Russia. Despite this, he joined the Left Opposition and was involved in Cannon's Communist League. He and I contacted each other. Later, I gathered he had left the Communist League. But next, at the time of the Moscow Trials, Zack gave to the Dewey commission an affidavit on some of the Comintern's methods. In this, he substantiated part of Trotsky's testimony. Zack had been an intensely Communist intellectual, capable – or so I was told at the time by his friend, Charlie Krumbein – of sitting all through the night to produce a thesis on the American union movement and of taking it down to the RILU the next morning. But now the preface to this completely bitter book of his mentioned what was surely the key to his life – his wife and child ended in the camps.

By early 1929, Trotsky came once again to be seen by the dominant faction as the main threat both within Russia and worldwide. Thus, in February 1929, all party members in the school were called together to hear Kirsanova relay the latest bits of information on him: as Trotsky was stubbornly corresponding, from his exile in Alma Ata, with Oppositionists in their various places of exile, the party Political Bureau had, despite protests from Bukharin, come to the conclusion that the only solution to his, as she called it, 'counter-revolutionary' activity was to expel him from the country altogether.

One cold February morning only a day or two after Trotsky had actually left, I was crossing the school forecourt on my way to the street when I happened to meet Rudas. His eyes flashed merrily as he stopped me: what did I think about the great Trotsky being bundled out of the Soviet Union? Guardedly, I answered I was on my way to buy a paper; I was mindful of our clash over the abolition of the party maximum. I found the newspaper kiosks festooned with a massive number of copies of a tiny five kopeck pamphlet. The cover had as its background the *Daily Express* headline, 'Trotsky's exclusive story ... by Leon Trotsky'. The pamphlet was by Yaroslavsky: *Mr Trotsky in the Service of the Bourgeoisie*. Its opening theme was to the effect that the first thing Trotsky had done on arriving in Turkey was to spit at Soviet Russia. Yaroslavsky around this time was also lambasting Trotsky at greater length in *Pravda*, almost every day. And his contribution for that day filled almost the whole of the front page. Presumably, this was the source of Rudas' bonhomie.

Kirsanova's addresses echoed her husband's polemics. Just as with the story about Trotsky spitting, so as regarding the area of Russian party history (something we had become very well versed in) Kirsanova seldom rang true: these polemics seemed to me, at the time, not to add up. Soon after, by a nice coincidence, one of the London Sunday papers (I think it was the *Observer*, which was regularly available in the school's library) serialised Trotsky's *My Life*. So I was able to read this in Moscow very soon after the authorities had gone to the lengths of deporting him.

Gradually throughout Russia, the records were being weeded. As early as 1928, on visits to the Museum of the Revolution, I noticed more and more gaps in some of the displays. Things were taken down without being replaced, and no indication was given as to what had been removed. It was obvious to me – and I can't possibly have been alone in this – that the history was being rewritten.

And Trotsky in particular was being erased. But this process did not occur at the same speed everywhere. In the summer of 1928, during that year's Crimean holiday, I went along to have a look inside the main library in Sebastopol. I have always enjoyed browsing around in libraries – as may by now be clear. This one turned out to have the air of a run down branch library in Britain. It obviously lacked resources. But, running my eye along some of the shelves, what should I find but Trotsky's *Collected Works*? These had begun to be published during 1924. In Moscow, such a find would surely have been inconceivable. But here, I was able to dip around without any fuss. I assume my opportunity resulted merely from an oversight. I have no evidence either way, though.

That was in 1928, but as late as May Day of 1929 the Left Opposition proved to be more than a quarter of a shelf full of possibly overlooked books. It remained active – under the very nose of Stalin. Hitherto, school students had always been able to go, with their passes, to the side of the Lenin mausoleum (along with Comintern functionaries and suchlike) and watch the parade go through Red Square. (The Politbureau would be up on top, and the diplomats in front.) But, very shortly before this 1929 May Day, Kirsanova informed us of the possibility that some Left Oppositionists would try to do something within the procession itself. So we students were to be distributed to different factories around Moscow. Each of us would march with a particular group of workers.

By good fortune, I was put to march with aero workers from the Avropribor factory. As usual, the march was terrific, accordions and bands playing. Apart from banners, many people were carrying articulated plywood caricatures of Western politicians. By the time we had reached Tverskaya (nowadays called Gorky Street) which is the main thoroughfare into the Square, we were marching 20, 30 or even 40 abreast. We were tightly packed. And we were becoming even more compressed as we neared the Square, because the organisers wanted to keep people flowing through it as quickly as possible, the parade goes on for hour after hour. So now we entered Red Square. As we did so, our wide column was funnelled between two sides made up of Red Army men and GPU (secret police). So we were even more compressed and were hurrying even more. We came level with the mausoleum. Up there, we could see Stalin and the Politbureau. And at the very moment when we all tended to look up, up went a flutter of duplicated Opposition leaflets from our part of the demonstration! They were floating down over us, but to grab one was impossible, the GPU men continued hurrying us along. Obviously, the informants whom the GPU had planted within the Opposition had been able to alert the authorities that something or other would be attempted, but evidently not to this defiant throwing of leaflets under Stalin's nose.

No time to stop, we continued being hurried along. Instead, I was now to observe something else which also opened my eyes a little further, though in a different way. After you cross Red Square, you come to the Moskva river. Here the march was to disperse. These beautiful models which must have cost many hours to make, what did the workers do with them? As I stood on the embankment by the river, one group of workers after another pitched their woodwork into the water, with an air of 'That's that!', or even of 'Good riddance'.

Enforcing the 'Third Period'

As Lenin School students, we were directly involved in all the international conferences which took place during our time in Moscow. And those conferences which coincided with my time there had particular worldwide importance.

The Comintern's Sixth World Congress opened during July 1928 and lasted nearly seven weeks. Previously, such conferences had been held in the Kremlin itself, but developments such as the Arcos raid had encouraged attempts to separate the Russian party from the Comintern, if only symbolically. This congress therefore took place in the Hall of Columns, outside the Kremlin, if only just. All day every day, we were sitting in that hall or moving around its corridors, through weeks that happened to be appallingly hot.

And the corridors were the place where we were supposed to be most important. During the run-up to the congress, Kirsanova switched the emphasis of her addresses from the 'Left Deviation' to the 'Right Deviation'. And she began hinting that this deviation was having to be fought against, not merely within the American, German and other parties (and thus among some of their students within the school), but also within the Russian party at its very highest level. This was why she wanted our wholehearted involvement in or near the congress. At this time, the students from the first intake were about to go home, so they in particular were instructed to meet the delegates from their home parties so as to brief them and make them aware of the differences within the Russian party. Thus this congress became very much what was known as a 'corridor conference'. In other words, the official discussions were one thing, Bukharin gave the main report, in which he even referred to a 'Right danger' within the International, but backstage or in the wings, the word was being put round among the delegates that he himself was a right winger, due for the chop (politically speaking). Often, that vast hall was pretty empty, the real congress was taking place wherever Stalin's supporters could lobby the delegates.

Another aspect of the political preparation was to do with Trotsky. During the weeks before the congress, we Lenin School students were given typed copies of the critique which he had written from Alma Ata of the Comintern programme. We were to sit and read it, but to return it at once to the party organiser. The worry was that it might be leaked. In the event, it certainly was; Cannon smuggled it out of Moscow, thereby helping to inaugurate Trotskyism in the USA. As for the congress itself, only the heads of delegations along with members of the programme commission were made aware of the document's existence. They were allowed to read it under the same conditions. However, amid the heat and the nervous tension, things occasionally slipped. I was vitally interested in the factional struggle going on in the American party, and was friendly with some of the Fosterite faction. One day, I was in the hall, listening to my American namesake, Harry Wicks, who was addressing the congress. Wicks started attacking Cannon for continually talking about Trotsky's document. Yet, officially, his audience were still supposed to be ignorant of the document's existence!

Another incident which showed the strained atmosphere occurred when Tomsky (who was one of the three leaders in Bukharin's faction, Rykov was the third) rose to speak. During that congress at least, spotlights were often switched on to allow the press to take photos. When Tomsky began his speech – soon after Bukharin's – the lights came on brightly. He objected angrily and had an altercation with the people controlling them. This, too, showed extremely frayed nerves.

This atmosphere within the Russian party was bound to effect the delegates; almost anything Russian enjoyed prestige or even worship. I experienced this again on the night the congress opened. Russians had a habit, before going into a cinema, theatre or meeting, of promenading up and down in the entrance lobby to greet each other and chat. On that evening, I happened to be standing with Arthur Horner. One of the Russian bigwigs parading up and down happened to be Lozovsky, who still headed the RILU. His style was worlds apart from that of an ordinary Russian trade unionist, though. He was wearing a beautifully embroidered Ukrainian shirt, his hair was magnificent and he had an impeccably dressed woman on his arm. Horner had great admiration for Lozovsky, as one trade unionist for another. He also had glasses of great thickness. And I remember how far his eyes seemed to stand out from his head as he gazed in wonderment at his hero.

Of course, such worship was to continue to be widespread for some decades more, but its importance at this congress was that more than three-quarters of the British delegates nonetheless came out in open opposition to the Comintern analysis of India. Looking back on this 'decolonisation debate' (as the Russians insisted on calling it), the curious thing is that, whatever the disagreements on **analysis**, few if any of the British delegation disagreed with the leftward turn in the Comintern **line** on India (as also internationally). This new line laid down that the Indian Communist Party renounce any alliance with bourgeois nationalists or with other non-Communist groupings. Indeed the main publication in English which expounded the British delegates' analysis (that a major though subordinate industrialisation was taking place in India and in the other Asian colonies and semi-colonies) was Palme Dutt's *India Today*. And Dutt had long led among those seeking to push the line leftwards on India, Britain and anywhere else. (Curiously, in Russian, Dutt was not the only British theorist associated with this analysis, in 1928, the Communist Academy published Harold Rathbone's book on decolonisation, which was never issued in English.)

In other words, the disagreement was never over what line or strategy to adopt, but simply over the analysis behind that line. A clear majority of the British delegates remained convinced that the official Comintern analysis, which minimised the scale of industrialisation and thus of the creation of a proletariat in India, was being overtaken by the facts. Unlike any other delegation at this congress (or at any subsequent ones for decades afterwards) the British one remained obstinate. But I doubt whether any of them, even so exceptionally clear a mind as Arnot, fully understood the thinness of the ice onto which they had put the Comintern leadership, or therefore the hysteria with which they were answered.

For, less than a year previously, there had been the catastrophe in China. The line which the Comintern had encouraged within the Chinese Communist Party had been one of subordination to the nationalist bourgeoisie and its Guomindang organisation. The GMT had repaid this by turning on the Communist Party and massacring it out of the cities. And now the Russians were trying, mainly for their own internal reasons, to switch the Comintern line from one extreme of subordination to the national bourgeoisie to the opposite extreme of total rejection of such a bourgeoisie in the other great country of Asia, as organised in the Indian National Congress. The reason why the ice was so thin was that, before December 1927, the Left Opposition had been warning precisely against the pro-GMT line: so that old line had now to be dropped without admitting that the Left Opposition had been correct in denouncing it. Further, any mention of so recent a cataclysm as the Canton insurrection, where the Chinese Communist Party had belatedly tried to make a come back, would be embarrassing – not least because one of those who spoke against the British delegation, Lominadze, had himself been one of the Comintern 'instructors' in Canton at the time. In effect and unawares, the British delegation were calling attention both to the thinness of the analysis underlying both the old line and the new, and to the disastrous nature of both.

This was the position from which the Russian delegation had to refute the British theory. No wonder that the Russians gave this theory the smear name (twisted from the title of Rathbone's book) of 'de-colonisation'; as if the British comrades had ever asserted that British imperialism was benevolently allowing an Indian bourgeoisie to become its rival. Dutt, Rathbone, Arnot and other British participants who defended their line were denounced as 'Mensheviks', 'Social Democrats', 'objectively pro-imperialist' or anything else that could be flung. But they too were in a tricky corner. If they mentioned China in a critical way, they might be smeared also as conciliatory to the Left Opposition – something which, as we know from their expulsion of AE Reade, they never had been. All this accounts for the extraordinary viciousness of the discussion and also for the way in which, once it was over, both sides immediately tried to smooth things over, however difficult this sometimes was temperamentally.

The person who suffered the most from that smoothing was Petrovsky. This is an important dimension in British Communists' silence when, within a year, he was taken to a camp. Petrovsky did not merely address the congress in support of the British delegation, throughout the debate, he tirelessly heckled the speeches of the Russians. 'Was Stalin a Social Democrat?', was one interjection which, as I remember, caused particular fury. So his rapport with Arnot, Dutt and the others was surely of the closest. He had stuck his neck out in their defence. He turned out to have gone far beyond the limits which a former Comintern emissary was now supposed to observe in relations with a foreign party. And, when he was punished for this, those he had stuck his neck out for kept silent.

This angle on the Comintern's Sixth World Congress also illuminates some murkier aspects of the next international gathering I attended. A year later, in July 1929, I returned from travels to Daghestan and Leningrad. I intended to write my report on my 'practical' work (that is, on my trip to Daghestan), something we were required to do. I also intended to catch up on some other written work. But as soon as we reached the school, we found its hall alive with electricians and carpenters who were rigging up facilities for simultaneous translation. This, we now discovered, was the preparation for the Tenth Plenum of the ECCI. As with the Sixth Congress the previous year, the Russian leaders remained scared that the capitalist countries might invade, and were therefore eager to be able to show that Comintern meetings took place outside the Kremlin and were therefore independent of it. As a result, I needed to walk a mere 12 yards from my room in order to sit in on this plenum. Quite a few of us did this – for longer than was good for our academic work, if my experience is typical. I saw it as a unique chance to listen to or even meet leading figures in the movement, from all over the world, and to weigh up what was going on.

Two particular impressions were left in my mind by that plenum. The first was immediate. On the platform where the lectern was, an enormous map had been placed. This was of the Soviet areas of China. Hunan and Chekiang were of course magnified to seem vastly significant, and to blur out the rest of the country where all was defeat. In contrast to the 1928 congress when the policy of the Stalin leadership had already laid in ruins for months, there was now something positive to show – if only through a magnifying glass. By these means, strategic defeat could be obscured by tactical reassertion.

The second impression intensified gradually. The personnel of the Comintern had completely changed during the intervening year. Bukharin had been reduced to the status of an intellectual ornament, as in January 1929 when I heard him give a most beautifully cultured speech marking the fifth anniversary of Lenin's death. Instead of Bukharin giving the main report on the international situation, the speaker was Molotov, who had previously been known, if at all, as a diplomat, but who had recently been switched to the top level of the party. Instead of Tomsky giving the main report on trade union work, it was Lozovsky and Thälmann. On Asia, the speaker was Manuilsky. So the new Stalinist leaders of the Comintern were making their premiere appearance before an international plenum. And the audience had changed similarly. Since the 1928 congress, there had been a turnover in the leadership of nearly all the parties around the world, because of the struggle against the so-called 'conciliators of the Right' – against those who did not want the new line applied in too sectarian a way.

The new line, of course, was that we were now entering a 'Third Period' in which class would once again be ranged against class; something which was now taken to mean Communist against Social Democrat. The latter, along with the reformist trade unions, were to be seen as 'Social Fascist'. Apart from 'Ercoli' (Togliatti), almost all the faces seemed new. This fresh international cadre had been called together to applaud this disastrously sectarian departure.

One had read about Molotov in the papers. We awaited his speech. When he began, you regretted waiting for it. It was so sterile, that it seemed to go for hours and hours. Partly as a result, at least one listener nearly went to sleep. My seat was near the front of the auditorium, and I noticed Gusev – who had once been to America for the

Comintern, an old Bolshevik and opponent of Trotsky. He was quite
elderly and very paunchy, his girth would have stood comparison with
George Hicks' or Lon Swales'. His eyes closed, he began nodding and
his head dropped. His neighbours had to jerk him awake more than
once. It must have been the speech's content, Molotov's delivery was
not entirely soporific. He droned certainly, but he also stuttered.
Though he was to remain on the world stage for some decades, I have
never seen any mention of this sharply staccato stutter that kept most
of us awake in the Tenth Plenum. Assuming he did not normally stutter,
this suggests how nervous he was.

Molotov's speech was splashed all over *Pravda* and issued in pamphlet form. What was its content? It heavily underscored the danger of
a capitalist invasion of Russia and the role of Social Democracy in
aiding the bourgeoisie in this. It outlined the initial successes of the
planned economy, of the Five Year Plan. But it was based on a **complete**
overestimate of the revolutionary potential in country after country.
What was being projected was an imminent revolutionary upsurge,
when actually a downturn was taking place, not only in the revolutionary movement but also in the working class movement as a whole.

After his speech, we heard a joint presentation by Thälmann and
Lozovsky. We now know that this was to be Thälmann's last but one
appearance at an international gathering before the Nazi victory en-
gulfed him. He and Lozovsky fleshed out the trade union aspect of
Molotov's line; an upsurge was taking place, the Social Democratic
trade unions were becoming Social Fascist. The word 'Fascisation' was
used, horrible word. And they advanced the idea that the task of
Communists now was to take over the leadership of the working class
movement – independently of the Social Democrats and of the Social
Democratic unions. How was this to be done? By first recognising that
there now existed within the working class a tremendous revolutionary
potential among unorganised workers. With these, it would be possible
to build – independent of the Social Democratic formations – movements of factory committees, which would embrace not only the Social
Democratic trade union rank and file but also those unorganised
workers. And with these attracted to your banner, it would be possible
to build an alternative machine which would become a trade union
opposition, and would thus lead the revolutionary struggles that were
about to break. This was, really, the content of the Tenth Plenum.

Of course, such a fantasy needed to be accompanied by a heavy
emphasis on the struggle against those within the International who
resisted it, against the 'conciliators'. This, along with the newness of the
participants, helps explain why the discussion was so flat. This flatness,
which contrasted so much with the heat of the previous year (whatever
the manipulations involved there too), became my outstanding impression of the Tenth Plenum.

In Britain, the new line completed the decline of the Communist Party, which was to hit me on my return. In Germany, it completed the split in the labour movement, and thus helped let the Nazis in. Such consequences are well known. Less well known in most countries was the result in India. The British party had always been the sponsor or ideologue of the Indian party (just as, say, the Dutch was of the Indonesian). Manuilsky insisted that, not only were we to have no alliance any more with Congress, this line had been laid down the previous year. But we were now to fight it. And not only Congress as such, we were to make the Congress Socialists, such as Nehru, our main focus of attack. (This was coincidentally – or rather not – an obvious mirror opposite of what had been the line on China into 1927).

For a long time, the British party had had an alliance with the Indian nationalists. This was merely the normal line of the international League Against Imperialism. But now, with the Tenth Plenum, the 'Class Against Class' line meant that the Congress Socialists became the Indian incarnation of 'Social Fascism'. Previously, they had been our main avenue into the Congress movement as a whole. We were now told to close that avenue off. Similarly, we now had to split the All-India TUC. As a result, India's organised Communist trade unionists were reduced during the early 1930s to a tiny sect. Even more important, we were approaching what turned out to be the great nationalist upsurge of 1930, which brought the Indian masses (worker as well as peasant) to their feet behind Gandhi. Thus the line dictated at the Tenth Plenum isolated the Communists from an upsurge of subcontinental proportions. Only in 1934, with the hasty but overdue burial of the 'Third Period', did their situation begin to mend again. And this utterly unnecessary defeat – self-inflicted – underlines again the significance of Radek's silence during that seminar at the Communist Academy. This was to occur less than six months after that 1929 plenum, at a time when the Indian upsurge was gathering strength.

'Practical' work in Russia

Britain and India were merely small parts of these decisions internationally. But within Russia itself, we students experienced, from a special perspective, not merely some of the consequences of party policy but also some of the restraints within which the party was forced to operate. We were expected to do this, as part of our curriculum. This, as I explained, alternated academic with 'practical' work. Just as the academic work was structured according to one's year, so too was the practical.

Our first year practical involved studying, at the base, how a factory was run and how the party operated within it. Groups of students were dispatched all over the country, but the six or eight people I was put with were sent no further than Mytishchi, 100 or 200 miles away. With us was an interpreter, the Bulgarian who surfaced about 20 years later as president Chervenkov. Every group also had to do a survey of some working class families' budgets, of how much money was earned and spent. The idea was to build up a geographical comparison from a very wide area. To concentrate our minds, we were given to understand – with a strictness I have never fathomed – that we were not to return to Moscow under any circumstances till our six weeks were over.

Mytishchi was a small village with two factories. One was presumably producing armaments, because it was guarded night and day by militia people. The other constructed railway carriages and engines. Our job within the factory was to collect and store heavy scrap metal. This stuff seemed to be lying around all over the place. I was struck by the wastefulness.

We were housed in a dormitory alongside the militiamen who were guarding that other factory. But Chervenkov took care to link each of us to a family connected with our workplace. And Bob MacIlhone and I had the great luck to be allocated to the family of an engineering worker named Paul. Sadly, I've forgotten his second name. Paul turned out to be most interesting. He told us how he had deserted from the Tsarist navy during the First World War. He had done this in Plymouth and had made his way to South Wales. Till the end of the War, he worked in a pit in Merthyr. (He was still corresponding with some of his former workmates – or had for some years.) Then he had made his way home, via Canada and Vladivostok. What rendered him even more interesting for us was that he had obviously picked up some Western ideas about housebuilding and physical planning. And he was very active in a little housing cooperative which had got hold of some land outside the village proper and had built some houses there. Inevitably, these were all wood. But their layout and other features were distinct from the run of the mill round about them, the pine trees had been kept in place, and the houses were grouped around their own somehow more intimate bit of ground. Obviously Paul had ideas.

We got on very, very famously. There wasn't a day when we were not involved with him, his wife and daughter. Sometimes we also went along to them for an evening meal. There was less of a language barrier than with anyone else in Mytishchi, probably – and anyway, surrounded at last by workers, we found our Russian come alive as it never had in the school. Paul was also a party member. Yet despite all this, try as we might, we could not get anywhere with our assigned task for which we had been allocated to him, the family budget. The fascinating thing was, that when we got back to Moscow, all of us turned out to have drawn the same blank, irrespective of where we had been. As party organiser of the English Land Sector, I can remember the nucleus meeting where I tried to summarise the results of the practical, that it had been a flop.

And the same verdict came from the Slavs and from others who cannot conceivably have had any shadow of a language barrier. My personal conclusion is that the Russian workers regarded us, not so much as foreigners (Paul, for example, was surely very internationalist), but rather as people connected with the higher-ups, with the government.

Foodwise, we felt we had had a rather frugal time at Mytishchi. There, the diet was basically a peasant one; milk, eggs, kvas (a fermented but non-alcoholic drink), kasha (from buckwheat) and black bread (though, when necessary, this could make a meal in itself). For eating with, ornamental wooden spoons were used. So obviously, the first thing some of us did, on arrival at the School, was to get hold of our pay and go down to the NEP restaurant in the Arbat, about five or 10 minutes' walk away. Who should be sitting in the restaurant – rosy-cheeked and nicely dressed as ever – Kirsanova! She saw us, smiled at us – no calling over – and went on eating.

My second year's practical, that of 1929, was more ambitious. This time, we were deemed sufficiently fluent in Russian to be able to fend for ourselves. There was to be no Chervenkov figure. We were to decide for ourselves who to go with. So 'Magharab', Séan Murray, Jim Larkin, Charlie Stead and 'Porter' (a Canadian whose real name I never knew) decided that we fitted each other's temperaments and interests.

The question then became: where shall we go? What shall we do? The options seemed wide open for us. I put my oar in. We should think in terms of getting off the beaten track, away from any Intourist circuit. Now, Kirsanova had mentioned that Rakovsky was currently exiled in a place called Barnaul. So I read up about Barnaul a bit; a small but important Siberian town, situated on a lake. But the sole requirement on us beforehand was to tell the school authorities the theme of our thesis – the highfalutin word for the short report we would have to do after the trip was over. The authorities turned out not to like our Barnaul idea. Siberia, they said, was too far.

Our second proposal was to go to Daghestan, an 'Autonomous Soviet Socialist Republic' bordered by the Caucasus, the Caspian and Iran. This scheme was approved. We set out. As usual, we were privileged in some ways, we needed only to show our passes at the GPU office which dominated most railway stations, in order for facilities to be flung open to us, wherever we were. But we were travelling 'hard' – that is, all-wooden – for four days and nights, solid. Apart from clothes, we were allowed to take no more than our school blankets (though these, by local standards, were good).

It was a tremendous journey. But eventually we were over the mountains and arriving at Makhachkala, the capital. It had no heavy industry and seemed a nice little town. Economically, its three main activities turned out to involve seal products (I hadn't dreamt of the existence of seals in an inland sea, thousands of miles from polar ice), fruit canning and caviar. We went and saw some of this activity. In one small department of the cannery, they were keeping samples of American canned foods so as to see how well these kept for various lengths of time. Caviar – if only in its cheaper varieties – was something on offer in the school every day. So I knew I could not stomach it. We were shown into a lift and taken on a tour of inspection of the processing plant, which was deep underground. Outside, the heat was terrific, but the cold in the plant seemed frightful. We were given enormous sheepskin hoods and coats, and shown the seemingly enormous range of colour and fineness of caviar which the plant produced. And we were offered a little sample of stuff which, we were proudly told, was sent 'to the embassies of the world'. I had to refuse it and caused offence. I suppose I was silly, it was their most famous industry.

But we had officially come to study Daghestan's political and administrative system, not its economy. We therefore went to party meetings at every level – from the factory to the city soviet and also to the national soviet which of course met in Makhachkala.

We also began to realise how much the culture of the people we were among differed from that we had become accustomed to in Moscow. It wasn't that we were fêted by the top men in their own homes – which of course we would never have been when in Moscow. Rather, the utter lavishness of the hospitality was something strange to us. Tables were creaking with rich food, and any wish – even when only half-expressed – was granted instantly many times over. We were spending many hours on end with these men, and were beginning to feel that they were not only incredibly hospitable but also no less bureaucratic. What really jarred on my guts was the relation between men and women. I knew little about women then, and may not know so much now. But I know what is offensive and slave-like, and what is not. And this slave-like relationship instantly jarred against my concept of Socialism.

So, the more we were entertained and the more access we had to Daghestan Soviet politics in the capital (not, of course, that we had any language in common beside Russian), the more we wondered about realities away from the centre. We therefore decided to go to the other extreme, to Shamil. This place was named after a famous guerrilla leader whose long resistance against Tsarist attack is one of the famous exploits in military history – or should be. We expected Shamil to be the least accessible point we had ever been to.

We were not disappointed. After a train journey, we transferred to a lorry which climbed for the best part of a day. Shamil lies right by the top of a pass through a mountain range. At one stage, the driver had to get out and put chains round the wheels, because of mud. For us, another problem turned out to be the heights. Sometimes the drop seemed vertiginous. 'Porter', though normally tough, was almost sick with the altitude, the jolting, with the looking down and with the looking up! A third problem was what we were told was banditry. On the top of the lorry crouched a militiaman, scanning the road around us with his rifle at the ready – responsible for our safety. Occasionally, when the lorry seemed almost wider than the road at some point where the drop seemed particularly frightening, we had to pass a man with his few goats. I can remember the utter fury of those goatherds as we pushed them and their animals even nearer the edge.

Finally, we reached Shamil; a tiny hamlet consisting of a few houses, plus a stone prison and the stables and barracks from which the militia operated in the interior. There was also one stone building where we stayed. I suppose it had at one time been something like a monastery. My reason for imagining this is that someone associated with it at some time had had some concept of sanitation; it included a toilet, built over a stream.

By and large, our food was similar to that in Mytishchi. From time to time, we were also given a chicken by a chap who was one of the officials in the local soviet. We were living under extremely primitive conditions – but we were mobile. The man who was locally responsible for the party commandeered some militia horses. This was where our riding experience came in. We were **away**; a ride of 15 minutes would take us to what was more or less a plateau. This was a truly beautiful place for riding. It had only short trees, down below, we could see vast forests, earmarked for exploitation under the Five Year Plan. On the way up to the plateau, we would sometimes pass a line of 20 or 30 prisoners doing heavy work, hacking and piling heavy stones, possibly building some fortress at this higher position. They were under guard; bandits – or so we were given to understand, but this was really a non-subject. They were housed in a low, dungeon-like stone building which lay at one end of Shamil's 200 or 300 yard long parapet on the edge of a precipice. I remember walking along there once and trying to peer in, but I was gazing into blackness and saw nothing.

Our horses had been given us, though, for a serious purpose. Around Shamil, we aimed to gather as broad an impression as we could of the ways in which the party's message was getting through at the local level. The locally most frequent word for hamlet or small village can be transliterated as 'aul'. We did an extensive survey round from Shamil. The houses in every aul were primitive mud arrangements, no windows. You sat on the floor to eat, and the eating was from a communal bowl. The women seemed to do all the work. If there was a donkey or ass, the man rode it and the woman trotted along with the load. I can remember being shocked at the women collecting cowdung which they formed into pancakes and slapped onto the outside wall so as to dry in the wind and sun for fuel. If we had been educated people, I imagine we'd have had some inkling before we arrived that things were like this.

But now the word that kept coming into our discussion was 'primitive'.

And all this came to us entirely raw, immediately following all the political turmoil and academic disputation about 'Socialism in One Country'! Our desire to be loyal to party concepts was stretched. I was, as I've claimed, the most critically minded – certainly in our group. But I too was shocked. Others, such as young Jim Larkin, simply could not stop talking about it. With our heads full of Socialism in One Country, our eyes showed us social relations which were pre-feudal. Often, no discussion was necessary, we could see each other's faces.

As for the party message! Such was the terrain, that the area was exceptionally diverse linguistically. Neighbouring auls might speak mutually unintelligible dialects or languages. People of very various backgrounds were living amongst each other. We came across Jews living as goatherds, for example. But there was still the propaganda being put out by the central authorities. In or outside the dilapidated hovel, there'd still be the official slogan exhorting everyone to fulfil the Five Year Plan. The words would be Russian. But Russian was not generally known where we went. Even our crude Glaswegian, Battersea, Indian, Dublin or Canadian versions of it were seldom understood. And even where people did seem literate in some script, such scripts were not Russian. So, in terms of communication as well as socially, Makhachkala was a peak in comparison with the Shamil area. Around that time, Daghestan's Komsomol or YCL was mounting a campaign to try and persuade the young men to part with their daggers. Just as the German businessman walks around with his little umbrella, so here every young man wore as part of his manhood a dagger with a beautiful handle of hammered silver (locally mined, I assumed). This campaign seemed to be making no progress at all – up in the mountains, at least.

The Five Year Plan also envisaged some enormous hydroelectric projects, mountain streams could be heard roaring almost everywhere. Undoubtedly, this was where we blundered – we drank. Whether directly because of this or because of the primitive conditions in general, Charlie Stead and I were struck down, the most violent dysentery I have ever had. We were soon in a pretty bad state, and there were no medical facilities. Ultimately the local party chap became worried and went over the mountains to where there was an afforestation scheme. There, he fetched some sort of medic who brought us castor oil. I can remember drinking this in quantities, to try and throw off the dysentery. In the end, we did. But it was very debilitating, and it restricted our range, even on horseback.

After two or three weeks at Shamil, we wanted to come out. The only question was: how on earth? On the eve of our departure, the local militia commander gave us a feast. I don't know if he himself was from Daghestan, but his wife certainly behaved as if she was; once again, all the chores were done by her. She offered far more food than at least Charlie and I could eat. But the other reason why this particular feast sticks in my memory, is that our host was apologising, time and time again, for our being without transport, there was no longer any possibility of getting a lorry up through the mud to carry us back down again. The next day, we were sat on the back end of a peasant cart with its wheels taken off. The horse heaved forwards or lent backwards, depending on the slope. And the peasant steered – but no more than approximately, as the cart slid, swinging from side to side. It was a frightful journey (not least for the horse). At least we were going down though!

We returned to Makhachkala and journeyed south to a place called Derbent. Under that Five Year Plan, a big glass industry was being built up. Derbent had two things at hand, the right type of sand on the beaches and, in addition to that, enormous reserves of natural gas. You could feel the vibration of the ground as you stood there. And you could see, in places, gushes of burning gas. And they had tapped this for making glass of many kinds. This glass complex was the biggest industry that we saw anywhere in Daghestan.

At that time, amid a population of about 400 000, Daghestan had a party membership of 4000, a tiny fraction. And the higher up the party hierarchy you went, the larger the minority of Russians in key positions. This, along with the linguistic insensitivity of distributing slogans in Russian to people who could neither read nor understand it, made the warnings of Lenin which I had read in an academic way against 'Great Russian chauvinism' come alive. And I couldn't see much impact of Socialism in One Country or even, come to that, of the abolition of serfdom in 1861. To my mind, most of the women were still the absolute slaves of the men. This may connect, in the longer run, with the naming of our hamlet after Shamil. Our friend the militia commander who was, of course, a key party cadre for the area, described Shamil as a great national hero who had welded disparate peoples together for the fight against the Tsarist armies. In the late 1940s though, Shamil was demoted to a mere bourgeois nationalist. Whether the name of the place was altered as a result, I don't know.

As in the previous year, I was entitled to a month's holiday. Again I went to the Crimea, this time to a former monastery in Novi Fond, near Sochi. But after a fortnight I decided to break off. It wasn't only the heat. I also wanted to go to the celebrations of International Youth Day in Leningrad. So, via Moscow, I travelled there. While in Leningrad, I addressed a meeting for the YCI in the centre and one in a workers' district. I spoke most of the time in English via an interpreter, the idea was to strengthen among young people the feeling that the movement was international. Two things struck me in Leningrad. The first was the shortage of food. As a guest speaker, I was given something to eat. But my hosts around me were sitting or standing there with nothing in front of them. My embarrassment was acute. This was in September 1929, clearly collectivisation was having problems. My second shock was the housing shortage. This seemed even worse than in Moscow. Academically we had read Engels on the housing question under capitalism. But this was a country officially constructing Socialism – the same slum conditions. This produced in my mind another violent contradiction between what was supposed to be and what actually was.

This concluded my travels for 1929. But the same tension between dogma and actuality was to recur even more massively the next summer. The aim we were given for our 'practical' work for the late spring of 1930, was to build up an overall picture of the progress of the Five Year Plan in terms of heavy industry and of the collectivisation of agriculture. Collectivisation was currently at its height. Kirsanova, in her morning talks to the School, had for some time been setting the scene. With the defeat of Bukharin, with the 'liquidation of the kulaks (rich peasants) as a class', with the progress in the Five Year Plan, the economy was surging towards the main goal of 'catching up and surpassing America'.

But also during the same months, we became unavoidably aware that tensions over collectivisation were building up. We had two indications. In the middle of the academic term, the Russian Land Sector – which included Russians as well as Russian speakers – were all given a Komandirovka; they were to go off and campaign in the villages to aid the collectivisation effort. Each of them was to report to the Central Committee building on Dzerzhinsky Square, and be told where to travel to. Our second indication came via those of us who had Russian girlfriends from outside the school. Those girlfriends who were party members were likewise taken off their jobs and sent away. One of the British students was a Scot, school name of 'Andie Auld', who met and married a Russian girl. (Incidentally, he was another who had all manner of difficulty getting his wife out. I never heard of him after 1930.) She was sent to somewhere down at the southern end of the Volga, probably near Astrakhan. Via such sources, you got hints of the difficulties the party was experiencing in the villages; 'difficulties' was the favourite word.

So, these echoes clashed rudely with the line that was being splashed for month after month in *Pravda* and *Izvestia* about progress in collectivisation. This too caused tensions in one's mind. And it was in this context that our academic courses at the school were drawing to a close. On paper, to examine on the ground the construction of Socialism would round our three years off very nicely.

On our side, we anticipated that this would mean our being given a sort of roving commission, as in the previous year. But that was not to be. Instead, all of us in the English Land Sector third year were sent en bloc, as one single tour group. Also in our group were some of those from the British party who, in late 1929, had begun the nine month short course. For some reason, not all of them were given this grand tour, but some were. The leader of our group was to be none other than Professor Mints who was thus dragged away from his books. We were to see both agriculture and industry. As we were to travel as far as Baku and Batum on either side of the Caucasus, we were given a railway engine and two coaches. Even more important – in view of the growing difficulties with the food supply, even in Moscow – we were also given cooking utensils and a supply of food. This was plentiful. I helped load our train: pots and pans, tea, black bread and salami or kolbasa. These supplies lasted for weeks and did us proud. We were not going to depend on hotels or party dormitories or headquarters, we were going to be self-contained – though, admittedly, on 'hard' seats all the way.

Around the time that we moved off, Mints initiated a discussion on the concept of a planned economy and on the bottlenecks which the Five Year Plan was experiencing because of the shortage of foreign currency for purchasing machinery abroad. He was trying to prepare us for such problems as he could anticipate.

Our first stop was at Orekhovo-Suevo, a large textile centre. To me, a textile factory is a mystery. But Maggie 'Jordan' was from Shipley in Yorkshire, and had been brought up in the woollen industry. She remarked that the number of workers per loom was higher than what she was used to. After touring the mill, we had an interview with its party leader, who seemed very able. She talked about communication with the workers. This was done in a very pictorial, graphically lively way, not only about production targets but also about local conditions, and the blending of party policy with these. We had seen her wall posters all round the workshops.

Next, we had a look at the workers' housing. This was of two types. First we were shown the new housing that was still being built; boxlike suburban structures such as you have nowadays almost anywhere. Of course, those dwellings that we saw were beautifully furnished – so that I, at least, began to feel I was on a sort of royal visit. But, after that, we were taken to where most of the workers still lived. And this was really as grim as one could conceive. Mind you, it was very durable, stone walls, slate floors and suchlike. But it gave the impression of being a very sordid barracks, a room for each family, with the inadequate facilities on a communal basis. So I got very mixed feelings at Orek-hovo-Suevo.

We went on to Kharkov and saw round the new industries that were being established there. Similarly in Rostov. By this time, another feeling was surfacing within me. As I've mentioned, acute shortages of commodities had been evident in Moscow even when I arrived. But till now, the further south you moved, the less these problems had seemed; the climate and soil were better and the peasants had more to sell. This time, though, the further south we progressed, the more observable the shortages of food became. We understood better and better why we were transporting our own supplies.

No less significant was the new attitude at the top of the party. Wherever we went, the first thing we did was to try and make contact with the local leadership. In previous years we had sat with such people for hours, talking about projects and other things. As before, we were supposed to be studying the practical workings of the troika – of party, union and managers – in the running of any workplace we visited. But now, from Kharkov on, these leaders seemed almost too busy to even see us. It must surely have been obvious to them that we had come in order to get an impression of what was going on in their district. But not only were they harassed and run off their feet. We were an **embarrassment** to them. During the whole tour, this became an outstanding impression, revived again and again.

At Kharkov, instead of giving a little of their time, what the local leaders laid on was hospitality. Lavishly: we were given everything. And after we had eaten our guts full – you **must** try our national dish, and a sucking pig was brought on. But we were surrounded by grim shortages. I was not alone in my feelings. We didn't need to talk, we could see from each other's faces that each was reacting similarly.

On we went to Dnieprostroy. This was to be the climax, to see such a huge dam being built. But our train was shunted to a siding, in the middle of nowhere. We waited – passing the time and playing chess and becoming increasingly pissed off – for a couple of days! We tried to imagine the reasons: illness, political problems? We were still aching to see this high spot of the Plan.

Ultimately, we pulled into the site. On one side were the offices. We were kept well clear of those where American engineers were working, but we were shown plans of the areas and villages that were to be flooded and of the shape of things to come when the dam was completed. Then we were taken outside again. At that stage, much of the work involved blasting the rocks which were submerged in the river Dniepr and which hindered navigation. But roughly one-third of the dam was already up. We moved further, on to a construction site. I had acquired a smattering of knowledge about such places – what with one brother and my two closest Battersea friends being building workers. But I had simply never seen anything like the size or the conditions which I witnessed here. One of the dam's vast pillars was being filled with concrete. After being poured, concrete has to be compressed so as to prevent pockets of air occurring which would make for unevenness of strength. Normally, or so I had gathered, the stuff is vibrated down in some way. But now I witnessed something I had never heard or read about, what seemed an enormous number of large peasant men, wearing shoes of mere straw, standing on this half-set concrete, inside this caisson – like a colossal wine vat – treading it down. This army of straw feet struck me as primitive in the extreme, treading, treading, treading.

After we had come away from the dam area proper, we ran into the only workers with whom we were able to try and converse during the whole tour, a huge grouping of besprizornye. We sat down and got talking with them – or rather to them. One of our bilingual Americans, 'Clark' (a leading Lovestoneite among the American students) started making them a little speech. But to start any discussion among them was an impossible effort, they seemed not to have a political concept between them. All the things uppermost in our party-impregnated minds for projecting into theirs – about the Plan, about living on a collective farm and suchlike – were dead to them. There was not the remotest resonance.

From Dneprostroy, we travelled into the Donbas coal district, halting at a place called, I think, Kramatorsk or something similar. Here, we were taken down a mine. In terms of the Plan, this was obviously a showplace, it had modern cutting equipment in use at the face. For me, it was my first such trip. Despite our protective clothing, we all got soaked on our way down in the cage. And when we reached the bottom, we had to walk a very long way to the face, there was no conveyance of any kind. The headroom was such that you walked bent, and the timbering creaked and didn't seem so very good. But finally we reached the face, and the engineers explained the mechanisms to us. One of our short course students was a Welsh miner, and he seemed to come alive in these conditions, with the damp, the creaking, the noise and all the frightful dust. I didn't know what to think of it all.

But there again, apart from the people near the cutting machine, we seemed to be meeting remarkably few workers. In addition, on previous tours as also in Moscow, it had been normal to attend union or party or shopfloor meetings and to feel we were making some contact in that way. But now we never did. Apart from that interview with a party **leader** in Orekhovo-Suevo, we saw again and again the physical aspect but not the political. And this registered with me uneasily. During nearly three years, it had become part of life to go to such meetings, observe people's faces, meet some and generate some rapport with them. But now the outstanding feeling was that we were missing out on people.

This became forcibly clear in three places. One workplace we saw in Rostov was a huge tractor factory which was still being built. Again, we saw tons of concrete but no meetings that had either been organised for us or which we were invited along to observe. Next, we went to a collective farm in the foothills of the Caucasus. At that time, we had heard much propaganda about 'Gigant' – situated really beautifully and covering the equivalent of many English counties. It turned out to be indeed in an extremely fertile area and to embrace hundreds of villages. But we never saw a single one of these.

A third place was a town (whose name I forget) in the same region. Here, we were not even taken to any workplace, but were simply put into a building and told to wait. We hung around for many hours. Eventually, the workforce (I can't remember what of – if we were told) marched down and stood in the triangular piece of ground in front of the building we had been put into. And Mints and one of the students – probably 'Clark' again – addressed them. Obviously, our contact with them was non-existent. Again, in my reactions to this, I did not feel myself to be alone. All my colleagues were Stalinist in their views and, like me, very highly committed party members. And I could see what they were feeling, no less than me. After all the propaganda about the urgency of devoting every possible minute to fulfilment of the Plan, here were all these workers being taken **away** from production, simply to stand in front of a group of foreigners, none of whom they would ever see again.

Whether my companions attributed all these oddities to political tensions which the local party bosses were trying to conceal, my suspicions certainly lay in this direction. For, during the previous year while returning from my holiday in the Crimea, I had chanced to see a crowd of people in cattle trucks, in transit: obviously 'kulaks'. At this time, the propaganda was unremitting against these 'rich kulaks' who were sabotaging collectivisation. But here were men, women and children in rags, obviously in the depths of poverty. From the train, one could see their faces.

By the time we reached Moscow, after going down to Baku and Batum, we had covered thousands of miles. Back at the school, our Land Sector met to exchange opinions as to whether the tour had been a success. Here, we encouraged in each other a state of mind which I can best label as 'gigantism'. The way in which we, persons who were supposedly saturated in concepts such as the forces and relations of production, solved whatever problems we had had to notice, was by concentrating on the physical hardware. We regurgitated to each other the almost photographic propaganda about bigness, projects, buildings in course of erection, unprecedented feats of productivity.

Not that we were peculiar in this. To the extent that you were in touch with ordinary Muscovites – or rather with those younger people, not least girlfriends, who tended to be politically active – they seemed to be caught up in enthusiasm for the Plan. This was despite or because of the poverty which, even in Moscow by now, was particularly terrible – so serious that, even in the Comintern and the school, the food situation was deteriorating sharply. The British, German and other Western delegates who came over for the Tenth Plenum in 1929 were eagerly awaited for the food they would bring.

Our tour had been designed to show us the unfolding of collectivisation and of the Plan in general. And yet, those officials in charge of implementing this were nearly always too busy to see us – although we were a very select international group of fast track cadres, travelling by special train, led by one of the best known Communist professors and under the auspices of the Central Committee. Although – or was it because? There were great class tensions underneath – however suppressed or distorted. And what, by now, did the Central Committee mean to these officials? Everywhere, it meant terrific pressure to overfulfil impossible targets. On the farms, it meant they had to carry on 'liquidating the kulaks', irrespective of the human or political costs. And increasingly, this pressure from above was contradictory; our tour more or less coincided with Stalin's 'Dizzy with Success' speech in which he counselled a little sensitivity over collectivisation. Either way, local officials were going to be saddled with the blame for any negative impressions we might come away with. So, the closer they imagined us as being to the holders of supreme power up in Moscow, the more they must have felt our approach as a threat.

This was the significance – dawning to me at the time – of the third year 'practical' part of the course. But a far briefer tour which was also important to me, in its way, was to the Marx-Engels Institute, a mere stroll down the road from the school. As explained, we students were given unlimited access to any institutions relevant to our studies. The only constraints were time, and pressure of work. But in 1929 David Riazanov, who was director of the Marx-Engels Institute, let it be known via the party nucleus bureau that he was aware of the British students' presence in the school, and wanted to bring to their attention the rich resources on their labour movement in the Marx-Engels Institute. He allegedly expressed surprise that we had not visited the Institute. Arising from that message, arrangements were made to visit it.

But first of all, it is necessary to say who Riazanov was. He was an outstanding Marxist scholar and historian, who, from the moment of the October Revolution, had spent his time fulfilling an ambition (which he had had when an emigré in Germany) of collecting all the writings and materials of Marx and Engels, and housing them in a library. So, shortly after the end of the First World War, his work started in earnest. A building was made available, the archive began to be collected, efforts were made to purchase – from here, there and everywhere – materials connected with Marx and Engels' life. Now, as early as 1924, Riazanov started the publication of their *Collected Works*. Four or five years later, in the second hand book market along the 'Chinese wall', I bought Volume One of that first edition (printed on the most primitive paper conceivable). It opened with a long introductory preface by Riazanov.

Pressures of work reduced our visiting group to those very few who were immediately interested and could spare or make time. I was one. The Institute was housed in a street of sumptuously pre-revolutionary buildings, high ceilinged and chandeliered. As we entered, we were greeted by a veteran Italian Communist, Peluso, a very portly, happy sort of a man. He spoke English perfectly, which made things easy for us. In addition to that, he turned out to be extremely knowledgeable about the British movement, and about Britain itself. He started his introduction off with a little talk on the wonderful asset he had with an English Burberry. As we were all proletarians, a Burberry coat meant nothing at all to us. His opening gambit flopped, he saw the dumbness of our expression. So he immediately switched to another topic (the German Max Beer's writings on British labour history).

Then he took us around the exhibition room with these lovely chandeliers and beautiful cases, to illustrate what there was. Among the manuscripts of Marx there was almost a child's school notebook, where he was learning the Russian language. There were Marx's early pamphlets in their original editions. This exhibition connected for us with our reading. It also gave us a nice introduction to what he next showed us. He took us into another room, the library of the development of the British labour movement. There was Thomas More's *Utopia*. There was the Winstanley Collection in a safe. Another special iron safe was opened, the *Northern Star*. And other Chartist papers were brought out, in mint condition. I remember thinking at once: Christ, how beautiful. This enormous library of books. By merely glancing at the book titles I could assemble a synopsis for our studies on the West European labour movement. A magnificent collection there, in such order. Masterly.

Peluso next showed us the library's general facilities and how, at that time, there were very few people at the desks working. And compared with Battersea or Westminster reference libraries the place did seem empty, given what it housed. His point in showing us was to invite us back, an admission ticket was handed to each of us. But before leaving, as we were moving towards the entrance, we looked up. In the inside portico over this beautiful entrance, there was an ark of the *Communist Manifesto* in different languages. Peluso, with a bright eye, showed us this collection, which he had concentrated on. I agreed: what a sense it gave of belonging to an international movement.

Although one did not have the time to work there properly, I did go back to see old Peluso again and have my second look at those Chartist papers, not only to be able to see them open, but to browse around in Harney's *Red Republican*, and in the *Northern Star*. To me, this was a sort of aesthetic joy. Peluso died in a camp, like Riazanov.

Before we leave Moscow, I must surely mention some other fascinating people to be encountered during the time of my stay there. In 1929, I was with a Chinese comrade called Yen – whom I was great friends with and who was among our group that holidayed in Kastropol – in the Bristol hotel to welcome a Chinese delegation to the RILU. And who should come to join in the welcome? – Heinz Neumann, who for some years had been Thälmann's righthand man in the German party. Neumann immediately broke into fluent Chinese. He was heavily involved in discussions over China. But he was, already at this time, seen as a friend of Bukharin. In the 1930s, he was shot.

Another person whom I knew (rather than merely stood near) was a student at the school. Not that he seemed to do any work there. He was a black American called Harry Hayward or 'Hall'. He hoped to become the Comintern's specialist on black America. In particular, he saturated himself in writings on black territorial self-determination. One of his obsessions was Marcus Garvey, the theorist of 'Back to Africa'. During the Third Period, the American party did come out for territorial self-determination. So Hayward was not over-ambitious. But our sector also had a South African student, whose name escapes me. Because of Hayward's advocacy of black self-determination, there was outright hostility between them. That policy was indeed disgraceful. But there certainly were extenuating circumstances. Till talking to Hayward, I had never imagined the depths of racism to which the American movement at that time could go, how trade unionists organising in the South could segregate their audience – blacks on one side, whites on the other – and how some Communists tolerated this or even, allegedly, did so themselves. With my Battersea background, this was something utterly inconceivable.

Not that American comrades were the only ones open to occasional accusations of racism. By the main entrance to the new building, the school displayed its regular wall newspaper, which was open to contributions from any student. One issue carried a cartoon of Harry Hayward while 'on practical work': this 'work' amounted to being surrounded by a bevy of pretty girls. It was not designed to flatter my friend. Possibly it would now be seen as sexist, let alone racist. Hayward later wrote an autobiography and, not surprisingly, recounts this incident. Something I could have told or reminded him of, though, is that this open criticism of a student in the public part of the school's premises was raised at the party nucleus bureau. As noted, I was on this and I remember Rudas and Kirsanova rightly insisting that criticism between students should be kept out of the newspaper and, instead, channelled via the student representatives on the bureau. The point is, the artist – technically most able – was Siqueiros who, back in his native Mexico by the late 1930s, was to carry out a machine gun attack on Trotsky.

Now and then, I have mentioned one or two interesting people who dropped by at the school, once or more often. There were others too: Bertram Wolfe, author of *Three Who Made a Revolution*, came to discussions during the crisis within the American party. Another visitor was big Jim Larkin. I've mentioned his son, my friend. I suggested he should invite his old man along. So Larkin came and addressed the English Land Sector students. His talk was to be on the current situation in Ireland – particularly on the decline of the trade union movement since the foundation of the Free State. He opened by casting his eye round us and making some sneering remark about 'all you little Lenins!' His main theme turned out to be the unlikelihood of a Communist Party ever taking off in Ireland. What stuck in my gullet most was that, for some reason or other, he was very critical of James Connolly. Emphasising the stranglehold of the Catholic church, he went out of his way to note that even Connolly had died in its arms. Now, that may well have been. But Larkin was loading the blame for his current difficulties onto Connolly. This seemed to me worse than silly.

Leaving Moscow

Before we left the school, we had a month or six weeks in which to produce our final piece of work. At that time, many people were complaining quite rightly about the British party's theoretical poverty. So, among the British students, I put the proposal round that we should produce a textbook for training cadres. It was agreed. I took it to the party nucleus, who agreed too. So we met and allocated the chapters. In those days, the poverty of the British left was historiographical as well as in its level of theory. So, what we ended up producing was a really voluminous tome – one of those too weighty for anyone to actually read. It transposed Rudas' historical course, starting way back with the Civil War. Luckily, there was a comrade called Danny Richards, a referencer. He took on the task of pulling our work together, so as it could function as a training manual. Years later, I bumped into him and asked what had happened to it. He said how appalled he had been when he first saw its size! Nonetheless, when the British Communist Party finally produced a series – one on Chartism, one on trade unionism, and so on – some parts were recognisable as derived from our grand tome.

Anyway, the school did not hand it back for rewriting! Next, each student was to be assessed individually – according to theoretical attainments, party work and every aspect of participation in the school. I've already mentioned the extraordinary lengths to which the school authorities went in consulting with students. This continued into the final moment. Not that every student was necessarily present at every assessment. But many did sit in on these discussions and often took part in them. In these meetings, the actual assessment was done by the tutors, the party organisers and the student representatives. So, as party organiser, I was present throughout. One of the criteria was 'independence of thought'. When the discussion came to me, Charlie Stead made the point that, if anyone in the whole school displayed such independence, it was 'Jack Tanner'. I blushed, but remain proud of the memory.

I left the school building along with Stead, Séan Murray and possibly one or two others. As we got into the car which was to take us to the station, who should be standing on the school steps – I recognised him from newspaper photos – but Béla Kun? After I was back home, I heard that Kun had been appointed to succeed Bukharin as the school's head. I wondered how Rudas was getting on, he and Kun would surely never abide each other in the same building.

We came out of Russia through Lithuania and East Prussia. We brought virtually no luggage with us. The official idea was that all school students should arrive back for work within their various countries unencumbered. My main interest during the journey was merely to do with clothes. An Anglo-Russian comrade, who had been deported from Britain, had been interested in acquiring my suit. This I had bought from Rust when Rust had been on a visit. So I sold it to this comrade in return for his promise to send successive volumes of the Marx-Engels *Collected Works* – which I had placed a subscription for – on to me as each was published. When I arrived in Berlin, I was determined to nip out to buy some clothes to go home in. But this proved impossible, Berlin was having some sort of public holiday. So we jumped on the next train and were in Berlin for only an hour or two. The first thing I did on arrival at Liverpool Street was to get a No 11 bus to the Strand where I bought a suit. I walked away in it, leaving my Russian suit in the shop.

A journey that is much more interesting was that of my books and papers. I had accumulated a big collection. Most of the students were in no position to take such things with them – because of distance, illegal conditions at home or other reasons. But I was determined that I wanted my stuff. If we wished to have anything packed, we were instructed to simply put it in our rooms, the packing would be done for us. What is interesting is not merely the quantity – I happened to be out of London when the crate arrived in Battersea, but my mother and stepfather told me how, when it was delivered from Hay's Wharf, it was so huge that they had to unpack it in the street!

Rather, the interesting thing was the content. I had those two copies of Trotsky's *Our Political Tasks*, plus whatever of his writings for *Nashe Slovo* (his wartime Paris paper) had been translated in the school, and his articles on the internationalist meetings at Zimmerwald and Kienthal. Not least, there were his writings in the internal party controversies. There was the 1927 re-edition (somewhat falsified, as was later proved) of the 1917 minutes of the Petrograd Bolshevik Committee. There was also the third edition of Lenin's *Collected Works* with its notes and bibliography by Bukharin and Kamenev who, by 1930, had become more than controversial. And the school let it all go! I can only assume that that laborious packing was done by some unpolitical or even illiterate labourer and that, as everything would have had to have been carried down flights of stairs, batch by batch to my crate, no-one noticed – even accidentally – so much heretical material accumulating. Subsequently, a number of comrades used my collection for their research. CLR James did so for his *World Revolution* and, after the Second World War, Isaac Deutscher did so for his books on Trotsky and Stalin, as did Hugo Dewar for his unpublished study of Saint-Simon.

What did the British party get from us 12 students? As we'll see, it got from me some service for a year or so, but I soon grew too critical for its taste. Of course, after expelling me, the party got less than nothing. But none of the other 11 became major heretics, as far as I know (and I have always, for more than 55 years now, kept my ears open for news of them). So from them, what did the party get? I have mentioned how prominent some of my contemporaries from other countries were to become during the next decades. None of my British ones became anything like as important. Some quickly became untraceable: did any drop out, sooner or later? Certainly the shock of return was immense (as we will see next), and must have been as serious for them as it was for me. But it would have been no less serious for students returning to many other countries too.

Perhaps there was an additional factor at work in Britain – anti-intellectualism. My impression from both before and after my Russian years, is that an acceptable way of undermining some person's arguments was to say 'oh well, he's an intellectual'. This is no more than my impression, but it is a constant one. And it is despite the important role of intellectuals – sometimes whole groupings of them – in the party's development since its formative years.

And we had indeed led the life of intellectuals for at least three winters, had lived at an intellectual rhythm continuously for three years and had been taken clean out of our original working class milieux. Charlie Stead was an extreme. The South Wales Miners Federation had sent him to the Central Labour College, Penywern Road, for two years. And then he had three years in the Lenin School. So indeed he was fortunate, in that! Or was he? By late 1930, we had all been remote from British struggles for three years. Unlike the earlier school intake, we had not been involved in the party at the national level (or in my case only to an extent, via the YCL executive). So the type of role – let alone post – we might fill, once we returned, was unclear. It still is! In our no doubt various ways, we must all have been in a political and personal quandary of an unprecedented nature.

Chapter 5
The Shock of Return

VERY quickly, this quandary grew acute. For me at least, the first months, or even days, in Britain were as if calculated to magnify it. Within an hour or two of our arrival in London, Charlie Stead, Séan Murray and I went to party headquarters in King Street, Covent Garden, to be assigned our new functions. Mine had already been decided in Moscow – after a slight disagreement, as I had learned. Apparently, some international comrades had wanted me to go to Berlin to work for Willi Münzenberg. There, his 'cabinet', as it was called, ran a sheaf of satellite organisations, such as MOPRA – International Red (or Class War Prisoners') Aid – the Friends of Soviet Russia and the League against Imperialism. But Pollitt and Rust, while visiting Moscow, had put paid to that idea. As far as they were concerned, I could be of more use in Britain. Rust had long been involved in the YCL and still was, partially. But he was now editor of the *Daily Worker*, was identified very much with the Comintern's new 'left' line and wanted to get out of youth work entirely. The YCL already had one secretary, a young Aberdonian called Alec Massey. He and I together were now to work as a secretariat, with me as the London organiser.

So this was to be my new sphere. I went home. But I had spent no more than a single night there with my mother, new stepfather and young sister when a telegram was delivered, ordering me instantly back to King Street. There, I was told to proceed at once to Shettlestone in Glasgow where Saklatvala was fighting a by-election. Once off the train and through the city into the committee room, I found two others from my Lenin School intake: Bob McIlhone and Willie Spence.

Three super-trained young cadres we were, fresh from three years in the motherland of Socialism; great things were obviously expected of us. Quickly we were put to work writing a leaflet. What could be simpler? Our great international minds sat down to this trivial chore – and promptly hit paralysis. For me, it wasn't that I was psychologically somewhere on the way back from Russia still, nor that I was in Scotland for the first time. For none of us was geography the main problem. Rather it was politics. We were stuck as to what to write and, worse, even more as to how to write it. It wasn't simply that three years of academic discipline take something out of you. Rather, a new political dialect had developed for party pronouncements. In Moscow, we had been in at the beginning of this as an international language. But now we suddenly had to jump into the British dialect of this language, almost from outside, and make it our own. It symbolised a change whose weight in Britain we were only just beginning to feel.

Another symbol was the mere fact that Sak's opponent in this by-election was no right winger, but John McGovern, a left ILPer. The last time I had been in Britain, those three intense years ago, there had still been strong fellow feeling within the labour movement; we Communists were still bonded with the working class, were respected and had a fair amount of sympathy. But during our absence, the party had thrown away whatever it had gained from its support for the miners during the General Strike and during the bitterly long rearguard action into the following winter. We were now in a different political country. We had become an even smaller party (roughly 3000 instead of 10 000) with, worse, negligible political contact with the organised labour movement: a sect. We three disoriented Muscovites could not yet formulate the matter quite so neatly, but we were surprised to find, in that committee room, that we had time on our hands. We spent some of it sharing our feeling of concussion. It just had not seemed possible that our party could become so isolated.

I suspect – though this I cannot prove – that the Pollitt/Rust leadership feared that our experience of Russian party dissensions and methods would make us dangerously quick to sense whatever the next changes in Comintern policy might be, before these were officially trumpeted. In this perspective, we would constitute a threat. Pollitt and Co would want to filter our party careers into dead ends as deftly as possible. Consequently, they sent us into a situation where we'd be likely to flop. In a party where anti-intellectualism was a reflex, 'those people from Moscow' would perform like intellectuals, too fond of sitting around talking for tackling practical tasks. Of course, any such manoeuvre presupposed the usual sterile counterposing of intellectual to practical.

In Shettleston, I was put up with Peter Kerrigan. He had done the nine month course at the Lenin School and was the most Stalinist of Stalinists. But, as it turned out, I was stuck with him for only a couple of nights before another telegram arrived: back to London, this time YCL headquarters.

Here, as I soon discovered, the situation was appalling. But this was merely part of the Communist Party's general problem. Not only had any gains from around 1926 been dissipated but also, as far as membership was concerned, this was mostly unemployed. This made our unemployed organisation, the NUWM, our one bright spot. Both of the new left unions which party members had led in forming, in the Fife coalfield and, in London, out of the Rego garment workers' strike, were in the doldrums. Our leading comrades in South Wales were in trouble. Arthur Horner was now seen within the party as a right winger, and was being hounded for his views.

Not surprisingly, therefore, the YCL was a shadow of its former self. Although it was then publishing a paper, *Young Worker*, there was not enough manpower to circulate it to any effect. The *Daily Worker* was facing a severe distribution problem. Party members had to be up early in the morning to meet the trains, take the papers round the shops; then, in the evenings, fagged out, they were on the knocker trying to sell. It was a crushing burden on such a small membership. So YCLers, too, had to be called on to help, to the neglect of their own work. This applied not only in London but throughout the country.

The Young Communist International, like the Comintern, had the practice of sending over instructors to ginger things up organisationally and politically. Our pair of trouble shooters were an American with an Ukrainian background named George Morris (real name or assumed I don't know) together with a German girl, Kitty (whose family name we never learned). Alec Massey and I first had for our office a sort of annexe in the basement at King Street. This was very poor accommodation, and we did not even have a typist. Later we were given space in the staff canteen of the *Daily Worker*. But in any case, the YCI reps kept well clear of party premises. Massey and I had to meet them almost daily elsewhere. This was a problem, because we were being tailed by plain clothes police. Any number of times Massey and I would leave the office together, get into a tube train and leap out just as the doors were closing, sometimes leaving our tail bottled up as the train accelerated out of the station. It was really babyish. Quite often, though, not even this was necessary, as only one plain clothes man was apparently available. So all Massey and I had to do was split up. Whichever of us was not being followed would make for the rendezvous. This varied between Hyde Park and, incongruously or not for prominent Young Communists, the Peter Pan statue in Kensington Gardens. There, our YCI reps were bursting with sound ideas about what the YCL should be doing. But these presupposed a membership and an organisation which simply no longer existed. It was as if they didn't want to see that they were talking to Big Chiefs who virtually lacked Injuns.

About this time, Massey was sent to some lengthy meeting or other at the YCI secretariat in Berlin. By now, I was more than a bit fed up with the YCI instructors' impossible demands. So I wrote a highly critical paper. This was not the sort of document which Massey would ever have approved. As a person, he was very diplomatic and cagey; he did not believe in sticking one's neck out. Well, I did. And, strangely enough, Rust seemed to concur with my paper. I was at the party politbureau meeting where he successfully argued for it to be pulled together and sent to Berlin. This editing was left to him, and I never saw the final version. But the point is, poor old Massey was sent no warning as to what was about to arrive while he was there. His embarrassment must have been total. Worse, all manner of difficulties ensued with the YCI leadership, and not just for him.

So the upshot of my criticism was a decision to remove me from the YCL secretariat. Instead, I was sent up to Bradford to help Jessie Sweet. Jessie, who was then aged 21 or 22, came from Maerdy and, in normal times, would have followed a more famous Maerdy man, Horner, into the mine. But he had been continuously unemployed since leaving school at 14. He had been trained for six or eight months at a YCI school near Moscow, and was a very able and charming fellow. But Bradford nonetheless deepened my disillusion.

Not that I travelled up there with many illusions undamaged. My first few days had shown me our grim position within a massively working class part of Glasgow. And during my time at the YCL secretariat I had, of course, been picking up some of the threads of my Battersea life – or rather, discovering many to be dangerously frayed. As noted, into the months when I had been preparing to leave for Russia, we in Battersea had been able to boast an impressively large YCL with its own premises and a cadre of people who were really good. Some, like Jimmy Lane, were used as speakers by the party nationally. But now, I was finding that London YCLers consisted of a few isolated pockets in Stepney, Hackney, Hammersmith and even Battersea.

But what hurt me most was that, when I contacted my oldest and closest YCL friends, they nearly all turned out to have left the party in disgust. Worse still, Communists like me were supposed to denounce them as 'Left Social Fascists'. (They quickly waxed ironic about this!) But they could not in any conceivable sense be accused of having moved rightwards. Alf Loughton and Jimmy never ever sold out. Alf went on to give a lifetime of service to the labour movement, ending with a stint as mayor of Wandsworth during which he dispensed with the flummery of office, and fought tooth and nail against council corruption. Jimmy was likewise to remain at least incorruptible for the rest of his life (unlike his successor as chair of the council's housing committee, Alderman Sporle, who was to go to prison for corruption). During the mid-1980s, on my last visit to his small house on the Shaftesbury estate, I was to notice with horror and admiration that this man, whose activity in housing had made him quite something in national discussions on the question, possessed no more than an earthenware sink in his kitchen and had never had a bathroom. Now, in 1930, they had no difficulty in showing me the idiocy of hitting non-members of the party on the head with jargon like 'Social Fascist'. As far as I was concerned, they remained the cream of the Battersea Socialists of my generation. I would obviously have to work alongside them in some way.

Nor was it only the YCL that had shrivelled. As mentioned, Labour's national leadership had disaffiliated Battersea Trades Council and Labour Party for refusing to cut links with us Communists. The situation in which there were two trades councils and two Labour Parties was frozen throughout May 1926 and after, as both sides rallied round the miners. (And even the right wing Labourites always happily opened Latchmere Baths for hunger marchers to sleep in, free of charge.) Meanwhile, the Communist Party leadership continued its ambiguous stance towards the left leaders in the unions and even towards not-so-left people outside the unions. As late as 1927, the Brussels Anti-Imperialist conference (an occasion controlled by the Comintern) had included middle and upper class progressives and not merely union and Labour leaders such as Hicks and Lansbury. So, despite the organisational splits, ideological differentiation was not always sharp. The left still had considerable legitimacy among Labour voters. Just before I had left for Russia, Jack Clancy, as candidate for Battersea's disaffiliated Labour Party, had beaten the official Labourites in a by-election for a seat on the borough council. This had occurred in Winstanley ward which, situated around Clapham Junction, was overwhelmingly working class. And in elections for the London County Council too, the left wing candidates, standing under the auspices of Battersea Trades Council and Labour Party, often had a good chance. The left dominated many wards and enjoyed the support of the Coop Women's Guild and of many union branches. In several dozen of the latter, when the membership found that their union officials were transferring to the official Battersea Labour Party the money paid in the political levy, they set up a contingency fund for the left wing Labour Party. (Here, though, the situation became really convoluted. As the victorious Tory government was legislating precisely against any automatic political levy, left wingers could not afford to be heard advocating taking money away from even the official Labour Party – particularly as the government was being echoed by a handful of renegades from the Labour Party itself!) Outside Battersea, this party was linked with more than 20 others in a National Left Wing Movement. Many people, including CPers like Clancy, hoped that this would allow the left to build up a truly Labour Party to replace the official one at the national level. In this, he was in agreement with many non-Communist Party left wingers, such as WT Colyer, the NLWM's secretary, who believed they saw a chance to build on a growing undercurrent of rank and file resentment within the Labour Party and ILP against the parliamentary leaders.

Within the Communist Party, though, Clancy was increasingly in a minority. The bulk of our membership grew worried that, if we helped replace the right wing Labour Party, we would merely be building 'another ILP', another barrier between ourselves and working class politics, or, at best, another rival to ourselves among left organisations. When this view triumphed within the party, our members moved within the NLWM to differentiate the good revolutionaries from the bad reformists. They behaved with growing insensitivity, and finally put forward a programme so advanced as to be virtually Communist. This was the last straw for Clancy who walked out of the Communist Party. So, 'Social Fascist' was now an accusation I was supposed to spit at my old political mentor.

All this, I was in the process of catching up on by the time I joined Jessie Sweet in Bradford. Here too, the gains which the party could show for its efforts since before 1926 were by now negligible. The area had just been through a bitter strike in the woollen industry, during which the party had done everything possible. But unemployment was now three times as high as it was in London. The dire poverty hit you. So in such mills as were still working, we had no members, they had all been excluded long ago and were now unemployed. Worse, we had no contacts. Most of those we had influenced were now amongst our unemployed fringe. We were isolated from the working remnant of the working class.

During the second half of 1930, the party was becoming conscious of how extreme this isolation was. So it was starting an effort to formulate a National Charter around which to rally the class. There was a long and tedious discussion as to whether the demands within this Charter should be all-embracing or narrowly particular. Predictably, the YCL was supposed to slot in here with its subsidiary National Youth Charter Campaign. In the party press, Dutt enthused that all this would 'open the way to the class again'. Big efforts were made. But they were all too 'Third Period', both in some of their motivation (our isolation from the class) and in their theory. The Comintern's Third Period line, whose proclamation in Moscow I had been present at, was that the unemployed and unorganised were more radical than other workers. This was as if designed for making a virtue out of our isolation. But it couldn't do much towards lessening it. Rather, it had helped cause it, and it now reinforced it. So the small numbers in the party and YCL were reduced to fund raising for sending delegates to a National Charter conference and rally in London. These twin events took place. But they were a fizzle. They never got to grips with the labour movement as such.

During these months too, there was a parliamentary by-election in Shipley, very near Bradford. Here, if anywhere, there seemed a good chance to put up Gallacher as candidate. Not only had Communists in the Bradford area invested considerable energy in the woollen strike, but they also had in Ernie H Brown, his wife Isabel and his brother, cadres who had been rooted in the labour movement since the pioneering days of the ILP, 40 years earlier. Symbolically (or so we hoped), the Communist Party had somehow acquired the ILP's hall in Shipley. As things turned out, though, the Shipley contest only confirmed our isolation once again. The hall became our committee room. But I remember no bustle of activity in it, no comings and goings, no-one seeking advice or offering help. Things were just as dead in our committee room in Bingley, the town next door which was also part of the constituency. Of course, some big Communist names did turn up. Beside Gallacher, Jim Larkin junior – my old Moscow friend – came over from Ireland along with a left wing nationalist called Peadar O'Donnell. Even Pollitt came up. As a speaker, he was among the ablest; but usually the audience he was able to attract onto the little triangle opposite our shop in the centre of Bingley were – just us. The only one of us who enjoyed slightly less of a flop was a Lancastrian called Harry Webb, who could work poetry into his speeches. Given our virtually zero level of support, our canvassing was reduced to flogging the *Daily Worker* from door to door. Inevitably, our sense of irrelevance surfaced into jokes between ourselves. Our political strategy presupposed our moving the 'vast masses'; so, when Pollitt, Gallacher or others of us were struggling out of a committee room to yet another non-meeting, we would sigh ironically about our 'going off to address the masses'. It was patently obvious to anyone: we were in the midst of a flop. Those we were trying to move were going to vote either Labour or Tory. Indeed, the Labour Party held big meetings addressed by, among others, Ellen Wilkinson. I bumped into her there; despite our warmth from Wimereux four and a half years previously, we were now on opposing sides. The ILP had been Labour's parent organisation, and this area had been one of the ILP's main seedbeds. Now, despite the Browns, Labour was obviously holding on to this tradition. On election day, the Tories narrowly won. Gallacher's total of votes was futile.

To any party member who had not been in the constituency with their eyes open, this result came as a shock. For me, it only deepened my unease at the line the party was pursuing. And only a little later, another Bradford experience was to underline this in another way. For, at around this time, the YCL decided that the best antidote to its isolation would be to adopt a lighter touch: to boost our emphasis on leisure activities and to try and build up a British Workers' Sports Federation. Sometimes, particularly during my Bradford months, I too dreamed of building a mass movement analogous to the Labour League of Youth, or even to what the Vienna Social Democrats had built: a broad based youth movement whose politics would be coloured by party conceptions. One effort we made towards realising such dreams was when we managed to attract some 50 to 100 young people for a ramble at Shipley Glen. As, we had discovered, many of these youngsters had never been in a train – such was their poverty – we laid on a ride to Shipley (some three miles or so) as an extra attraction. Many of them were so thrilled by this, they seemed almost ecstatic. Apart from Jessie, myself and a local Communist Party organiser whose name (I think) was Ernie Wooley, my old Yorkshire Moscow comrade Maggie Jordan was also involved in organising this outing. Predictably, where there were girls and boys, all too many of them started pairing off and disappearing in all manner of directions once we had reached the Glen. So, we four high calibre comrades were running around like mother hens trying to keep everyone together for the ramble. I doubt if we always succeeded. For many individual participants, that day may well have proved historic. But politically it seemed to me a farce.

On the broader canvas too, a development occurred which simply disgusted me. I noticed that Dutt's *Labour Monthly* was lambasting David Riazanov. Less than two years previously, I had been feasting from the fruits of Riazanov's years of interest in the history of the movement I had grown up in. Often, when I had visited a bookshop in Moscow, there had been fresh Marxist classics, edited and historically introduced by him. Another book I had picked up in Moscow had been a 1924 copy of V Adoratsky's *Fundamental Questions of Marxism* (its fourth edition in two years). What suddenly became relevant to me was that its back cover advertised a number of major works by Kautsky, translated into Russian **since** 1917. Now, in July 1931, *Labour Monthly* carried extracts of a letter from Marx characterising Kautsky in particularly acerbic tones. Dutt here asserted that Riazanov was 'in fact carefully concealing the original of this letter in order to safeguard the authority of Kautsky'. But the quoted phrases of Marx were personal, not political; the 26 year old Kautsky was described as 'a mediocrity', 'too wise by half' and as 'belonging from the year of his birth to the genus philistine'. The Stalinist charge was that Riazanov was secreting documents in his institute which would harm the Mensheviks if published and, in particular, this allegedly devastating critique of Kautsky, their political mentor.

I began wondering how Riazanov might answer these accusations. Here, I recalled my readings of *Inprecorr* in January 1924 – all the more vividly while its arrival was being disturbed by Clynes, Labour's Home Secretary. The number of 4 January, which I had read more or less as eagerly as anyone in Britain, had included a lecture to the Communist Academy in Moscow by Riazanov, in which he not only emphasised that the publication of some of those Marx/Engels letters (which he had obtained from Kautsky and Bernstein) was 'dependent on special conditions'; he also made accusations against the two Germans politically very similar to those now, in 1932, being made against him. Bernstein and Kautsky had 'edited [these letters] without any respect for the memory of Marx and Engels', notably by omitting embarrassing passages.

Even in Bradford, I knew the charges against Riazanov to be refutable from the British party press of a mere eight years previously. Now, though, this was all too evidently of no help to him; his side of the argument was not being heard. He was turfed out, not only of the institute which had been the central achievement of his life, but also out of the party for which he had once gone into exile. In 1939, he was to die in a camp. But in 1931, his expulsion gave me profound misgivings.

In the foreground of this, though, my own Bradford experiences were now by themselves enough to impel me into writing ever more critical letters to the YCL Secretariat. I felt I had had a gutful; the party and YCL were progressing nowhere. Worse, the movement and the party in which I had grown into adulthood had gone separate ways. At YCL headquarters, one of the new lights was a lad, surnamed Douglas, whose reasoning I never understood; he seemed to have no political opinions at all. But, because he had been in the bourgeois Boy Scout movement, he was regarded as the cat's whiskers for promoting that turn to lighter work. Douglas now wrote me a letter in which he announced that 'the Panjandrums' – a word beyond my ken – had 'decided to shift you out of the YCL'. That was the decision.

So I was recalled to London. The Central Committee of the party met in special session – to which a wide range of other party members were invited – to consider the future of the YCL. In that meeting, I vigorously attacked current developments, contrasting the class based party I had known into 1927 with the isolated sect I now found on my return. My criticism was no less vigorously rejected by all the others. After the meeting but in front of many participants, Pollitt remarked to me that my speech had been 'your swansong, Harry'; by being too clearly critical, I had condemned myself.

More immediately, I had also catapulted myself into the unemployed. Battersea had a lively movement of unemployed. I was soon speaking outside the Beauchamp Road labour exchange almost every day. In addition, as the party still clung to the idea of factory organisation, its Battersea unemployed grouped themselves into so-called 'concentration groups', focusing on a given workplace. My group concentrated on Morgan Crucibles. So I used to take part in meetings outside the gates there.

For some trivial reason, I was arrested during one of these. To get me to Lavender Hill police court, a policeman got with me into a Number 34 tram. One of the comrades who had seen my arrest came with us. This was Jack Tierney's ex-wife. In the tram, she struck up a conversation with me in Russian, her first language. The policeman's face showed great alarm! Anyway, he immediately brought me before a magistrate called Cairns. My line was to emphasise how John Burns had for years and years used precisely the same spot for **his** meetings, some decades ago. Whether or not this argument was what told with Cairns, he dismissed my case. Subsequently, though, another member of our concentration group, a comrade named Edwards, was arrested at the same spot, some months later. And his case came up, not locally, but at the Old Bailey. Although I happened not to have been present that day, I was subpoenaed to go up to Central London (a journey for which I was given the traditional one shilling towards the bus fare). I intended to take exactly the line I had to Cairns. But I only got as far as the witness box, when the judge intervened in a rather contemptuous way and stopped the trial; it had taken up too much time, he said. Thompson, the Communist Party's barrister, was powerless to intervene. Instead, Edwards was immediately given three months in Wandsworth Prison (where I was one of his visitors). Evidently, free speech did not count so weightily with higher authorities – perhaps all the less after Morgans had apparently begun complaining that our unemployed meetings were worrying the office staff.

But at least I was back in the Battersea I had known. The local branch of the Union of Shop Assistants, Warehousemen and Clerks – a large, lively and left wing one that used to meet weekly – immediately admitted me to membership, even though they knew I was unemployed and had never been anything other than a railwayman. The person who sponsored my entry into the branch was Alec Richardson. His family had had a photography shop locally, but Alec had joined the navy and been involved in the intervention in Murmansk and Archangel. He had long been a Socialist, though, and extremely friendly to me through many years. As he was now working as a civil servant in Somerset House, he tried his utmost to get me a temporary job there, but to no avail. Within the union, he had greater success; perhaps because he was important within its Metropolitan District Committee, he helped me attend some of its meetings alongside him as a delegate from the branch. Also via the branch, I was able to become a delegate to Battersea Trades Council. I was getting back into the swim of the movement.

I also attended the London District Committee of the party. On these occasions, I sometimes met the London organiser, RW Robson and also a former assistant of Pollitt's, called Ralph Bond (who later became quite a figure on the cinematic and cultural side). By chance, a depot of Russian Oil Products was sited very near where I lived. And, one night in late 1931 after I had been unemployed for some months, I found a message awaiting me when I got home. It came, to me, totally out of the blue. It was from a party member called Frank Smith and told me to report to ROP's headquarters in Moorgate, in the City. Smith had earlier been a Sheffield shop steward alongside JT Murphy and Ted Lismer. He had subsequently been a founder member of the party, and heavily involved during the 1920s in getting up the London bureau of the Red International of Labour Unions and on the London Trades Council during the General Strike. By 1930, he had ended up earning his crust as an ROP rep, a job which involved the use of a car. Relatedly or not, he always supported the party leadership during internal discussions. The decision to employ me cannot have been his alone (or perhaps at all); it can only have been a party one. Many comrades were already employed in the Russian trading agencies, and my long Russian experience made me seem very much one of the gang – at first.

At Moorgate Hall, the scene was often tense. Russia – in the grip of forced collectivisation and breakneck industrialisation – was desperate to earn foreign currency. But world demand for oil products was slumping, we were all in the depths of the world depression. So the Russians had begun dumping their oil cheaply on the British market. This became known as the 'oil war'. ROP put me into its economics department where my main job was to calculate profits. Their significance was this. Not only was the price of the exported Russian oil subsidised by the Russian government, but ROP itself also offered 'discounts' (in effect, bribes) to bus and other transport companies. Each month, our district reps would inform Moorgate Hall of the amounts of different oils sold, the sums received and the sums paid out in so-called 'rebates'. My job was to receive all these details via a giant Hollerith machine and then to calculate from them the net monthly profit per gallon for each district. Usually, any profit came to point zero something per cent of a penny per gallon. And the Russians in the building used to be simply desperate to get that monthly figure. Not only in the building, either; Sokolnikov, the ambassador (the 1929 Labour government had restored diplomatic relations), would often be on the phone, anxious for the same details.

Soon we were into the summer and autumn of 1931. The economy was collapsing and the Labour government along with it. Although working for ROP full time, I still used to address unemployed meetings at the 'Prince's Head' and elsewhere almost every night. More and more often, the crowds seemed to stretch along the streets, almost as far as the eye could see. One night, from my platform, I glanced across at an *Evening Standard* placard outside the 'Falcon' pub. I could read it vividly: '**The Navy on Strike.**'

In my opinion, the potential of these months has been underestimated. What might have happened is therefore particularly hard to say. But what seems clear to me is that the mood of whole swathes of working people was much harder bitten than in 1926, however big the landslide won by the National government during the snap autumn 1931 election. During the general strike, millions of working people had suffered from a whole range of virgin illusions, whether left or right. In 1931, it was clear that the capitalist system had failed, that Labour (whether led by Macdonald or, soon, repudiating him) had nothing distinctive to offer and that the Tories hardly pretended to have anything positive either.

And there was an even more important contrast: in 1926, you could hardly help observing the power of the state to move supplies, food, troops and ships, and to clear us off the streets. In 1931 the ruling class lacked confidence and became jittery. The Invergordon naval mutiny and the international run on the pound merely brought this to a head. From the other side, workers and unemployed had already begun to appear on the streets in great numbers. They were not merely protesting. They were disillusioned, looking for answers. That was the mood, however fleeting. There were tremendous demonstrations during those months. Early on, these coincided with the floodlighting of public buildings in central London. Jumbled up with the large numbers of people who had travelled in to look at this, there was a huge demonstration of unemployed, called for Parliament Square. At the very gates of St Stephen's, the crowds became so massive that they virtually blocked the road. A number of Labour MPs were standing at these gates and became witnesses of the seething anger of those unemployed workers. The police drew batons and charged at us again and again.

Similar events seemed to be brewing within Battersea. Around 1931, Alf Loughton was working for the council as a bricklayer on the St John's estate. He and I, together with Johnny Holmes and 'Workhouse Waller' (two of the ex-SPGBers whom I mentioned in Chapter One) organised what we anticipated would be a modest demonstration to pressure the council into setting up a public works programme to counter the exceptional level of unemployment. When we saw the numbers who turned up, no-one could have been more astonished than we were. It was one of the biggest ever seen in Battersea; colossal. When we reached the top of Lavender Hill, we found a dense cordon of mounted police round the town hall. They let us through gradually, though. Normally, when a council in full session deigns to receive a deputation at all, it allows them a few seconds to state their case to the assembled Establishment, and then out they go. But on that night, the galleries were packed and vocal. So when the mayor (a Catholic right wing Labour man) asked me, as leader of the deputation, to state our case, I ignored procedure by ostentatiously turning my back on the Tories – the class enemy, as I emphasised – and addressed the Labour people at some length. After this, a number of councillors spoke up. One of these was Ivor Thomas. He was a right wing careerist (who later became an MP) and was hoping to throw me off balance. His behaviour produced dissension among the Labour ranks. Charlie Powell, a former Burnsite, rose up to defend me: 'This boy is Battersea born and bred. We know him.', he shouted. (Thomas had grown up in Wales.)

After leaving the council chamber, Alf and I led these masses of people down the hill of Latchmere Road towards the 'Prince's Head', which was the traditional place for demonstrations to hear any closing speeches and then to disperse. On the way, we passed Latchmere Baths. Gazing out through the window panes in the boardroom of that building were some faces, pressed against the glass. It was the Battersea branch of the Communist Party – my branch was completely extraneous to this vast demonstration which they could see me at the front of. The only other party member to be seen in it was Tom Bell, probably one of the few non-Battersea persons there. He had obviously been sent by King Street to keep an eye on things and, as we came down the hill, he was taking the opportunity to lecture me most didactically as to how much more revolutionary and Third Period I could have been during my report back (which I had just given to the crowd when our deputation emerged from the council chamber). And what were my party comrades discussing on that evening? 'Leninism!'

Not that the Communist Party was the only organisation to be uninvolved in such developments. We had tried to bring the local ILP in, but it had approached the prospect of this demonstration in a gingerly fashion. Around the autumn of 1931, so many illusions momentarily seemed to be cracking up, that many people felt danger in the air. Many politicos, once they have recognised a situation as potentially revolutionary, prefer not to engage with it unless they feel they know what to do with it. And such situations can be short lived.

Unfortunately, at this of all times, I suffered an apparent haemorrhage in my lungs. At the time, it looked serious. The party had a comrade called Dr Hart who worked as a house surgeon or something in Hampstead General Hospital. He gave me a thorough examination, said it might be TB and persuaded me to enter that place for a few days' observation. Though the alarm soon turned out to be false, he still strongly advised me to take a break from Battersea for rest and fresh air. So it was arranged for me to stay in Weston-super-Mare for a couple of months. This I did – during the late autumn of 1931! But, soon after I returned, my frustration at having to be absent was soon tempered by a tiny experience. One of the ideas which my friends and I had been hammering away on – apparently unheeded – down at the labour exchange, was the need of the younger unemployed to form their youth sections so as to help make people of our age feel at home in the movement. By chance or not, the first march of unemployed that I saw, after my return, included a youth contingent. So sometimes, ideas which appeared not to have registered were after all revived by at least some people. I feel as strongly as I did then that this can apply in the long term as much as in the short. This, for me, is the value of history. When people are in turmoil, they turn to ideas. And such ideas don't necessarily come from their own heads, but often from previous heads. Whether they are accurately or appropriately revived is another matter; obviously, there is no automatic register. But they do come, not only from what people have thought on their own experience, but also from other people's reflections on **their** experience. Thoughts are not necessarily cut off at 40 years or even at four generations.

At the time, something far more important was that, before my TB scare, I had come into contact with more people of my own generation (in addition to Alf and Jimmy) who strengthened my determination to engage further in revolutionary agitation among workers, absolutely irrespective of the party line.

Already working at ROP was Reg Groves. He was in the pump department, not the economics. But he would drop by for a chat. Increasingly we would continue after office hours in local branches of ABC or Lyons. There, he introduced me to other critical party members. On the whole, they had first made contact via the December 1929 Leeds conference of the party. Apart from Reg, the most important for me were Henry Sara and Stewart Purkis. With these, discussions quickly progressed from criticising the party for misapplying the Comintern line, to a position of thought out opposition to the main thrust of that line, and thus of the party. I had come into the process of starting the Balham Group – so-called because that was where Reg, his wife Daisy and some others lived. I soon discovered that my new friends had not only shared in the dissatisfaction – which had been general throughout the party by 1929 – at the then right wing line of the leadership, but had also realised for some time that the party's conversion at Leeds to the Comintern's recent left turn had been thoughtless and superficial; the dissatisfaction with the pre-1929 'old guard' had not been based on clear political perspective, and so there had been virtually unanimous support for the Stalinist line, with no understanding of it. Only when faced by an even steeper decline in the party's fortunes – despite the leadership's loud and cliché-ridden commitment to the 'correct' line – did the doubts raised in some critical minds turn into serious questioning of that very line. For each of us, the first significant break had come when he or she had rejected the nonsense that all people in the labour movement who did not directly support the party were 'Social Fascists'. This break came via practice, via an instinctive understanding that the vital need of the hour was united working class action, particularly in face of the international growth of Fascism.

But this break was also reinforced by such few writings as were available by Trotsky, particularly his 1929 *Criticism of the Draft Programme of the Communist International* (For a possible answer to the riddle of how this reached the West, see the appendix under 'Weston'.) Reg, in his 1974 pamphlet *The Balham Group*, takes the view that we reached our oppositional stance without any external Trotskyist stimulus; that the group formed, and only **then** entered into correspondence with the International Left Opposition (abbreviated then to ILO). This is too simple. To take one instance, Reg himself and Henry were members of the party's central agitprop committee, chaired by Murphy. I remember Henry recounting at the end of 1931 how there had been comments at this committee on the lack of official information about the situation in other countries. Here, he and Reg had remarked that, in Charing Cross Road just round the corner from the committee room, there was a bookshop selling Trotsky's writings. So both of them were surely, almost from the start, aware of Trotsky's arguments.

That bookshop, Henderson's, had for decades been known on the left as the Bombshop, ideas being bombs. Around 1931 particular reverberations were caused by two pamphlets which Trotsky wrote from his exile on the Turkish island of Prinkipo. The first was on the significance of the trade credits being given to Russia and their relationship to unemployment in the capitalist countries. The second was on Spain. And we ourselves were particularly worried about the situation in Spain and Germany. In that year, Trotsky published the *Spanish Revolution in Danger*, in which he argued that Spain was now the weakest link in the chain of world imperialism. Meanwhile, the Comintern's *Inprecorr* had nothing to say on Spain, there was virtually a blank page, as also in the British party's *Communist Review* and *Daily Worker*. Nor was Trotsky exactly silent on Germany either. In addition, it was via the Bombshop that Reg had first come across copies of the American Trotskyist paper, *The Militant*. Soon – under a pseudonym, of course – he was writing a 'London Letter' for it.

Because of this contact with the Americans, Max Shachtman came to see us on his way back from Prinkipo, early in the autumn of 1931. When he met a few of us – including Billy Williams (a railway clerk like Stewart), Reg, Henry, a chap called George Weston (who, like me, had spent some time in Russia) and me – he insisted absolutely on our bringing out our own paper as quickly as possible. He admitted that this presupposed someone giving their address and thereby incurring instant expulsion from the party. But the need was to establish a British section of the Opposition. So, which of us was going to be the sacrificial lamb? Not a bleat was heard! Even our less than a dozen CPers in South-West London made us a significant minority in a party of such diminished size, tiny ponds make almost any fish significant. Politically, each of us had much to lose. Our fields of activity added up to something wide: union branches, Coop Guilds, the Battersea and Wandsworth Trades Councils, among the unemployed and at speaking pitches in Brixton, Balham, in Undine Street, Tooting, and at 'Prince's Head' in Battersea. We engaged in all of this activity as party members, and, at this stage, saw little point in jettisoning that status, not least because other party members were among our most promising targets for recruitment. If we stood out so early, we would risk losing our integration in the movement.

The only activity which we as a group were already engaging in involved taking a speaker's platform to Clapham Common regularly every Sunday at 11 o'clock. Here, Hugo Dewar, Reg, Henry, myself and a few others covered a wide range of topics – not at all like the party's normal propaganda meetings. Spain and Germany figured prominently, but also the situation of the labour movement in Britain, unemployment, the right to work and the right to be lazy. Some of this was basic marxist stuff, and some of the material we sold – and often heavily – was no less basic: *The Communist Manifesto* or *Wage Labour and Capital*. We were attempting to pull into our orbit those people we had more or less influenced in our separate activities, to realise politically the energy we had invested in these. By the early summer of 1932, King Street had become aware of these Sunday morning meetings. My old friend Wally Tapsell began turning up on the Common. It was lovely to see him and to crack jokes with him. But Reg voiced suspicion at Wally's sudden interest in our activities. Quite rightly, he suspected Wally had been sent along to keep an eye on us. There were also comments from the London District Committee on how basic our literature was; it included nothing advocating distinctive party policies.

These public meetings were immensely successful, not only because of the range of topics but also in that they did indeed work in well with our political and union activities. Among these was the ILP. Hugo Dewar had joined it in 1928 (only in mid-1932 did he join the Communist Party as part of our Balham Group's tactic of maximising our presence there). Hugo and Reg had a particularly close relationship with Clapham ILP This branch owned some large premises in Bedford Road and boasted the biggest membership in London. It was to play a considerable role in the development of the Trotskyist movement between 1932 and 1935. I myself had connections with Battersea ILP, where Jimmy Lane was a member. When in 1930 the Labour Party rejected some unorthodox proposals on combatting unemployment which had been put forward by (among others) Sir Oswald Mosley, who was still a left wing Labourite, quite a few Battersea people switched to the ILP. This party was riven by disputes, not least on the question of the Communist Party There was the Revolutionary Policy Committee among London ILPers, which was wide open to Trotskyist ideas at this time, though not later. It was led by Jack Gaster, CA Smith, a doctor from Poplar called Cullen and – particularly friendly to us – Bert Matlow. So this ferment in the ILP connected directly to our Sunday morning meetings and was one big reason for the success of the initiative which flowed from them.

The summer of 1932 also showed that the Communist Party's leadership was grievously underestimating this liveliness in the ILP. Jimmy Lane was a delegate to the ILP's national conference which was held in Bradford during July. I went up there with him and with Jim Barrett, a Balham Group member. Of course, orthodox CPers had no relations at all with the ILP which was, in the Comintern's jargon, 'Left Social Fascist'. That conference – in the ILP's beautiful Jowett Hall, passed by 241 votes to 142, a resolution to disaffiliate from the Labour Party. I was in the gallery during that debate, and so were Gallacher and Pollitt, along with quite a few local YCL and party friends of mine. Gallacher openly expressed astonishment – both to me and generally – not only at the size of the majority but also at the strength of the bitterness voiced against Labour during the debate. Apparently the Communist Party leadership had no idea of what was going on in the ILP or of the mood.

But that gallery also saw a tiny incident which pointed towards my own political future. My old Lenin School friend, Maggie Jordan, was sitting with me. She had long been in a comradely relationship with Alec Massey. I was still friends with Alec despite the embarrassment I had helped cause him in Berlin. (Indeed, during that summer Alec almost managed to get me on to a boat up from London to his native Aberdeen to spend a brief holiday with him – an idea I dropped instantly when he let on that Bill Rust was going to be there too. Apparently these two discovered the failure of their last-minute indoctrination manoeuvre, only when they came to the quayside at the Aberdeen end and could not find me among the disembarking passengers!) Pollitt now called Maggie over to his side of the gallery. When she returned, what had happened was only too obvious from her entire change of manner. He had cautioned her about me: I was already suspect. From his point of view, he was undoubtedly correct. For I had taken with me to Bradford some copies of the first issue of *The Communist* (subtitled the *Organ of the Communist League, International Left Opposition*), which I circulated as discreetly as I could among comrades I knew within Bradford and Leeds Communist Party, and also at a YCL camp outside Leeds.

An irregular, duplicated little paper was all we had promised Shachtman at that meeting where he had vainly sought his 'sacrificial lamb'. May of 1932 had seen the first issue. Trotsky's *Germany, the Key to the International Situation* provided the main meat. What finally decided us to publish at all was the dire relevance of his warnings against the split in the German labour movement. For, our reluctance to publish had lasted many months. As early as December 1931, Reg and I had taken time off from ROP to view a cellarful of typewriters and duplicators elsewhere within the city. We purchased a huge, wide handturned machine. At first we sweated blood and wasted a ruinous amount of paper, even though the folding of the duplicated sheets was done by hand. But then two of our members had turned out to be experts (Billy Williams and a man called Francis), and soon our paper was being so nicely produced that Trotsky was to praise it as an example for the rest of the international movement to follow. How we solved our pre-expulsion problem of a contact address I do not know; an organisation called Monomark did exist for such purposes, but I gather it refused for some reason. Anyway, despite all the obstacles, we were able to continue our illicit work within the party for many months – up to our expulsion in August 1932 – even though the leadership was well aware of Trotskyist material circulating within the ranks. That we lasted so long may partly have been because we knew, as any revolutionaries should, when to avoid trouble, and partly because the leadership had no thoroughly convincing political arguments available against us.

Our most reverberative involvement during those 12 or so months was on the question of war and Fascism. During mid-1932 the Comintern began calling for an international congress to counter what it saw as the very great danger of an imperialist attack on the Soviet Union. For this purpose, it sought support, not from working class organisations (given that most of these were non-Communist, this would have infringed its Third Period sectarianism), but from every shade of middle class pacifist of any level of commitment. The manifesto appealing for a congress, to be held in Amsterdam, was written by or for the French pacifist, Henri Barbusse. As it happened, our friends in the Battersea movement and in Clapham ILP had already called a conference to which the whole of the Balham Group managed to be sent as delegates from political or union organisations. That conference had been against Japanese aggression in China. But, out of it, came an organisation with a broader focus, the South West London Anti-War Committee. Unlike most of the other bodies formed in Britain around the time of the Barbusse manifesto, this Committee was a representative body (60 regular delegates from 30 local organisations, as Reg's pamphlet recalls). Further, around or shortly after our expulsion, an internal Communist Party document was to lament that the only place in London where a really representative Anti-War Committee existed was in the South-West, where, unfortunately, Trotskyists were in control.

Our immediate political aim within the SWLAWC was to see, not merely a good delegate elected to Amsterdam, but also and more important a good mandate for her or him to take there. In the first aim, we failed. Reg stood, and was beaten by a man called Davey Wild who was able, as an AEU member, to emphasise his status as a manual worker. After Wild had come back from Amsterdam, I never heard of him anywhere in South-West London again.

But when it came to the mandate, we were able to incorporate into it a number of Trotskyist emphases, particularly in its seventh and last demand: for 'untiring explanation that the only guarantee of victory for the workers of Russia lies in the development of world revolution'. This mandate issued from a heavy debate in which many leading orthodox spokespeople participated (not least Dave Capper, a high-powered technical teacher who was quite a figure at the time among local Communists). And yet, despite this involvement and despite giving itself five days during which to mull things over, the *Daily Worker* greeted our effort enthusiastically as a 'militant mandate'! Only three days later, though, it admitted its mistake; the mandate – which was now demoted to a mere 'South-West London resolution' – was, wrote JR Campbell, 'not militant but mischievous' for containing 'phrases which conceal Trotskyist meanings'.

With a section of its own membership being subjected to such prominent denunciations, the party was obviously going to have to strike soon. And so, on that very day, Henry, Reg and I were invited (that is, as Reg puts it, 'summoned') by RW Robson to see him at district headquarters. Reg's account cannot be bettered:

'When we arrived we found Willie Gallacher, Harry Pollitt and Kay Beauchamp – a well-connected mediocrity – waiting for us. Where, asked Henry Sara, was Robson? He would not be present, was the answer. Henry rose. "Robson invited me here", he said, "and if he is not coming, then I'm not waiting." And he walked out. It was neatly done, and probably Harry and I should have followed, but we were too surprised to move, and remained to face the inquisitors. Pollitt, startled and annoyed, dismissed Henry's act as "mere liberalism" and turned to us. Would we cease our opposition to party line and leadership particularly on the World Congress Against War? We would not. Gallacher blinked at us over his spectacles – did we realise that we were doing harm to the party? Encouraging sinister forces? "Some very strange circulars are going round the country", he said. The individual was nothing, the party everything, he went on. To talk about doing our own thinking was petit-bourgeois.'

The pressure continued, but neither Reg nor I responded to it. Two days later, both of us were expelled, as was Henry soon after.

The party quickly convened the other members of the group, in the hope that they would prove more malleable. None did. All soon shared our fate. That meeting also chanced to have another dimension to do with my sacking from ROP which I must now recount.

At ROP, the spring of 1932 had seen a relative relaxation of the political atmosphere, a temporary development which occurred in the Soviet Union generally, after the smashing of the Left and Right Oppositions. In our economics department there were four employees apart from me: three Russian women plus Eleanor Burns (a party intellectual, like her husband Emile). During coffee breaks, though, we five were usually joined by, among others, the heads of other departments – all Russians, of course.

The head of the department was called Abramov and was reputed to be an Old Bolshevik. It was his presence that attracted the other Russians to our room. But, to me, he was a continual source of bewilderment. His desk, to the side of mine, always had a lovely collection of the latest economic journals, in Russian and English. Yet he never seemed to more than browse through them. Instead, his main interest appeared to be philately. I formed the opinion that his stamp collecting must be an escape from the pressures of internal party politics. Certainly one morning, over coffee, I overheard him expressing a sacrilegious thought: 'Last night's bureau meeting was quite pleasant, it passed without all that business of left and right deviations.'

So, those discussions, as we stood around, were fascinating to listen to. One of these Russians was the son of A Tsiurupa, an economist who had been president of Gosplan (the official economic planning organisation) since 1924, and a member of the Central Committee of the Party. Young Tsurupa remarked on one occasion that Trotsky's sons were very fine chess players. This was almost certainly a statement of at least vague sympathy with their father's politics. My reason for thinking this, is that I was aware that some of the Russians were buying and circulating the Russian language *Bulletin of the Opposition* from an international newspaper shop, hard by Leicester Square tube station. Conceivably, they were in or near the Russian opposition movement in London. Not that I let on about my own growing Trotskyist sympathies. But, all in all, I managed to get on rather intimately friendly terms with my Russian colleagues. Of course I knew that, once we came out politically into the open, Reg and I would be out on our ear, and back among the unemployed (minus our relatively marvellous pay). And sooner or later we would in fact have to attack, for we were bound to be kicked out as Balham Groupers eventually.

One day, a meeting was called of all ROP's British employees – the party cell. Percy Glading, the politbureau member responsible for liaising with the Russians, explained that there was some labour dispute down at Hay's Wharf which was delaying some Russian ships and thus sabotaging the Five Year Plan. He made it crystal clear that the Plan should take priority over any mere strike in Britain. Reg and I attacked; this was an absolutely basic union issue. We could not possibly regret British workers going on strike, 'however much we applaud the Russians', and so on. Glading complained that I was being far too heavy: 'Laying it on with a trowel.' This hardly put Reg or me in the bureaucracy's good books.

Reg got the sack soon after, and mine followed two days later. Neither of us were given any notice beforehand. Now, Eleanor told me, on the spot, not to discuss my dismissal with any Russian colleagues. But I was not going to stand for **that**. With two of the Russian women in my department I had been on extremely friendly terms. So I wrote them a letter. The problem was how to deliver it. I was barred from going up the stairs to the office. So I left it for them over at the Moscow Narodny Bank, across the road, with a lad I had virtually grown up with; Ben Smith had been in the Hammersmith YCL at the time I had been in the Battersea one. He was now a teller in that bank. The point here is that that letter was waved by Dave Springhall in the face of our Balham Group comrades; the party leadership apparently hoped that such a revelation (that I had been trying to 'undermine' the Russian party) might shock some of them into recanting.

Such hopes were forlorn. Our members were far too aware that the international dimension was the key to our disagreement with the party line. Issues of how best to prevent war were increasingly converging with those of how to prevent the Nazis coming to power in Germany. We felt Trotsky to be all too correct in emphasising the danger which this possibility posed to workers everywhere. The divisions there between SPD and KPD undermined working class resistance to this threat. During the summer of 1932, which saw Nazi strength growing by leaps and bounds, not just electorally but also in street battles against the left, there was complete disbelief among British Communists and sympathisers that Fascism was on the agenda in Germany or, even if on the agenda, that any Fascist triumph could prove durable there. We had emphasised our fears on this score from the start of our agitation. By July, we were infuriating the party orthodox with it at the aggregate meeting of London members. Eleven days later, the Nazi vote reached its peak. We next appealed to the party leadership, urging a national campaign in solidarity with the German working class. We nourished hopes – desperate, as we knew – that we might just somehow persuade the British party which, in turn, might just somehow persuade the Comintern to switch its line on collaboration with the SPD before all was lost.

After our expulsion, we of course continued our emphasis on Germany. Before as after, the party from its side sent some of its heaviest guns along to the SWLAWC's monthly meetings to try and beat us down. Thus it was that Tom Bell somehow became an at least honourary resident of South-West London and therefore a delegate to the committee from some organisation. Dave Springhall was another. The language in which our disputations were couched was not one of Stalinism versus Trotskyism, but rather in terms of divergent conceptions of a 'united front'. We attacked theirs – the so-called 'united front from below' – as ad hoc and not class based, as compared with ours which emphasised representative working class organisations coming together with each other. Their united front seemed to us a paper thin bureaucratic creation which could all too easily be thrown into the waste-paper basket.

It was not surprising that the party went to such lengths to deploy its big guns; the level of sophistication among many ordinary members was often pathetic. Shortly (by chance or not) before our expulsion, there was an enlightening incident at a SWLAWC demonstration. As usual, processions were to converge on Clapham Common from Battersea, from Tooting (picking up a Balham contingent on the way) and so on. On the Common, the speakers were to include Dave Capper, Reg and Henry. It proved a very big occasion. And we produced the posters for it. In these, we counterposed the united front of Barbusse with that of Lenin. 'Not Barbusse, But Lenin' was one slogan. Among other people, many CPers accepted these posters, carried them aloft in all innocence! Of course, those party members who did have some understanding – but who happened to be watching on the Common as the marchers arrived – went into hysterics when they saw this. So, possibly the timing of our expulsions was not so accidental. However indirectly, the barrenness of the Comintern line reinforced the ignorance of many party members. And ignorance rendered them – or so the leadership must have thought – easy prey to us Trotskyists who had at least an analysis that was not a string of clichés.

Armed with our analysis, we appealed through every channel – not least during that last interview with Gallacher and Pollitt – for the calling of a party congress to thrash out the question of our party's isolation from the class. By now, a party congress was anyway two years overdue. A few days after our expulsions, the leadership did announce one for November, to be prepared by 'the most democratic discussion in the history of the party' – but forgot to say what about .

By good fortune, the congress was held in Battersea. During the intervening months, we had time to write a leaflet, appealing to the delegates not to confirm our expulsions before hearing our case. Theoretically, this was the right of any party member but, just in case, we also painted slogans on walls opposite the entrance. One about which Pollitt was to express particular rage in his closing speech at the end of the congress was 'Not National Socialism But World Revolution'. Our leaflet reiterated our position, particularly on union work, Germany and the Amsterdam Congress. But most of its copies were wasted. Split seconds after each incoming delegate had been handed it while crossing the pavement outside, my old colleague Will Rust would be waiting to confiscate it in the entrance foyer. I remember the sheepish look on Wally Tapsell's face as he handed his copy to Rust. But other delegates seemed, or tried to seem, anything but embarrassed. Bob McIlhone, whom I had shared a room with in Moscow for three years, refused to look at me, he simply turned his face away. There were threats to beat us up, but nothing came of these – not least, perhaps, because Reg was a very big fellow. The Congress endorsed our expulsions on the say-so of the leadership – as also, symbolically for more important developments which the decade had in store – the Comintern's expulsion of the politbureau of the Spanish Communist Party.

Thus ended the first and last significant opposition within the British Communist Party until, as it turns out, the protest led by John Saville and Edward Thompson in 1956.

Chapter 6

With Trotsky in Copenhagen

JUST after the Battersea congress, I experienced, for me, a momentous episode – a chapter in itself. Trotsky, after his exile from the Soviet Union in 1929, had been more or less marooned on the Turkish island of Prinkipo. Try as he did, he could not persuade any West European government to offer him exile. Macdonald in Britain and, in France and Germany, the Radical and Social Democrat governments barred him. But in 1932 the Social Democrat students of Copenhagen invited him to speak during the fifteenth anniversary of the October Revolution. This was Trotsky's first visit to Western Europe since before 1917. As things turned out, it was also to be almost his last, as also his last speech in public. The visa which the Danish government gave him was for only eight days (lengthened later to a total of 10). But it did represent a rare chance to confer with oppositionists from various countries.

My ejection from ROP was, as it transpired, to inaugurate five years of unemployment for me. From the start, I had to do most of my newspaper reading in public libraries. This, surprisingly, was how I found out about Trotsky's impending visit to Copenhagen. Although, immediately after our expulsion from the Communist Party, we had formed ourselves into a Communist League, we were not only tiny but also, as I gradually discovered, organised oddly as regards international contacts. As Reg had been the one among us who had been the London reporter for *The Militant*, he naturally became the channel for international correspondence. He turned out to have simply kept much of this for himself. Reg was a wonderful friend of mine through five and a half decades, but everyone has their quirks. Some pages ago, I have noted how his 1974 *Balham Group* pamphlet underplays the rôle of Trotsky's writings in our germination. At the time too, he wanted to keep the group, and now the Communist League, as British as possible. Rightly or wrongly, he found the style and rhythms of the Third, and soon of the Fourth, Internationals unbearable. (This was certainly his reaction – recalled in his pamphlet – to the February 1933 meeting of the International Secretariat in Paris, which he went to before informing us!) In the early 1930s, Daisy's and his large Balham house was shared by Jim Barrett, the Dowdalls and Henry Sara. Henry's austerely intellectual lifestyle involved an early start; part of his early morning routine was to pick the post off the floor. So Henry was aware that Reg was getting mail from abroad, and rather resented not being privy to this international correspondence.

Many or most of our 40 or so members were unemployed too. So I wasn't the only avid reader of newspapers. Most of us agreed that it was imperative that one or other of us should take the chance to contact Trotsky. But a return fare was out of the question. By scraping our pennies together, though, we found we could afford one ticket as far as Copenhagen – although not enough to come back! Reg would have liked to go. But, during those months, he felt very lucky to have even a part time job (in some bookshop in Hampstead). Understandably, he hardly wanted to risk losing that. So Stewart and the others asked me if I'd like to go. I seized their proposal with both hands. To me, it meant an opportunity to meet, not only Trotsky but also one of his sons, Sedov, who was roughly my age and with whom, I imagined, I could develop a particular rapport. Meanwhile, on 14 November, Trotsky began his long journey from Prinkipo, along with his life companion Natalia Sedova and one or two close comrades. The bourgeois papers vied with each other to invent reasons for his trip. Was it to negotiate with a representative of Stalin for his return to Russia? Was it to act as adviser to the KPD? This bourgeois nonsense was actually excelled on the Stalinist side: 'Spearhead of the attack on the Soviet Union', 'pensioner of capitalism', 'renegade', 'imperialist agent'. It even shrieked that, at Copenhagen, he would renounce the Russian Revolution itself!

Via Liverpool Street and Harwich, I reached Esbjerg on 20 November and went on to Copenhagen. Trotsky and Natalia had not yet arrived. So I checked into a cheap hotel that Reg had told me to go to. I was given a tiny room up many steep flights of stairs and virtually in the roof. I had been told to wait here till Pierre Naville came to fetch me. My wait in that room – self-evidently the hotel had nothing so luxurious as a lounge – was punctuated by trips to look at the streets and to browse around bookshops. On my return from one of these, I found a note for me with the address of Naville's hotel. I immediately made my way there and found him in his pyjamas. He could speak English. Yes, Trotsky and his group had arrived safely in the city, but would I please return to my hotel and wait. Back in my room, I still had enough reading matter with me from England, but the light was as lousy as ever.

I felt increasingly disconnected and bored, when suddenly bang bang on the door, and in walked Naville and Raymond Molinier. They took me in a car (with Molinier driving, as usual) through the city to a large restaurant opposite the town hall. Here, a number of people were already enjoying a slap-up meal. But before I could join their feast, one of them stopped eating, came over and introduced himself as Jan Frankel from Czechoslovakia. He sat me at a separate table where he took down details of my personal history. (He was to remain Trotsky's secretary for some years.) He and Naville then introduced me to the table. There or soon after, I met Anton Grylewicz (who edited the Russian-language *Bulletin of the Opposition*), Oskar Cohn (a lawyer) and Oskar Hippe, all from Germany; Gérard Rosenthal (Trotsky's French lawyer) and 'Bruno' (a German emigré, based by then in Paris); Lucienne Tedeschi and her husband Julian, both exiles from Italy; and Léon Lesoil, a Belgian from the Charleroi coalfield and an obvious miner himself. I'll mention a few others as we go along. Most of those I met in Copenhagen were to die at the hands of the Nazis within a decade or so. One shining exception was to be Hippe, whose Trotskyist cell in Berlin was, after Stalingrad, to issue a leaflet, 'Down With The War!'; he was destined for two years in Nazi cells and later for 25 in Stalinist.

The ride back to my hotel was a bit scary, the car was so overloaded. The next morning, I went to Naville's hotel again and met his wife Denise who spoke English too. They filled me in further as to the political situation. The previous afternoon (the 23rd) there had been booing, whistling and shouting while Trotsky and his group were landing at Esbjerg (from Dunkirk). It became clear that one of our main jobs in Copenhagen would be, not merely to confer with Trotsky, but simply to guard him from physical danger. Apparently, Denmark had virtually no Left Oppositionists, as Trotsky complained soon after, 'we badly needed a Danish speaking comrade' there.

The Copenhagen Stalinists were led – all too effectively, it seemed – by a man called Aksel Larsen who had been at the Lenin School with me. I remember him as a real charmer (and, incidentally, as the person who had got me into that Indian party where I sat on the sitar). Ironically, he was, in 1958, to lead a significant number in breaking with the Russians, though he never came near any Trotskyist movement. I gather he was a marvellous orator. But he and other Stalinists were now organising a virulent campaign against Trotsky's presence in their city. Apparently, at about this time, some of us went to the headquarters of the Danish Communist Party and offered to have Trotsky defend his views before the party's members in whatever manner its leaders chose. In those days, some of us were obviously still a little optimistic about Stalinist methods or, at least, had not fully expected the icy-cold water poured on this proposal.

So, instead, some of us wrote a tiny leaflet in explanation, and had it translated by someone into Danish. I was one of those who took these tiny black on red leaflets – though we didn't have many – into meetings in one or two working class parts of Copenhagen. It sought to explain as simply as possible that Trotsky was not attacking the Russian Revolution or the Soviet Union, as the Stalinist press was claiming. Most people accepted our leaflet. But the hostility with which they did so – big, proletarian docker types, many of them – hurt me distinctly. Worst of all, I had not a word of their language. Here, Molinier was outstanding. At one particularly full meeting, he pushed his way through up to the platform to speak (in German). He even got them to listen to him! As Molinier was later to become rather unpopular among

Trotskyists for his disagreement with Trotsky, I think the courage he showed on Trotsky's behalf needs remembering all the more.

On that morning after my meal with Frankel and the others, I was taken along to a small villa (owned, I gathered, by a dancer). The street was a modestly suburban one. The interior of the house remains with me like yesterday. There was a small front room. Thick curtains separated it from another small room, off which there was a tiny kitchen. The stairs went up from a tiny hallway. At the top were two bedrooms situated over the two ground floor rooms, plus a very narrow box room. This was where Trotsky worked. During all our time in that house, we were confined to the ground floor. And at first, even the front room was out of bounds; it was assigned to Danish plain clothes men. So – assuming they weren't there merely to keep tabs on us – we were not the only people who believed Trotsky to be in some physical danger.

One result of these preoccupations was merely pathetic. The hall-way was lit by a tiny window to one side of the front door – or normally would have been. But the glass was now obscured by a suitcase; against bullets, we were solemnly told. Anyone with a grain of common sense would have seen the uselessness of such a shield. Another result was that there seemed to be quite a collection of revolvers and similar weapons in the house. Anyway, we took it in turns to stay indoors, on guard duty, night and day. Obviously, we spent most of this time talking. So, during the night, we would confine ourselves to the kitchen so as to minimise the disturbance to those upstairs.

In effect, Trotsky was a virtual prisoner, in the sense that his face was too well known. We, by contrast, were able to go out, when not on duty. There was an understanding with the Danish government that Trotsky's exact whereabouts were to remain confidential. So we were asked most emphatically not to draw attention to the house by unnecessary comings and goings. Once we were out, we should stay out for many hours at a time. So I spent further periods trudging pleasurably round the streets of Copenhagen.

I still had virtually no money in my pockets, but luckily another inmate of the villa turned out to be in the same situation as me: with Georg Jungclas I was to become lifelong friends. A Hamburg docker, he was now an agitator among the unemployed and as broke as me. Like me, he sometimes felt very restless in the atmosphere of the house; all that intellectual gossip in languages we didn't understand, about people we had never met, was no atmosphere in which to do any reading even. Best of all, he and I shared the immediate problem of being poorer than those around us; even in such a small movement, you hardly wanted to feel like a beggar. In the face of this intellectual coterie, we knew we were both outsiders. Our eyes met: let's go out. He certainly knew his Copenhagen. (Within 10 years, he was to be involved in the Danish resistance, before the Gestapo caught him and took him back to Germany where he was lucky to survive). Most important now, he knew one or two working class cafés where a few even of our coins could put in front of each of us a bowl of soup, which was a meal in itself. Then he took me under his wing and showed me much of the city. By the evenings, we would be back at the house.

Apart from the lecture, Trotsky's main purpose in coming to Copenhagen was to talk with as many European comrades as possible about the problems of the movement in each of their countries. That little box room was where he met and interviewed a succession of arrivals from various countries. I assumed that everyone kept a tight schedule. My turn came. As I went up those stairs, I reflected how really **piddling** were the activities I could report on: the Balham people, plus a few individuals, a tiny fragment in Hackney, and a tiny accession to our ranks in Camberwell, plus really good connections with some members of the ILP. So I reminded myself to tell Trotsky about the political mood that I had sensed among the Russians at ROP up to my dismissal the previous August. As I was about to find, names rang bells with Trotsky and he knew Tsiurupa.

So up I went. There was a desk by the window and, along one wall, a couch. Sitting on that was a man I had just met, an American academic called BJ Field. Field had travelled to Prinkipo to see Trotsky, and had come along with him to Copenhagen. (Quite soon after, he was to break with Trotskyism; the reasons for his entry and exit I have never known.) Trotsky got up from the desk and embraced me in a beautifully warm, Russian way. My mind went blank at this unexpected warmth and took some minutes to recover.

Trotsky was speaking English, but very faultily. Now and then, he would speak to Field in German, checking some word or phrase. He must have sensed my confusion, for he began by emphasising the urgency of being completely factual on our situation in Britain: 'You start from **what is**', was his phrase. He was particularly concerned that we should not fritter away the gains from our work within the British Communist Party: 'You must retain the initiative and choose the moments.' We would have to build up our forces gradually. Obviously, his hope was still to reform the Communist Party from within (and this was to remain ours too, till 1934 when Labour was to recover much of its lost electorate and to capture the London County Council). A precondition for our advance was to make our *Communist* a regular publication; he was most fulsome in praise of our duplication efforts so far. He also asked whether we couldn't send him a British comrade to work with him in his secretariat at Prinkipo.

We then spoke about my Russian colleagues at ROP and about my experience in Moscow. Rightly, I had imagined that the military aspect would particularly interest him. So I told him about our studies of the political background and the military mock ups we had done of Hamburg, Warsaw and Dublin, among other places. About the 1916 Irish rising he was so interested, that I promised to send him my duplicated material from the Lenin School. (This I later did, via Weston and presumably Cannon; possibly it is now in Harvard's Trotsky archive.) Next, Trotsky mentioned that he had already written his speech for the meeting at the university. He said:

'It will be in German but, as you don't speak German, I will have George Fischer [one of his secretaries] give you the English version to read before the lecture. This you can take to the British comrades.'

Downstairs, we now included people from Italy, France, Belgium, Germany and the Netherlands. So there was continual political gossip. Trotsky was beavering away upstairs and never participated in this. But every day, after he had had his supper, he would come down and sit in a chair and we would sit around on the floor (so as to save space) and have a discussion. Apart from the main issues (Spain and Germany, obviously), a number of others came up.

There was the question of the Bordigists or independent Left Communists in Italy and their disagreements with the Comintern over a United Front against Fascism, as well as over the correctness of decisions made at the first four congresses of the Comintern about Syndicalism, about the need for a democratic centralist party and other vital matters. Another issue was the Brandlerites, or right wing Communists. In Germany, they had some presence; but in America, as the Jay Lovestone-Wolfe grouping, they controlled the party. Elsewhere, two heretical Communists were in prison, apparently forgotten by the Comintern: Chen Duxui and, in India, MN Roy. Trotsky suggested we should try and see that Roy's case was raised within the Comintern's organisation, International Red Aid (MOPRA). Given Britain's role in India, our response was going to be important here.

On the day (coincidentally) of Trotsky's lecture, something happened which deepened my admiration for him. A rumour went round – Zinoviev had died. He had ratted on Trotsky at least once. But that evening, he spoke most feelingly of Zinoviev's contribution to the revolution, as someone who had shared exile with Lenin in Switzerland, as co-author with Lenin in 1914 of *Socialism and War*, denouncing the Social Democrats' capitulation to patriotism. In other words, he spoke about Zinoviev's positive aspects in a way redolent of the power of comradeship in the old movement. It shone through, despite long years of Stalinist dividing and manoeuvring.

The crucial country, Germany, brought us to the problems of our own section in that country. This numbered about 600 members altogether, including 60 or so in Berlin. It was bedeviled at the time by a feeling that it had been penetrated by Stalin's GPU Later, this fear was to turn out to have been correct – the agent was Soblen who, in a later role of his (as a spy during the 1950s) was to commit suicide while being flown to an interrogation in the USA.

Another contact in Berlin was Sedov. I had been disappointed that he could not be with us now. Instead, there was his girlfriend, Jeanne Martin des Pallières, who could speak English; but she could not make the reasons for Sedov's absence clear to me. (She also wondered why I was there at all; after all, the only British comrade they knew of had been Reg.) In the hall of the house, there was a phone on a small table. On more than one evening, the usual chatter would be going on in the middle room when that phone rang. I heard Jeanne answering it. Natalia came round the door with her finger to her lips: 'Pipe down, my son Sedov is on the phone from Berlin.' This vivid little memory was something I was able to make good use of some years later.

Even during the evenings, Trotsky could not always spend the time with us. On one occasion, a few Danish Social Democrat MPs and intellectuals paid a call on him. And, towards the end of our time in Copenhagen, some Social Democrats entertained most of us (though not, of course, Trotsky) to a meal in the parliament building. The person who sat beside me to give some inkling of what was being said (in German) was Henk Sneevliet, a Dutch comrade whom I will deal with soon.

An evening or two before Trotsky was due to lecture, the tension heightened sharply. As ever, the Stalinist hate campaign remained ferocious. But the right wing were not dormant either. One middle ranking member of the Danish royal family who had served in the French foreign legion, Prince Aage, reminded his people that the Czarina, for whose murder Trotsky had ultimately been responsible, had once been a Danish princess. Ergo, there was 'something rotten in the state of Denmark' as long as Trotsky remained. Up to this moment, the Social Democrat prime minister, Stauning, had been reasonably accommodating. But now the pressure was really on. Would our protection be sufficient? I can remember the worry reflected on people's faces around our evening meetings; would hooligan behaviour by the Danish Communist Party reduce the lecture to a fiasco? At this point, Jungclas made a suggestion. There were Hamburg comrades of his, dockers for the most part. Some of the older ones had been with him in the paramilitary Rote Front (which, by now, had been banned). He said they and some younger ones were sympathetic and would readily cycle up to Copenhagen – it would take only a day – to act as a protective screen between the platform and any thuggery in the hall.

It was agreed that to get Trotsky to the hall, Molinier would drive the car, with Trotsky, Natalia and me as passengers. We drove to the back of the university building, to what I remember as an empty space, partly laid out as sports fields. Trotsky was soon striding across this at some speed, he had a very military step. But poor Natalia wasn't built for this sort of exertion, and came shuffling along on my arm, trying to keep up. We were all borne along by the tension as to what would happen at the meeting itself. We reached the back of the building where we were met by two or three Danish students, and taken into a small ante-room which turned out to be underneath and at the back of the stage. We sat there, trying to unwind, while two of these students got Trotsky to sign their copies of the first of the three volumes of his *History of the Russian Revolution*. We waited.

Then Molinier came and said it was time for us to go up on the stage. So up Trotsky went, followed by Natalia, Molinier and me. In front of us, between us and the audience, were Jungclas's dockers with their backs to us; our protective screen. We were expecting, at any moment, some verbal or physical explosion from Stalinists or right wingers such as we had nearly witnessed in Copenhagen itself. But, at that instant, something very different happened. As Trotsky was stepping up to the lectern with his notes and was about to start speaking (Molinier and I were behind him on the platform, slightly to one side) – over the loudspeaker system came the strains of the *Internationale*. Within a split second, an atmosphere of astonishingly deep and unanimous warmth towards Trotsky filled the hall, where about 2000 people must have been listening. He then began his lecture. I had already read it and, judging from people's faces, I could tell it was enjoying a colossal success. Not only was no voice raised in opposition, but there was hardly a cough to be heard at any time. I have seldom experienced such a rapt audience. To this day, I am puzzled by this. After all, there was an enormous Stalinist demonstration outside – or so we had been told. I can only presume that the organisers had been discriminating as to who they issued tickets to. But certainly, that playing of the *Internationale* had an overpowering effect too.

And no less an effect would have flowed from the speech itself. Almost its opening words were: 'I stand under the same banner as I did when I participated in the events of the Revolution.' It magnificently defended the Russian Revolution as a stage in the historical rise of humanity. On the way, it emphasised the contrast between Socialist planning and the chaos of capitalism; any Stalinist would have had to have been super-clever to heckle **that**. Five years had passed since Trotsky had addressed a live audience, but he had obviously lost none of his verve as a speaker. I have been privileged during my life to hear many revolutionary orators: CLR James, Arthur MacManus, Tom Mann, Bukharin, Togliatti, Saklatvala and the old Polish Communist Felix Cohn, to name but a few. Yet, allowing for all of the extraordinary impact that Trotsky has had on my life, his Copenhagen speech was the most impressive. It managed this without heavy rhetoric. Frequently since then, a photo has gone the rounds of the picture agencies of a passionate – even desperately plaintive – Trotsky with an indefinite number of people sitting behind him; Copenhagen allegedly. All I can say is, we totalled three people on the stage behind him, and it was a lecture.

At the end, the applause was thunderous. But meanwhile, Naville had informed Molinier that there was still a dense crowd of hostile demonstrators in the street at the front of the building. So we left the way we had come; scurrying behind Trotsky across this sports field, into the car and back to the villa. There, the relief that it was all over was intense. We were excited and enthused by the success of the meeting. The desire to talk well into the small hours was natural. But that house had a strict working rhythm.

The next day I accompanied Trotsky to a radio station to record a broadcast for an American radio company. But the idea that the lecture itself should be broadcast live had been vetoed after a meeting of the Danish cabinet. More seriously, the evening after the lecture, when Jungclas and I were returning from one of our forays into the city, we found the house besieged by news reporters who jostled us as we went in.

Any confidentiality had obviously been blown. Possibly this was a broad hint from the authorities that Trotsky had better not overstay his welcome, now that he had given the lecture – the official purpose of his visit. So the decision was quickly made that he had better be moved from the house. That night happened to see Sneevliet, Jungclas and I doing our turn as guards in the kitchen. We were told of the arrangements: at 2 or 3am, a car would come, pick Trotsky up and take him to some friend or Social Democrat who had agreed to take him in temporarily. Natalia would remain behind for the moment. So, we three were keeping ourselves awake when the car drew up. Trotsky came downstairs, into the car, and was whisked away; there was no-one about, not even a reporter.

Immediately after, Natalia came into where we were sitting. The tension of the previous few days seemed to have taken its toll; she looked an old woman. Two days or so later (on 2 December), she and Trotsky were reunited on the boat at Esbjerg. And a few days after that I too passed through the port on my way back to London. Pierre Frank, another of Trotsky's secretaries, had given me the fare home.

I returned to Britain with two documents and one important detail. The first document was, of course, the English translation of Trotsky's speech. But my London comrades remained as poor as me. So, could we find a publisher? This took us years. In the end, it was brought out by the ILP, after Reg had got Trotsky's permission. But something that we were able to do much more quickly was to hold a meeting in Morris Hall, Clapham. After their big fuss about Trotsky's journey to Copenhagen, the British papers had had virtually nothing about his actual speech, apart a fraction of a column in the *Manchester Guardian*. But quite a few non-Trotskyists in Battersea were interested enough to come along. So there, with the help of Hugo Dewar, I read it to them.

The other document was more private, but not insignificant. When talking with Trotsky over my experience at ROP, I remarked that any further approach which I might be able to make to Russians was going to be easier if I could have some introductory letter to show them. For obvious reasons of personal survival, Russians were understandably very guarded towards anyone who tried to speak to them about Trotsky or Trotskyism. So, more or less there and then, Trotsky wrote out a credential for me (in Russian obviously, but I am giving the Pathfinder translation):

'Dear Comrade

'I am not sure whether you know my handwriting. If not, you will probably find someone else who does. I am profiting by this fortunate occasion to write a few words to you. The comrades who sympathise with the Left Opposition **are obliged** to come out of their passive state at this time, maintaining, of course, all **precautions**. To communicate with me directly is not always easy. But it is possible to find an absolutely sure way, of course, not direct; for example, through my son in Berlin. You can find him through Pfemfert (I am enclosing his address) through Grylewicz – through personal acquaintances, etc. Keeping all precautionary measures, it is necessary to establish communications for: **information**, to distribute the *Bulletin*, aid with money, etc, etc. I am definitely expecting the menacing situation in which the party finds itself will force all comrades devoted to the revolution to gather actively about the Left Opposition.

'I will wait for a written (typewritten) affirmation that this letter has been received. It can be written to: M Pierre Frank, Post Restante, Pera, Istanbul.

'I clasp your hand firmly.

'Yours, L Trotsky.'

In the event, that letter did, once or twice, come in handy. And I held on to it for possible further use. This proved a lucky decision. For, at the time of the Moscow Trials, I realised that this constituted evidence as to how Trotsky in reality (as against in Stalinist fantasies) behaved towards Russians during his exile. So I sent it to Sedov who, since 1933, had been in Paris (where the GPU killed him in 1938). Sedov sent it on to his father in Mexico, which is how it ended up in the report which Harper and Row published of the Dewey Commission on the Trials.

And the detail (which I've mentioned along with these two documents) was directly to do with Sedov, and was also useful in our effort to refute the Moscow Trials. For the allegation was made during one of these that Sedov had been an active participant in Copenhagen during those 10 days. Of course, he had been nowhere near, and I was able to recount the detail of Natalia hushing us, so that she and his girlfriend could hear his voice from Berlin.

Three individuals

Here some biographical information is relevant which would have slowed the flow of this and the previous chapter. Politically, these persons belong together.

George Weston (sometimes also surnamed Morris) was possibly the earliest British Trotskyist after Reade – although not, at first, while resident in Britain. He was involved in at least the very early meetings of the Balham Group, including the one with Shachtman, and remained a Trotskyist till the end of the decade at the very least. Reg's pamphlet never mentions him. Let us meet him.

Weston was an engineer by trade. He was an old party member from Sheffield. In the early 1920s, he was involved in some sort of activity to do with Ireland. Conceivably in connection with this, he was sent to Moscow where he ended up working in the secretariat of MOPRA under Lenin's old friend Stasova, with whom his relations were most cordial. I knew him and his wife as part of the Lux Hotel assemblage of foreigners. By the time of the Comintern's Sixth World Congress in 1928, Weston was a supporter of Trotsky. James Cannon, the founder of American Trotskyism, liaised with him around that time. Cannon was on the Programme Commission of that Congress, and was, as I mentioned, instrumental in getting Trotsky's *Critique* of the International's programme beyond the circle of top delegates (who, as I explained, were supposed to return it immediately after reading it).

But Weston too was involved. He travelled now and then to Berlin anyway as part of his job, and had contacts with the Left Opposition there. But exactly how the *Critique* reached the West has always been a mystery till now. The mystery was never cleared up in print, certainly never by Cannon. Even Hal Draper has drawn a blank. But when I met Weston's widow at Tamara Deutscher's flat during the early 1970s (in the presence of a tape recorder brought by a comrade called Ken Tarbuck), we discussed our Moscow years.

By the time I first met the Westons, they already had a daughter and, while I was still in Moscow, their son Vladimir was born. As Weston's job ended with that World Congress, he and his family returned to Britain at about this time. Mrs Weston remembers this *Critique* being inserted into Vladimir's teddy bear. This was how it reached the Fischer-Urbahns group in Berlin. I do not know whether Weston's copy was Cannon's or someone else's. If the second, then conceivably that person would have been Stasova. Weston remained personal friends with Cannon for many years.

During those arguments within the Balham Group as to when and how we should break with the Communist Party, Weston very much shared Shachtman's impatience. Here, his differences with Reg were particularly sharp. This, I suppose, was the main reason why Reg wrote him out of the pamphlet. But this is to distort the truth.

Through the 1930s, I was frequently fed by the Westons at their flat in Mill Hill (by the end of the decade, along with my wife Marjorie). Weston was earning what passed for a living as a salesman of radio sets. At one stage during my five years of unemployment, he hoped to bring me into the same line. To this end, he tried teaching me to drive his car. At the start of the war, there was considerable short-term dislocation and direction of labour. Alf Loughton (Marjorie's brother) had been unemployed and was directed to an engineering factory in Hendon. By pure chance, who should be convenor of shop stewards there, but Weston? Alf was never a Trotskyist (though he had attended our Sunday morning meetings on the Common). Together, they worked in opposition to the line of the Communist Party during those early war years.

Weston, as a good revolutionary, knew how to place himself in useful positions without compromising his principles. He was extremely able. At one particular moment, he may well have been crucial in the germination of Trotskyism as an international movement. He should not be suppressed from the record.

Henry Sara spent decades of his life fascinating and stirring audiences all over the country and further afield. A major tragedy was that he published virtually nothing.

He was so stimulated by ideas and was intellectually so self-reliant, that I have often doubted whether he ever had any formal education. He was born 19 years before me, but I'm sure he must have been one of those children who take to books from very early, like ducklings take to water. He was active in the Anarcho-Syndicalist and Socialist movement from his boyhood (and in the secularist, as a follower of Guy Aldred). For him, his unconditional opposition to the First World War followed automatically. He became what was called an 'absolutist' conscientious objector. In prison and, later on, when he was forced into the army, he refused to wear uniform despite pressures so terrible that Philip Snowden MP – hardly a revolutionary even by Labour standards – tabled a Commons question specifically about Henry's mistreatment.

After the War, he was among the last COs to be released. He joined the Communist Party very soon. He earned his money by lecturing up and down the country, often about revolutionary personalities such as Lenin, Luxemburg and Liebknecht. He made one or two trips for the Comintern, notably to Austria and other European countries, but also, around 1926, to China on a delegation which included Tom Mann. He also lectured in America.

Henry had an extraordinarily deep knowledge of the British labour movement and of its history. He had been aware of Trotsky's position on Germany and on other vital questions from the first. He was among the earliest of those who became the Balham Group. It was far more than his strong voice which made him such a marvellous speaker. I wouldn't call him a great political leader, but he was one of those outstanding personalities to whom younger people look to for strength. And this he gave. We had no single leader, but he was our main personality.

Though much of his lecturing was for the NCLC, he must also have been one of the last lecturers to make a living, into the mid-1920s, independently of any organisations. Or at least, this is what I assumed till recently when I noticed in the autobiography of the historian AJP Taylor that Taylor's mother, who was well off, had for many years a liaison with Henry and had helped him financially!

During his years in the Communist Party, Henry never lectured under party auspices. I imagine this was partly so as to retain his intellectual freedom. For he could be effective not only in his main fields of interest, but also in his sidelines. One of these was opposition to spiritualism. For some time during the interwar years, the *Daily Herald* journalist, Hannen Swaffer, was being invited all over the country to preach spiritualism. Henry made a habit of following him as closely as possible from town to town so as to debunk him. Again, during the years that party members, from Clemens Dutt in the *Daily Worker* down, were falling for the fraudulent biology of academician TD Lysenko, Henry was able to refute it – for those who would listen to a Trotskyist, of course.

Henk Sneevliet's name first swam into my ken during the NMM conference at the Latchmere Baths as signatory of a telegram of solidarity from a federation of Dutch Syndicalist unions. At this time also, he was barred by the British authorities from attempting to attend such a conference.

Sneevliet supported the Comintern from 1919. He was also involved in founding the Communist movements of Indonesia and China. This activity obviously enhanced his prestige within the Comintern, whose second and third World Congresses he took an active part in, while retaining his revolutionary Syndicalist views. Though for some years he remained as a sort of loyal opposition within the Comintern, he parted company with it well before Trotsky's expulsion from the Russian party. Nonetheless, when he arrived at the villa in Copenhagen, during an evening session with Trotsky downstairs, the deep warmth of their meeting was unforgettable.

Sneevliet spoke excellent English, and he and I spent many hours more or less alone together, including on guard duty through more than one night. There was much he wanted to catch up on; notably, the General Strike and the Minority Movement. He very much wanted to know how involved we were in the trade union movement. He felt particularly close to my old namesake Jack Tanner whose pro-Comintern Syndicalism made them very much akin. (I'd say Sneevliet was by far the more political of the two, but that's an aside.)

Within a year or two, Sneevliet was to enhance his reputation by a courageous defence, in the Dutch parliament, of Indonesian sailors who had mutinied against their Dutch naval officers. But his relation with Trotskyists was soon to be dominated by something more divisive.

During our guard duty in Copenhagen, he and I exchanged opinions about the Comintern and on international organisation generally. Trotskyism was, of course, not invariably the automatic choice for every individual or group excluded from under the Comintern. There was, for instance, the Sozialistische Arbeiterpartei, which formed from members of the KPD and SPD before Hitler came to power, and which stood for working class unity and a 'New Beginning'. Their ideas went back to the early KPD leader Paul Levi and to the right wing Communism of Brandler and Thalheimer. They were far from ignoramuses. And they were particularly critical of the haste with which Trotsky tried to found a new International before, in many or most countries, winning a minimal amount of support.

Relatedly, they saw him as dominating the International's Secretariat too much, and were suspicious of the speed with which it put out declarations on Russia or wherever. Instinctively they were critical of the way in which arguments in or about Russia polarised arguments about anything else. So, these dissident Communists were less interested in Trotskyism than in the project for what became known as a New International of Left Parties. The ILP – from CA Smith to Fenner Brockway at least – were also attracted by this and also by the Dutch comrade, Schmidt, who visited Britain during the mid-1930s in support of this idea. Not surprisingly, Sneevliet supported this also. In addition, he was not the sole revolutionary Syndicalist leader to have supported the Bolshevik revolution from the earliest years; he remained friendly with Andrés Nin, leader of the Spanish POUM. During the revolution and Civil War in Spain, it was inevitable that he would rally vocally to him.

For all these reasons, Trotsky's rift with Sneevliet was anything but unexpected. What did surprise me, though, was the bitterness of Trotsky's attacks. For example, he damned Sneevliet for being Syndicalist. But obviously Sneevliet's Syndicalist federation of unions had always been his main power base in the Netherlands. Further, disagreement between Bolsheviks and Dutch Syndicalists plus other revolutionaries were a well remembered feature, not simply of the Comintern's early years, but also of the years before. So Trotsky must have known all this for a very long time before that evening in Copenhagen. Their disagreements had surely been clear and **amicable**.

The subsequent bitterness was perhaps not a matter of political divergence alone. I suspect that, in addition, Sneevliet's suspicions preceded Trotsky's as to GPU penetration of the International Secretariat in Paris. There was at least one GPU person, 'Étienne', who worked in the closest proximity to Sedov. Trotsky and Sedov were not alone in making such a mistake; even Lenin had once defended Malinovsky who later turned out to be a Tsarist agent. 'Étienne' was exposed by Ignace Reiss, an agent who broke with the GPU (courageously enclosing his Order of Lenin with an open letter to Stalin) and who was gunned down by GPU killers. While on the run, Reiss's wife stayed some time in Sneevliet's house. But the bullets that, in 1942, ended Sneevliet's life were to come from a Nazi firing squad.

Chapter 7

Defeat and Survival 1933-46

Editor's Note

UP to this sentence, every word of this, final, version of this book had either been written by Harry Wicks or minutely chewed over by him. To understand the last phrase, readers need to know how the whole book came to be written. Particularly during 1976-77, but intermittently up to 1988, I transcribed 380 or more foolscap pages of interviews with Harry. He corrected these transcripts week by week. Early in 1977, I arranged what we so far had into chronological order with a rough index. The aim was for Harry to use these, plus documents in his possession, as the basis for his autobiography. He was never sure of his ability to do this. On the other hand, he repeatedly made clear what he did **not** want done. Thus in 1977 two friends of us both, in the early 1980s a third and, in 1987-88, a fourth comrade attempted to pull some chapters together for him. Each time, Harry was deeply upset at the result. So far I had avoided making any such attempt, as I still felt too close to what had passed through my ears and typing fingers. On the rebound from the last episode, however, Harry sounded so despairing that I relented. On taking back the materials, much of which I found I had become somewhat rusty about during the intervening 10 or more years, I found that Harry had in fact made lengthy drafts of the opening parts of the first three chapters himself. These I have obviously used. This use, too, he closely approved.

So the main breakthrough was that we were now able to exploit the immense word processing professionalism of my Bremen colleague, Christine Weber. This meant that Harry was totally involved in rewriting each draft (sometimes two or three times) till every word was completely to his satisfaction. I had anyway continued to visit him once or twice a year. From now on, I was also on the phone to him, usually from Bremen, at rhythms that varied from roughly once a month to four or five times a week. Some of these conversations turned into 45 or 50 minute history sessions in themselves. These were presumably untaped, unlike those of the face to face interviews during 1976-88 which, together with their transcriptions, will eventually be deposited at the Modern Records Centre at Warwick University, along with Harry's documents.

From the start of the decade, Harry carried the main hour to hour burden of caring for Marjorie, whom a stroke had paralysed. His selflessness was reciprocated by younger members of his family, not least by sister Rose, and by Reg and Sue Wicks (who had placed him and Marjorie in a small bungalow flat next to them and the children).

Increasingly stretched though the Somerset health services may have been during the 1980s, periods seem to have occurred with increasing frequency during which Marjorie would be taken into hospital for a fortnight or so to give everyone, not least Harry, a break. In Chapter One, Harry has described his mother's love for Dr Bean, who perhaps saved his life around 1910. Whether he got on well with individual medics is probably none of our business. But I do know that for them as a lump his word remained 'quacks'. Whether for this or other reasons, I gather he may not have been swallowing his high blood pressure pills as consistently as he should have. Conceivably too, our longer phone conversations became a strain as well as a relief. But then again, as I also discovered after his death, he was also continuing to do solitary exercises in German grammar; hardly a pastime famous for regulating stress! Anyway, late in March 1989, he suffered a big stroke and died eight days later.

My main reason for mentioning this is that anyone and surely everyone will remember that Harry remained as razor sharp as, say, any reader of these lines or, of course, the writer of them. Harry continued into 1989 to do most of the checking of dates and other details, using among much else such works of reference as he had managed to bring from his larger collection at his house in Twickenham, which he had let soon after Marjorie's stroke. For every page so far, he is entirely responsible for the accuracy of facts and interpretation. The words are approximately 80 or 90 per cent those spoken or written by him at least once at one time or another. Some of the linking sentences are more often mine.

The pages which now follow were keyed in after his death, and therefore self-evidently could not benefit from an interactive rewrite with him. Their main source remains, as before, his transcripts plus a number of unrecorded phone conversations with him. In addition, I found among his papers a number of contemporary documents which I have quoted clearly and extensively. Whether Harry would have wanted this, I doubt; but they do express themselves more pithily than any paraphrase of mine ever could. Nor have I implied any conscious position of my own on the exact degree of political correctness embodied in these documents or in Harry's words; any nuances of self-criticism are those expressed by Harry. Above all, whatever knowledge I accumulated of some fundamental aspects of the life of Harry Wicks, I am no expert on the history of Trotskyism. Here I have benefited greatly from Al Richardson's and the late Sam Bornstein's *Against the Stream* and *War and the International* (both of these published by Socialist Platform in 1986), two thickety but significantly under-reviewed explorations.

Harry had at first intended his book to stop with September 1939. Given that his transcription materials for the period from 1940 to 1945 were often scrappy, I would have inclined towards this. However, he became increasingly aware that the London building workers' struggle of 1945-46 and the by-election flop of 1946 would mark an ending more appropriate to postwar themes. There are some good reasons.

Firstly, he became increasingly aware that the builders' movement, with which, as we will see, he was heavily involved, was one of those unofficial upsurges which are, not romanticised but rather, at the other extreme, coolly ordered to 'dis-happen' themselves. Secondly, Harry insisted during 1988 on recording with me a description of that episode. Thirdly, I later discovered among his papers some pages of manuscript in which he had begun what was evidently intended to be a full account of it. The fact that it breaks off after a few pages is surely not from any uncertainty as to its value, but rather from some urgent call; maybe from Marjorie in the same room, maybe from me in Bremen. Fourthly, there was also in Harry's papers a copy made by Margarita Dewar of the political parts of the sometimes twice-weekly letters which she wrote to her husband, Hugo, while he was in the army during 1944-46. I use them here, with her enthusiastic permission, to produce clearly demarcated comments by her and me on Harry's words. Aside from meetings with her, I have also been warmed and helped by a conversation with Daisy Groves on 28 February 1990.

The British Library's Newspaper Library in Colindale also afforded the opportunity to wade for days through microfilms in search of the building workers' movement. For these I am grateful, unlike my eyes.

To sum up, Harry too would have seen what follows as a dangerously premature child.

∴   ∴   ∴

My expulsion had economic consequences and not merely political. In common with millions of workers, I spent years on the dole – five, in my case. The 1930s were a particularly intolerant decade for heretics. But what restricted us even more was a lack of resources, nearly all of us were down on our luck economically. The effects of this were psychological too.

My own situation was both alleviated and aggravated by my mother having remarried while I had been in Moscow. On the one hand, her new husband was personally warm towards me. Not that he was left wing, we never discussed politics deeply. But he was a Labour supporter, and had shown his basic solidarity while I had still been in the Communist Party. For he worked as a supervisor at Lavender Hill post office. I had given the Comintern my brother's place in Percy Road as a cover address. Unfortunately the Comintern did not proceed to behave very discreetly. Often its letters and other materials simply **poured** in at my brother's. Now, my stepfather tipped me off that all this was being 'sent up': 'You're not the first person to open your mail,

Harry.' On that basis, I took immediate steps, via Berlin, to close that avenue. And personally too, he was supportive. For much of the decade, I had at his and my mother's house in Gwynne Road, Battersea, a bedroom with another room where I kept my books. So I had a base and was part of the family. On the other hand, even though my stepfather never ever complained, I knew I was bringing not a single bean into the family budget. I was living off a stepfather whom I had acquired at the age of 22 or 23. This was an indignity which often depressed me. It made me powerless in all sorts of little ways. For example, I could no longer enjoy vegetarian meals such as Reg and I had done while working at ROP.

Talking of meals, another thing which hardly added to life's joys was my teeth. Two or three years after I arrived back from Moscow, I was told that the dentist there had not removed all the decayed matter from around some holes he had been plugging. In those days, people still thought nothing of having all their teeth out. So I decided to. At the Anti-Vivisection Hospital, it cost a few pennies for as long as the gas lasted. The trouble was, dentures were for some years beyond my pocket. During these years, eating was complicated, and public speaking was a bit of a trial.

As I said, my situation was common to much of the Balham Group. As the Groves, the Dowdalls, Henry Sara and Jim Barrett continued for some years to live in the Balham house, some of us were reduced to arranging for a firm in Grimsby to supply us with boxes of fish. Regularly once a week, these would arrive for us at Balham station, which is high up a long flight of steps. We would heave the fish down these, borrow a barrow from the station people, trundle it up the hill to the house, unload it, pack our fish into little boxes and then sell these door to door at 6d or 9d a box. On one or other day in the week we also sold eggs. And this was at a time when we were financing and producing the *Red Flag* – as near to monthly as we could afford!

At one stage in 1934 or 1935, I became so depressed that I resolved to go on the tramp around the country, looking for work. Luckily, I first discussed with Alf a variation on that solution; that I should go into a camp for unemployed at Hollesley Bay – normally known as Botany Bay. This had a workhouse-like regime but did teach you a trade. And the trade I proposed to learn was bricklaying. As mentioned, Alf was a bricklayer. He had married and was trying to raise kids in extreme poverty (living in the Battersea house where he was to remain for virtually the rest of his life). He now said: 'Harry, no need to go off to Botany Bay – I'll teach you bricklaying.' So I went up Garrett Lane and bought 100 bricks. For months and months, day after day, I spent myself while he taught me to build walls and then corners and arches. In the reference library, I consulted all the available books, studied the theory of bonding and so on. Our idea was that, when he got a job again he would get me in as his mate. Luckily, I found myself unexpectedly a temporary job as a clerk to the registrar of births and deaths. In 1937 I began, also as a clerk, at Battersea's municipal electricity undertaking.

But the 1930s were politically far worse. The reasons for this were as self-evident to my comrades and me then as they are to most people now. We had, physically, experienced the bitterness with which the Communist Party had rejected the central precondition for a working class fightback against Nazism: an end to sectarianism between the KPD and SPD. For standing against this, we had been expelled – Reg and I onto the dole.

But the very magnitude of the defeat allowed the Comintern to seem to be leading the fightback. It proclaimed a new period which culminated in calls for a Popular Front. This trend answered pretty well to the needs of many leftish people in the labour movement. For them the decade had opened shamefully in 1931 with what seemed to them the 'betrayal' by their leader of many years' standing (Ramsay Macdonald) when he formed a National Government, and then won a landslide election victory against his former followers. Their political bankruptcy only fuelled their fury further.

In addition to this, the world economic crisis, which had helped trigger such 'betrayals', accentuated the seeming contrast between the capitalist world and Soviet Russia. At one stage, the capitalist countries were calculated to have a total of 16 million people unemployed and, at the peak, three million of these were in Britain. But Russia had no unemployed at all; apparently, apart from kulaks and saboteurs, everyone was in an ecstasy of collective achievement, fulfilling the Plan. Increasingly, the Labour Party echoed the idea that Socialism had the answer: a planned economy. Of course, the British movement, like others, was living in a fool's paradise. Admiration often grew limitless for the gigantic scale of Soviet construction. In and around the Communist Party, the promise was frequently heard: 'Give us five years to fulfil the Plan, and we'll **show** you the difference between Socialism and Capitalism.' This was the mentality that we were up against. Anyone seeking to puncture hopes as deep as these was going to be vulnerable for a very long time to lies as big.

Nonetheless, at the local level we were not easily forgotten for our energetic campaigning throughout our part of London, before and after our expulsion, for the unity of the German working class. In particular, this gave us some credit among many ILPers. And not only locally; at the national level there were people like Fenner Brockway. He had worked with and admired Ramsay Macdonald for decades, and felt shattered by the events of 1931. He also felt threatened by a group of Communist sympathisers within the ILP. From the point of view of him or Jimmy Maxton, Trotskyism was something to flirt with in one's ideas and to use as a tactical counterweight in a balancing act against one's CP-influenced comrades.

So we did not yet feel isolated. Rather, on May Day 1933 we brought out the first printed issue of our *Red Flag* in an optimistic mood. (This is something that Reg, in his book on the Balham Group, omits simply by ending his story beforehand, on a downward note.) And when this May Day number sold out all its 500 copies, we thought we were really making an impact! We sold it at ILP and Communist meetings from Hyde Park to nearer home. Further afield, copies went to Edinburgh, Glasgow and Oxford. Also to South Wales. Here and in Yorkshire and elsewhere, Henry Sara sold it during his lecturing for the NCLC. Our joy at such tiny sales is a measure of the effort we amateurs had had to put into producing it – all for the cost of between five and 10 pounds. We kept it going, though with breaks, till October 1937.

Six weeks or so after starting *Red Flag*, we formed ourselves as the Communist League. As our new name implied, we still saw the Communist Party as our main focus. Our 'immediate programme' sought to demonstrate to any CPers who might be growing uneasy at official policy how to relate to other left wingers. It spoke of our task as being 'to unite the advanced workers within the already formed organisations for the winning of the mass of the workers to revolutionary principles and understanding... by participation in the day to day activities of the workers... within the labour, trade union and cooperative movements'. In a paragraph which now seems to look not only backward at the Socialism of the Labour Party and ILP but also forward to the Stalinists' impending turn towards Popular Fronts, we demanded:

'The preservation of the leading role of the working class in the struggle for Socialism. Not "Socialism" to suit the middle classes but the middle classes for Socialism.'

There was much else in this little document which expressed the line most of us were to follow for many years yet.

We began to win a few adherents. Our first breakthrough was with a number of people in the Camberwell Communist Party, led by Francis Cooper. But outside South London our earliest sympathisers had been in Chelsea and in Hackney. From Chelsea, in particular, came Lee and Gerry Bradley. Both were experienced speakers in Hyde Park. Lee was outstandingly intelligent; her husband, Gerry, had done a short stretch in jail for involvement in a confrontation between unemployed and the police. They and our other Chelsea comrades eventually got hold of a small press and actually printed four issues of *Red Flag* – handsetting the type, a most laborious task. In Hackney there was a man named Max Nicholls and another called W Graham. Graham had actually been chosen as a delegate to the Communist Party's 1932 conference which had voted our expulsion. At that moment, he was our lone secret sympathiser in the hall. After a time, he and Nicholls had been thrown out on a matter of principle, and so had joined us openly, remaining for some time. There were also stirrings among Communist Party members at the London School of Economics, led by Margaret Johns, Denzil Harber and a friend of his called Stuart Kirby, who was anyway always about to go off to Japan.

But all such individual gains brought us up to a mere 30 or 40 people. By focusing on the Communist Party we were fishing from a very small pond. And they were predominantly unemployed fish – rather like us! And many less surefooted unemployed people were going through the party as through a sieve; things were rather chaotic. And we regarded ourselves as a left faction of the Communist Party and of the CI – a faction which had been expelled but was still trying to relate to them. Thus we were striving against very heavy odds to relate to a tiny party which was itself almost totally isolated from the working class. By itself, this was a recipe for peripheralisation compounded.

As I've recounted in earlier pages, though, we had for a long time been trying rather successfully to open out to the wider labour movement. In fact the Communist Party's London District Council had specifically complained, in its letter expelling me, that I had carried out a policy of a United Front with the ILP for May Day 1932. And obviously we were not going to drop these dimensions now. Rather, they helped us in the following way. Many of us, both from the original Balham Group and among our later adherents, had spent years heavily involved in the Communist Party. The party had been our life, and to be divorced from it and from many people with whom we had had deep bonds was a tremendous blow. Many of us had built a life's friendships on commitment to the Communist Party, or had expected to up until expulsion.

All of us felt traumatised and bereft. What saved the situation was our ongoing activity, we were very active in the Unemployed Workers' Movement, we had an active propaganda at all the speaking pitches in our parts of London. And we continued with our involvement on the South West London Anti-War Committee. The Balham Group's central issue was the unity of the German working class.

So, in local practice, we were often working alongside ILPers. Jimmy Lane, for example, had helped found a Battersea branch of the ILP. This branch was involved in our continued campaign for solidarity with the German working class. However, these exceptions apart, the ILP had always seemed a wishy-washy middle class outfit – not only to me but also to most of the original Balham Group. Sara had been absolute in his refusal to participate in the First World War, and felt the utmost contempt for those ILPers whose refusal had stretched to working in agriculture. For him, non-revolutionary pacifism was a self-righteous sham. Again, Stewart Purkis and I had edited factory papers. To us, the ILP had also meant its then leading members such as Macdonald, the Labour leader who had condemned Red Friday as undermining the British Constitution. And Groves was another who felt similarly on the ILP.

Now, the point of this is that in 1934 Trotsky made a new assessment. Internationally, he drew an analogy between the collapse of the German movement against Hitler and the collapse of the Second International in 1914. For Britain, he argued that this meant we should limit ourselves less to the Communist Party, and concentrate instead more on the ILP. Not that many of us knew Trotsky's full argument; once again, Reg seems to have been keeping some of the correspondence away from Henry, myself and the rest of us. Thirty-odd years later, I was astonished to read one of Trotsky's letters to him. Ironically, though, most of us would have agreed with Trotsky about the situation.

As mentioned, I had watched the ILP's 1932 conference which had disaffiliated in such disgust from the Labour Party. The eagerness of even its MPs to do so had been understandable; given Labour's political bankruptcy and given the unprecedented level of economic crisis, the rigidity which Attlee and Morrison were seeking to impose was unbearable irksome. The discipline wielded by the party whip and by the right wing union leaders was isolating ILPers from a working class, growing numbers of whom were looking for new answers. Since 1932, though, the ILP had been unable to provide any of these. Relatedly, it never worked out a role for itself. Many of its members developed the most ultra-left fantasies on the situation. For example, the idea was propagated very seriously of trade unionists refusing to pay their political levy to the Labour Party. This was something which would have completely isolated many working class people from **any** politics.

Another feature of this mess was that the party was split at least three ways. There was the main working class base in the north which was dominated by the right, many of whom eventually returned to the Labour Party. Secondly, there was the Revolutionary Policy Committee of Jack Gaster and others, which was moving towards the Communist Party. And in between were Brockway, Maxton and other leading lights who were wavering between some sort of link, even affiliation, to the Comintern on the one hand, and, on the other, inviting Trotskyists in so as to oppose the Stalinisers. There was also a growing segment of the membership, led by Bert Matlow, who were developing Trotskyist sympathies.

All this was clear. But what Trotsky forgot, in my estimate, was the materials he had to hand. As I've explained, we were already relating to many ILPers very successfully anyway, in our area at least, but would have felt silly and out of place as members of their party. Our personalities had been shaped in a Communist revolutionary movement, and we saw the idea that we should enter the ILP as unnecessarily sacrificing our independence.

Nonetheless, this was Trotsky's advice. So we held a meeting to discuss it. Something we acquired or reacquired at about that time was an ability to discuss things rationally, with everyone making their contribution and with a consensus being arrived at. Subsequently, some of us liked to think we retained that ability too. The consensus we arrived at in that meeting was that we should not go into the ILP but should maintain our separate force and carry on relating to both CPers and ILPers.

But also at the meeting, of course, were Harber, Kirby and a number of others around that recent recruitment to our ranks from LSE and elsewhere. They opted for Trotsky's tactic, for going in. Soon after our meeting, the ILP's *New Leader* announced that our Communist League had wound itself up and was entering the ILP. As a result, the outside world assumed for a time that we had gone out of business. Groves wrote to the paper a note of correction. This was never published. Brockway's eagerness, as the *New Leader's* editor, to persist in his exaggerations underlines his broader longing to welcome us in as allies against the Stalinists.

So the Harber-Kirby group marched into the ILP during the summer of 1934. What happened? Kirby quickly went off to teach at a Japanese university.[1] By early 1935 the others were marching out again and into the Labour Party's League of Youth. I call that very quick footwork – but without serving the purpose for which they had left us! Now, everyone makes mistakes, but I'm still waiting to see a balance sheet of **that** brilliant operation. Harber and his friends exploited to the full something that I don't see as any kind of advantage – lack of roots in a local labour movement. Consequently, they had no-one to whom to account for their actions. I thought they had some accounting to do.

Nonetheless, 1934 saw major developments to which we, too, reacted. In the spring, the Vienna Social Democrats fought back and were suppressed with howitzers. A month or two later, the Labour Party revived with a big victory in the London County Council elections. Within Labour, there were the beginnings of what became the Socialist League – a grouping of Socialists accumulating their own 'educational force', and aiming to get their party to adopt leftish policies. Reg was in touch with some of these people. The Labour League of Youth, which had previously been a skeletal outfit, became a really lively organisation for the first time, far outdoing the ILP's more and more ailing Guild of Youth.

We took stock of ourselves again. We were a small propaganda group, organisationally far from the Labour Party where the main action was now likely to be. The word 'Communist' in our name guaranteed that we would never have a hope of joining the party. And anyway the Communist League was listed among the organisations prohibited from affiliating. So we changed our name and became the Marxist League. We kept the *Red Flag* going, though not always regularly. We also published a closely printed eight page pamphlet of mine replying to Ralph Fox's biography of Lenin which we saw as the best example of 'the Stalinist treatment of history'.[2] (Some years later, we reissued it with a tribute to Fox, who had joined the International Brigade and been killed.)

Our main interest was in the Labour League of Youth and in the Socialist League. The LLY soon grew to more than 10 000 members. It became the main focus for most of us. It had an enormous Stalinist faction led by a Battersea trade unionist, Ted (later Lord) Willis, a right wing one led by George Brown (Harold Wilson's deputy during the 1960s), and a Trotskyist one led by Hugo Dewar's sister, Roma. The LLY had the right to elect one person to Labour's Executive Committee. On one occasion, Roma was the successful candidate. My own contribution was a course of Sunday afternoon classes at the North Battersea Labour Party rooms on the history of the working class movement.

The LLY members who came to these – often packing the room chock full – included much of the generation who were to become Labour councillors after the war. I was also on the executive of North Battersea Labour Party and on the trades council. From 1934 till after the war, I was also one of North Battersea's delegates to the London Trades Council. Partly because of being unemployed myself, I was also active among the unemployed, where for a time there was considerable activity independent of the Communist Party's front organisation, the National Unemployed Workers' Movement, which had been temporarily undermined by Third Period sectarianism in the familiar way.

But all too soon after we had started along a promising road with the right equipment, a massive obstacle was thrown across our way. This was the Moscow Trials. At times, we felt as if it was rolling onto us and crushing us. It first appeared with the assassination of Kirov in December 1934. From that winter, there was a succession of trials which increasingly poisoned our whole environment.

Nearly a year previously, we had had a pretaste – a deceptively sweet one, as things turned out – of the support we might expect against Moscow's manipulations. Back at the Copenhagen meeting, as I mentioned, the decision had been made to demand that MOPRA (International Class War Prisoners' Aid) extend its support to those dissident Communists whom Moscow was trying to keep silent about. The Balham Group decided to focus on Chen Duxiu. Like many of the beneficiaries of the Trotskyists' international campaign, he was not himself a Trotskyist. But when Henry Sara and Tom Mann had visited China for the Comintern in 1926, alongside the Indian, MN Roy, and the American, Earl Browder, he had been prominent among those Communists they had met. Subsequently, he had been swallowed up in the nationalists' repression of the Communists, and MOPRA seemed entirely indifferent to his fate. Tom Mann was still head of the National Minority Movement (what was left of it) and of course in the Communist Party. Nonetheless, we approached him with the argument: surely Chen, too, was a class war prisoner?

To our surprise as well as joy, Mann showed his calibre by writing a letter to *Red Flag*, which we published in our September 1933 number, promising to do everything he could 'to continue to develop opinion till it shall be equal to demanding and securing the release of our comrade'. And in its January 1934 number, *Red Flag* was able to publish a letter over his signature jointly with those of Alex Gossip (who normally could hardly have been closer to the Communist Party's line) and of seven other members of the Executive of his Furniture Trades Association, plus three national officers of the Chemical Workers' Union, two of the AEU (one of these Jack Tanner) and John Jagger of the Distributive and Allied Workers. From the ILP, Brockway and Maxton also signed. With this letter, we at least broke the silence. And this brief shout should not be forgotten.

But our small success early 1934 was to prove a flower on the edge of a desert compared with our efforts during the Moscow Trials. Time and again, the feeling was brought home to us that we were a tiny handful standing against almost the whole of the left and of the media (though HN Brailsford in *Reynolds* was an oasis there). So much so, that we ourselves sometimes felt like wavering. I distinctly remember Reg – one of the leaders of British Trotskyism at that time – saying: 'Harry, this represents curtains for us.' I do not mean to denigrate him; in public, he spoke as courageously as any of us, though he wasn't as consistently active as some on this issue. But, at the time, the idea that absolutely all these viciously trumpeted accusations could be inventions was hard even for us to believe wholeheartedly. We had yet to hear about modern techniques of interrogation.

But from the Stalinist side, too, some people obviously had difficulty following through the logic of the accusations. The first meeting which the Communist Party called about the trials was at Conway Hall. At its very start, while the announcements from the chair were still going on, one Indian journalist who used to float around the left at the time did an extraordinary thing. Amid this tense gathering, jam packed both in the gallery and on the floor, he threw everything into confusion. Up he stood:

'Mr chairman, would it be in order for us all to stand in one minute's silence for Lenin's companions, the Bolshevik leaders, Kamenev and Zinoviev, who have been executed?'

And they did not know whether to stand or sit! The confusion was astonishing! But JR Campbell stepped in to crush that idea at once. As the main speaker, he set out the indictment: Trotskyism was Fascist and counter-revolutionary. In the meeting at least, we were a small group. One of us was George Padmore, the black American revolutionary who had himself spent some time in Moscow. We were vociferous enough for me to be allowed onto the platform to speak against the trials.

But, next to its opening, my other vivid memory of that meeting was of standing outside as the crowd came out. There was virtually no support there for the view I had just put over. For the one time in my life, I felt aware of a Jewish influence in the Communist Party and on the Communist Party's periphery. The audience was disproportionately East End Jewish. Given Hitler, one can hardly blame the East End in particular for seeing nothing other than Stalin for stopping him.

The second meeting – in the same hall, overflowing no less than before – was called by the Friends of Soviet Russia. This audience was made up more of intellectuals. The main speaker was DN Pritt, a prominent barrister. After he had finished, I was allowed onto the platform to oppose him. Part of the indictment he was putting forward was that the Trotskyist Opposition in Russia were for armed struggle against the Soviet régime. Now, I chanced to have in my pocket a copy of the Russian Opposition's *Bulletin* where the actual phrase was **political** struggle. So I said to Pritt: 'There's your documentary evidence.' His retort – uttered as if aside – left me breathless: 'I've seen all manner of documents in my time as a lawyer.' What also left me breathless was that this produced from the audience an instant **laugh** of agreement. (The *Manchester Guardian* reported both our speeches.)

By the late summer of 1936, I was secretary to the Provisional Committee for the Defence of Leon Trotsky. We managed to bring out a tiny printed leaflet. But of all the people whom Reg and I approached for signatures, only seven or eight gave their names. These included HN Brailsford, JF Horrabin, Irene Rathbone and Conrad Noel (the 'Red Vicar' of Thaxted, and a former mentor of Reg's). At most, only one half were trade unionists, two of them in the Railway Clerks' Union (one of these our friend and former comrade, Stewart Purkis). Yet the content of this leaflet could not have been more modest. It called merely for an 'International Commission of Enquiry' to be 'set up by the international labour movement'. Even this was too much for the *New Statesman* to print. Indeed, only the *Daily Herald* and the *Guardian* consented to run it. But we ourselves circulated that appeal as widely as we possibly could; only a tiny handful of additional signatures came back. One of these was from the novelist Ethel Mannin, and another was from Sidney Silverman, Labour MP for Nelson and Colne. During the autumn, CLR James and I addressed a meeting. Henry Sara was in the chair. The main Communist Party heckler was Pat Sloan. In print, too, he was most prolific and aggressive on the subject of the trials; Moscow's prize hack in Britain. So I challenged him to hold a properly organised public debate with me. But he never took my challenge up. [But see Bornstein and Richardson, pp231-2, where a second Essex Hall meeting is mentioned where Sloan **was** billed as the opponent.] Two weeks previously, also during February 1937, some hundreds of people also filled the Memorial Hall, Farringdon, where Purkis and Silverman spoke, alongside CLR, Reg, Henry and Harry.]

We tried every conceivable avenue. Back in 1931 I had bumped into AE Reade for the first time in six years. This had occurred at an unusual pub in Soho where I had gone with some Battersea ex-YCL friends. It was known as Kleinfeld's and was an odd place to meet him for the first time since my days on the Victoria train indicator. On one occasion, I remember one end of the pub singing the *Internationale*, while the other sang the Nazi *Horst Wessel Song*. The tension was extreme, but was spiced by the presence of some curious regular customers. Someone pointed out two of them, Alistair Crowley and Betty May, as devotees of black magic. Anyway, this man walked in whom I instantly recognised as Reade. He was carrying a little sack which contained a barrister's whig. He turned out to have just passed his final exam for the bar.

Now that I was secretary of the Trotsky Defence Committee, I remembered how warmly Reade had greeted me in Kleinfeld's. Trotsky was now hoping to gain some publicity by having us sue, in his name, some newspaper wholesalers for distributing one or more foreign journals which might be judged to have slandered him. I decided to look Reade up. His chambers were in Lincoln's Inn Fields. Once again, Reade was personally warm. However, he said, he wanted to make something very clear to me: 'I'm no longer a Trotskyist, Harry.' He had anyway, he said, a wife and child. He had 'great admiration for Trotsky as a **man**, but I've moved away from that type of politics.' That aside, I had asked his professional opinion. This was, that no possibility existed of bringing an action for libel such as I had outlined. No London jury would be likely to be moved by the plight of someone like Trotsky. (That, as it happened, was the last I saw of Reade. In 1945, a friend of mine from the YCL days,[3] who was by now working for the NAAFI in Germany, came across Major AE Reade.)

A far worse disappointment, also during the autumn of 1936, was a visit to Fenner Brockway. Up to this time, the ILP's *New Leader* had been saying critical things about the trials. And Brockway in particular had the ability to give the impression that he was always enquiring, always keeping an open mind. Sara, Purkis and I were becoming deeply worried at the failure of our efforts to obtain left intellectuals' support for a commission of inquiry. Purkis, as an old Socialist living in Hampstead Garden Suburb, had contacts with many such people and was struck by their unwillingness to speak out. He – I think it was – suggested we go and ask Brockway whether the ILP could not sponsor a meeting on the trials. So we made an appointment to see him at his office above the ILP bookshop off Ludgate Circus. (The bookshop's manager, Jon Kimche, later became a Zionist, but at that time was a Brandlerite; on the trials, we had a warm rapport.) Upstairs, Fenner began warmly: 'Ah, yes, the Moscow Trials. One moment please, gentlemen.' He plunged into the room behind and fished out an elaborate Spanish grandee's red velvet uniform. His words now were:

'The Spanish Revolution is on. So, the problem is: if the sky were clear and blue, then we'd really **do** something about the Moscow Trials. But the situation is that the Russians are supplying arms to the Spanish Revolution. Therefore we can't do anything for the present.'

Little more than a week later, he followed up his private refusal with a leading front page article in the *New Leader* on 'the methods of the Trotskyists' in which he denounced us as, in effect, obsessives and disrupters. Of course, he never mentioned his having met with us. Purkis sent a reply which was never printed. Instead, *Red Flag*, with obviously a tinier circulation, was the only journal to carry it. Its gist was that mainstream working class politics was being sacrificed yet again in order to cover Soviet foreign policy.

For me personally, though, the most horrible episode of all was the meeting we called in the lower hall of Battersea town hall. Unlike some of our meetings elsewhere on this subject, it was not overflowing. I had intended to give more of a lecture than a speech. This was underlined by the charge we made for entry, to help prevent us being swamped, we had hoped. Part of the indictment in the current trial mentioned Sedov as being present in Copenhagen with his father. Well, as I have recounted in the last chapter, this was utter nonsense. I had been particularly disappointed that he had **not** been there, and Natalia had had to ask us to pipe down in order that she could hear his voice on the phone from Berlin. So I was now intending to offer a careful refutation, based on my direct experience, of that part of the indictment and therefore of the whole.

But this time, CPers came along, not to argue, but really to wreck the meeting. The only word for the behaviour of many of them was hooliganism. Here, though, there was something much worse for me – in **that** hall, I could see the faces of people I had known from my boyhood, people who had known me when we had been growing up in the local labour movement. I could **see** that most of them either disbelieved me or did not understand. Or, if they understood a thing, then they inclined towards the Communist Party's indictment of Trotsky. This for me was a bitter, bitter experience. But somehow I rode it by reminding myself that I knew, as distinctly as I had ever known anything in my life, that Sedov had simply not been in Copenhagen, whereas the indictment hinged on his having been there.

This range of reactions between puzzled suspicion and outright loathing of us worsened with the international situation. The pressure mounted day after day and year after year. The best of the wider spread reactions to our views was one of non-involvement. Alf Loughton, for example, had around 1932 been along, with his two children, to our Clapham Common meetings. He never touched Trotskyism as such, but he remained willing to collaborate with us.

And he shared with me an interest in the fate of a person who, as I have mentioned, had been sent to those same meetings so as to keep an eye on us, our old comrade, Wally Tapsell. Wally we had known since the early 1920s. He died in the Spanish Civil War rather mysteriously. I gather (from Charlotte Haldane's *Truth Will Out* and from other sources) that he had differences with the British Communist Party and was sent from the British brigade, where he was serving, to find out what was going on in Barcelona. As is clear, he had long been aware of our general analysis. Many years later, Alf was sent by his building trades union to a printers' union convalescent home at Rottingdean. And there, what should he find but a room dedicated to Wally's memory! As the place seemed to be crawling with CPers, Alf proceeded to pump some of these as to how Wally had met his death in Spain. But they were as mystified as he. Again after the war, I too confronted one CPer with the question. The reply added enigma to the mystery: 'Wally was a great guy, but he was no soldier.' This could mean almost anything.

Altogether, in Britain as in so many other countries, the history of any Trotskyist movement, from December 1934 at any level, has to be seen against the background of this mounting international hysteria. Anything one did or attempted was in almost all directions systematically ignored or distorted.

The autumn of 1935 saw the Italian attack on Abyssinia. Now that Stalin's Russia was in the League of Nations and in alliance with France, it supported sanctions against Mussolini via the League. Predictably, these turned out to be ineffective. As against this, the ILP and the Socialist League (which was financed and mainly controlled by Stafford Cripps, one of the highest paid barristers in the land) came out with a correct position for class sanctions: an embargo on all materials to Italy. Thus the Communist Party found itself in tandem with the Labour right. This was symbolised at a conference called by

Labour and the TUC in the big hall of Friends' Meeting House in Euston Road. I was present as a delegate – though whether from Battersea Trades Council or my union branch I can't remember. The speech by the TUC's General Secretary, Citrine, was followed by one from JR Campbell. The two boiled down to the same League of Nations line. The opposition came from ILPers and SLers. For some months, there seemed a possibility that these two small organisations might converge in class conscious opposition to the two larger ones. Had this occurred, some reactions to the Stalinist repression in Spain, and to much else, might have been different.

Reg Groves had just been elected onto the Socialist League's Executive, and was chair of the London Area Committee. Around 1936 the situation which developed was that the Communists achieved an alliance with Cripps, and, during the autumn of that year, brought to a climax their negotiations both with him and with the leaders of the ILP. Both Cripps and they were acting behind the backs of their membership. We were against this Communist Unity Campaign, not simply because it was obviously designed to open the way for the Communist Party to affiliate to Labour and thus to further its Stalinisation, but, even more, because it was transparently designed to silence left wing criticism of Soviet foreign policy. All this was another part of the context of our interview with Brockway about the trials. This context also coloured his swift denunciation of us.

The Socialist League held a special conference at the Scotch Café in the Strand during January 1937 to consider the Unity campaign. Groves and I were among the main speakers. I vividly remember our feeling of elation there that no absolute majority of delegates could be won for that campaign. Nonetheless, the largest minority was for it. Participation in the Unity Campaign was clearly going to entail expulsion from the Labour Party. We were not going to risk the loss of working class contacts that this would entail, merely for the privilege of joining up with a Stalinist front where we would have been tolerated even less. Instead, we put some of our still pitifully few pennies together to bring out *Socialist Left*. Its aim was to rally SLers for staying in the Labour Party; we were trying to retain the gains we had made at that special conference. *Socialist Left* had one issue only. Our funds were too overstretched with *Red Flag* to be burdened with a second publication.

Not that the Socialist League lived much longer. Reg had had a shrewd suspicion that the Communist Party saw it as an encumbrance on their intended path into the Labour Party, and were aiming to have it closed down. As is now known, the Communist Party did indeed put this idea to Cripps as something which would help the Unity Campaign. In May 1937, he implemented it. As the League's financier, he was effectively responsible to no-one, least of all to his membership who would surely have outvoted him on this switch in his barrister's brief. Within a few months, the Communist Party were suggesting that its sympathisers within the Labour Party should, to avoid expulsion from Labour, cease their public participation in the Unity Campaign. By 1938, the Communist Party was going for a Popular Front of all anti-Fascists, whether Socialist or anything. The Unity Campaign was silently forgotten. (In by-elections, Socialists were to be publicly opposed unless they supported the Communist Party's version of anti-Fascism. This was what happened to Reg when he stood as Labour candidate at Aylesbury in 1938.)

In this connection, I vividly remember watching one huge Popular Front demonstration in Trafalgar Square, if only because it was led by Dave Springhall. He had been the man sent down by King Street to hammer the Trotskyists in the South-West London Anti-War Committee. Now here he was marching into the Square with a Union Jack over his shoulder! At about this time I also saw a Popular Front pageant portraying an English revolutionary tradition since Winstanley and the Diggers. It was interesting, but it fitted neatly the need of left intellectuals to find common roots between revolutionaries and liberals. We now know that Springhall was fated to be the person who, in September 1939, brought from Moscow to the Communist Party's Central Committee the order that the new war was not anti-Fascist but between rival imperialisms. So much for Union Jacks – for the moment.

Although our marginalisation was on the whole not our fault, it was to a minor extent. For it increased our fragmentation. By 1937, there were no less than four groups of Trotskyist allegiance. There was the one, led by Harber and Margaret Johns, which the Fourth International officially recognised: the Militant Group, Bolshevist Leninist – you know, grandiose name! – which was active in the Labour Party. There was the Marxist Group led by CLR James. It was tightly organised and was giving battle to the leaders of the ILP. Here, it was really winning influence against the Stalinisers. There was our organisation, the Marxist League. And fourthly, there was the Hyde Park group of people who had come from South Africa, plus Jock Haston and, from 1937, Gerry Healy. All of us had the same principles but different tactics. The Moscow Trials rammed home to many of us the lesson that this was not good enough – but not to all of us.

During my efforts to form a broad committee in response to the first Moscow Trials, my mother's home was positively bombarded with letters and even cablegrams from our American comrades asking why on earth we could not launch a publicity campaign and enrol the left intellectuals onto a defence committee on the scale as huge as what they had achieved in America. Why couldn't we do this and that and the other! I have already mentioned the deep disillusion with our left intellectuals that I was undergoing. (Indeed, the file of replies that I got from them would make priceless reading today had I not turned it over to the RCP during the late 1940s.)

But another disillusion, almost as deep, was with many Trotskyists. Each little group was peddling its particular little line, its particular focus on this or that arena. On the trials, each said its little piece in its little paper about the need to do something about them. But to become part of this committee which some of us were trying to put together, for that they were too pure.

And as if non-participation were not bad enough, when they did participate they were sometimes almost worse. At one meeting at the Essex Hall early in 1937, I can remember some Harberites (or was it Hyde Park people?) heckling about the need to build a Fourth International. This was at a meeting to try and broaden the pressure within the working class movement to look objectively at the whole question of Trotsky's alleged guilt! This sectarian flying of our flag disgusted me and, together with the feeling of failure and isolation, depressed and demoralised me so much that I decided to resign the secretaryship of the committee. I gave way to Charles Sumner. Also, as he was an intellectual, I was sure he could type letters far quicker than I. Not that I left the committee, I continued participating in all the meetings and doing as much speaking as anyone on the trials.

These experiences intensified my longing for a fusion of forces. I was hardly alone in this. By the second half of 1937 there was a widespread feeling that our movement's growth was going into reverse, that individuals were leaving us in exhaustion and that we were failing. CLR James shared this longing as much as anyone. He had arrived from Trinidad in 1932. He and I were very frequently together during 1936 while he was writing his book, *World Revolution*, which Secker brought out the next year, on the misadventures of the Comintern. As mentioned, he made extensive use of the documents I had brought out of Russia. No less important, I commented on each chapter as he drafted it. He laboured through an enormous literature, working from a small room in Gray's Inn Road, heated by the smallest of gas fires. Working as his typist and secretary was Dorothy Pizer, the companion of George Padmore. (On one occasion in 1935, James and Padmore had taken me to meet a number of politically minded African students, one of whom I'm certain was J Kenyatta.) James and I became rather close. Not only did we share a frustration at the lack of unity, but we also agreed for each of us to push the idea within his own organisation.

Within the Marxist League, our main opponents were Reg and Daisy, along with Hugo, Arthur Wimbush and Vic Carpenter. As mentioned, the trials had depressed Reg even more deeply than me, and he had not been very active over them. He now viewed all the undoubted sectarianism of the various grouplets through a magnifying glass. As a consequence, he would have nothing to do with fusion. At the personal level, though, our relations remained warm. We knew what a tactical difference was. But most of us decided for fusion. So the Marxist League officially dissolved itself in October 1937, and in February 1938 a fusion conference was held. The Haston-Healy group and the Johns-Harber group refused to have anything to do with it. The Harberites objected that there had been insufficient political preparation. Some comrades of CLR's shared this objection. It had much truth in it. But, to my mind, at a time when war was looming up and when the trials were continuing, the need for unity was paramount.

Henry Sara chaired the conference. James summarised its main discussion and I presented its opening Political Statement which had been drawn up by a committee made up of three members from both organisations. I proposed that those comrades who were in the Labour Party should continue there, while those outside should continue there. On this basis, the conference set up the Revolutionary Socialist League. Our *Red Flag* was incorporated into the joint paper which took the title of James' group's paper, *Fight*. Its first number came out in April 1938. This contained an inspiring proclamation of the new League by CLR. After warning that 'the capitalists respect democracy only as long as democracy respects the capitalists', he went through the disasters engendered by the existing leaderships, from the Comintern to the ILP. He declared:

'Our heritage is mixed. We have Marxism... We also to some extent carry the burden of Stalinism, its crimes and errors. For many, the nightmare of Stalinism proclaiming itself as Socialism condemns every form of Marxism. It is not without irony that we who, for many years and still today, are denounced as the enemies of the Soviet State, now increasingly have to stand between the USSR and a devastating disillusion. As people turn in... disgust from the... Stalinist megaphones, they... are beginning to distinguish between the solid gains of the October Revolution, the failure of the world revolution and – direct result of that failure – the fungoid bureaucratic lump that is now fathered on the Russian workers and peasants.'

Clearly, when James declared that 'for thousands of people... the Moscow Trials have opened their eyes', he was optimistic. The trials closed many more minds than they opened.

Some months later, further trials and the continued need for further regroupment persuaded the International Secretariat to send both Cannon and Shachtman over to bang heads together. The result was a further unity conference during September. Our name remained the same, but we officially fused with the Harberites. Our League did not make much progress. Alongside Sara, I was on its Executive. The first thing we were confronted with was that Cannon turned out to have arranged for James to be sent to America. In the event, he was to remain there till deportation in 1953. To my mind, James was the outstanding British Trotskyist of the 1930s. Not only was he a good speaker, but his speeches evidenced wide culture and deep reading. Above all, he could think mightily for himself. The Brockways and Maxtons could hardly dismiss him as a scruffy Trotskyist. The immediate result of his departure was that Henry and I were left to face the Harberites alone. These manoeuvres by Cannon have always smelt to me of Comintern-type manipulation – something Cannon himself had considerable experience of. So, in this situation, I now felt very lukewarm.

But in effect, the terms of both fusions allowed every organisation to carry on doing what it had already proved best at. During the autumn of 1938, with war seemingly nearer than ever, those of us who had been in the former Marxist League – including Reg, back from his rather successful by-election at Aylesbury – decided to tie ourselves as closely as possible into the workers' movement. For this purpose, we decided to revive our old tactic of the SWLAWC, this time under the more manageable title of the Socialist Anti-War Front. For this, certain things were moving in our favour. The ILP's leadership had learnt something from burning its fingers with the Communist Party. Transfixed by the war danger, it swung back towards its old pacifism. Within the ILP, there remained a body of people with revolutionary backgrounds sufficient for seeing the need to organise on immediate issues.

At this moment, the government presented us with one such issue. For the first time in British history, conscription – or at least registration for it – was introduced in peacetime. At the time and since, our activities against this have brought accusations from other Trotskyists that we were making concessions to bourgeois pacifism. The accusations ignored the fact that Continental bourgeoisies had long had peacetime conscription, whereas ours had not.

As for such accusations that came from our local comrades at that time, the best reply is the history of our agitation itself. It climaxed at the Bermondsey conference of the No Conscription League a few weeks after the start of the war. This conference gathered revolutionaries and pacifists both within the ILP and outside. In terms of the representation of meaningful working class organisations, the conference proved formidable. We participated via the SAWF, in which Reg and those comrades in Wimbledon and Balham who had kept closer to the Labour Party than we had were also involved. The line of the pure pacifists was made clearest of all by CA Smith, then a leading ILPer. He could, he said, think of nothing more magnificent than the spectacle of individuals throwing themselves against the might of the state. (Shortly after, he was to volunteer to go and fight the Russians in Finland; but this was a deviation from his normal pacifist instincts.) The line that Reg and I advocated, by contrast, was that the answer to conscription was to develop a shop stewards' movement such as had been so important during the previous war. At the time, of course, any such movement was as dead as a dodo, outside the aircraft industry. The conference's final resolutions were a hodge-podge. But Reg was on the drafting committee, so our line featured in them very clearly.

The opening resolution declared:

'We wish to destroy Hitlerism. But the practice of Hitlerism is not confined to the Nazis. The oppression of colonial peoples in the British and French Empires and all encroachments on the rights and liberties of British and French workers are to us as abhorrent as the Nazi oppression of Poles and Czechs and the suppression of German Socialists and trade unionists...

'The overthrow of Hitlerism in Germany depends mainly on the German working class. The task of British workers is to end the domination of the British capitalist class, and to win power to build a Socialist Britain which can take its place in a Socialist Europe.'

Consistently with this, a whole section headed 'The Way To Do It', demanded a revival of the shop stewards' movement.

Curiously, though the Harber-Johns group – our comrades in the RSL – strongly disapproved of our initiative in forming SAWF, the Bermondsey conference was too big for them to ignore. Indeed, I can remember one of their leading members, Starkey Jackson, coming up to me during the session to ask if we could do anything to give him the opportunity to speak. This dumbfounded me. Reg had got the opportunity by virtue of being one of the initiators of the resolution, but I had seized it in the same way as anybody else, by sticking my hand up. Jackson's uncertainty is, in my submission, another example of the Harberites' disconnection from the labour movement. In many milieux, they did not know how to operate. And in general, they seemed unable to utilise even an ambiguous occasion such as this conference in order to put their ideas forward.

So this strengthened my opinion of them as people without background or feel. For this reason, I let my links with the RSL loosen to vanishing point. I never formally broke with them, and to this day I don't know whether I was expelled by them. I doubt if I was.

From the winter of 1938-39, Henry, Reg, Hugo and I were energetically going round union branches speaking for SAWF and calling for a revived shop stewards' movement. For the day when the young men were supposed to go to the labour exchanges to register for conscription, we brought out a leaflet which we handed out there. I happened to be doing this at Beauchamp Road when the War Minister, Hore-

Belisha, drew up in his big car to see how things were going. Naturally, I gave him a copy.

Also during this winter, there was a big struggle in Battersea Labour Party over whether to collaborate in government air raid precautions, the distribution of gasmasks and the digging of shelters. I was on the General Management Committee as a union delegate. The leader of the Council, FR Douglas, put a right wing viewpoint, for participation. (He was later to be Governor of Malta and a member of the House of Lords.) The meeting packed the Latchmere Baths. I put the opposing viewpoint, and won.

Later, however, during the weeks in which the war actually started, the borough Labour Party called another meeting, which was again full to bursting, to consider the question of the war. Tom Pocock, my old mentor of two decades earlier, was in the chair. The only resolution allowed was based on an official pamphlet by Attlee, Labour's national leader; any amendment would have to be to his *The Labour Party and the War*. The motion was now moved by the Labour agent, who carried the day – but only narrowly. I was not going to participate in the war, even indirectly. So, on that issue, I walked out of the Labour Party, along with my other comrades. Obviously, though, I stayed in the trades council.

So, during the year or so before the outbreak of war, we became quite well known within the Labour Party for our stand against the coming conflict. As CLR had argued in his April 1938 proclamation:

'Where the Duchess of Atholl, the Archbishop of Canterbury, Winston Churchill, Citrine, Bevin and Harry Pollitt are all united... in their many keyed chorus for a war to preserve peace, the voice of Marxism can be heard more clearly if only by simple contrast with the prevailing mass of lies and hypocrisy which stands for 1914 all over again.'

And now SAWF made some considerable gains for us. Hitherto we had been known only within our locality. But now we were attracting sympathy from some people in Manchester, Bradford, Liverpool and elsewhere.

Our first vehicle was a penny pamphlet which Hugo published in February 1939, *Resist the Draft*. In the longer term, our vehicle was SAWF's paper, *The Call*. It came out in October 1939. Reg edited it. But its contributors were not confined to our group. George Padmore wrote for it. So did the Bradford railway clerk, Rowland Hill (who had previously figured as one of our few signatories against the Moscow Trials). So did the independent Marxist, Frank Ridley, as also an old Socialist writer of children's stories called Will Morris of the No Conscription League; lovely name, lovely man.

The Call had five or six issues. One of its numbers reported a march to Battersea Town Hall by building workers involved in constructing shelters and repairing bomb damage, for better wages and conditions. Reg at this time also attracted further attention to us by publishing his penny pamphlet of 11 pages, *It is an Imperialist War: A Reply to Harold Laski*. Laski was one of the leading left wing thinkers of the time. Here, Reg ironised that Laski 'urges the German workers to overthrow their capitalist government, but urges the British workers not to overthrow theirs', and argued that 'the blows of British workers against their own imperialism will awaken wider reverberations in Germany than all the leaflets and radio appeals made by Labour men serving as the mouth-pieces of an imperialist government'. In this opinion, we were express-ing the view of more than our own group.

Though Reg remained in the Labour Party, we drew closer together personally. In December 1937 I had married Alf's sister, Marjorie. We had set up house in a flat on the Battersea side of Wandsworth Common, and soon were starting a family. When the war started, I felt I could not know what might happen to me: would I be arrested, or what? I wanted to go on being active, but was worried about Marjorie. She agreed that she would also be worried about her mother. So we moved in with her. Then Reg made a suggestion. Following his good showing in the Aylesbury by-election of the previous year, he had moved up there. But when the war started he got a job in London. This meant he was commuting in trains which were blacked out and where he could not do any reading. So he now suggested that Marjorie and I set up house and live communally with him and Daisy. I broached the question to Marjorie and she was favourable. So Reg said: 'Get the two girls together and let them sort something out.' So they sorted out a place at the side of Wandsworth Common. We began living together during October 1939. It was there that we edited *The Call* and where Reg wrote his reply to Laski.

With hindsight, we were taking an impossible stand on ARP: refusing to protect our own people. Not only were we taking a 'clean hands' attitude (the phrase was much used by us and by those who agreed with us in these debates). But also, worse, we were much too directly influenced by the movement's experience during the First World War. In this, we happened to be in agreement with Trotsky's *Transitional Programme*, though we had arrived at our position before reading it. Our position was that the new war was between rival imperialisms and was going to open the path for the unfolding of a European revolution – certainly by or at the end of the conflict (as in 1918-19), but probably even more quickly this time.

During these months also, the Trotskyist groupings were in ribbons. Leading Trotskyists, such as Harber, Healy, Haston and Grant, de-cided that the bombing and the repression would be so severe as to necessitate going underground. For a time they themselves went to Ireland. To us it seemed they had left their membership (such as it was) high and dry. Only later in the war, when industrial unrest began to flare up, did they gain some strength.

The outcome of our prewar efforts was that, for the beginning of the war, we were able to formulate a manifesto which clearly and readably explained our position. Hugo did the final write-up, but we all discussed it at every stage of its production. At that time, gasmasks had by law to be carried at all times. So, on the morning that war was declared, we put copies of our leaflet into our cardboard gasmask containers and distributed it in that way. In addition, one of Reg's followers, Fred White, had a handpress with which we printed stickers. These went up around a number of railway depots and other places.

That manifesto acted for us as our guide to our position throughout the war. It saw the conflict as one between rival imperialisms:

'In the colonial Empires of France and Britain millions live at starvation level under an oppression equalled only by that existing in Fascist Germany. And it is for the right to exploit these territories rich in men and raw materials that the rival imperials of Europe go to war.

'The responsibility for the present war lies therefore with no one government, but with the profit making system and the men that maintain it.'

It then denounced the 'leaders of Labour' and of the Communist Party. The first had 'once again ranged themselves on the side of the exploiters in this country. In the name of freedom and democracy they support... the piecemeal destruction of freedom and democracy' and had therefore 'forfeited the right to speak on... [the workers'] behalf.' The second had:

'... proved no less traitorous to the principle of international Socialism. By their "Peace" Front policy they have fostered the illusion of "peace loving" as opposed to "aggressor" nations. They hailed the Russo-German pact as a "victory for peace and Socialism" when in reality it set the seal on Stalin's abandonment of Socialism. Now they stand behind British imperialism and call its struggle to hold its vast possessions the "fight against Fascism".

Men without principles or shame, they have well earned the contempt of the workers. In these circumstances the rank and file of the labour movement must look to itself for aid.'

So, most of the next 150 words led up to the final slogans to:

'**Make the trades councils the vigorous committees of labour!!! Build the shop stewards' movement. Defend trade union conditions. For a United Socialist States of Europe.'**

The only mention of mainline pacifist activity was to 'members of the No Conscription League' to make 'the fight of the conscientious objector part of the wider struggle of labour'. Even this was open to misinterpretation, though: it was implicitly calling on those of our sympathisers among working class men who were not **yet** conscripted, to refuse to be conscripted – something which would have tended to isolate us from the class. A more fundamental fault was that its talk of 'efforts to impose military and police dictatorship upon the workers' was to feel an overestimate of the immediate level of repression.

During the first weeks of the war, before the Home Guard got going, the authorities started what was known as the Local Defence Volunteers. For Battersea at least, this involved learning to fire a rifle in your employer's time. As a revolutionary (**not** a pacifist, please note) I obviously had nothing against that. Another attraction was that it was on a sort of people's militia basis, in the sense that there were no sergeants and also no generals. Within months, though, they did transform this into the Home Guard, in which the foreman became the sergeant and so on. That was the moment for me to hand in my rifle and tin hat. And some others at work did similarly, for similar reasons. We felt we had been taken for a ride.

Apart from continuing our activity in SAWF, our main efforts were directed at the factories. Some advances were soon made. At Napier's in West London, one of our comrades was a works convenor, though the Communist Party soon ousted him. Secondly, a stroke of luck occurred with Alf Loughton. Though still a bricklayer, he was ordered into other employment, more related to the war effort. So he ended up in an aircraft factory in Hendon. Here, the works convenor turned out to be my old Moscow comrade, Weston; good revolutionaries always know how to position themselves. Together, they struggled to develop the shop stewards' organisation. But they too were ousted under Communist Party pressure.

The months around Dunkirk are often said to have strengthened national unity against an expected invasion. This often felt true. But it has been exaggerated. For example, much has ever since been made of the 'little ships' whose crews volunteered to go over to rescue the British forces. All I know is, that Marjorie's brother-in-law was a Thames lighterman who served three months in Wandsworth Prison for refusing to volunteer. So it wasn't always as voluntary as all that.

During the autumn of 1940, we discussed what to do, given that we expected to be made illegal. The Labour Party, normally a mass electoral machine, had ceased to exist as such, given its agreement to an electoral truce for the duration of the war. So our discussions turned towards the ILP. Its politics remained internationalist and opposed to the war – however clouded by straight pacifism. So, given this, we decided to recommend the SAWF to go into the ILP. Many did, though

Reg stayed with Labour. On the ILP side, Walter Padley, the London and Southern Divisional Organiser, was said to have welcomed our presence as at least inoculating the party against Stalinism. At the turn of 1940-41, we went in with the serious perspective of turning the ILP towards industrial struggle. Alf was already a member. He, Bill Hunter and I were soon on the ILP's London Divisional Council. Through its Industrial Sub-Committee, we started a small paper, *The Shop Steward*.

From 1942 as the industrial struggle picked up again, we were able to keep in touch with it. One issue was dominated by the strike at Barrow-in-Furness. In the North-east apprentices' strike, one or two Newcastle ILPers were involved. Obviously we were not. But we were not isolated either. I was a Battersea delegate to the ILP national conferences at Morecambe, Bradford, Blackpool and Southport. So I participated in fraction work with leading members of one or other faction of the Revolutionary Communist Party such as Roy Tearse and Healy (though Healy in particular was siphoning off many of the youngsters we were building up in the ILP).

For a time we ran, with them, an 'open' publication called *Free Expression*. It had articles on historical things, commented regularly on the war and reproduced an article of Trotsky's on Plekhanov. When Haston and Tearse were arrested for strike agitation, there was quite a degree of activity from the ILP and elsewhere on their behalf. The ILP's *Socialist Leader* carried many good articles on industrial struggles, including from Hugo.

The line of many Trotskyists was for the ILP to go back into the Labour Party. This we were vigorously opposing; even assuming Labour resurrected itself, there was a vital need for an alternative to its left, untainted by Stalinism.

What with the call up, our forces in Battersea became smaller and smaller. Hugo, for example, had originally been a conscientious objector; but in 1944 he had to go into the army, on the Trotskyist line that we ought to be wherever the working class was. I was spared such a choice, the old scare with my lungs was enough to bring me exemption from the call up.

I continued with my job as a clerk in the mains office of Battersea's municipal electricity. Here, the only episode worth remembering amounted to merely a tiny echo of the Communist Party's total war on Trotskyists. One day, I was working as usual, typing at my desk next to that of my three bosses who were university trained electrical engineers. Suddenly, in burst one of the workers, a Communist. As he did so, he let loose a flood of venom at me: Trotskyists were Fascist 'fifth columnists' who should be crushed, spewed out, etc, etc. He was obviously aiming to get me sacked. My bosses also knew all too well what he was up to. To their credit, whatever their own right wing or apolitical views, they quietly asked him to leave the room, and then carried on as if they had never heard anything. Neither they nor anyone else ever mentioned this outburst again.

The other, personal, incident occurred later in the war when I was a sparetime firewatcher in Battersea power station. I heard a V1 (doodlebug) coughing overhead. By now, anyone knew very well that this meant the thing was likely to come down on top of us. At that moment, I happened to be in the mains room, many storeys up within it, half way up a ladder. Luckily for me, somewhere else got hit instead. But, during those long seconds, I was totally unable to decide whether to climb up that ladder or down it!

My moment of terror contrasted with the everyday attitude one had normally had for some years by then. For example, the trades council continued its regular meetings throughout the war, bombing or no bombing. In particular, I can remember participating in terrific debates which arose out of the Communist Party's campaign for a Second Front. Our opposition to the Communist Party attracted an amount of sympathy which still surprises me – not least given that the air raid warnings went off during the discussion. But everybody had become too blasé to interrupt the meeting to go down to a shelter. We simply lay down on the floor when the explosions came too near.

Particularly during the later stages of the war, we did some regular open air speaking for the ILP. Bill Hunter and I used to speak regularly on Clapham Common and for Chiswick ILP on Turnham Green. Although we were putting an anti-war position, we always got a hearing. One reason was that, until June 1941, the Communist Party had itself been anti-war. So we were often assumed to be carrying on a tradition from which they had departed. But apart from this, a considerable segment of the audience was sometimes made up of Italian prisoners of war.

One particular internationalist occasion which I am proud to have been present at was a meeting organised by the Labour Party on May Day 1943 in Denison House, near Victoria Station, for German prisoners of war. At that time, German prisoners of war were forbidden to use public transport, yet the meeting seemed enormous. It was addressed in German by a member of the London County Council who was speaking officially for the Labour Party. Margaret Dewar and I went there to participate and to meet some of the audience. Around these months, we also used to go to places where they were housed, to exchange opinions and cigarettes. At one such place – a Catholic monastery in South-west London (or possibly it was no more than a day centre) – we got talking also with some people who were in Sir Richard Acland's independent left party, Common Wealth. This was the origin of some activities in Battersea which we engaged in jointly with this grouping.

One activity which we engaged in via the London ILP was to

distribute a leaflet during the winter of 1944-45 called *Four Ways to Help the Flying Bomb Victims*. It demanded:

'The requisitioning by the government of country mansions for evacuees. Empty property in the West End of London to be taken over, and furnished with whatever is necessary to adapt the cellars for shelter purpose, [a big increase in billeting allowances, and] rent relief in the case of damaged property.'

The leaflet was drafted by Bill Morris and me, and was directed at 'all local working class organisations'.

Bomb damage was also the occasion for my most direct involvement in industrial struggle for many years. This began from around the end of the war in Europe and hinged on Alf Loughton.

Along with his age group, Alf had eventually been called up. In the army, he used all educational forums to maximum political effect. After a year or two, he was discharged as an invalid because of a chest problem. Immediately, he returned to his trade as a bricklayer. For a time, he was in a position to move around the country. He remained very much in his element, agitating and organising among unorganised building workers. When in London he had found his previous base in Wandsworth Labour Party dormant. So, without compromising his membership, he allied himself with us in Battersea ILP because of our industrial activities. When those Trotskyists in the RCP stood Jock Haston as candidate in the Neath by-election during May of 1945, Alf found work down in South Wales as a bricklayer so as to help them. Next, he found employment with Battersea Borough Council building works department on bomb damage repair.

During the later stages of the war, Battersea had been particularly heavily hit by V1s and V2s, So much so, that a virtual army of labour was recruited to carry out first aid repair on large segments of housing. This was to help those people who had been bombed out, as whole streetfuls had been, and who were having to live in overcrowded school buildings and air raid shelters.

Throughout the war, Ernest Bevin and the Labour part of the government (aided from June 1941 by the Communist Party) had been developing so-called Joint Production Committees: in return for greater productivity, workers were supposedly to help plan production. So Battersea Council organised a committee of stewards elected from every site. This committee elected its own chairman. But, taking the minutes as its secretary, was a council civil servant whose job was to report back to the town clerk. The committee's size can be gauged from the fact that its monthly meetings filled the small hall of Latchmere Baths. Although that committee was officially restricted to considering how work was progressing, social issues and questions of wages and hours entered its agenda increasingly. This was hardly surprising. The workers were recruited over a wide area. Many had come as volunteers from up North, others from the South Coast towns. The expense of being away from home – many, for economy's sake, were sleeping rough on the sites – simply thrust on to the committee the issue of wages and hours.

Alf, who soon represented the men employed on the south side of Lavender Hill, tried to get the committee to expand union membership on the sites. He formulated a series of demands. Outside war factories, most wages were more or less pegged. In the building industry, the official unions had lost power considerably. At that time, the Building Workers Federation was talking of an increase of a few pence an hour. So Alf started a campaign against piecework, for what became known as the 'three bob an hour'. This slogan was designed to draw in the mass of the unorganised as well as organised. It won overwhelming approval at the committee, which he persuaded to sponsor a petition for these two aims. His own aim, with the petition, was to collect addresses. When these came in by the hundred, he, Jimmy Lane and I resolved to publish a duplicated paper, *The Builders' Forward*. Alf and I produced it on a hand worked flat bed machine. Soon, dozens of workers were selling it on the larger bomb damage sites all over London. Of course, this circulation spread the petition further and gathered more addresses. Our machine became worn out, trying to keep pace with the tremendous circulation.

We were aiming, too, at countering the Communist Party which also had a considerable following among building workers. But the Communist Party was hamstrung by its industrial line which was for **spreading** piecework and 'payment by results'. This left it without a figure around which to campaign, such as so much per hour. So our campaign really hotted up. Alf was elected to the London Divisional Committee of the Amalgamated Union of Building Trade Workers. He already had a number of other building workers as part of his team. Battersea's 'production' committee had assumed a new role, one more favourable to the workers. Clark, the council servant, became worried.

The climax came early in October 1945. The committee decided there was sufficient support to call a London-wide demonstration. Leaders such as George Coppock of Alf's union were still hoping that a few more pence an hour would defuse the movement. But the massive proportions of the demonstration on 8 October amazed us all. Alf came under pressure from the Communist members of his union's district committee (which they dominated), wanting to know what he intended to do with the movement he had initiated. From the demo, Alf and a delegation detached themselves to go and deliver the petition to Nye Bevan, the new Minister of Health and Housing. The delegation received the usual string along from some civil servant and reported back to the mass meeting in the park. The question now became: what next? So, there and then, Alf and his friends organised a committee to represent each district. This committee convened a conference at Holborn Trades and Labour Club.

By now, though, the Communist Party was aware of the movement which it had had no part in developing. Indeed, the party was still trying to sell its building workers' paper along the lines of homes for the people, and payment by results. This, even though the building trades, with the exception of the electricians, had always viewed PBR as anathema. The Communist Party and the right wing union leaders (some of them involved in what later became Catholic Action) were also unambiguously for Bevan's idea that Labour councils should publicise the figures of houses they had erected, and that this should be used to stimulate building workers' ardour for productivity.

Alf intended the conference to elect an even more representative committee in order to carry the agitation deeper into the union. But at this stage the Communist Party stepped in with rough hand methods. Of course, as a non-building worker, I could not be at the Holborn meeting, but I did attend the committee meetings, which Alf chaired and where I heard his subsequent account of the Holborn defeat. At the entrance, the tables where the delegates' credentials were being examined were swept aside; into the conference, people forced their way. Their status was unclear and they may not have been building workers. The complexion of the meeting was completely changed, and Alf found that the agitation he had built had been snatched out of his hands at what seemed to be the moment of its breakthrough.

One outcome of this, though, was that the Communist Party itself lost some important building workers who now came over to Alf's view. Some of these went further and joined the RCP.

Editor's note

At this point, I can plug some gaps, but must also signal the existence of others.

Harry is indisputably correct on the large size of the 8 October march. If we take the papers of the following day, the *Daily Herald* speaks of '50 000 bomb damage repair workers' marching from Hyde Park, through the West End and back to the park, causing 'London's worst traffic jam for years'. Relatedly perhaps, the paper also mentioned 'more than 5000 of Croydon's 6000 bomb repair workers' doing similarly on that day for the same demands. On the West End, the *News Chronicle* speaks of 45 000 and lists the deputation as Alf, plus Philip Young 'of Durham County' and Alan McCleery of Paddington. Alf is reported to have 'emphasised' that that day's half day strike had been 'a token'. The men would probably down tools again, 'perhaps for a day, perhaps for a week and would go on doing so' till their demands were met. These demands can be read from a Lambeth banner in the *Chronicle*: three shillings an hour for craftsmen with labourers getting 80 per cent of that, plus (as the *Herald* confirms) a 44-hour week.

Alf's threat of further action was made on discovering that Bevan was unavailable to see him. The message which he had left for Bevan to mull over ended on an upward note:

'In view of the opposition which will be forthcoming from the employers and investors, we submit that the same answer which you gave to the building rings – to set up government plants to supply the national needs of building materials – would be appropriate. That is, the Labour government should instruct local councils to take control of all building operations under a direct labour scheme.

The committee was in no way far ahead of its supporters:

'When the demonstrators returned to Hyde Park some of them called for an immediate strike, but... were told that the rank and file committee must have an opportunity to consider what further action should be taken.'

Meanwhile, up in North London, 'an immediate strike' was reportedly 'voted for' by '75 per cent of Southgate's bomb repair workers': 'Suggestions of a token strike, a go slow policy and continuing at work while an ultimatum was issued were all rejected.'

But the Hyde Park crowd had to be content with a resolution for the resignation of Coppock as General Secretary of the AUBTW. Possibly some of them were aware of a more sedate gathering, a mere five days previously, in the Dorchester Hotel, a building they had just passed. This had been to commemorate 'the twenty-fifth year of the National Joint Council for the Building Industry'. Here Coppock, 'in recognition of his services to the Council for 25 years', had been presented with 'an inscribed silver tray'. This had occurred in the presence of Bevan and of Herbert Morrison, with the latter congratulating the industry on 'not having any official strikes for 22 years' (*The Times*, 4 October 1945). The Hyde Park resolution was apparently unanimous, but Coppock merely retorted that the demonstration had been 'attended by only one per cent of the men in the London building industry' (*The Times*, 9 October 1945).

Two other things seem clear. One is the immediate trigger for demonstrating. 8 October was a Monday. On the previous Friday, as one 'shop steward, working in South-west London' stated to *The Times* of the Monday, 'the men [had] found their pay reduced by about 30s [a week] owing to the reduction in hours from 54 to 44' at the end of summer time. Here too, Coppock had been on hand to round this report off with a belittling remark: the movement was, he said, 'an annual threat – an attempt to bully us to concede the principle of Sunday work'. But, as we have seen, the Monday was to prove more than an autumn ritual. And the 11-strong committee was already claiming to represent about 30 boroughs. As Alf (if we can surmise it to be him) remarked, negotiations 'had been in progress for several months' and the aim now was to speed them up.

The next evening, no doubt flushed by the demonstration, the committee was said to be calling a meeting 'for the coming weekend' so as to 'elect a more representative committee'. Whether this occurred so speedily and, if so, whether this was the occasion which saw the CPers' misbehaviour mentioned by Harry is not clear. Alf is quoted by Margaret Dewar (in her letters to Hugo which were mentioned at the start of this chapter) as reporting the Communist Party's thuggery by mid-January of 1946.

The other thing is even more important. The autumn 1945 builders' movement took place against a background of widespread dock and other strikes which were often reported on the same newspaper pages. Viewed from Hugo's vantage point in Germany, 'the whole union organisation' seemed to be 'beginning to crack, the crust... being broken from below' (quoted in Margaret Dewar's transcript, 1 and 5 November 1945).

What is not clear is the length of the builders' movement and also of Harry's involvement with it. Margaret Dewar's letters speak of Harry as 'immersed in work with the builders', and, even more tantalisingly, of a builders' petition and of an 'enormous' meeting in Hyde Park by **May**. Conceivably, the papers were so obsessed with wider affairs as simply to miss it. In any case, demonstration sizes are always hard to estimate: during October, Alf was to mention 90 000 to Margaret.

At all events, by January 1946 Margaret was writing that the movement had 'obviously... at present petered out'.

Her letters give further dimensions of Harry's activities. Around the winter of 1944-45 he seems to have felt restless about the ILP, fearing that it would reaffiliate to Labour and that the counter-affiliationists were hopeless. In 1944, he had resigned (Margaret wrote, 'impulsively') from the ILP's London Divisional Council. For a few days during late April 1945, he even toyed with joining the RCP. Whatever problems he was going through – whether political, personal or both – he kept going. Most important, he did so in a creative way. Apart from the builders' struggle about which he seems to have felt optimistically all along, he was reported during and after April 1945 as being 'involved in some research on the Battersea Labour Party over the past [words indistinct] years and is interviewing old people and digging up old books'. With Daisy and Reg Groves, he had been doodlebugged. Luckily, Marjorie and the boys had already been evacuated. But most of his books and papers had been destroyed. He had had to go and live in Twickenham. Conceivably, the wartime disruptions and destructions had made him fear for the continuity of the Battersea labour movement's memory.

By 9 August, he 'seems to regain his old fighting spirit'. He was now for approaching Labour Party members with a revolutionary Socialist programme so as to help them fight their right leaders. He was also prepared to envisage that 'we' (Margaret's words) affiliate to the Labour Party. As before, such a question was merely tactical, his friends and closest neighbours, the Groves, had stayed with Labour throughout. And it did not stop him making a 'very good speech' to the ILP's London Divisional Council. Here, the right wing took its lead from that party's parliamentarians who had long been for reaffiliating to Labour as a body. Harry and others helped outvote this line. However, one test of the ILP's significance in **any** perspective came in Battersea during 1946 with a parliamentary by-election. Here, high hopes and heavy efforts were shattered by a derisory vote of a few hundred. This blow seems to have knocked the stuffing out of Battersea ILP. And at this point, he and his circle seem to have ceased to act as an even informally coherent group.

Notes

1. By 1945 Kirby had reached quite a high rank in British Intelligence in India. Harry Wicks had instinctively mistrusted him.
2. This article appears in the Socialist Platform pamphlet **Harry Wicks: A Memorial**.
3. Bill Brown. As he was for some decades a very dear friend who will otherwise be forgotten, I'd like to say some things about him here, even though these come under various headings. Before 1914, his father, a German, had had a baker's shop in Poplar. During that war, this was smashed up by a mob, and his father was interned in the Isle of Man. At Poplar workhouse, Bill and his mother were either refused entry or after a time turfed out. After the war, they came to Battersea. It was being bilingual in German that was to give him that senior administrative post in the NAAFI. But, in 1923, it helped impel him into going to Germany where the revolution seemed to be coming along faster than in Britain. So he went there on the tramp, sleeping in shelters, workhouses or suchlike. When the revolution failed to arrive, he returned to Britain by getting the consulate in Hamburg to put him on a boat. This dumped him in Newcastle without any money to get back to Battersea. He later recounted his solution – to lie down in the road (there was rain falling at the time). He was rushed to hospital and eventually sent home. In 1931 and out of the YCL, he was involved with Mosley's unstable New Party – though only for a few weeks. But the next year, he and his wife were working in the Russian trade association. So they hardly wanted to become involved in our agitation for the unity of the German working class. But, by 1935 or '36, he had his own bakery business and felt able to come to our meetings in defence of Trotsky and to speak from the floor. He retained to the last his adventurous streak. In the 1950s and still comfortably married, he upped and went as a pastry cook on a luxury liner to New Zealand, where he later died.

Endnote

A S readers will have noticed, the pages after Harry's meeting with Trotsky feel flat when compared with the liveliness and sophistication of struggle which precede them. This difference is of course partly or mainly explicable by Harry's no longer being around to add, delete, relink and rethink. But another, no less inescapable, reason is surely the nature of the period they deal with – years of defeat and growing isolation. The isolation was not simply a matter of being hated and outrageously misrepresented (something Harry has just described so vividly). It also involved being treated as irrelevant by the disastrously stampeding mass of one's contemporaries.

Harry's life after 1946 was something he somehow never talked about. I now regret bitterly my failure to ask him. All I gather is that he made contact with the International Socialism group (forerunner organisation of the Socialist Workers Party) late in the 1960s. He was active in many types of IS activity. In 1975, with some of those workers and intellectuals who had left the International Socialists or been expelled during that year, he collaborated in the shortlived Workers League. But at the personal level he remained in lively contact with numerous SWPers as well as ex-International Socialist members and other comrades. And during the late 1980s most of his last public speeches were to Socialist Workers Party gatherings – for which he travelled up from Somerset to London.

Jobwise, he spent the final decade or two of his working life as an electoral registration officer in Battersea. ('What did you do in the war?', a right wing Labour interviewer had asked this applicant for the job, hoping Harry would once again commit economic suicide. 'I was a firewatcher in Battersea power station', Harry had truthfully replied.)

At the start of the 1980s, Marjorie suffered a major stroke. The move that she and Harry made from Twickenham to Somerset was in order to be near two of their three sons, plus, no less, many other members of the family. Harry's nursing of Marjorie was epic, as was the family help they received. As we have seen, his very young life may have been saved by a Dr Bean. But his collective word for medics was 'quacks'; in this too, he was continuing a generations-old working class tradition – here, an ambiguity about medical orthodoxy. Possibly he was not taking the pills he had been prescribed against high blood pressure. Anyway, during the early spring of 1989, he had a massive stroke which ended his life a week later. There were many older SWP members as well as other Socialists at his funeral, and their feelings were well drawn together, humanly and politically, in a moving speech by Duncan Hallas.

Selected Biographical Notes

Aage, Christian Alexander Robert, Count of Rosenborg (1887-1949). Prince, grandson of Christian IX, and thus a first cousin to the Danish King. He served in, and wrote a book about, the French Foreign Legion in the First World War. His mother was a princess of the French House of Orleans, and one of his grandsons has married a Bowes-Lyon, a relative of the British Queen Mother.

Archer, John Richard (1863-1932). Born in Liverpool of Irish Afro-Caribbean parents. Lived in Battersea at 55 Brynamer Road (1898-1918) and 214 Battersea Park Road. A photographer. Progressive Councillor for Latchmere Ward 1906-19, Mayor 1913-14, Labour Councillor Latchmere Ward 1919-22. Candidate Nine Elms Ward 1925, Alderman 1925-31, Councillor Nine Elms Ward 1931-32. Manager St Joseph's Roman Catholic School, Trustee Walter St Johns School, Trustee Battersea Charities. Member of the Health and Tuberculosis Committee and Board of Guardians. Pan-Africanist activities included attendance at 1900, 1919 and 1921 Congresses. President African Progress Union 1918-21. See *Battersea's Black Activist* (South London Record No 2) and Peter Fryer, *Staying Power*, 1984.

Carmichael, Duncan (1870-1926). Lived at 8 Bennerley Road, SW11. Secretary Battersea Social Democratic Federation 1908, Delegate for Shop Assistants Union to Battersea Trades and Labour Council 1905, Treasurer Trades and Labour Council 1911, Secretary British Socialist Party Battersea Branch 1912, spoke on women's suffrage at BSP first annual conference 1912. Took a prominent part in official trade union activity during the war. A member of Workers Welfare League of India with Saklatvala. See *London Trades Council 1860-1959: A History*, Lawrence and Wishart, 1950. He died shortly after General Strike, very stressed after motorcycling around London to coordinate activity.

Clancy, Jack. Of Irish descent and member of Battersea Herald League and later Plebs League, founder member of the Communist Party representing Battersea Socialist Society at Communist Unity Convention 1920. Unemployed workers' leader in first half of 1920s. In 1921 chaired lectures in Battersea by the National Council of Labour Colleges. Chairman Battersea Council of Action 1926. Active in disaffiliated Battersea Trades and Labour Council, won Winstanley Ward by-election after death of Duncan Carmichael against official Labour. Resigned from the disaffiliated party in 1928 and did not stand for re-election.

Clancy, Daisy. In Clarion Scouts and helped to run Battersea

Socialist Sunday School. Her father was railwayman and secularist. Wicks did not know whether he left the secularists with Burns to join the SDF.

Fitzgerald, Jack. Irish bricklayer, great speaker, member of Clarion Club and leading member of Socialist Party of Great Britain. Taught building at Brixton School of building in Ferndale Road (1921). Alf Laughton remembers him. See Alf Laughton, *I Remember: Autobiography of Childhood and Youth*, unpublished manuscript (nd), and is mentioned in Robert Barltrop, *The Monument*, Pluto Press, 1975.

Frankel, Jan (1906-). Czech Trotskyist, came from a poor rabbinic Jewish family. Spoke several languages perfectly. In a TB sanatorium in Italy he met the future founder of the Czech Communist Party, Lenorovic. Was a friend of Kafka. Joined the Left Opposition and went to Prinkipo to see Trotsky in 1930. The Czech police thought him responsible for all Left Opposition activity in Central Europe. Worked underground in Nazi Germany. Went back to Czechoslovakia using the name Keller or Verny. Worked with Trotsky but left Coyoacan for personal reasons in 1937. Known as John Glenn or Glenner in the USA. Briefly married the novelist Eleanor Clark. Took the side of Shachtman and Burnham in the faction fight and went with the Workers Party in 1941. Later gave up politics and became very bitter and cynical. Renamed himself John Frank, and became an American businessman, and very rich after involving himself in the Patiño tin empire. Probably now dead. See *Cahiers Leon Trotsky*, No 1, January 1979, pp67-71.

Grylewicz, Anton (1885-1971). Joined the SPD in 1912, later the USPD and KPD. German Trotskyist. Berlin district secretary of KPD. Expelled in 1927. A leading Trotskyist and Trotskyist publisher. Exiled to Paris and later the GDR. Went back to Berlin in 1955.

Hall, Otto (1891-). Elder brother of Harry Hayward. Recruited his brother to CP and studied at Lenin School 1927-30, a friend of Harry Wicks there. Took part in the expulsion of the Lovestoneites and served on the Central Committee of the CPUSA. Active in civil rights cases such as that involving Angelo Herndon. See *Black Bolshevik* by Harry Haywood for numerous references.

Haywood, Harry (1898-1985). Born Hall. Afro-American recruited by CPUSA in 1925 and studied at Lenin School in Moscow 1927-30. Initiated debate on self-determination and prominent in the 'Black Nation' thesis. Fought in Spanish Civil War. Expelled in 1959 for 'Left Sectarianism'. Became associated with the Revolutionary Action Movement and the League of Revolutionary Black Workers. In the 1970s his writings were collected and published by Maoists seeking to create a new Communist Party. They also helped him to write his autobiography. Details of his life and thought in *Black Bolshevik: Autobiography of an Afro-American Communist*, Lake View Press, Chicago, 1978. See *EAB* for a summary of the debates in which he was involved.

Harling, Horace (1887-1969). A woodcarver living at 100 Grandison Road, SW11 in 1919, and at 122 Grandison Road in 1940. Councillor for Shaftesbury Ward 1919-34, Mayor 1923-24, candidate St John's Ward 1934, Alderman 1934-45, Councillor Winstanley Ward 1945-59, Alderman 1959-65.

Holmes, Johnny. Ex-SPGB, Secretary of Wandsworth Unemployed Committee and member of Communist Party. Very active in 1921 and 22. See Michael Ward *The Unemployed in South West London 1918-23* (draft manuscript), and *Red Flag over the Workhouse*, Labour and Social History Group, 1980.

Joy, Bert. Member of the Amalgamated Society of Woodworkers, CPer in Tooting. On CC of CP. Known as the 'Tooting Trotsky'. Supported the South West London Anti-War Committee in the 1930s. See Reg Groves, *The Balham Group*, Pluto Press, 1974.

Kirby, Edward Stuart (1909-). Professor, once of Aston University. After leaving the Marxist Group and teaching in Japan, he spent a period as an economic researcher in the League of Nations before the war. He spent the entire war in Indian Army Intelligence and censorship, rising to the rank of Lieutenant-Colonel, in Eastern, Southern and Western Asia. In the latter two parts of the world there were no dangerous Japanese soldiers but many nationalist movements. His academic work has consisted of somewhat tedious economic geographies of Siberia and Asia – the unkind might call them bomb-aiming manuals. (Like him, many of the authors of similar work, such as Connolly, Wheeler etc, have an intelligence or Foreign Office background, though they often do it better.) It is unknown whether he maintained some kind of link with the security services after the war, though some students were suspicious of him during the student agitation of 1968-70. He contributed articles and letters with extreme right wing views to military journals during the 1970s, and in whose correspondence columns puzzled Lieutenant-Colonels had to assure him that they did not think the Greens were part of a sinister Communist plot for world domination. Curiously, he is not named in John Archer's unpublished thesis, *Trotskyism in Britain 1931-37*, though the reference to 'another man' on page 108 is probably him. According to Al Richardson he may have been almost as important as Harber in the early period. Though there is little reference to him in the documents, his name crops up a lot in interviews – just in passing. (Research by Ted Crawford. A list of his publications and record of service in the Indian Army is available in Socialist Platform Archive.)

Krumbein, Charles (1889-1947). Joined Socialist Party in 1910 and a founder member of the Communist Labor Party in 1919. Chosen for the first class at the Lenin School in 1926. Worked for the Comintern in the 1920s and 1930s. While in China in 1927 used the name Isadore Dreiser. Did six months in prison in Britain (1930) for using a false passport. Arrested in the USA (1934) and served 15 months for charges relating to his links with the Sorge spy ring in China (1930-31). From 1938-47 the Treasurer of the CPUSA. See *BDAL*.

Lanchester, Elsa (Elizabeth Sullivan) (1902-1986). A dancer from Battersea, later well known, danced in aid of Russian Famine Relief. Married Charles Laughton in 1928. Played in numerous films, but most famous as the mate of the monster in *Bride of Frankenstein*.

Lane, James Frederick (Jimmy) (1905-1986). Ex-Socialist Labour Party, once apprentice bricklayer, lived in Elsey Road on Shaftesbury Park Estate for 45 years. Labour candidate Park Ward 1925 and candidate for disaffiliated Battersea TLC in LCC elections 1928. Councillor Park Ward 1934-37, Councillor Winstanley Ward 1937-45, Councillor Vicarage Ward 1949-56, Councillor Bolingbroke Ward 1956-65, Mayor 1950-51, Housing Chair 1945-61. Retired from Council in 1965 when it merged with Wandsworth. Chairman of Battersea Society.

Larsen, Aksel (1897-1972). Went to Lenin School, became a Zinovievist. A letter in German to the Danish CP told the party to give no key post to him but this was ignored, either because the party was so small or because nobody could read German. Became party President in 1930 with the eviction of the Jensen-Thogersen group. Elected to Parliament in 1932 as a result of his unemployment work. Arrested in the war in 1942, survived Sachsenhausen camp, and was minister without portfolio in the first postwar government. A loyal Stalinist until after Hungary. Expelled from DKP in 1958. Helped found the Socialist Peoples Party which had 11 members of Parliament in 1960. Led it until his death.

Manning, Henry G. An old Independent Labour Party member, working as signalman in Victoria South Box and a delegate to Battersea TLC for Battersea Branch of Amalgamated Society of Railway Servants.

Mason, Charles Edward (Charlie) (-1942). Journeyman compositor, lived at 455 Battersea Park Road 1900, and 'Mulbera' Victoria Road, Farnborough, Hants 1928. Once a Burns supporter. Member of Battersea Labour League from 1890s. Progressive Councillor Latchmere Ward (1900-06), Delegate for the London Society of Compositors on Battersea TLC and on Executive Committee of TLC 1908. Treasurer Battersea Labour League's Coal Club (1908), Labour Councillor Latchmere Ward 1912-19, Charlotte Despard's agent in 1918 election, Secretary Battersea TLC and delegate to National Conference. Labour Councillor 1919-34, Mayor 1924-25, Labour agent in Battersea.

Okines, Wally. Of 37 Middleton Road and later 49 Lavender Hill, Battersea Rise. Insurance agent for Planet Friendly Insurance and later Cooperative Insurance Manager (1919). (Insurance work was often a refuge for victimised militants and left wingers.) Veteran member of Battersea Socialist League, very interested in cultural matters. Represented Battersea Socialist Society at Communist Unity Convention 1920. Labour Councillor Winstanley Ward 1919-28. Supporter of the *Herald*.

Pocock, Tom (-1945). Born at Crowhurst, Surrey. Signalman at Victoria North Box. Lived at 49 Odger Street, SW11 1909, 51 Odger Street 1919, 27 St Matthews Street, SW11 on Latchmere Estate 1925. ILP member 1908 and its Secretary 1910-11, candidate Shaftesbury Ward 1909. Member Amalgamated Society of Railway Servants and their delegate on Battersea TLC, later NUR. Represented NUR at Labour Party Conference 1918. Labour Alderman 1919-25, Alderman 1937-45. On EC of NUR, often at odds with Henry Manning, and very hostile to the CP in 1920s.

Smith, Frank. Lived at 24 Salcott Road 1925. Ex-SLPer. Member of AEU. Battersea TC delegate to London TC, Red International of Labour Unions. Labour candidate Latchmere Ward 1925. On EC of Battersea TLC. Member of London TUC. AEU Presidential candidate 1945. From 1945 lived at 17 Wolverton Avenue, Kingston-upon-Thames and stood as Labour candidate in Kingston Canbury Ward.

Soemus (spelt Soermus in Cabinet Minutes). A violinist, arrested in early 1919 for making 'violent speeches'. See Wrigley, *Lloyd George and the Challenge of Labour*, Harvester Wheatsheaf,1990.

Tapsell, Wally, Walter (-1938). Joined CP at 16, becoming a member of the EC and National Organiser of the Young Communist League and manager of *Daily Worker*. Joined International Brigade, arriving in Spain in February 1937. Killed near Belchite. See *The Book of the XV Brigade. Records of British American, Canadian and Irish Volunteers in the XV International Brigade in Spain 1936-1938*. (Commissariat of War, XV Brigade, Madrid, 1938).

Thompson, Bonar (1888-). Well-known orator in Battersea, called 'the Hyde Park Orator'. An anti-war speaker during the First World War. See RH Foy, *Bonar Thompson: The Old Days at Carnearney*, Antrim Historical Society, 1991, and his autobiography, *Hyde Park Orator*, Jarrolds, 1936.

Varran, Mrs. Labour activist in North Battersea Women's Section of Labour Party, taxi driver husband, visited Moscow and saw Harry there.

Wicks, Harry (1889-1957). Harry's American namesake. During his long career as a member of many radical groups he was also an undercover agent for private investigating firms. After his expulsion from the CPUSA in 1938 he sold information to the FBI and the Immigration Service, but his FBI file concludes that he was unreliable and he may have remained a dedicated Communist all his life. Before the formation of the CPUSA he was active in the Industrial Workers of the World and the Socialist Party. Became an important leader in the Proletarian Party which came out of the Michigan Socialist Party which had been one of the five founding groups of the CP. It refused to join new groups, and was based mainly in Michigan and adjoining states. He joined the CP in 1922 and was at one time editor of the *Daily Worker*, representative to the Profintern, district organiser and overseas traveller. Wicks later edited the *Southern Worker* under the pseudonym of James Allen. His real name may have been Richard Proctor. See *EAL* for organisational histories and *BDAL* for biography.

Zack, Joseph (Kornfeder) (1897-1963). Known in the CPUSA as 'Joseph Cass' on some occasions. Joined Socialist Party in 1916 and was also attracted to the IWW. Joined the Communist Party as a founder member 1919. From 1927-30 attended the Lenin School. A strong supporter of dual unionism, expelled in 1934. He was associated with various political groups, including some with IWW and Trotskyist connections. He could not get his wife and child out of Europe, and they died in the camps. Later a bitter anti-Communist. Became a friendly witness for the US government in investigations of the left. See *BDAL*.

References

DLB: *Dictionary of Labour Biography*.
BDSU: *Biographical Dictionary of the Soviet Union*, Cambridge, 1990.
BDAL: *Biographical Dictionary of the American Left*, edited by Bernard K John Poll and Harvey Klehr, Greenwood, NY, 1986.
EAL: *Encyclopedia of the American Left*, edited by Marie-Jo Buhle, Paul Buhle and Dan Georgakas, Garland, NY, 1990.

The above information was supplied by the following members of Wandsworth History Workshop: Sean Creighton, Mike Squires, Martin Tupper. Information also came from Dave Nellor and Chris Wrigley. Dan Georgakas supplied information on the American left.

Name List

Aage, Christian Alexander Robert, Count of Rosenborg (1887-1949), see biographical note

Ablett, Noah MP (1883-1935), see **DLB**, Volume 3

Abramov, Arkady Mikhailovich

Acland, Sir Richard (1906-), leader of Common Wealth Party

Adams, Ted, boxing instructor at Caius College, Cambridge Settlement in Battersea

Aldred, Guy (1886-1963), Anarchist

Amanullah, King of Afghanistan (1891-1960)

Andrews, Councillor, left wing member of Council of Action

Archer, John (1863-1932), see biographical note

Arnot, Robin Page (1891-1986), leading member of CPGB

Askew, JB, old member of SDF, who died in Moscow when HW was there

Astbury, Mr Justice, Rt Hon Sir John Meir (1860-1939)

Atholl, Duchess of, Murray, Katharine Marjory (1874-1960), see **DNB**

'Auld Archie', a Scot at Lenin School

Baldwin, Stanley (1867-1947), British Conservative Prime Minister

Barbusse, Henri (1873-1935), French writer, apologist for Stalinism

Barrett, Jim

Bax, Ernest Belfort (1854-1926), British Socialist

Bean, Doctor in Falcon Road

Bell, Tom (1882-1940), CPGB leader

'Bennett, AJ', Comintern representative (David Petrovsky but really Max Goldfarb)

Beauchamp, Kay (1899-1992), well-born Stalinist hack

Bevan, Nye (Aneurin) (1897-1960), left Labour MP

Bierut, Boleslaw (1892-1956), Polish Stalinist

Bond, Ralph

Booth, Charles (1840-1926), reformer

Bradley, Gerry

Bradley, Lee

Brailsford, Henry Noel Archibald (1873-1958), see **DLB**, Volume 2

Brandler, Heinrich (1881-1967), German Communist leader

Brockway, Fenner (1888-1988), left Labour MP

Browder, Earl (1891-1973), CPUSA leader during Popular Front period

Brown, Bill

Brown, Ernie H (1892-1967), CPGB member

Brown, Isabel (1894-1984), wife of Ernie

'Bruno'

Budden, Olive (Mrs Page Arnot)

Bukharin, Nikolai (1888-1938), see **BDSU**

Burns, Emile (1889-1972), Stalinist intellectual

Burns, John (1858-1943), trade union leader

Burgess, Joe

Cairns, a magistrate

Cadman, F, bricklayer, founder member of SPGB

Campbell-Bannerman, Sir Henry (1836-1907), British politician

Cannon, James Patrick (1890-1974), US Trotskyist leader

Canterbury, Archbishop of

Capper, Dave

Carmichael, Duncan (1870-1926), see biographical note
Carpenter, Vic
'Cass, Joseph', see Zack
Chaloner, headmaster of Harry's school
Champion, Harry (1857-1928)
Chen Tu Hsu, Ch'en Tu-Hsiu, Chen Duxiu (1879-1942) Chinese Trotskyist leader
Chervenko, Vulko (1900-?), later Bulgarian Prime Minister, at Lenin School
Mde Chervenko, Dimitrov's daughter, at Lenin School
Churchill, Sir Winston Spencer (1876-1965), Tory Prime Minister
Citrine, Walter (1887-1983), right wing TUC leader
Clancy, Jack, see biographical note
Clancy, Daisy, see biographical note
'Clark', a leading American Lovestoneite, a **Daily Worker** reporter
John R Clynes (1869-1949), union leader
Cohen, Rose, British Communist, sent to the camps
Cohn, Felix
Cohn, Oscar
Cooper, Frank (Arthur Francis George), (?-1982)
Coppock, George, Secretary Building Workers Federation
Cousins (a busman arrested during General Strike)
Crawford, Helen, ILP intellectual, joined CPGB, then left
Cripps, Sir Stafford (1889-1952), Labour MP
Crowley, Aleister (1875-1947), well-known Satanist and upper class degenerate
Cullen, Dr CK

Despard, Charlotte, (née French) (1844-1939)
Dewar, Hugo (1908-1980), pioneer British Trotskyist
Dewar, Marguerite (1901-), wife of Hugo
Dewar, Roma, sister of Hugo
Dewey, John (1859-1952), American philosopher
Dobb, Maurice (1900-1976), economist and Stalinist
Douglas, FR
Dowdall, Steve (1896-1982), and family
Duncan, Kathleen, took a party of left wing women to Moscow
Dutt, Clemens brother of Rajani Palme Dutt
Dutt, Rajani Palme (1896-1974), leading CPGB theoretician

Edwards, a public speaker convicted (possibly Bob Edwards, ILP, 1905-1990)
'Ercoli' (Togliatti, Palmiro) (1893-1964), leading Italian Stalinist

Fenn, bricklayer, SPGB member
Ferguson, Maurice, CP member in Moscow
Field, BJ (Max Gould) (1900-1977), US Trotskyist
Findlay, TUC General Council member
Fitzgerald, Jack, see biographical note
Foster, William Zebulon (1881-1961), CPUSA leader
Fox, Ralph (1900-1936), CPGB member, killed in Spain
France, Anatole (Jacques Anatole François-Thibault) (1844-1921)
Frank, Pierre (1905-1984), French Trotskyist
Frankel, Jan (1906-?), see biographical note

Gallacher, William (Willie) (1881-1965), MP, CPGB leader and teetotaller
Garibaldi (1807-1882)
Garvey, Marcus (1887-1940), see EB
Gaster, Jack, Stalinist lawyer

Geard, Walter, old SDF member
Gilbert, Mrs, friend of Harry's mother in Lombard Road
Glading, Percy, CP member in Moscow, sent to prison in UK for espionage
Gossip, Alex, furniture workers' union and CPGB leader
Graham, Wally (Nardell) (1912-?)
Groves, Reginald (1908-1988), pioneer British Trotskyist
Grylewicz, Anton (1885-1971), see biographical note
Guser, Sergei Ivanovich (Yakov Davidovich Drabkin) (1874-1973)

Haldane, Charlotte
Hall, Otto (1891-), see biographical note
Harler, Mr
Harling, Horace (1887-1969), see biographical note
Harber, Denzil Dean (1909-1966), early British Trotskyist
Hart, Dr Alex Tudor, Stalinist
Haston, Jock (James Ritchie) (1913-1986), British Trotskyist
Hayward, Harry, 'Hall' (1898-1985), see biographical note
Haywood, 'Big Bill' (1869-1928), American trade unionist
Healy, Claude, Westminster CPGB organiser, Secretary of Typewriter Mechanics Trade Union
Healy, Gerry (Thomas Gerard) (1913-1989), British Trotskyist leader
Hicks, George (1879-1954), TUC GC
Hill, Rowland
Hippe, Oskar (1900-1990), German Trotskyist
Holmes, Johnny, see biographical note
Hopper, station superintendent at Victoria
Horner, Arthur Lewis (1894-1968), see **DLB**, Volume 5
Horrabin, Frank (1884-1962)
Horrabin, Winifred
Hore-Belisha, Leslie (1894-1957), Conservative politician
Hunter, Bill (1920-), British Trotskyist
Hunter, stationmaster at Deal
Allen Hutt (1901-1973), CP member in Moscow

Ibsen, Henrik Johann (1828-1906), Norwegian playwright
Inkpin, Albert (1884-1944), CPGB leader

Jackson, Thomas Alfred (1879-1955), CPGB philosopher
Jackson, E Starkey (1909-1943), British Trotskyist
Jagger, John
James, CLR (Cyril Lionel Robert) (1901-1989), West Indian Trotskyist and writer
Jessop, Sam, an activist in the NUR in 1920
'Joss', on Agitprop work, Comintern functionary, sent to the camps
Joffe, Adolf Abramovich (1883-1927), see **BDSU**
Johns, Margaret (1912-), British Trotskyist
Joy, Bert, see biographical note
Jungclas, Georg (1902-1975), German Trotskyist

Kautsky, Karl (1854-1938), Austrian Marxist
Katayama, Sen (1859-1933), veteran Japanese revolutionary
Kenyatta, Jomo (c1894-1978), Kenyan nationalist leader
Kerrigan, Peter (1899-1977), Stalinist functionary
Kimche, Jon (1909-)
Kirby, Edward Stuart (1909-), see biographical note
Kirov, Sergei M (1896-1934), see **BDSU**

Kirsanova, wife of Yaroslavsky and director of Lenin School
Klugmann, James (1912?-1977), CPGB leader
Krumbein, Charlie (1889-1947), see biographical note
Kun, Bela (1886-1939), Hungarian Communist leader

Lanchester, Edith, mother of Elsa
Lanchester, Elsa (Elizabeth Sullivan) (1902-1986), see biographical note
Lane, James Frederick (Jimmy) (1905-1986), see biographical note
Lansbury, George (1859-1940), see **DLB**, Volume 2
Larkin, 'Big' Jim (1876-1947), Irish union leader
Larkin (jnr), Jim, friend of HW at Lenin School
Larsen, Aksel (1897-1972), see biographical note
Laski, Harold J (1893-1950), Labour Party intellectual
Lavey, a labour dustman
Lawlers, family
Lenin, Vladimir Ilyich Ulyanov (1870-1924)
Daniel de Leon (1852-1914), American Socialist
Lesoil, Léon (1892-1942), Belgian Trotskyist
Lisner, Ted
Loring, Alice, labour activist, great friend of Wicks, died in Swaffield Road Old Peoples Home (ex-workhouse)
Loughton, Alf, an apprentice bricklayer, later Wicks' brother-in-law, later Mayor of Wandsworth
Lovell, Bill, boxing instructor at Caius College Cambridge Settlement in Battersea
Lovenadze, actually Lominadze, Vissarion Vissarionovich (1897-1935), Comintern delegate to China, regarded as a 'left', committed suicide
Lozovsky, Salomon (1878-1952), see **BDSU**

Macdonald, James Ramsay (1866-1937), see **DLB**, Volume 1
Macfarlane, CJ
McLaren, John
McLeery, Alan
McManus, Arthur, CPGB leader
Mace, Rodney, labour historian
McIlhone, Bob, leading Scottish CPGB member, close friend of HW
McSwiney, Terence (1879-1920), Mayor of Cork
'Magharab', upper class Indian at Lenin School
Mahon, John, CPGB leader, biographer of Harry Pollitt
Malone, Colonel l'Estrange, MP (1890-1965), see **DLB**, Volume 1
Mann, Tom (1856-1941), pioneer CPGB member
Mannin, Ethel (1900-1984), novelist
Manning, Henry G, see biographical note
Manuilsky, Dmitri Z (1883-1952), Comintern General Secretary
Marx, Eleanor (1855-1898), daughter of Karl
Mason, Charlie (?-1942), see biographical note
Matlow, Bert (Albert) (1898-1987), early British Trotskyist
Maxton, Jimmy (1885-1946), MP, leader of ILP
May, Betty
Mayakovsky, Vladimir (1894-1930), Russian writer and poet
Mints, Professor Ivan, Israel Israelovich (1896-), see **BDSU** and **Biographic Diction-ary of the USSR**, 1954
Molinier, Raymond (1904-), French Trotskyist, now living in Paris
Molotov, Vyacheslav M (Scriabin) (1890-1986), see **BDSU**
Morris, 'Donkey', a raconteur at Battersea Labour Club
'Morris, George', a Ukrainian at Lenin School

Morris, William (1834-1896), writer, designer, social theorist
Morris, Will, wrote children's books
Mosley, Sir Oswald (1896-1980), British Fascist leader
Mott, George
Murphy, John Thomas (1888-1966), early CPGB leader
Murphy, Jack

Naville, Denise, French Trotskyist
Naville, Pierre (1904-), French Trotskyist
Neuman, Heinz (1902-1937), German Stalinist, murdered in purges
Newbold, JY Walton (1888-1955) pioneer CPGB member, MP
Newbold, Marjorie
Nicholls, Max
Noel, Conrad Reverend (1869-1942), see **DLB**, Volume 2

'Ochlov', a lascar seaman at Lenin School and friend of HW
O'Donnell, Peadar (1891-?), Socialist and Irish nationalist, alive in 1980
Okines, Wally, see biographical note
Ernie Osborne, painted a banner for Battersea Plebs League
Henry Osborne, brother of Ernie

Packman, Lydia, Labour Research Department
Padley, Walter (1916-1984), ILP MP
Pallieres, Jeanne Martin des, wife of Leon Sedov
Paling, Wilfred (1883-1971), Labour MP
Palmer, Mr, farrier in Lombard Road
Pauker, Anna (1893-1960), Romanian Stalinist
Paul, Willie, ex-SLP member, ILP member, joined CPGB
Peluso, librarian at Marx-Engels Institute, died in camps
'Percy', a Czechoslovak, Comintern functionary
Perry (Ernie), Ernest George (1908-), Labour MP
Price, Morgan Phillips (1885-1973), Liberal then Labour politician
Pizer, Dorothy
Pritt, Dennis Nowell (1887-1972), Stalinist lawyer
Pocock, Tom (?-1945), see biographical note
Pollitt, Harry (1890-1960), CPGB General Secretary
Pollitt, Marjorie, wife of Harry
'Porter', a Canadian at Lenin School
Postgate, Daisy (1892-1971), see **DLB**, Volume 2
Postgate, Raymond (1896-1971), see **DLB**, Volume 2
Potter, George (1832-1893), see **DLB**, Volume 6
Powell, Charlie
Pugh, Arthur Sir (1870-1955), Labour politician
Purcell, Albert Arthur (1872-1935), see **DLB**, Volume 1
Purkiss, Stewart

Radek, Karl (1885-1939), see **BDSU**
Feodor Raskolnikov (1892-1939), see **BDSU**
Rathbone, Harold, LRD
Reade, Arthur E
Riazanov, David B (Goldendach) (1870-1938), see **BDSU**
Richards, Danny, a referencer at the Lenin School
Richardson, Alec, USAWC
Ridley, Frank (Francis Ambrose) (1897-), ILP member, author
Robson, RW

Trotsky, Lev Davidovich (Bronstein) (1879-1940)
Tsiurupa, AD (1870-1928)
Turner, Jack, TUC GC

Varran, Mrs, see biographical note
'Vuk', probably Svetoslar Vukmanovic, Tempo, a Yugoslav, later party historian in Yugoslavia

Waller, Tom, known as 'workhouse Waller', ex-SPGB, led agitation against the workhouse
Watts, Bob, a signalman
Webb, Henry at Lenin School
Webb, Sydney (1859-1947), and Beatrice (1858-1943), see **DLB**, Volume 2
Weston, George (Morris), British Trotskyist
White, Fred
White, George, Secretary of Battersea CPGB
Wicks Ben, HW's uncle
Wicks, FR, HW's father
Wicks, Harry (1889-1957), see biographical note
Wilkinson, Ellen (1891-1947), Labour Minister
Williams, Bert (1895-1958), fellow student at Lenin School
Willis, Ted, Lord (1918-), Stalinist youth leader
Wilson, Sir Henry Hughes (1864-1922), British Field Marshal and reactionary, killed by IRA
Wimbush, Arthur
Wincott, Len (1910-), mutineer at Invergordon, sent to Russian camps (see **Invergordon Mutineer**, 1974)
Wolfe, Bertram David (1896-1977), CPUSA member, later biographer of Lenin
Woodburn, Arthur (1890-1978), Labour politician
Woolley, Ernie, CPGB organiser in Shipley

Yaroslavsky, Yemel'yan Mikhailovich (Emilian), pseudonyms Minej Israelovich Gubelman (1878-1943), see **BDSU**
'Yen' Chinese friend of HW's at Lenin School
Young, Phillip

Zack, Joseph (1897-1963), see biographical note
Zamenhof, Lazarus Ludovic (1859-1917), founder of Esperanto
Zinoviev, Grigorii Yevseyevich Radomyslsky (1883-1936), see **BDSU**

References
DLB: Dictionary of Labour Biography
BDSU: Biographical Dictionary of the Soviet Union, Cambridge, 1990
BDAL: Biographical Dictionary of the American Left
EAL: Encyclopedia of the American Left

Index

SOCIALIST PLATFORM LTD
Other Books Available

Harry Wicks 1905-1989
A memorial pamphlet, it includes four essays by Harry: an introduction to the Comintern's *The Organisation and Construction of Communist Parties* (1973), 'Notes on the History of Bolshevism' (1934), 'British Trotskyism in the Thirties' (1971), and 'Labour and the War' (1938), plus an interview given by Harry to Al Richardson in 1978. An excellent companion to this book.
Special offer: £1.00 + 40p p+p

FA Ridley, *The Assassins*
The classic account of the famous Islamic sect.
Special offer: £2.95 + 80p p+p

RS Baghavan, *An Introduction to the Philosophy of Marxism*
An excellent introduction to materialism and the natural sciences.
Special offer: £1.50 + 50p p+p

Sam Bornstein + Al Richardson, *War and the International*
The British Trotskyist movement from 1937 to 1949.
Special offer: £2.95 + 80p p+p

Sam Bornstein + Al Richardson, *Two Steps Back*
The Communist Party of Great Britain and the working class from 1935 to 1945.
£3.50 + 50p p+p

CLR James and British Trotskyism
An interview.
£1.00 + 30p p+p

For multiple orders, p+p is 10 per cent of the total price. Overseas rates available on request. Overseas payment in Pounds Sterling by International Money Order. Cheques/IMOs payable to Socialist Platform Ltd. Send orders to:

Socialist Platform Ltd, BCM 7646, London WC1N 3XX

Revolutionary History
The leading English language Marxist history journal

Since its appearance in March 1988, *Revolutionary History* has established itself as the foremost Marxist history journal in the English language. In the first four volumes we have featured a wide range of documents, statements and articles from the revolutionary Marxist movement which have been unobtainable for many years or have never appeared before in an English translation. We have also published historical studies which have either been commissioned or submitted, or translated from such prestigious publications as the *Cahiers Léon Trotsky*. Each issue of *Revolutionary History* also features an extensive book review section and a lively correspondence page.

Revolutionary History, Volume 4, nos 1/2 is a 400 page book entitled *The Spanish Civil War: The View From The Left*, and is a unique collection of eyewitness accounts, contemporary analyses and modern investigations from a whole range of non-Stalinist viewpoints. The cost is UK: £10.95, elsewhere: £12.95. Volume 4, no 3 is an intensive account of the Trotskyist movement in Bolivia during the Revolution of 1952, and Volume 4, no 4 investigates the Trotskyist movement in South Africa. The cost for each is UK: £3.50, Europe: £4.00, elsewhere: £5.00.

Volume 5 of *Revolutionary History* will appear in 1993. Subscriptions cost UK: £14.00, Europe: £16.00, elsewhere: £20.00. Copies of most back issues of *Revolutionary History* are still available, write in for details.

Overseas orders in Pounds Sterling by International Money Order. Make cheques or IMOs payable to Socialist Platform Ltd. Send orders to:

Socialist Platform Ltd, BCM 7646, London WC1N 3XX

Introduction

During the 1950s and 60s, metal, grease, oil, leathers and attitude bucked tradition and sprouted a revolution in machine masculinity, discarding ephemera for stretched tanks, clip-on handlebars and linear lines. Owning and riding a café racer was about elemental emotions, where the relationship between man and machine was visceral, borne out of intuition and a unique vision that was thoughtful, intuitive and insightful. To some it may have appeared illogical, whilst to others it was akin to pure freedom of expression honed out of rebellion. Gleaming in the sunlight, a new breed of bike roared between suburban cafés. Eyes flicked from road to speedo as the needle quivered towards the magic ton, with riders intent on returning to their Nescafés before the 45rpm single had finished spinning on the turntable. Straddling their bikes, adrenalin pumping through their veins, perhaps a hint of fear slowly fading behind crinkled eyes blasted by wind. Kudos. Maybe the odd tall tale. No one would know otherwise. Best to grab it while you can as a member of the Ton-up Club. Magical moments. Pumped up, proud moments. Glory days.

Time fades, and trends die out. To the public at large, the greasers had decided to smarten up their act, wed and have families and become respectable in suits, holding down 9-5 jobs and saving up for semis in suburbia. Come dusk, however, with the children safely tucked up in bed, down in the garden something stirred. Passion. The shed boys would be once again out in their leathers and grease-encrusted jeans, spanners in hand, never having forsaken their dreams. That was never an option. Someone may have pricked the bubble, but it had failed to burst. Far from it. The true converts had continued putting pencil to paper, designing and creating their dream machines. That was when the mythology adopted a new persona, outsmarting the cynics and the 'I told you so's' who had perceived it as a passing fad. Something was definitely stirring here. Coming out of the woodwork. Wheeled out to the street to be drooled over by fellow bikers. Bike manufacturers sat up. What's this? A stark simplicity devoid of adornment. Darkly masculine. Clinical. But beautiful at the same time. Those perfected linear lines working towards the genesis of a next generation café racer style. And God said: 'Let the land produce living creatures according to their kinds: the livestock, the creatures that move along the ground, and the wild animals, each according to its kind.' And it was so. God saw that it was good. As did the motorcycle fraternity. By the 1970s the postwar disaffected may have become mainstream, but the stereotypical leather-clad, anti-social iconoclasts had never buried the shared passion that called for mechanical acumen and social enterprise to the common good. Like their brothers before them, they headed up the nouveau avant-garde, acting as conduits for yet further experimentation and aesthetic innovation. Like their wheels, they were on a roll. And just like before, we all sat up and took notice.

Thank goodness we [...] dust alongside other co[...] witnesses only short-term popularity before being filed for posterity in the backs of sheds. For we live in a world of collectibles, desirous objects that remain so for their age and beauty and rarity and condition and utility and personal emotional connection. Objects that represent a previous era or time period in human history are deemed antique if they are at least a century old. No older than antique, but less than 20 years old, and we enter the 'vintage' world.

True vintage is at least 50 years old. Confusion then reigns as vintage is often termed as retro, a style that is consciously derivative or imitative of trends, modes, fashions, or attitudes of the recent past. Many new bikes are clothed in retro, because whilst they do not have to be old, they should be made in a style of the time they are trying to replicate. Where vintage refers to the actual construction, retro refers to the appearance, which is how we have retro styling in motorcycle clothing and helmets.

Type in 'retro motorcycles' in Google, however, and you note the following: 'In the last few years, the retro motorcycle market has boomed. Timeless brands like Norton, Triumph and Royal Enfield have seen their popularity rise, causing manufacturers across the globe to take note and launch their own modern classics and neo-retro machines.'

Whilst some manufacturers are happy to blend retro style with contemporary technology, other models need little improvement when style is to spare at re-release time. I test rode the Royal Enfield Continental GT 650 to enjoy this unique retro café racer. On looks alone it deserves a place in these pages. There are more, lots more, with amazing throwback styling and a punch that leaves you breathless with excitement. Take the BMW R nineT, a supremely primed bike that first hit the street six years ago. Viewed by many custom builders as a blank canvas for re-configuration, personally, aside from the occasional visual accent to draw one's attention, I do not see why you would want to. With its state-of-the-art technology, superb lines and characterful air-cooled boxer engine, it commands an unmistakeable presence and is the embodiment of passion and innovation honed from 90 years of motorcycle construction. It does not come much better than that.

And so to Café Racer International. Much has been written about the scene, historically and otherwise, so it seemed pointless to waste valuable time and space to reiterate what you no doubt know already. In reality, I wanted to bring you the scene as it is today, although in these pages we are hardly rippling the surface. With so much more to say, we hope you will watch out for us in the near future. For now, enjoy the read.

MICHAEL COWTON
EDITOR
MCOWTON@MORTONS.CO.UK

Contents

FEATURES

ON THE ROAD

EDITOR/SCRIBE:
MICHAEL COWTON
DESIGN:
GARETH WILLIAMS
PUBLISHER:
STEVE O'HARA
PUBLISHING DIRECTOR:
DAN SAVAGE
ADVERTISING MANAGER:
TOM LEE
MARKETING MANAGER:
CHARLOTTE PARK
COMMERCIAL DIRECTOR:
NIGEL HOLE
THANKS TO:
DAVE MANNING, ROSS MOWBRAY, ROGER JONES, GARY CHAPMAN, BMW, TRIUMPH, SUZUKI, DUCATI, HONDA, HUSQVARNA, KAWASAKI, ROYAL ENFIELD

PUBLISHED BY:
MORTONS MEDIA GROUP LTD, MEDIA CENTRE, MORTON WAY, HORNCASTLE LINCOLNSHIRE LN9 6JR
TEL: **01507 529529**

PRINTED BY: **WILLIAM GIBBONS AND SONS, WOLVERHAMPTON**

ISBN: **978-1-911639-37-4**

COVER IMAGE:
CODYMONSER FROM PIXABAY
BACK COVER IMAGE:
SPLITSHIRE FROM PIXABAY

MORTONS
MEDIA GROUP LTD
Independent publisher since 1885

MADE IN METAL'S TRITON

UNKNOWN PERFORMANCE: The ubiquitous combination of Triumph engine and Norton frame has long been a popular one in the café racer idiom, although this usually entails using an old engine built in the Triumph Meriden factory at some point more than 40 years ago. Neil Adams at Made In Metal knew that a modern Triumph engine from the Hinckley factory would not only make more power, but also be smoother, more reliable and easier to source than a good Meriden motor. And, of course, that extra power requires modern brakes and suspension too, all taken from the 1200cc Hinckley Thruxton version of the Bonneville, bringing hitherto unknown performance to the classic Norton frame. – *Dave Manning* CRI

ACE CAFE REUNION

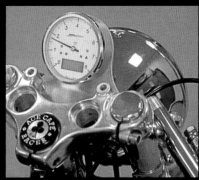

ROCKING UP TO THE ACE CAFE

IMAGES: MORTONS ARCHIVE
(MORTONSARCHIVE.COM)

I DOUBT THERE IS A BIKER OUT THERE THAT HAS NOT HEARD OF THE ACE CAFE, THE FORMER TRANSPORT CAFE LOCATED IN STONEBRIDGE, NORTH WEST LONDON. HEAD ALONG THE OLD NORTH CIRCULAR AND YOU CAN HARDLY MISS IT.

ACE CAFE LONDON
NORTH CIRCULAR ROAD
STONEBRIDGE
LONDON NW10 7UD
TELEPHONE: **020 8961 1000**
EMAIL: **ENQUIRIES@ACE-CAFE-LONDON.COM**

TOP NOSH

A few more suggestions to tempt your tastebuds when out on the bike...

IRON HORSE RANCH HOUSE
2 HIGH STREET, MARKET DEEPING, LINCOLNSHIRE PE6 8EB
01778 346952
IRONHORSERANCH HOUSE.CO.UK
Try a slice of American pie. Custom bike nights. Rustic approach. Hearty food from the grill. Lively atmosphere.

JACKS HILL CAFE AND TRUCKSTOP
A5, WATLING STREET, TOWCESTER, NORTHAMPTONSHIRE NN12 8ET
01327 351350
ADMIN@JACKSHILL. CO.UK
Wide range of all-day breakfasts and additional dinner options within 120 seater cafeteria. Free Wi-Fi.

RYKA'S CAFÉ
BOX HILL, DORKING, SURREY RH5 6BY
01306 884454
RYKAS.CO.UK
Bikers' hangout for half a century. Hot and cold food. Famous for its burgers and milkshakes.

SQUIRES CAFÉ BAR
NEWTHORPE LANE, NEWTHORPE, SOUTH MILFORD, LEEDS, WEST YORKSHIRE LS25 5LX
01977 684618
INFO@SQUIRES-CAFÉ. CO.UK
SQUIRES-CAFÉ.CO.UK
Popular with bikers for over 40 years. Breakfast, brunch, pub grub. Campsite. Speedstyle bike accessory shop in the grounds (**01977 689933**).

THE BIKE SHED
384 OLD STREET, LONDON EC1V 9LT
0207 729 8114
THEBIKESHED.CC
Settled in the heart of London, you can enjoy a coffee and a chat as bikes trundle through the popular venue.

THE HUNGRY HIGHLANDER
14 INVERCAULD ROAD, BRAEMAR, ABERDEENSHIRE AB35 5YP
01339 741556
FACEBOOK.COM/ HUNGRYHIGHLANDER
Roadside diner. Breakfast, lunch, dinner. Fancy trying haggis or venison, or a tasty burger? The choice is yours.

THE TRIUMPH 1902 CAFÉ
NORMANDY WAY, HINCKLEY, LEICESTERSHIRE LE10 3BZ
01455 453088
TRIUMPHMOTORCYCLES. CO.UK
Stylish surroundings and a warm welcome. Hot and cold refreshments. Barista-style coffees. Free Wi-Fi.

WILLINGHAM WOODS KIOSK
WILLINGHAM WOODS.COM
The Picnic Kiosk, Willingham Wood, Market Rasen, Lincolnshire LN8 3QT
Affectionately known as Willy Woods. Attracts hundreds of bikers, usually on Wednesday evenings and Sunday afternoons between May and October. Wide range of hot and cold food, drinks, ice cream.

The roadside transport cafe first opened its doors in 1938 in order to accommodate traffic on the then-new A406, known locally as the North Circular. The venue suffered serious damage during an air raid in the Second World War on the nearby Willesden railway marshalling yards, and was rebuilt in 1949.

Due to its proximity to Britain's fast arterial road network and remaining open 24 hours, bikers were soon drawn to the venue during evenings and weekends, and its popularity grew exponentially during the 1950s and 60s when Rockers came on the scene. The social hub saw hordes of bikers gathering to share gossip, drink coffee and play rock 'n' roll on the jukebox. It was during this period that the Reverand Bill Shergold invited them to join the 59 Club.

By 1969, the Ace Cafe had become the victim of changes in social order, the growth of the car market and the expansion of the motorway infrastructure. With the opening of Scratchwood Services at what was then the southern end of the M1, the cafe had served its last meal. Its ground floor was converted to a tyre sales and fitting shop, whilst the first floor was occupied by a vehicle delivery company.

Fortunately for the many bikers young and old caught up in the folklore and increasing popularity of the Rocker revival, discussions were held between original members of the 59 Club, and as a result the first Ace Cafe reunion was organised by Triumph fan Mark Wilsmore and a group of friends on September 4, 1994, marking the 25th anniversary of the cafe's closure. It was estimated that over 12,000 people gathered at the site.

The following annual reunions, wich became known as 'Ace Days', took place on Brighton's famous Madeira Drive. With the Grand Opening of the original London premises, the Ace Cafe Reunion Weekend developed into the critically acclaimed 'world's coolest motorbike event'... every September attracting tens of thousands of riders partaking in the Brighton Burn Up Run from the Ace Cafe to gather for a free-to-attend motorbike and rock 'n' roll party on Madeira Drive.

Three years later the cafe was once again open, having undergone a complete refurbishment, which was completed by 2001. Whilst it was no longer open 24 hours a day, bikers from throughout the world frequented the establishment, enjoying themed meetings.

After the 2001 Grand Re-Opening, more openings gathered apace throughout the world. In June 2011 the all-new Ace Cafe Lahti celebrated its Grand Opening. In June 2015 the all-new Ace Cafe Luzern celebrated its Grand Opening. The following month saw the opening of the Ace Cafe Beijing. On the weekend of April 21-23, 2017, the all-new Ace Cafe Barcelona celebrated its Grand Opening. And in May 2017 the Ace Cafe Orlando opened its doors for the first time.

The Ace Cafe also has seen fame on the silver screen and television. In 1964 it was used as a location for Sidney J Furie's British gay-interest kitchen sink drama, The Leather Boys, which starred Rita Tushingham. The Channel 5 programme Fifth Gear used the venue in the seasons 10 to 13 (September 2006 until March 2008), and for the ITV programme Used Car Roadshow. The cafe has also been featured in the BBC TV series By Any Means with Charley Boorman; mentioned as a favourite for Ewan McGregor by his wife in the documentary Long Way Down; and the 2008 film Freebird. You might also have caught it in an edition on Car SOS, Season 1, Episode 9, presented by Tim Shaw, filmed during 2012 and shown in the UK on the National Geographic channel. TV presenters Edd China and Mike Brewer also filmed at the Ace Cafe on a Hot Rod night in early 2014 during a sequence to sell a Chevrolet Camaro, as part of Wheeler Dealers series 11.

There have been a number of books recording the history of the Ace Cafe and the culture it spawned, including Winston Ramsay's 2002 offering The Ace Cafe Then and Now, Johnny Stuart's 1987 book Rockers!, and Mick Duckworth's Ace Times, published in 2011. **CRI**

DANIEL ANDERSSON'S NORTON

ECLECTIC TASTE: While the café racer phenomenon is thought of as being a strictly British affair, the influence has spread throughout the globe. Daniel Andersson lives in Sweden, and has an eclectic taste in custom motorcycles, having built choppers with Japanese inline four cylinder engines and classic British single cylinder engines, as well as this stunning Norton café racer. Using a recent Norton parallel twin from the factory based next to Donington Park race circuit (before the concern went through its recent financial issues and subsequent sale), Daniel built his own frame to suit the engine using the finest suspension and braking components available, all topped off with bespoke bodywork and impeccable paint. – *Dave Manning* **CRI**

IMAGES: MORTONS ARCHIVE
(MORTONSARCHIVE.COM)

THE BIKE SHED

A MEETING PLACE FOR LIKE-MINDED ENTHUSIASTS

**BIKE SHED
MOTORCYCLE CLUB**
**384 OLD STREET
SHOREDITCH
LONDON EC1V 9LT
+44 (0) 207 729 8114
THEBIKESHED.CC**

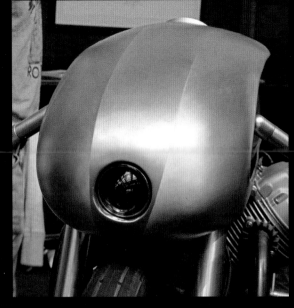

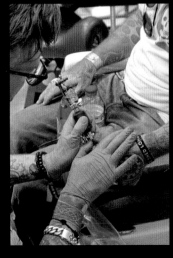

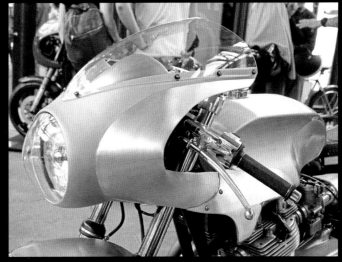

For the past nine years, one of the most popular UK haunts for bikers to share their passion for two wheels has been the Bike Shed. Located in the London Borough of Hackney, Shoreditch is an arty area adjacent to the equally hip neighbourhood of Hoxton, so it could not be better placed. Young creatives and trendsetters fill the fashionable clubs and bars that surround Shoreditch High Street, Great Eastern Street and Old Street, while an eclectic dining scene features everything from trendy chain restaurants and smart gastro pubs to artisan coffee shops and noodle bars, vintage and design shops.

The interesting thing about the Bike Shed is that although it is a motorcycle club (BSMC) for riders, one does not have to be a member or a rider to enjoy the hospitality and equally unique experience. Visitors are treated to an inclusive, welcoming moto-cultural space.

Back in November 2011 bikers enjoyed reading online about Anthony 'Dutch' van Someren's journey as modern sportsbike rider and his take on the new bikes and builders on the scene at that time. In just two years van Someren had grown to become one of the most popular commentators around, clocking a global following. In May 2013 the Bike Shed blog migrated from a virtual community into hosting their first pop-up motorcycle event, which celebrated the creative scene around motorcycle custom culture.

profile

Attracting 3000 visitors, around 70 bikes were featured across two arches in Shoreditch. Aside from the bikes, also on show were art, photography, a barbershop, plus retailers, food and hospitality. It was to prove a major success, and it was not long before people started talking about the possibility of creating a permanent home for the Bike Shed.

Those tentative doors were opened finally in November 2015, and today the Bike Shed at 384 Old Street welcomes 2500 people every week to enjoy the facilities, which include a café and restaurant, curated retail space, galleries for bikes and art, a barbershop and an event space, plus the BSMC's offices.

Such has been the worldwide popularity of the Bike Shed, that 2020 saw the expansion of the name in Los Angeles, California, where a new venue was to open on a historical 30,000 square foot property featuring a similar theme to Shoreditch with a restaurant and café, bar and lounge, retail emporium, barbershop, gallery space, plus a tattoo studio.

The building, which was constructed in 1945, lies in the heart of the Arts District downtown, a thriving area of Los Angeles with its cafés, individual traders, markets and restaurants,

If you have not visited the Shoreditch base before, then it might be time to check it out, enjoy a coffee and a meal, having a beard trim (if you've got one), see some fabulous bikes, and chat with fellow bikers. Oh, and don't forget to join the club! **CRI**

BIKE SHED SHOW

While the Bike Shed venue beneath rail lines in Shoreditch is a permanent fixture in the capital city's custom bike scene, once a year (with 2020 being the Covid-led exception), the Bike Shed team ups sticks and moves just down the road to the impressive Tobacco Dock venue for the annual Bike Shed Show – where all of the pics you see here were taken.

As the name suggests, the Wapping site was once a dockside warehouse, with the 19th century building now converted into an astounding brick, steel and glass edifice that provides a suitably historic, yet trendy, venue.

While this year hasn't seen the expansive display of café racers, bobbers, street scramblers, flat trackers, choppers and street fighters spread liberally around the multitudinous halls and rooms of Tobacco Dock – thanks to the social distancing that has affected every aspect of life – the previous years have seen a continually expanding number and variety of machinery, with a strong focus on the subject style of this publication – café racers.

From budget small capacity singles through to forced induction speed freaks, the show encompasses anything and everything that epitomises the performance and style of café racers, with music, clothing and even films to suit each and every fan of the style. If you like custom motorcycles, the show should be on your list of places to visit, but if your particular passion is café racers, then it's compulsory! – *Dave Manning* **CRI**

JIM CAMPBELL'S RYCA SUZUKI 650

CORNER CARVER: The Suzuki Savage of the late Eighties was perhaps the most poorly named bike of the period, given that the 650cc air-cooled single cylinder was only capable of eking out around 30bhp, at best. However, that simple thumper does provide a traditional motive force for a traditional café racer, as Jim Campbell's Ryca proves. With reduced weight, and improved engine performance thanks to a free-flowing exhaust and air filter, plus the minimalist bodywork from Ryca Motors in America, the little Suzuki has turned from a flaccid and lardy cruiser to a scalpel-like corner-carving café racer! – *Dave Manning* CRI

THE TRANSFORMER

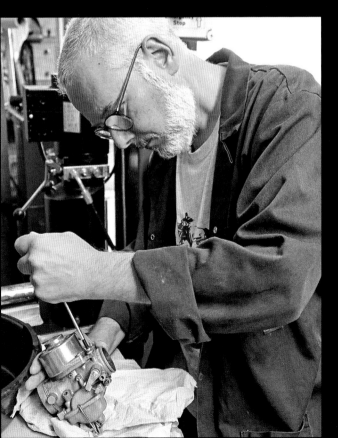

SHOULD YOUR TIMELESS CLASSIC BE IN NEED OF RESTORATION OR TURNING INTO A RETRO-COOL MACHINE, HIPSTER MOTORCYCLES IS HERE TO HELP

HIPSTER MOTORCYCLES
UNIT 19 PRIDE COURT
ENTERPRISE PARK
SLEAFORD NG34 8GL
TELEPHONE: **07580 135897**
SALES@HIPSTERMOTORCYCLES.COM
WWW.HIPSTERMOTORCYCLES.CO.UK

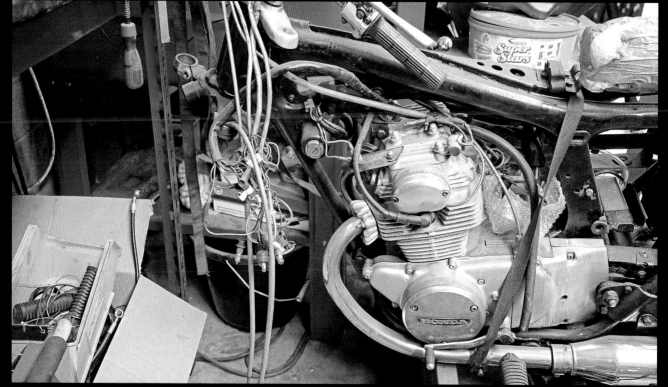

"BECAUSE I WANT TO ENJOY MY WORK, I WILL PICK PROJECTS THAT SUIT ME. THE CUSTOMER HAS TO BE SOMEONE I CAN WORK WITH; SOMEONE WHO UNDERSTANDS WHAT I DO AND WHY I DO IT"

Talk to Kevin Brennan about old bikes, and it does not take long before you come to appreciate his passion for carburettors and a naturally aspirated motorcycle engine. It could be something languishing in a shed, or a barn find; in fact, anything that requires care and attention to detail. From initial sketch to completed design, Hipster Motorcycles can take a timeless classic and transform it into a retro-cool machine or follow the full restoration route, according to the customer's needs, which is precisely why the business has grown to become a successful one-stop custom shop for many in Lincolnshire.

Kevin's father, a works engineer, came over from Ireland in 1957. With a love for classic cars, his son grew up around engines. Kevin, however, chose architecture as a career, but having completed a three-year university degree, he concluded that the profession was not for him and instead pursued a career in sales, working for the VKR Group, well known for its Velux windows, blinds and shutters. As part of the marketing and business management team, he was involved in political lobbying in Parliament. Always at the back of his mind, however, was that burning passion for motorbikes. "Aside from working on my own bikes, I also worked on those for other people, but that had always been on a part-time basis. Whilst I continue to maintain a passion for 70s bikes, particularly the Japanese marques, I went through plenty of different phases. I had a nice Ducati 749, which I sold about three years ago, plus Fireblades and R1s and a BMW GS, which I really enjoyed.

"When someone first starts tinkering with bikes, there is limited scope on what they can achieve, depending on what machinery they have. Electronics sometimes can get in the way and unless you are into engine re-mapping, which I am not, it is difficult to customise to a level that the customer really wants."

With Japanese bikes such a focus of his attention, Kevin admits to never having been much into British brands. "Closed shop is a strange term, but this area is extremely well serviced by a lot of talented and knowledgeable people, and I do not profess to be one of those. I think that's due to the fact that I never grew up around bikes, as my father was never into them. Even today, whilst I do get the odd British bike in the workshop, I do not go out purposefully to attract them, although it is a very valuable sector with a lot of money invested."

About a decade ago Kevin realised the growing trend amongst younger people looking for something a bit more unique, and the desire to move into more classic styled biking, but with a modern twist, and that is where he began to focus his efforts. He has a penchant for old commuter bikes such as the CB175, a standard bike manufactured by Honda from 1969 to 1973. It had a 174cc (10.6 cu.in.) four-stroke, straight-twin engine with a single overhead camshaft, two valves per cylinder, dual slide-valve carburettors, and dual exhausts. "I probably go through three or four of those a year in terms of restoration," he says.

"A lot of the time it comes down to having the facility to help people with projects, translating one's passion for work. I always say every biker is a home mechanic. We like to put our bike on a paddock stand and clean it and change things, but beyond that it gets into the realms of needing specialist equipment such as bike and tail-lifts, anything really that could make things easier."

Initially having set up shop in Bourne, Lincolnshire, Kevin started to attract attention before deciding to move to a unit on Sleaford's Enterprise Park. Coming up to four years this Christmas since the relocation, he has not looked back since.

"People simply turn up when I open the doors. It doesn't take a lot of promotion to create a brand locally and really that's where our focus lies. I believe there is a growing demand for specialist workshops such as ours. Admittedly, there are plenty of motorcycle franchises, dealers and general service garages

out there, but not many that try to offer what we do. Generally, the custom scene in the UK has followed that of America with choppers and bobbers, and being very heavily Harley focused. That's not where we have focused our attention, as we aim more for the younger, slightly trendier hipster market."

Kevin finds that finances play a crucial part in any restoration project, and a number of customers work on a rolling financial basis. "Customers will advance at the pace of their budget and for me that's great because they end up with a bike they really want, and it gives them an opportunity to think about design."

A classic example is a Honda CX500, which has been on a lift for nigh on a year at the shop. Hipster recently took delivery of a set of Ducati upside-down forks for the bike. The owner acquired them second-hand in very good condition, but they still cost £1200. A pair of wheels would come from America and that is a further £2000, so money can roll on very quickly if one is not careful.

Next to the CX500 stands a Kawasaki Zephyr 1100, which had been dragged out of a shed after 20 years. Kevin managed to get it running within a week. It had a factory immobiliser and trying to strip that out was hard work, but having achieved that, he cleaned the carbs and it is now running, although there is more work to be done. The exhaust design has changed three times. The seat has gone from being a twin to a slightly smaller seat to a race seat with a saddle that's going to be covered with Alcantara, so the design is ever evolving.

"If we take time we can be fluid," says Kevin. "It is when people make a commitment from day one. For example, the CX500 initally started with the idea of fitting an Öhlins monoshock, but within a year you have got hundreds of people out there following that route, so the owner came back and said he wanted to go dual shock, so we have now started to see how we can re-fabricate the frame to accommodate that. We will then get the owner to sit on the bike because it is a custom bike and has to fit him, his riding style and his size. He is quite tall so we have lifted the frame and the tank, and will lift the whole stance of the bike at the rear end, which will be reflected in the wheels and the rear suspension.

"I believe the biggest investment you can make is at the design stage. However, it is not a financial investment, but one of time. Unfortunately, bikers often come along with an ambition and vision of what they want the bike to look like. It is not until you start cutting and changing things, and they sit on it, that they realise it is not quite what they wanted or where they thought it might go. So, the more time you spend at the design stage the better, because when you start buying in brand new parts it can become very expensive."

Kevin's interest in design comes from having studied art and architecture at university. He is happy to invest his time in making sure the customer is happy, and will go through four or five different sketches before they get to understand where the bike is going in terms of the look. "The sort of market we are in does not have 40 grand to spend on a CAD drawing carried out by a company in London, so we have to tailor the work to suit that. Having previously run CAD teams, I appreciate what a great tool it is, although sometimes it can limit flair; it is only as good as the line you put on the drawing and you cannot change it as easily as something that is three dimensional, such as a bike.

"When I do a mock-up of a frame I will use copper tube because it is easier to bend and manipulate, and we can use that to fabricate the design, because sometimes aesthetics are as important to owners as function, if not more so. Most people that have a bike for modernisation or restoration, will normally also have a bike they use daily. One customer has a Ducati Monster that he rides every day, so what they are looking for is something that expresses their personality, and that is exactly what we are trying to achieve for them. I have the luxury of having retired early so I do not have the same financial pressures that other companies have, so all I have to do is cover costs and that then offers me the luxury of time.

"Because I want to enjoy my work, I will pick projects that suit me. The customer has to be someone I can work with; someone who understands what I do and why I do it. I will always say to people, I am not going to be the quickest because I want to take the time to get it right. It is not about getting it done, out the door and invoiced, but rather the customer going away happy and recommending me, which is the best and least expensive form of advertising."

If any painting is required and is relatively small and easy to manage, then Hipster will handle it. Recently a customer brought in a pair of tanks for a Harley-Davidson WLA. The WLA was produced to US Army specifications in the years during and around the Second World War and was based on an existing civilian model, the WL, and is of the 45 solo type, so-called due to its 45cu.in. engine displacement and single-rider design.

Kevin often adopts a trial and error approach to his work. "If something does not work out we will pay someone else to do it. We learn every day, and there is a lot of expertise out there one can learn from. I have up to four people that I can call upon to come in and help whenever is necessary. There comes a time when you need others on site."

One of his cherished bikes is a 1974 Honda CB350 Twin, a 19.87cu.in. ohc parallel twin cylinder, four-stroke. With its reliable engine and dual Keihin carburettors, it became one of Honda's best-selling models. "I built it five years ago. It was supposedly a running bike. I rode it round for a couple of months, but it had a lot of problems and a lot of rust. Originally I was going to restore it, but then I wanted to create something more of the style of a 50s or 60s café racer, so I tried to keep as much originality as I could, such as the front drum brake and existing clocks. I put ace bars on it, which was a challenge because the bike runs all of its electrics through the bars. We adapted the frame and went for the café racer seat. It will not run at the moment because it is dry. We took it to a show where it was on display in a marquee, so has no fuel or oil in it. Whilst it has been under wraps since we moved here, occasionally I will show customers what can be done."

Scooterboys also pop into Hipster, where Kevin has seen about eight going through the workshop in the last couple of years. Hipster has a reputation as the UK's largest supplier of spares stock for the Capri, a fact recognised by the Capri Scooter Club of Great Britain. Not complex machines, they do possess their peculiarities. The Agrati-Garelli 80cc Capri marque was made famous by the successes of its racing two-strokes in the 1920s. Garelli resumed postwar production with the Mosquito clip-on power unit and before long was producing proper motorcycles once again. In 1958 the firm merged with Agrati, another Italian concern that was already producing the Capri scooter in a range of engine sizes, through 50cc, 70cc, 80cc, 125cc and 150cc. Faced with intense competition from Piaggio and Innocenti in its home market, the Capri was widely exported, the majority being sold abroad. Kevin managed to acquire a Capri as a project bike. "It is nearly all paint and not a lot else," he says, tongue-in-cheek. "The engines have very simple electronics and are even simpler because they do not run batteries, so are pretty straightforward to work on."

So what of that abiding passion for Japanese bikes as opposed to UK marques? "In lots of ways Triumph saved the British bike industry by what they produced, and have to be applauded for that. They treated it as a business rather than a passion, and investors will put money into that. So much of the British-built market did not move on. They got hit heavily when the Japanese came in because the bikes were twice as quick, half the weight and twice as reliable. Others have tried and failed for other reasons and that is quite sad to see. When you see brands such as Norton end up in the situation they are in yet again, it is a great shame. It has a good, if not better brand name than Triumph, but it needs to do something different with its business model. If you look at a lot of the modern bike manufacturers and what they have done with their range, going down the retro-styled route, that has done a lot of good for them. Of 10 bikers I know, for example, only two are riding sports bikes in the same way they would have a decade ago. The majority are riding something a little bit different now. When I started riding you saw a lot more bikes, and the roads were safer in lots of ways, even if the conditions were not. The volume of traffic was different; the speed of the bikes was different; and the amount of street furniture was different. Today, riding a bike is a dangerous pastime and requires a different mentality."

When I mention that I enjoyed a recent test ride on a new BMW R nineT, he said a farmer had brought in an older version that had been languishing in a woodshed for 30 years. "When we fired it up, it filled the place with sawdust, despite us having blown it off with air before we brought it in! The owner simply wanted it restored to the point where it still looked like a 1974 bike. He wanted it running, useable and reliable, that was it."

Should you fancy having the cobwebs – or sawdust – blown off an old bike and have it tweaked, fully restored or given the retro look, pop in and see Kevin, he is always happy to chat. Say Hi to wife Karen and their lovely Bichon, Bridie, too! **CRI**

"CUSTOMERS WILL ADVANCE AT THE PACE OF THEIR BUDGET AND FOR ME THAT'S GREAT BECAUSE THEY END UP WITH A BIKE THEY REALLY WANT"

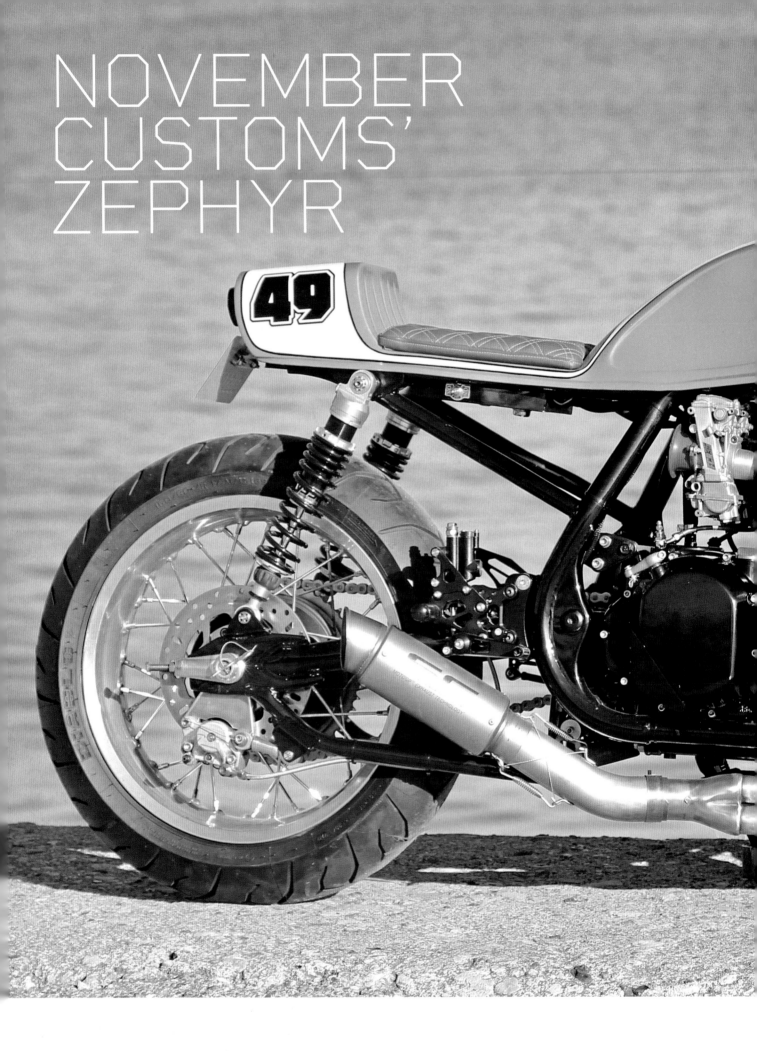

NOVEMBER CUSTOMS' ZEPHYR

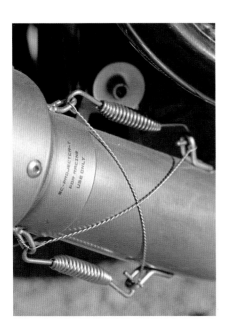

WORLD-CLASS PEDIGREE: Kawasaki's Zephyr 750 was never the most outrageous model in the Japanese manufacturer's arsenal in the early Nineties, but north-eastern custom bike builder November Customs made its Zephyr into a very special machine indeed! Uprated suspension and brakes (including mechanical anti-dive at the front) allied to improved engine performance follow the café racer idiom to a tee; show-winning attention to detail and the quality of finish on the one-piece seat/tank/fairing unit make this a bike with world-class pedigree. – *Dave Manning* CRI

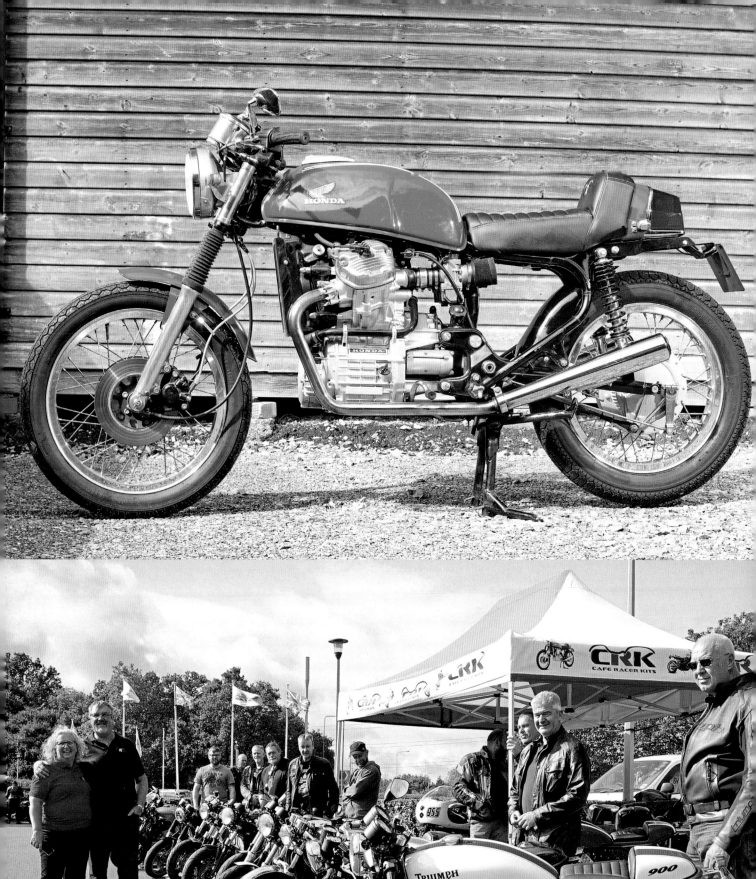

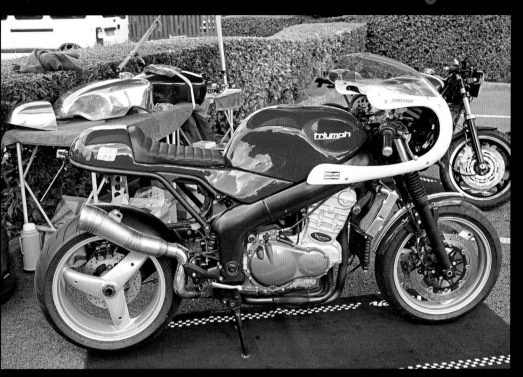

IMAGES: IAN SAXCOBURG & MICHAEL COWTON

CHOP SHOP

IAN SAXCOBURG OF CAFÉ RACER KITS DISCUSSES BIG IDEAS IN SMALL SHEDS

THE TERM 'café racer' has been with us since the 1950s, when the music of Eddie Cochran and Bo Diddley spun on jukeboxes in transport cafés, and Ton-up Boys began making headlines with their leather-clad look, sat astride stripped-back bike customisations. A new motorcycle culture had been born, as the bikes morphed into lean, mean machines with their single racer seats and low clip-on bars, racing petrol tanks, cone megaphone mufflers and swept-back exhaust pipes.

With home-made hybridisations continuing to flourish, specialist manufacturers jostled for space alongside those renowned manufacturers eager to grab a piece of the action, developing a new breed of café racer for the retro market.

Moving from Essex to the Isle of Wight aged five, Ian Saxcoburg grew up with bikes. Originally trained as a mechanical engineer, he admits to probably spending too many years on the drawing board and on 3D CAD systems, all the while thinking, tinkering or building bikes.

In 2011 he happened upon an American television programme called Café Racer, where a guy had customised a machine based on a Honda CX500. "I thought it was really good and told myself that I was going to make one similar," he recalls. "As my principal idea behind customisations had been to use older, cheaper and readily available motorcycles, I knew the CX would be ideal. Browsing the local free ads, there was almost always one listed, unused and unloved, and normally stashed in a shed or backyard. I managed to find one for £100, so I bought it. When I arrived to collect it, the bike was leant against a garage behind a hedge in the garden.

"As a youngster it had been possible to get almost anything made, but times changed, with people no longer having easy access to fabricators. As a result it became really hard to get even the simplest of things made. So I decided that while I was building this bike, I would draw everything I made and then make two of them, so that if someone else wanted to build a similar bike, they could buy the parts from me. My thinking was that the parts were not like vegetables, they would not go off, and therefore they could sit on the shelf until such time as they were needed."

With the customisation complete, in 2012 Ian and his wife Tracey launched Café Racer Kits, and took space at the Classic Motorcycle Mechanics show in Shepton Mallet, along with a batch of CX500 parts. Ian simply wanted to gauge interest. He hadn't expected the parts to sell out within a matter of weeks. Alongside the kit, they developed and produced a working manual, enabling even the most inexperienced of café racer enthusiast to have a go at a conversion themselves. CRK realised they were on to a winner.

"When we first launched the CX500 kit, I thought people might think we were wrecking all these bikes, but the first person on the stand at Shepton Mallet said it was great, because otherwise the bikes would end up in landfill," says Ian. "We were going to keep more bikes on the road by doing kits, because whilst the bikes were not worth the money to complete a full restoration, it made sense to convert them. As a result, CX prices have reflected that, because no longer can they be picked up for £100." CRK's 250/400 Café Racer kit went on to transform the Honda CB250N or CB400N into a stand-out old school racer, thanks to clip-on handlebars and a single seat, coupled with stainless steel instruments and Bates-style headlamp adding to the cool retro look.

After years of restoring classics and building specials, and keen to share his experience and expertise, in 2014 Ian began his next project – a kit for the Honda Superdream. Based on the Honda CB250N and CB400N Superdreams made from 1978 to 1984, the kit modules were to provide all the major parts and instructions required to transform a donor bike into a café racer.

With their revvy four-stroke motors and good handling, the bikes made a great

basis for a special, retaining the practical features that made the Superdreams a favourite, including electric start, centre stand, disc brakes, easy maintenance and electronic ignition. With the removal of 'excess baggage' from the machine, the bike's character would be transformed, improving performance and boosting riding fun. Despite their strong engines and reliability, the fact that Superdreams are not yet considered 'classic' in the secondhand market makes great news for specials builders, and whilst the CRK

kit did not set the world alight, donor bikes turn up to this day, and the kit is still readily available.

Ian then turned his attention to the early bulletproof Hinckley triples, with their great engine and solid chassis, but again weighed down by excess baggage. The first CRK Triumph kit was unveiled in February 2015, designed for the T300 series of 750 and 900 triples, built from 1992 to 1996, and which includes the Trophy, Trident, Sprint, Daytona and Speed Triple, but not the Tiger, Thunderbird or Adventurer. The kit proved a phenomenal success, with in excess of 240 sold throughout the world, many having gone into Europe. One kit is in Iceland, another in Peru, sold simply through the power of the Internet. "We advise people that if they already have a really good Triumph or CX500, for example, as there are so many tatty ones out there, they should source one of those rather than convert their pride and joy," says Ian.

"Building a café racer is about doing something of your own; it is a bit like Airfix kits. Some customers are much more interested in

building something to ride, whilst others will build a bike and then almost immediately sell it because they want to build something else. There are those riders that have built bikes that are very well used, whilst

others want something that is individual, a bike that they have put their stamp on, something to admire."

With strong engines, good spares availability and proven reliability, the early Hinckley Triumphs are deservedly gaining classic status. However, with prices of scruffy bikes suitable for conversion still very affordable, that can be nothing but good news for specials builders, plus having the word Triumph emblazoned on the tank makes it just that little bit more special. Riding on the success of the Triumph T300 Series kit, CRK's attention next turned to the Triumph Sprint ST 955, which was manufactured for six years from 1998.

With every kit, each aspect of the CRK process is repeated dozens of times and is fully documented, so owners can be confident that the parts will fit properly in accordance with the comprehensive project manual. Builders can also watch videos, guiding them through the build process. A CRK kit is pretty straightforward, essentially requiring the removal of the original rear subframe, and bolting all the new bits together, with a typical transformation taking anywhere from 50 to 100 hours to complete, depending on the builder's previous experience and how radical the overhaul is. Even so, as Ian happily points out, CRK has had several customers who before they build a bike have had to go and buy themselves a set of spanners because they have never worked on anything like it before.

"We put a lot of effort into the instructions, on the premise that the more information we give, the fewer questions will be asked, and that has paid off," says Ian. "Most people will follow the manual, but if people get stuck or if they want a bit of advice, we are always here for them. We do try and converse by email because it gives us time to think of an answer rather than simply speaking on the telephone. It is surprising when no questions come back! Often we send the kit off and then wonder what has happened to it, and the next thing you know we are sent a picture of the completed bike. We encourage people always to tell us how they get on."

Ian continues to handle all the design and prototype work, but because everything is designed using CAD, after the prototype stage he will rely on the expertise of others. "We try to use local people if we can for at least 80% of the parts, then we build in small batches. With the glassfibre, that is done by someone else, although I would make the original shape, then use that for the mouldings to be made. Some of the simpler metalwork is done by myself in-house, as that doesn't take up too much time. In the end it is a question of mixing and matching to get the desired look. That really is our while mantra.

"When you think back to the era of the Triton, it was more DIY, and we try to do that with CRK. In order to achieve that, the donor bike has to be a good bike and also very affordable. It also has to be a little bit tatty, perhaps with broken plastic, that sort of thing, a bike that is not worth rebuilding, but is worthy of customisation."

With the current café racer revival, CRK are riding the crest of the wave alongside big-name manufacturers such as Triumph with their new Thruxton RS, manufacturers that know the

demand is there, and are appealing to the more mature customer with cash in their pocket, willing to pay out for a bike that perhaps reminds them of their youth. "We, too, are

"WHEN WE FIRST LAUNCHED THE CX500 KIT, I THOUGHT PEOPLE MIGHT THINK WE WERE WRECKING ALL THESE BIKES, BUT THE FIRST PERSON ON THE STAND AT SHEPTON MALLET SAID IT WAS GREAT, BECAUSE OTHERWISE THE BIKES WOULD END UP IN LANDFILL"

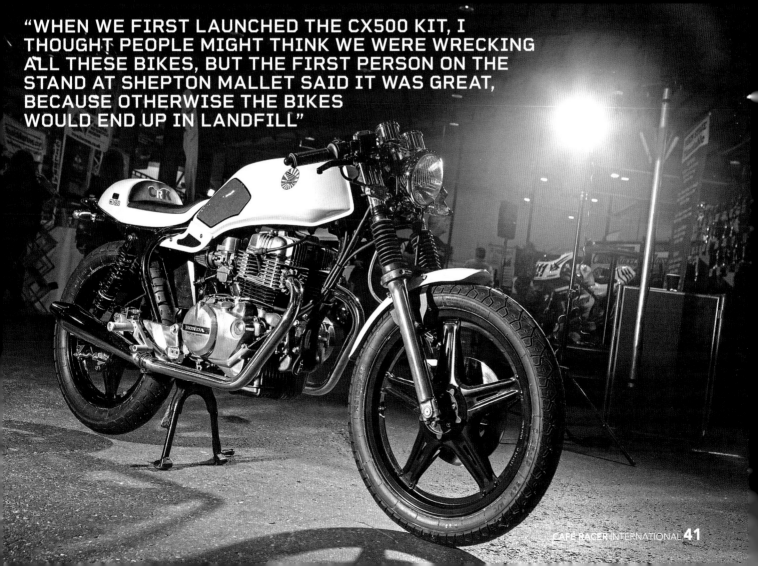

mostly dealing with a more mature clientele," says Ian, "older guys who may have a bit more time and enjoy being in their workshop. Having said that, we have customers in their 30s that want to end up with something that is theirs. Whilst we produce a kit, the customer can put their twist on it so they end up with a bike that is not like anyone other.

"You also have to consider that the younger kit builders probably cannot afford to spend over £10,000 for a bike like the Thruxton, but they can buy a donor bike. It's quite cool in a way, because buying a Thruxton is one thing, but when you say 'I made this', that is a very different thing altogether. Most people seem to like the hands-on approach. They take pride in the work. Café racers have become a genre again, with a lot of customers having had a café racer background, or are aware of the tradition through their families. One chap who bought a kit from us converted a bike as a tribute to his father, with the same colour scheme. It is all about nostalgia at the end of the day."

Ian remains conscious that the bubble eventually may burst as far as the trend in café racers is concerned. "Some manufacturers have done a fantastic job in getting on the bandwagon, and probably saw it coming five years ago, but it is like fashion, in that there will be a hit and then people will move on to something else. Take the Triumph Trident for example. There was a period when you could buy one for next to nothing, and then all of a sudden they became really desirable. From our point of view, we will always stick to our original idea, which is that the donor bike has to be cheap, the build has got to be fun,

and it is something you do, not particularly because the bike is going to be worth a fortune or esoteric. For a niche market like ours, hopefully people will continue to want to do that."

The best way to think of a CRK bike is by way of comparison to a restoration, inasmuch as with the latter you are going to have to do the whole bike if you want to do a nice job, but with a conversion you do not have to source the original parts. Some people may prefer to buy and convert an old naked bike because it is possible to see more of the original engine at point of purchase. Remove a fairing, however, and although the bike may be clean underneath, it can be badly corroded because of having been ridden through the winter. Road dirt could have made its way underneath the powder coating, causing it to peel off. The suspension linkage may have corroded, and the seals may have all gone. Despite being well engineered, the back can still be a vulnerable area. By this stage you would be committed to doing it all.

Such has been the popularity of CRK over the past few years, that a number of people have opted to convert more than one bike. Whereby some have built the same kit again, others have gone for something different. One man in Finland built two identical Triumphs – one for his wife and the other for himself to enjoy.

If you fancy transforming an unwanted Yamaha Fazer 600 into a stunning pocket rocket TZ lookalike, then CRK can help here too, as they have launched a FZS600 kit.

"When we began with the CX and the Superdream, they were simpler kits, particularly the CX, being the first one," says Ian.

"The thing with those bikes now is that they are so old, 40 years old, so even if you buy one now it is still an old bike. The reason for opting to do a Fazer kit was that being slightly more modern, in a way the bike acts as a replacement for both the CX and the Superdream. It still has carburettors, and is quite a simple bike to work on. With the Triumph we had to move away from the original shape of the bike, which meant making our own fuel tank and subframe, whereas the Fazer is different, and it was simply a question of chopping the end of the frame off and keeping the fuel tank, so it should be an easier build. With a café racer everything is about the line of the stock frame, and how your eye follows it. Unless you are making a frame from scratch, there is a compromise to be made.

"We try to choose donor bikes that are reasonably priced in the second-hand market so that your project won't break the bank," says Ian. "Then we build prototype bikes to get the look just right. During the design we use a mixture of experience, craft and

modern techniques such as 3D CAD to specify the parts. We work out all the headaches such as load stresses, wiring modifications, fasteners and clearances for tyres." Once the prototyping is complete, CRK concentrate on making all the engineered parts that are required for the conversion, before producing the parts in small batches to keep the cost competitive and the quality high. Ian then builds a second pre-production prototype and uses that to write the comprehensive instructions that are included with each kit.

As much as CRK components are built locally, it remains clear that Ian Saxcoburg is happy to roll up his sleeves, hammering, filing, shaving, bending, drilling, polishing, painting and deburring machined components to his heart's content, because it is all part and parcel towards helping big ideas to be created in small sheds.

CRK currently provide a range of kits, but whichever you fancy, bear in mind that not everything for your finished bike is included, with parts such as silencers, indicators and tyres being of your own choice, thereby allowing you to customise the build.

Similarly, the tank and mudguards are supplied bare for you to paint in your own personal scheme, thereby completing the personalisation. Each kit is made up of 'modules', giving you the choice of buying the complete kit or individual modules.

Anyone who has attempted to build a café racer from scratch knows how much time and money it takes. Thanks to Ian and Tracey Saxcoburg and CRK, the process and cost have been simplified, thereby allowing the average bike enthusiast to create a seriously cool café racer of their own. CBI

LEE STANAWAY'S GS/GSX-R HYBRID

STYLE AND PERFORMANCE: Building a café racer need not be the financial load that some may think it may be, nor does it entail having to find a Featherbed frame and classic Triumph twin engine in fine fettle, as Lee Stanaway knew. By taking a cheap and available Suzuki GS550 frame, and a later oil-cooled GSX-R 750 engine that produces nigh on 100bhp, fitting them together and adding some suitable rolling gear and stylistically appropriate bodywork, Lee was able to create a bike with the right style, at the right price, that has the right performance.
– *Dave Manning* **CRI**

BMW R NINET

SPREADING THE LOVE

THE R nineT GRABS BOTH THE
SOUL AND SPIRIT OF RIDING;
THE SOUND OF THE WIND
AND THAT GLORIOUS BOXER
V-TWIN PURRING LIKE A
CAGED ANIMAL

IMAGES: BMW & MICHAEL COWTON

Y ou know you are on something special when car drivers at traffic light intersections glance at your bike, wind down the window and give you the thumbs up. It was the same at several roadside pull-ins where I stopped for the occasional break. One owner even popped out of his burger van and asked the significance of the number 21 on the tank. Ah, that is where ignorance reared its head and I had to admit defeat, even though I should have done my research beforehand, anticipating that very same question. So when I arrived home I contacted Neil Allen, BMW Motorrad UK PR & Communications Manager.

"The number 21 is a reference to the internal model code that BMW had for the R nineT when building it," he explained. Glancing through the manufacturer's website, I then noted the number 719 on the side of a rather splendid red and blue coloured R nineT. This relates to the 'Option 719' customisation/ accessories arm of BMW Motorrad, where it is possible to spec up the heritage range with some lovely paint jobs, billet packs, etcetera. And lovely paint jobs they are, too.

Every time I took the bike out, it reminded me of a rather excellent quote (anon) I had once read: 'Only a biker knows why a dog sticks his head out of a car window.' That neatly sums up my passion for this bike. It is akin to donning one's favourite tailor-made suit, nothing being out of place, the fit perfect, the styling rather wonderful, and in this case, the ride pure pleasure.

As you may have gathered, this is proving difficult to explain in any clear sense, because until you ride a bike that truly fits with your psyche, you will not understand where I am going with this line of thought. Psyche, of course, is the goddess of the soul and the spirit. It was her husband Eros, son of Aphrodite, who spread love around the world. Whilst I will not go down that road, I will spread the word about how the R nineT grabs both the soul and spirit of riding; the sound of the wind and that glorious Boxer v-twin purring like a caged animal as it sends shivers of pleasure down the spine.

Looking at the aluminium seat hump cover, which on my test bike had been fitted instead of the pillion seat and included a small splash-proof storage compartment, I was pleasantly surprised at how nice the seat was, offering a comfortable backrest pad. Should you wish to, it is possible to upgrade and make the bike more individual by getting yourself a custom rider's seat with moulding and indicated cross steps, plus

Ridden

RIDING THE R NINET IS AKIN TO DONNING ONE'S FAVOURITE TAILOR-MADE SUIT, NOTHING BEING OUT OF PLACE, THE FIT PERFECT, THE STYLING RATHER WONDERFUL, AND IN THIS CASE, THE RIDE PURE PLEASURE

BMW R nineT | RRP £12,745

ENGINE: 1170CC, AIR-COOLED DOHC, FLAT TWIN (BOXER) 4-STROKE **POWER:** 110HP/81KW @ 7550RPM **TORQUE:** 88LB-FT/119NM @ 6000RPM **TRANSMISSION:** 6 GEARS **FRAME:** FOUR-SECTION (FRONT AND THREE-SECTION REAR SUBFRAMES) **FRONT SUSPENSION:** UPSIDE-DOWN TELESCOPIC FORKS, 46MM FIXED-FORK-TUBE DIAMETER **REAR SUSPENSION:** CAST ALUMINIUM SINGLE-SIDED SWINGARM WITH BMW MOTORRAD PARALEVER, CENTRAL SPRING STRUT, SPRING PRE-LOAD HYDRAULICALLY AND STEPLESSLY ADJUSTABLE VIA HANDWHEEL, ADJUSTABLE REBOUND DAMPING **FRONT BRAKE:** TWIN DISC BRAKES, FLOATING DISCS, DIAMETER 320MM, FOUR-PISTON RADIAL BRAKE CALIPERS **REAR BRAKE:** SINGLE DISC BRAKE, DIAMETER 265MM, DOUBLE-PISTON FLOATING CALIPER **FRONT TYRE:** 120/70 ZR17 **REAR TYRE:** 180/55 ZR17 **SEAT HEIGHT:** 805MM **FUEL TANK:** 18 LITRES **FUEL ECONOMY:** 53MPG (CLAIMED) **KERB WEIGHT:** 222KG **CONTACT:** WWW.BMW-MOTORRAD.CO.UK

such as aesthetics, the market and the cost, and it all adds up to something rather special. I write this purely from a personal perspective, as this bike will not suit everyone, I know that, just like a cruiser, or an adventure bike, or a scrambler will not be to everyone's taste. All bikes are subjective, and it just so happens that I have come across a bike that dials into my needs perfectly.

It has an unmistakeable presence and a wonderful soundtrack, the powerful air-cooled two cylinder boxer engine featuring a capacity of 1170cc and 110bhp of output, supplying the rider with a dynamic power delivery even when in slow-moving traffic. Not that you would want to be stuck in that for long, because once on the open road, the R nineT comes into its own.

As far as specs go, apart from the standard BMW Motorrad ABS and optional ASC traction control, that is about as far as it goes with rider aids. No more mods to distract you, instead leaving you with a good, old-fashioned, honest ride, the bike stripped back and ready for action. With the double instrument panel you do get an analogue speedometer and rev counter, and the brake and clutch levers are adjustable. Having said that, owners can customise the no-nonsense bike to their heart's content.

For starters, in addition to the Black storm metallic paint finish, there are three paint finishes from the individualisation offer under the umbrella of BMW Motorrad Spezial, the most expensive being 'Option 719', offering a part of BMW history as a self-starter conversation, so if exclusivity is your thing, this is a good place to begin. Excluding the classic Black storm metallic colour, you could check out two new special colour variants from

partially Alcantara look. Alongside the black with white double decorative stitching, you are treated to embroidered R nineT lettering in gold. Fancy, eh!

I rode and rode, through towns and villages, across open pasturelands and through wooded glades, on A- and B-roads, finding quiet valleys and stumbling upon sleepy hamlets, dawdling behind tractors and waving at hikers, all the

while clearing away the rubbish that had been festering in my head and causing me sleepless nights. Cobwebs were blown away and left to break up and die in the breeze. I labelled this bike 'The Hedonist', ordering up a constant quest for pleasure and satisfaction at every outing. And it never let me down.

It is somewhat of a peculiarity that this, the 'standard' version, sits at the top of the R nineT model variants alongside the Pure, Scrambler, Racer and Urban/GS. But then, the ergonomics are what count here, where BMW have paid special attention to the design, making sure it is the best possible for the end user, and the task to which it has been built. Balance that with other factors

the customisation range: Option 719 Pollux metallic/Aluminium with classic light and dark colour mixtures, so if you are after dark and characterful, then there you have it; or opt for the perfect colour triad of Option 719 Mars red metallic matt/Cosmic blue metallic matt, with the number 719 on the tank. My test bike came with Option 19 Black storm metallic/Vintage with its unified yellow application with the starting number '21', hand-brushed like the padded sides.

We are talking new levels of exclusivity and expert craftsmanship here, where you can tinker to your heart's content, upgrading and adding personal touches as you go, provided your wallet will stretch to it, or instead simply opt for the ex-works option. The possibilities are pretty much limitless as far as customisation goes, depending on your personality and vision.

The BMW R nineT is indeed a bike for all seasons. If I had been able to keep it for longer, I know I would have enjoyed a few longer distance rides, even though in reality this is a naked. I know, doesn't make sense, does it? But at the end of the day it's a blast, whichever way you look at it. CRI

CASTING A SPELL

TRIUMPH STREET TWIN

IMAGES: TRIUMPH MOTORCYCLES

THE STREET TWIN HAS MANAGED TO TAP SUCCESSFULLY INTO A FERTILE VEIN, OFFERING UNAFFECTED PLEASURE ON THE OPEN ROAD

Let's put modesty aside for a moment and reflect on Triumph's somewhat impressive stable of Modern Classics. There's the outstanding Thruxton RS, a true café racer if ever there was one; Bonneville and Scrambler ranges; and the Speed Twin, all with OTR prices across the board from £8900 to £13,000. Oh, hang on, what's that quietly minding its own business in the corner? A Street Twin. Perhaps you didn't notice it at first because it doesn't shout 'Look at me!' In fact, it doesn't shout anything because it doesn't have to. Neither does it pretend to be anything other than a truly honest, unintimidating machine with a price tag of £8100. That's as humble as its presence.

But then that's only half the tale. Because what we have here is Triumph's sales chart-topper. According to the manufacturer, the reason for its success has been down to a mix of entry-level price, classic looks and easy demeanour. Didn't we just say that? Anyway, it's good that we concur.

"That's nice," commented a biker as I parked up at Willingham Woods, Lincolnshire's Mecca for bikers drawn from across the county and Yorkshire's hinterland, where they enjoy tea and chit-chat, particularly on Wednesdays and Sundays. I happened to be there on a Thursday, and whilst there were fewer people around than the norm, bikers that were present

strolled up and down, ears pricked as they heard another machine approaching, the latter strategically altering speed as it passed the 'cash cow' van with camera poised to snap the unwary. Some might well be muttering 'Bugger' under their breath, steaming up the visor for their stupidity. Chancers, eh!

The 900cc parallel twin is a breeze to ride, and whilst not exactly a pure café racer, it sits comfortably in the retro mould, and if you are a sucker for a comfy seat and more upright riding position, then here you have it. Yes, there is something hugely likeable about this bike, whether it is its lightness, its power curve, or its willingness to please. For me it ticks all the right boxes.

First introduced four years ago, Triumph has been busy tweaking here and there, particularly with the upgraded high torque Bonneville engine, which gives the rider 18% more peak power, up 10PS to 65PS at 7400rpm. You are also treated to a higher rev limit, up 500rpm from 7000rpm. Then there are those Brembo front brakes, cartridge forks for better feel, and cast wheels, all locked into an improved finish and nice detailing. You are also treated to two electronic riding modes – Rain and Road. To be honest, you don't need any more than that. Road is there should you fancy a full throttle response, and you can easily dial in Rain to dampen (sorry!) things down, should you worry about reduced grip when it's wet.

Specification

TRIUMPH STREET TWIN | RRP £8,100

ENGINE: 900CC LIQUID-COOLED, 8 VALVE SOHC PARALLEL TWIN **POWER:** 64.1BHP (47.8KW) @ 7500RPM | **TORQUE:** 59LB-FT/80NM @ 3800RPM | **TRANSMISSION:** 5-SPEED | **FRAME:** TUBULAR STEEL CRADLE | **FRONT WHEEL:** CAST ALUMINIUM ALLOY MULTI-SPOKE 2.75 X 18IN | **REAR WHEEL:** CAST ALUMINIUM ALLOY MULTI-SPOKE 4.25 X 17IN | **FRONT SUSPENSION:** KYB 41MM FORKS, NON-ADJUSTABLE WITH CARTRIDGE DAMPING, 120MM TRAVEL | **REAR SUSPENSION:** KYB TWIN RSUS, WITH PRE-LOAD ADJUSTMENT, 120MM REAR WHEEL TRAVEL | **FRONT BRAKE:** SINGLE 310MM FLOATING DISC BREMBO FOUR PISTON FIXED CALIPER, ABS | **REAR BRAKE:** SINGLE 255MM DISC, NISSIN 2-PISTON FLOATING CALIPER, ABS | **FRONT TYRE:** 100/90-18 | **REAR TYRE:** 150/70R-17 | **SEAT HEIGHT:** 760MM **FUEL TANK:** 12 LITRES/2.64 GALS | **FUEL ECONOMY:** 72.4MPG (CLAIMED) | **KERB WEIGHT:** 198KG/436LB | **CONTACT:** WWW.TRIUMPHMOTORCYCLES.CO.UK

TRIUMPH HAS EMBRACED A SEA CHANGE IN SIMPLICITY, AND YET ENCAPSULATED IT IN AN EXTRAORDINARY DYNAMISM

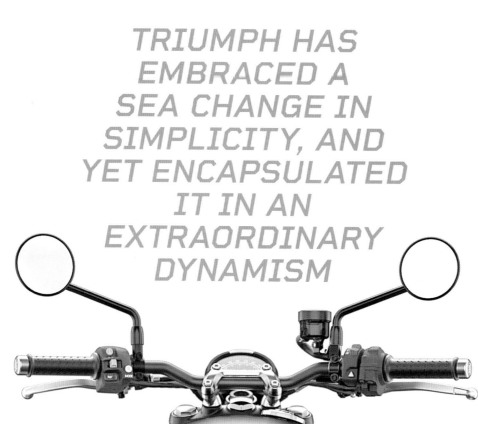

As part of the original cult revolution in both bike and biker identity when the original Bonneville engine first saw the light of day, I can look back fondly on those early years, and can see how that DNA has worked its magic on the current line-up, casting a spell over this new breed of updated modern classic. That contemporary look includes its own particular level of detailing and finish, from the blacked-out sculpted engine and sprocket covers, to the original machined engine fins and Triumph maker's mark triangle and Bonneville engine badges.

What's more, this bike is very much a blank canvas when it comes to aftermarket accessorising. Make it what you will, or leave it as it comes out of the crate, you can adapt to your heart's content with well in excess of 100 premium accessories at your disposal, designed, engineered and tested alongside the Street Twin.

I have been enjoying various rides this year, all with their own template of style and performance; all offering a feeling of expectation and hoping not to disappoint. The Street Twin has managed to tap successfully into a fertile vein, offering unaffected pleasure on the open road. It has a quiet charisma, one that alters your perception when you ride it, and little wonder, then, that it has proved such a prodigious success. It is like cracking open an oyster and hoping for a pearl. Bingo!

Head out into the countryside and into a tempest of wind, and soon you will be grinning. With a character all of its own, it is wonderfully indulgent no matter how you ride it, being dynamic in its handling, although this is not a motorcycle that will take kindly to abuse, and neither should you ever consider that. You need to ride this bike to fully appreciate all that it can offer, however, from its comfort to its wonderful level of control, its balance and its relaxed handling and, yes, its responsiveness.

So, if your desire is for a contemporary custom bike that oozes character even before you consider following the accessorising route; amazing detailing and finish; original styling cues; and, at the forefront, a modern, capable ride and a road presence to match, then here it is. It is an icon, whichever way you look at it. One with an outstanding British pedigree to match.

It is just that extra level of expressiveness that I hoped for and did not expect, that had me particularly warming to this bike. Yes, you can bung on all the bells and whistles, but sometimes less is more. Triumph has managed to embrace a sea change in simplicity, and yet encapsulated it in an extraordinary dynamism, articulated in a more accessible fashion than its contemporaries.

In the hierarchy of retro machines, it can indeed stand tall and proud. **CRI**

SUPERB ENGINEERING AT A GREAT PRICE... NOT MUCH MORE YOU COULD ASK FOR, REALLY

SUZUKI SV650X

PARTING IS SUCH SWEET SORROW

IMAGES: GARY D CHAPMAN

One word springs to mind immediately when it comes to the SX650X. One word comprising three syllables… fab-u-lous. Really? Yes, really. And yes, I know, that is setting the bar particularly high for Suzuki's newest member of the SV family, but my word, it deserves recognition. You want V-twin fun and performance with the manufacturer's latest innovations and the added twist of café racer flare, then here it is with bells and whistles.

Suzuki is clearly adept at neat conjuring tricks, having managed to drop the smooth revving power plant into a slim, lightweight trellis frame. And then there is all the advanced rider technology to go with it. Suzuki's Easy Start System engages the starter motor at a precisely timed pre-set interval to start the bike with a simple push of a button. A computerised 32-bit ECM checks the status and disengages the starter motor immediately after start. Neat.

Then we have Suzuki's Low RPM Assist function, a new feature which utilises the Idle Speed Control (ISC) to help boost engine rpm when powering up or whilst running at low speed, helping to suppress an engine stall, thereby resulting in better start control and operation, especially in heavy traffic when you find yourself constantly stopping and starting. These are aids that will certainly benefit less experienced or returning riders.

Being of the café racer style, you might imagine the SV650X is fine for weekend blasts, which, of course, it is, but then it has hardly fired out of the starting blocks at this point. For not only does this bike lend itself to commuter transport, but it is great also for day rides, despite those clip-ons and therefore a slightly more hunched riding position.

On only my second outing I enjoyed over 160 miles around North Lincolnshire, slicing across the Wolds to the Humber Estuary, bimbling around Barton-Upon-Humber, then out on the A15 and the A180 towards Immingham, looping back via Caistor, Brigg and on to Gainsborough, then back across some glorious countryside with sweeping A and B roads to Market Rasen, where we enjoyed a cup of tea at Willingham Woods, a popular biker rest stop, before I headed back to Lincoln.

I say 'we', because I had linked up with Peter O'Grady, who runs Barton Advanced Motorcycle Training courses. Due to the

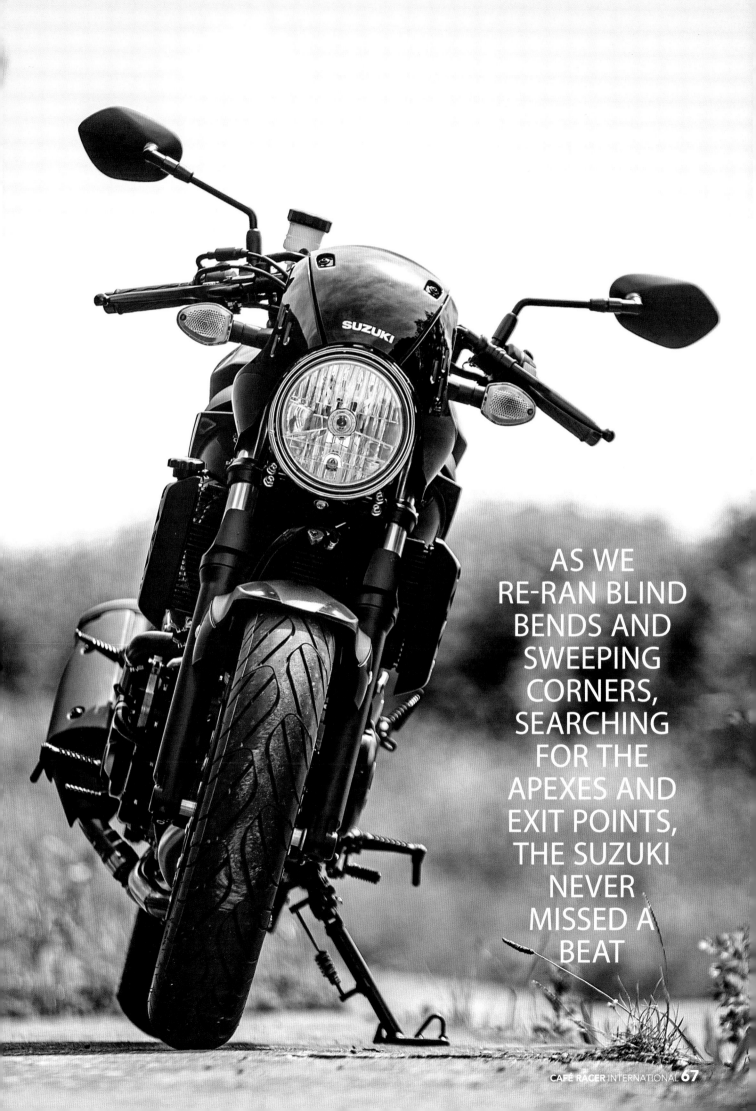

AS WE
RE-RAN BLIND
BENDS AND
SWEEPING
CORNERS,
SEARCHING
FOR THE
APEXES AND
EXIT POINTS,
THE SUZUKI
NEVER
MISSED A
BEAT

Specification

SUZUKI SV650X | RRP £6599

ENGINE: 645CC, 4-STROKE, 2-CYLINDER, LIQUID-COOLED, DOHC, 90-DEGREE V-TWIN | **TRANSMISSION:** 6-SPEED CONSTANT MESH | **CAPACITY:** 76BHP/56KW AT 8,500RPM. 47LB-FT/64NM @ 8100RPM | **FRAME:** STEEL TRELLIS | **FRONT SUSPENSION:** 41MM CONVENTIONAL FORK ADJUSTABLE FOR PRELOAD | **REAR SUSPENSION:** LINK-TYPE, COIL-SPRING SHOCK ADJUSTABLE FOR PRELOAD | **FRONT BRAKE:** DISC BRAKE, TWIN | **REAR BRAKE:** DISC BRAKE | **FRONT TYRE:** 120/70ZR17M/C (58W), TUBELESS | **REAR TYRE:** 160/60ZR17M/C (69W), TUBELESS | **SEAT HEIGHT:** 790MM | **FUEL CAPACITY:** 14.5 LITRES/3.2 GALLONS | **RANGE:** 70.62MPG (CLAIMED) | **KERB WEIGHT:** 198KG/437LB | **CONTACT:** WWW.BIKES.SUZUKI.CO.UK

coronavirus lockdown, I had already completed several online theory sessions with Peter, covering such topics as advanced braking, steering (cornering), line choice, moving on the bike, body position, and trail braking, some of which I was fine with, other areas I was certainly in need of brushing up on, as it is surprising how much one forgets after several months off a bike.

The core focus of the course is to give riders the tools to be the master of the machine itself, with a greater understanding of the skills and techniques that are an essential component of being in total control of the machine under any circumstance.

When I explained to Peter which bikes I owned, he initially suggested I take my Honda CBR 600 F1. But then along came the SV650X for test. Perfect timing, you may suggest, and you would be right, because that was my weapon a choice.

And what a choice. That smooth, predictable power never once lost its impact, and coupled with the bike's ease of handling and well-behaved suspension and brakes, there was never a senior moment when I felt anything other than comfortable, in control and planted.

As we re-ran blind bends and sweeping corners, searching for the apexes and exit points, making minor adjustments here and there, the Suzuki never missed a beat, and with the merest hint of a knee out it would lean to left or right, gripping the Tarmac as it hugged either the centre line or the curb. I do believe the bike was enjoying the ride as much as I was, as cornering improved and the speedo became ever more advanced. Even at low revs, the understated torque was always on standby, ready to take me to the mid-range at the merest twist of the throttle, and that power delivery just kept on giving. "Trust me," said Peter as I followed him at pace over several miles of twisties east of Gainsborough, en route to Caenby Corner. And I did, not once exceeding my limitations, but always at one with the bike. It was looking after me, ready to handle any of my foibles.

It is hard to imagine how a manufacturer can turn out such a superb piece of engineering at such a remarkable price. Okay, six-and-a-half grand is still a lot of money, but just look at what you get for it... a bike that is so versatile, so giving, with such attractive lines, and okay, I did stand up on the pegs a couple of times to relieve my butt, but I was more on than off the saddle for a good seven hours that day, so that was no mean feat.

It is hard to explain how someone can feel so at one with a piece of metal, but to me this was a living, breathing partner on the road, and we seemed to bond perfectly. When it came to the parting of the ways, loading her on to the truck, waving her a fond farewell, I was truly sad... silly old sod that I am. CRI

RETRO AUTHENTICITY

DUCATI SCRAMBLER CAFÉ RACER

THIS IS A BIKE FOR THE FREE OF SPIRIT WITH A SPRINKLING OF REBELLION

Men with earphones and radio receivers with antennae protruding skywards. Waiting expectantly, patiently, binoculars to hand, as their partners sit by their cars in fold-out chairs with a book. Could it be Boeing's 'eye in the sky' E3 AWACS (Sentry) Airborne Warning and Control System aircraft, or perhaps a Raytheon Sentinel R1 – no, not that R1, but a Bombardier Global Express modified as an airborne battlefield and ground surveillance platform for the RAF? Well, don't ask me.

I had stopped by at the Waddington Aircraft Viewing Experience (WAVE), which had recently re-opened its gates since the March lockdown due to the Covid-19 pandemic swept the country. WAVE plays host to military and aircraft enthusiasts, and has an on-site café, the Sentry Post Snack Bar… thus my stop. The popular site with its large parking area is located at the east side of the Lincoln-Sleaford A15, close to the landing lights of runway 20 at RAF Waddington.

Sat with a bacon roll and a cup of tea, I was fascinated to watch as the small pocket of dedicated enthusiasts with their hand-held scanners monitored ground-to-air communications – at least, I presumed that is the frequency they were tuned to. Anyway, as it clearly was not their thing because it was incapable of flying, no one really bothered about the bike, which I had parked strategically in front of the café as I wanted to take a few snaps while the weather held. Blue skies dominated as I sat in T-shirt, basking in the sun's rays and waiting for an aircraft to approach, but none did. Hell, you have got to have some patience for plane spotting.

People have a fascination for aircraft, just as others do for bikes. That was clearly evident when next I decided to attend a bike night at Olivers Motorcycles in Sleaford, which involved a pleasant backcountry jaunt from my home, mostly along a 50mph speed zone.

There are some lovely twisties along the B1188, which is probably why the law had decided to put a spoiler on things.

Once at Olivers, I had hardly had chance to park up and remove my helmet when I saw a biker eyeing up the Ducati. He strolled casually round it before stepping back, hitching up his jeans over an impressive beer belly, and commented: "She looks a lot better in the flesh than in the images," as if referring to a Page 3 model. I replied that 'she' was light and agile and accommodating and tremendous fun, okay, rather like a Page 3 model. He had been thinking about purchasing one (Ducati), but when I offered for him to sit on it, he declined, which I thought a bit odd.

IT IS ONE FOR BACKROADS CARVERS AS OPPOSED TO SMOKING RUBBERITES WHO THRILL AT SLAM DUNKING MOTORISTS AT TRAFFIC LIGHTS

Specification

DUCATI SCRAMBLER CAFÉ RACER | RRP £9995

ENGINE: 803CC AIR-COOLED, SOHC, V-TWIN **POWER:** 73BHP/54KW @ 8250RPM **TORQUE:** 49LB-FT/67NM @ 5750RPM | **TRANSMISSION:** 6 SPEED | **FRAME:** TUBULAR STEEL TRELLIS | **FRONT SUSPENSION:** UPSIDE-DOWN KAYABA 41MM FORK | **REAR SUSPENSION:** KAYABA NEAR SHOCK, PRE-LOAD ADJUSTABLE | **FRONT BRAKE:** 330MM DISC, RADIAL 4-PISTON CALIPER WITH BOSCH CORNERING ABS AS STANDARD EQUIPMENT | **REAR BRAKE:** 245MM DISC, 1-PISTON FLOATING CALIPER WITH BOSCH CORNERING ABS AS STANDARD | **FRONT TYRE:** 120/70 ZR17 REAR TYRE: 180/55 ZR17 | **SEAT HEIGHT:** 805MM/31.7IN | **FUEL CAPACITY:** 13.5 LITRES/3.57 GALLONS (CLAIMED) | **KERB WEIGHT:** 180KG/396.8LB | **CONTACT:** WWW.DUCATI.COM

Another biker then approached and asked if it was mine. I could have told a fib, but I did not. He then proceeded to show me a range of different bikes that he had either previously owned or longed for, that he had captured on his cellphone. I was not really sure as I had missed the start of the conversation because I still had my ear defenders in situ. Without being rude, I was gagging for a coffee so I wandered off to fetch one from the other end of the parking area. When I turned around from the burger stall a number of bikers had gathered round the Ducati, some leaning down and pointing, others chatting animatedly. Having returned to the bike and explained that it was, in fact, the Scrambler Café Racer model, that started a whole new line of questioning. What does it ride like? It looks rather small! (In fact, when I rode into the car park a friend noted that I rather dwarfed the bike!) What is it like on fuel? Is that a new colour scheme? What does the number stand for? Is it the V-twin? Loving those spoked wheels! But then we got down to the nitty-gritty. Is it a scrambler of is it a café racer? Is it mutually exclusive to one model, or the other? Now there's a dichotomy for you.

In fact, the first thing that struck me about the Ducati was the new 'silver ice matt' colour complete with blue frame, blue seat and classic black spoked wheels. If you fancy another colour, you will not get it, because that's it. But it looks lovely. And if you are wondering about the number 54 on the side-mounted plates, that is in reference (or deference) to Italian racer Bruno Spaggiari, winner of the 125cc edition of the 1958 Nations Grand Priz at Monza (on a Ducati, of course), and later Ducati Desmo team manager.

The 803cc, air-cooled, sohc V-twin is a blast. The one thing that I took issue with was the unexpected heat generated from the rear cylinder exhaust pipe. I first noticed the heat as it penetrated my jeans at my right cheek, and when I got off the bike and removed my gloves, part of the frame and side-mounted plate were almost too hot to touch.

On the other (not so hot) hand, there are plenty of things to love about this bike. The agility is hugely impressive; it feels as light as a feather; it easily, yet gracefully, tips into bends; and on straights it carves through the wind like a peregrine falcon on speed. It is about as far removed from its semi-knobbly tyred stablemate as it is possible to get. And should you fancy carrying a pillion, the seat cover is removable, although the solo look draws the eye easily to the rear section. Also gorgeous are the classic wire-spoked wheels wrapped in 120/70 ZR17 rubber at the front and 180/55 ZR17 at the rear.

A pair of inverted KYB forks float the front end and stopping power of this mid-sized ride is courtesy of a massive 330mm front disc with a four-piston monoblock Brembo caliper, plus the benefit of Bosch ABS delivering corner-sensitive antilock protection. The handlebar's end-mounted mirrors offer a clear view behind without any obstruction from one's shoulders or elbows.

Rewinding to Olivers' bike night, and I can understand why the bike drew so much attention. The 'silver ice matt' paint job is so uber cool; the exposed trellis skeleton frame makes you yearn to run your hands along it; the cut-back front mudguard harks back to the original café racer decades; and the handlebar mimics the upside-down, backwards way on bars that are so reminiscent of the original custom jobs that would park up outside the Ace Cafe.

Ducati is well into the mix of manufacturers offering sporty, café racer-styled models, and the Scrambler Café Racer would easily take its place on the podium, thanks in no small part to the upgraded rideability and its retro authenticity. With that improved riding experience, new graphics, uncluttered lines and adorned with both subtlety and finesse, the model offers opportunities for customisation, but personally, I do not see why you would want to.

Attired in leather jacket and sporting an open face helmet and goggles, this is a bike for the free of spirit with a sprinkling of rebellion. It is one for backroads carvers as opposed to smoking rubberites who thrill at slam dunking motorists at traffic lights. Nooo, we are far too polite for that. Anyway, if you do, the cops have got your number... 'cos it's on the side-mounted plates, so there. **CRI**

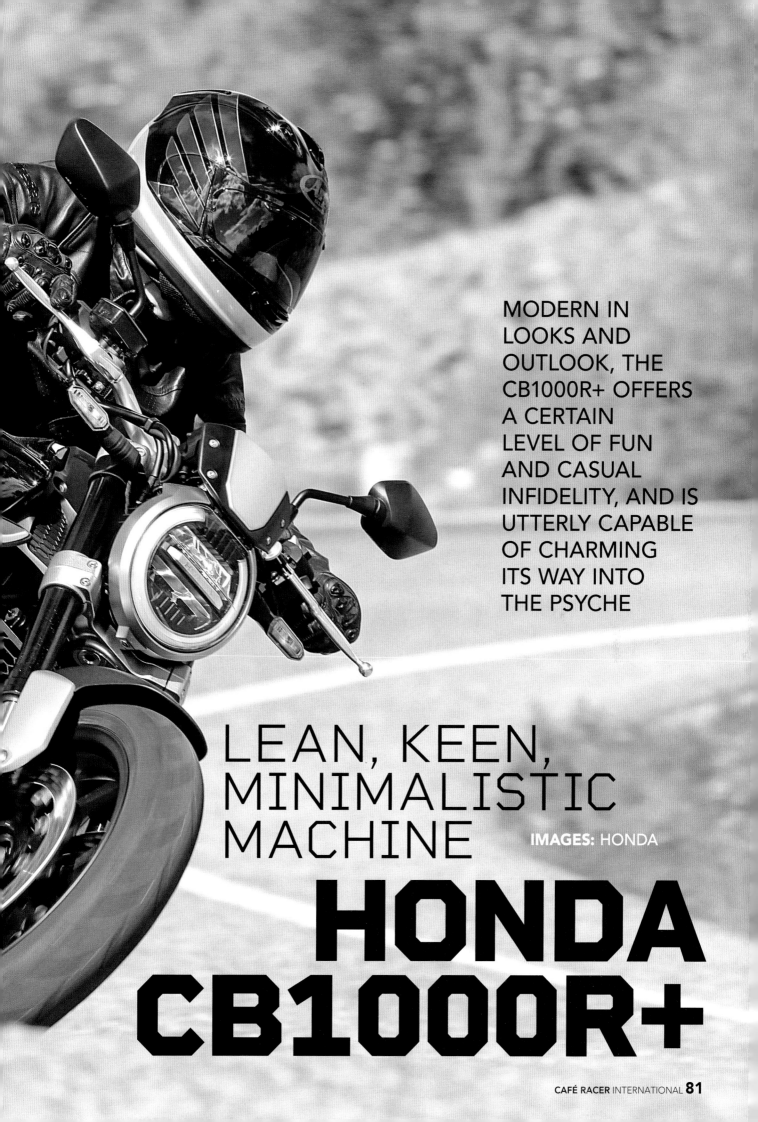

MODERN IN LOOKS AND OUTLOOK, THE CB1000R+ OFFERS A CERTAIN LEVEL OF FUN AND CASUAL INFIDELITY, AND IS UTTERLY CAPABLE OF CHARMING ITS WAY INTO THE PSYCHE

LEAN, KEEN, MINIMALISTIC MACHINE

IMAGES: HONDA

HONDA CB1000R+

A colleague likened the CB1000R+ to a digestive biscuit. It's dependable and inoffensive, he said, if a tad dull. It's not trying to be something other than a very nice, modern-day bike with a nod and a wink to nostalgia. I won't elaborate further, only to say that I beg to differ. I love this bike. It looks great, the engine is supremely smooth, the chassis is wholly reliable, and it's exciting to ride. Honda term it as a Neo-Sports Café, a prefix from the ancient Greek word 'neos' meaning something that is either new or contemporary. So there you have it in a nutshell. The CB1000R+ is modern in looks and outlook, and comes complete with a personality all its own. Revolutionary… on the verge. Streetfighter… most definitely. Cutting edge… that'll be a positive then.

The 998cc four-cylinder engine has been specially tuned for mid-range and top-end power, and it delivers in bucketloads. Light and responsive, the bike is a hoot to ride, and a fitting testament to the Honda design team's ability to create something that is, in fact, more than the sum of its parts; a lean, keen, minimalistic metal machine that is in itself a dichotomy, on the one hand a stripped-back naked, and on the other boasting myriad distinguishing features that are impossible to ignore.

So let's get down to those individual characteristics that give this bike such a road presence. For starters, there is the burnished alloy radiator shroud along with engine casings and airbox cover. The lighting is LED. I love the signature thin round headlight with its metal-tone painted rim, the shape a throwback to café racers of old. The dual front, radial-mounted disc brakes boast four-piston calipers, along with ABS, thereby providing the rider with a trustworthy braking force and feel in almost any conditions. Then there is the 4-2-1 exhaust system with its distinctive tone. The all-

new chassis is paired with high-spec Showa suspension.

As for the punchy inline four-cylinder engine, that is controlled by throttle by wire, three riding modes – Standard, Rain and Sport – plus a User setting, which offers the option to dial in one's own preferences, fine-tuning for traction and torque controls, and engine braking. Test riding over several weeks during the winter in miserable conditions, I kept it mostly in either Rain or Standard mode. The former offers a medium amount of engine braking and high Honda Selectable Torque Control, with lower levels of power and torque focused on the first three gears. By comparison, Standard Mode reduces the output of first and second gear, and uses a power curve that sits just below that of Sport mode. A reduced amount of torque at minimal throttle openings kept the bike smooth and steady when I was on and off the power, and it also allowed for small rear wheel slides and also kept the front wheel on the

Specification

HONDA CB1000R+ | RRP £9099

ENGINE: Liquid-cooled DOHC in-line four cylinder **CAPACITY:** 998cc | **BORE & STROKE:** 75mm x 56.5mm | **CARBURATION:** PGM-FI **CLUTCH:** Wet, multiplate **MAXIMUM POWER:** 107kW @ 10,500rpm **MAXIMUM TORQUE:** 77LB-FT / 104Nm @ 8250rpm **TRANSMISSION:** Six-speed **FRONT SUSPENSION:** Showa SFF-BP USD fork. 120mm stroke | **REAR SUSPENSION:** Monoshock with gas-charged HMAS damper featuring 10-step pre-load and stepless rebound damping adjustment. 131mm stroke | **FRONT BRAKE:** 310mm double disc | **REAR BRAKE:** 256mm single disc **WHEEL FRONT/REAR:** Cast aluminium **FRONT TYRE:** 120/70 ZR17 | **REAR TYRE:** 190/55 ZR17 **SEAT:** 830mm | **WHEELBASE:** 1455mm | Fuel capacity: 16.2 litres | **KERB WEIGHT:** 212kg | **CONTACT:** www.honda.co.uk

IF IT WERE A HUMAN BEING, IT WOULD BE OPEN-HEARTED AND SEXIST AND LIBERAL AND PROBABLY WOULD VOTE FOR TRUMP JUST BECAUSE IT WANTED TO WIND YOU UP

ground. I knew that Sport mode would have produced a grin-inducing blast, with maximum delivery through all six gears, but that was for another day, and another season.

With no traditional mudguard and only the Euro standard rear wheel hugger number plate mount, I got completely muddied up across my back from the collar to the top of my trousers. But then I do appreciate that these bikes are not really best for riding in wet, muddy, wintry conditions, so I will forgive it for that, because I love the styling.

This is clearly a bike for hitting the B roads of a weekend, the commute to work, or popping down the shops, which is exactly what I used it for. And for that it made for maximum enjoyment, with a suitably padded seat. In fact, the riding position is extremely comfortable, and the LCD screen clear with all the necessary information for an informed ride.

I did wonder about the capabilities of the Honda as a touring machine. Able it certainly would be, and I would have no qualms about heading off on a long weekend jaunt with a backpack.

Sit astride this bike, and you know instantly that it wants to be ridden, pulling away easily with gusto, the throttle response being particularly smooth, with plenty of power through the revs. Adopt the Assist/Slipper Clutch, and that smoothness is personified. Agile and well balanced, bends were a breeze and winding her up on straights was a pure tonic.

So that begs the inevitable question of whether I would buy one. If you have managed it thus far through the article, then you will know that I am sold on the Honda CB1000R+. I love its styling, its coolness and its rideability, and that

+ sign signifies factory-fit accessories including heated grips, aluminium front fender panels, flyscreen with aluminium inserts, radiator grille with CB1000R logo, and quickshifter, all making the package completely worthy of its price point.

Yes, it is a safe bet, being predictable and reliable and well behaved, with touches of luxury, and thereby quintessentially Honda, but then those things are right up there on my radar. Astride it at idle, and you will find no vibration through the seat or those comfortably set handlebars and decent height footpegs. Walk around it, and it looks good from any angle. It's got an understated personality, and I like that. Honda has pulled out all the stops in torquey-ness, so if you want an animal under your derrière, then here you have it. That's where the understatement occurs. You think this is a cuddly pussycat, calm and non-plussed, but then it growls and spits venom. Fab. That's down to the throttle response, which is wonderfully positive, even in sixth gear when you want to blitz past another moving vehicle, with all that torque on tap.

The more I rode this bike, the more I wanted one as a go-to machine. I love my Honda VFR Firestorm, and my Triumph Sprint RS, as they serve solely different purposes. The 1000+, by contrast, has it all: a modern-day bike with superb performance, great handling, comfort and reliability. You instinctively know that you can ride it harder, for longer, and it will comfortably eat up the miles. It's not exactly a Marmite bike, although it does divide opinion, yet the more I talk to bikers, the more the angle of lean veers to the positive.

The CB1000R+ offers a certain level of fun and casual infidelity. It's capable of charming its way into your psyche. It straddles the great divide between traditionalism and iconoclasm, whilst feasting on common ground; a half-mast epiphany to motorcycle building.

If it were a human being, it would be open-hearted and sexist and liberal and probably would vote for Trump just because it wanted to wind you up. Yes, it's easy to eulogise, but when an inanimate object sits so relentlessly breathless in the present tense, yet will stand in later years as a vidid reminder of a time and place that we have grown out of, it deserves to be remembered. But that's a long way off. And okay, it is a bit bonkers but, my word, it is all the better for it. If you get the chance, ride one, and then tell me I am wrong. **CRI**

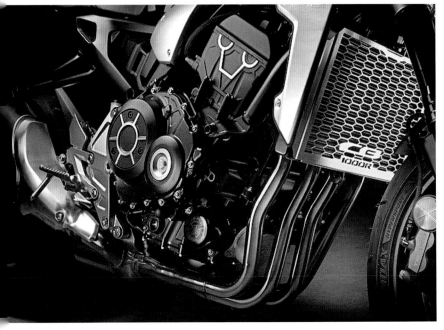

Ridden

'WHITE ARROW' HAS A POINT TO MAKE

VITPILEN 701

HUSQVARNA STRAYS FROM A BRAND STEEPED IN DIRT-ORIENTATION TO A STREET-SMART PERFORMER WITH THE LOOKS TO MATCH

IMAGES: GARY D CHAPMAN

IT is not often I have a pair of siblings land at my front door, but that is exactly what happened recently with the delivery of a couple of Huskys. No, not the dogs. They are unusual however, to say the least, which also makes them appealing, but then that beggars the question: Why have I seen so few on the road? In fact, I have seen precisely none. Is that because their looks are so off the wall, that after a cursory glance, potential buyers move on?

It is not that the Husqvarna marque is a sibling itself to the motorcycle world, having been rolling machines off the factory floor for over a century in Sweden as a subsidiary of the eponymous armament firm. Today, the company is owned by the Austrian KTM group, so there is pedigree for you.

As to the bikes, I have here a Vitpilen 701 and a Svartpilen 701. The names translate as 'White Arrow' and 'Black Arrow' in Swedish. The base plastics of both bikes are the same, and while the latter is flat-tracker inspired, the Vitpilen, which I will concentrate on here, features clip-on bars, road-focused rubbers and a totally different riding position.

I guess you can see where this going – yep, a nod and a wink to café racers, thus the more aggressive, forward-leaning stance. Yet another throwback to the 1950s, you may say... and you would be right, but that is because the retro scene is so prevalent in today's market, and if you have not got the knowledge or shed to build your own fantasy from a barn-find reject, then this could well be the marque that deserves your attention.

The 701 – big brother of the 401 and featuring the 690 Duke's powertrain – had been left dangling like the proverbial carrot for at least half-a-dozen years by the manufacturer, until the original concept morphed into the flapship production model we see today. While no doubt some baulked at the design, others were bowled over by its classy brazenness. If Husqvarna wanted to make a statement, they got that right. As to categorisation, that was to be another question entirely. Retro, roadster, street, classic... labels flew around, but no one was able to pin the tale on the proverbial donkey until Husqvarna Motorcycles introduced the swingtags 'Simple' and 'Progressive' to the new Husky

on the block, one that it was hoped would appeal to the masses, so there was definitely no stereotyping here. Suddenly, Husqvarna had strayed from a brand steeped in dirt-orientation to a street-smart performer with the looks to match. From the circular instrument pod to the tasteful silencer, styling cues abound and if you can get over the Marmite moment, then step away and appreciate that this is no modest commuter bike. Ride one and you will see what I mean.

At first glance it's a stripped-back, lean, mean machine. Simplistic might sound derogatory, but it's not meant to be. Because it is, and that is the whole point. Café racers were, and remain, great for those short bursts over brief miles, eating up the Tarmac in a blur. Yet whilst the 701 is indeed retro, it was never Husqvarna's intention to produce a throwback from the past, but rather capture the essence of nostalgia in all its modern form. The silhouette is there for sure, but strip anything back and it is crucial that you retain the lines and proportions, and the company has achieved that with the 701. Less is more, and all that. So, can Husqvarna be regarded as a pioneer in today's modern world? As far as the 701 is concerned, then yes, but only by getting it out on the road and checking if that intuitive and authentic feel are as hoped, and whether the bike will provide a whole new gateway to the world of retro motorcycling, will tell the tale.

Before I go any further, let us step back to those looks for a moment, which at once are compelling, quirky even... starting with the angular shape of the tank. Approach the 701 from the rear and we have all the hallmarks of a sportsbike, and do not forget to take note of the light cluster under the seat frame. That is one neat job. Husqvarna's designers were no doubt empowered to come up with a bike that would be radically different from the retro mainstream, and urban riders can rejoice that the manufacturer saw the light. The 692.7cc liquid-cooled,

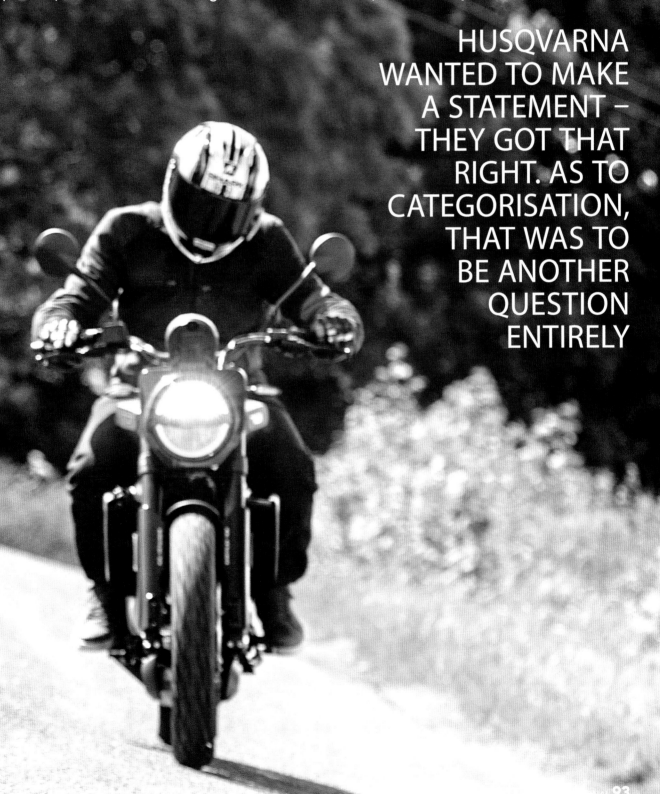

Specification

VITPILEN 701 | **RRP** 701 VITPILEN – WAS £8899 NOW £7549
701 SVARTPILEN – WAS £9349 NOW £7999

ENGINE: 693cc Liquid-cooled, single cylinder four-stroke **POWER:** 75hp / 55kW @ 8500rpm | **TORQUE:** 53LB-FT / 72Nm @ 6750rpm | **TRANSMISSION:** Six gears | **FRAME:** Steel trellis | **FRONT SUSPENSION:** WP fully adjustable 43mm forks | **REAR SUSPENSION:** WP fully adjustable single shock | **FRONT BRAKE:** 320mm disc with four-piston radial Brembo caliper. Cornering ABS **REAR BRAKE:** 240mm rear disc with single-piston caliper. Cornering ABS **FRONT TYRE:** 120/70 ZR17 | **REAR TYRE:** 160/60 ZR17 | **SEAT HEIGHT:** 835mm | **FUEL TANK:** 12 litres/2.64 gallons | **FUEL ECONOMY:** 80.7mpg (claimed) | **KERB WEIGHT:** 158kg | **CONTACT:** www.husqvarna-motorcycles.com

HUSQVARNA WANTED TO MAKE A STATEMENT – THEY GOT THAT RIGHT. AS TO CATEGORISATION, THAT WAS TO BE ANOTHER QUESTION ENTIRELY

four-stroke single cylinder motor comes courtesy of modern design and electronics trickery, the horsepower good for a claimed 75hp and 72Nm. Nothing remarkable about that you might think, but if ever a bike was to offer an honest ride, with a superb power-to-weight ratio, then this is it. What is equally as important is that it sets a benchmark for urban riding, which is exactly what Husqvarna was hoping for with this nod to the street bike scene.

Whilst the seat height at 830mm is more dirt-bike, the actual seating position is far more aggressive, tipping the rider forward over the mid-section as one grabs hold of the clip-ons. Turning the key in the ignition, the message display pops up immediately on the single digital display, making everything clearly visible. I then hit the starter and am struck immediately by the raspy tone of the engine. Everything about this bike would prove to be responsive, from the light slipper clutch to the six-speed box. Power comes via the ride-by-wire throttle, and that is when I discover how good this engine truly is.

Get the revs wrong, however, and it quickly lets you know about it. Taking it up to around 45mph at 5000rpm in third, and I feel a slight vibration through my hands… so I wind it on, and suddenly that engine noise turns into a growl as a secondary power band kicks in and fires me down the road. I am through the gears and heading towards the limiter, but goodness knows what that is exactly, because forums vary so widely, and I could not find any evidence of it on the Husqvarna website.

No matter. It was like a slam in the face, bringing a wide grin as opposed to a grimace. This is one mean, highly tuned machine, and any qualms I had of something lacking finesse were quickly binned. Light of weight, it is as agile as a ballet dancer and fantastic to punch out of sweeping corners. Point and shoot, point and shoot, tipping the

bars left and right and the bike follows my line and never misses a beat. This bike is style and substance rolled into one, and I am in a place where I feel securely planted. The up and down shifter and ABS enhanced the excellent rideability, and the handlebars were comfortably wide enough apart to offer good leverage. A quick check on the accessories part of Husqvarna's website lists bar end mirrors to complete the café look, should you wish to.

As to taking a mate for a ride on an afternoon jaunt, the smaller they are the better as there's no grab rail, so I doubt your pillion will thank you for the lift unless you are happy to have someone grabbing on for dear life to your leathers.

What Vitpilen's designers have done so well is to create a street bike for the 21st century, one with a unique look and a superb engine. Oh yes, they have thrown in a tank and a tail, and a seat of course, and said: 'There you are, we said we could do it, now you go and ride it and prove us wrong'. Well I cannot, and I will not, because the 701 takes me back to what motorcycling used to be, when riding was for exhilaration and fun.

For over a century, Swedish design has permeated the world consciousness. It is where design is woven into the fabric of everyday life, recognised for its emphasis on functionality. Swedes like things to look good, but they also like to keep things simple. It is a part of the fabric of life. Husqvarna fits perfectly into the equation. Whether the 701 competes in the buying stakes with other naked roadsters still remains to be seen, as some may argue that the price tag doesn't befit the simplistic styling, but let us not ignore the amount of high tech hidden away beneath the exterior.

There is a timeless, yet progressive energy to this streamlined bike and, yes, it is a multitude of likes once you are on the road. The 701 is made for high-end kicks, and if you want to scare yourself by prodding the hair trigger, it will do that, too.

Without doubt this trendsetter wears its heart on its sleeve. It sits on an honest platform, and when potential buyers get their heads around that, we might start to see a few (more?) on the road. I can only hope so, because it deserves to be seen. And if it is gimmicks you are after, then forget it and look elsewhere. No, you won't be bamboozled by all the modern technology and gizmo aides found on so many other modern bikes, so fear not my friends, because what you get is what you see… classic Swedish simplicity at its finest. **CRI**

KAWASAKI W800 CAFE

RETRO RIDE WITH A TWIN PERSONALITY

IMAGES: GARY D CHAPMAN

TOP MARKS TO
KAWASAKI FOR
KEEPING ITS EYE
ON THE BALL
WITH REGARDS TO
THE SEEMINGLY
UNSTOPPABLE
FORCE OF NEO-
CLASSICISM

Whilst I appreciate that most everything in life is subjective, I believe I may well be fawning over the epitome of a café racer, albeit in modern guise. Yes, I know, that is a bold statement, but having ridden a number of motorbikes of late, all great bikes in their own right, somehow the Kawaski W800 Café stands out for its sheer audacity.

Top marks to Kawasaki for keeping its eye on the ball with regards to the seemingly unstoppable force of neo-classicism. The timing of the launch of the W800 Café was impeccable, almost a divine intervention, drawing attention away from the sportsbike arena to one of spirit, minimalism and old-school character. Metalheads were drawn immediately to the modern materials assembled in an attractive package that oozed charisma. Having then dialled in an M-shaped handlebar, round-faced instrumentation, comfortable two-tone leather seat, bikini fairing and simple switchgear that a child could manage, Kawasaki pretty much nailed it.

Of course, looks make up only one aspect of the overall package, with the ride controlling the main factor. So, the first thing of note when firing up the 773cc fuel-injected, air-cooled, sohc parallel-twin is the low burble through the peashooter exhausts. Slipping it into first and immediately I felt how light the bike was as I moved off. Smooth and effortless, I was soon out of the village and joining traffic.

Getting up to speed, however, seemed at odds. It was not long before I discovered how comfortable the bike was firing at low revs in high gears, and quite happy to trundle along in 30mph speed limits in fourth. The issue seemed to be when I wanted to take it through the gears at a more smooth, but sensible, rate of knots, finding that each time the engine grumbled, nay, complained, before I changed up a gear.

On the flip-side, when I made it on to an open, clear stretch of road, I could wind up the throttle to max revs before changing, making full use of the assist and slipper clutch, and it was bang on, the chassis offering a smooth balancing act as I swept round curves. Yes, this is one capable machine when you ride it hard, or fancy a bimble at a leisurely pace in high gear, it is just that there appeared to be no middle ground. Was I dealing with some kind of Jekyll and Hyde here?

The reach from seat to grips was certainly comfortable, although after a while my neck began to complain and I found myself flicking my head from side to side to relieve the strain that was building oh so annoyingly slowly.

My first proper outing on the W800 was to a bike night. I had hardly switched off the engine when a fellow biker approached, said his mate had just purchased one, and asked what I thought of it. I explained about the engine's somewhat twin personality, particularly through the mid rev range. It would appear that I was not alone in that thought, as his friend had mentioned a similar experience. So it wasn't just me, then. I went on to say that whilst the engine pulled well enough, once one winds on the power, pushing above 4000rpm, it becomes far more mellow, thanks in no small part to the balance shaft, which reduces vibration.

The W800 pays homage to Kawasaki's legendary, and original, 1966 W1 650, its first parallel twin and, at the time, the largest capacity four-stroke machine manufactured in Japan and, without doubt, one of the most enduring and identifiable Kawasaki motorcycle families; with the classic looks and ride feel possessed by an older generation, particularly with its handling characteristics.

Don't misunderstand me. Alongside the W800 Café is a sister bike, the W800 Street, both having little in common with previous iterations, the newly born Euro4 compliant twins being 90 per cent new with a whole host of styling, technical and practical changes. For starters, they share a completely new chassis, and each machine has powerful new brakes – including a rear disc for the first time on a W – as well as ABS and, in another nod to contemporary riding, LED lighting.

Fully A2 licence compliant and with a targeted maximum power of 35kW, the authenticity, classic styling and seductive good looks of the W800 Café and its sister are bound to attract new riders... as well as tempting existing licence holders who will, no doubt, appreciate the carefully considered simplicity of form and function. Wherever I happened to stop on this bike, riders were drawn to it, commenting on its looks, asking how it rode... and how much it cost!

Kawasaki's designers clearly had their thinking caps on straight when they thought about how the vertical twin could talk the torque, the characteristically reliable handling that comes from a rigid new frame with large-diameter wheels, and the throaty roar from those twin, low-slung peashooter exhaust cans. Cleverly

cultivated and packaged to recall the bikes of yesteryear, it offers lighter, sportier handling and a certain feel-good factor once on board.

The designers also thought it might be fun to create a game of hide and seek, because beneath the classic look and feel of the W800 lay hidden a few modern concessions. The engine, for example, whilst remaining true to its air-cooled Vertical Twin roots, benefits from the addition of O2 sensors and revised catalysers to ensure clean

Specification

KAWASAKI W800 CAFÉ | RRP £9099

ENGINE: 733cc, air-cooled, four-stroke Vertical Twin, SOHC, eight valves | **POWER:** 47bhp (35kW @ 6000rpm) | **MAX TORQUE** 46lb-ft / 62.9Nm @ 4800rpm | **TRANSMISSION:** Five-speed | **FRAME:** Double cradle, high tensile steel | **SUSPENSION:** (F) 41mm telescopic fork, non-adjustable (R) Twin shocks with spring preload adjustability | **BRAKES:** (F) Single 320mm petal-style disc with two-piston calipers, ABS (R) Single 270mm petal-style disc with two-piston caliper, ABS | **TYRES:** (F) 100/90-18 (R) 130/80-18 | **SEAT HEIGHT:** 790mm/31.3in | **FUEL TANK:** 15 litres | **KERB WEIGHT:** 223kg | **CONTACT:** www.kawasaki.co.uk

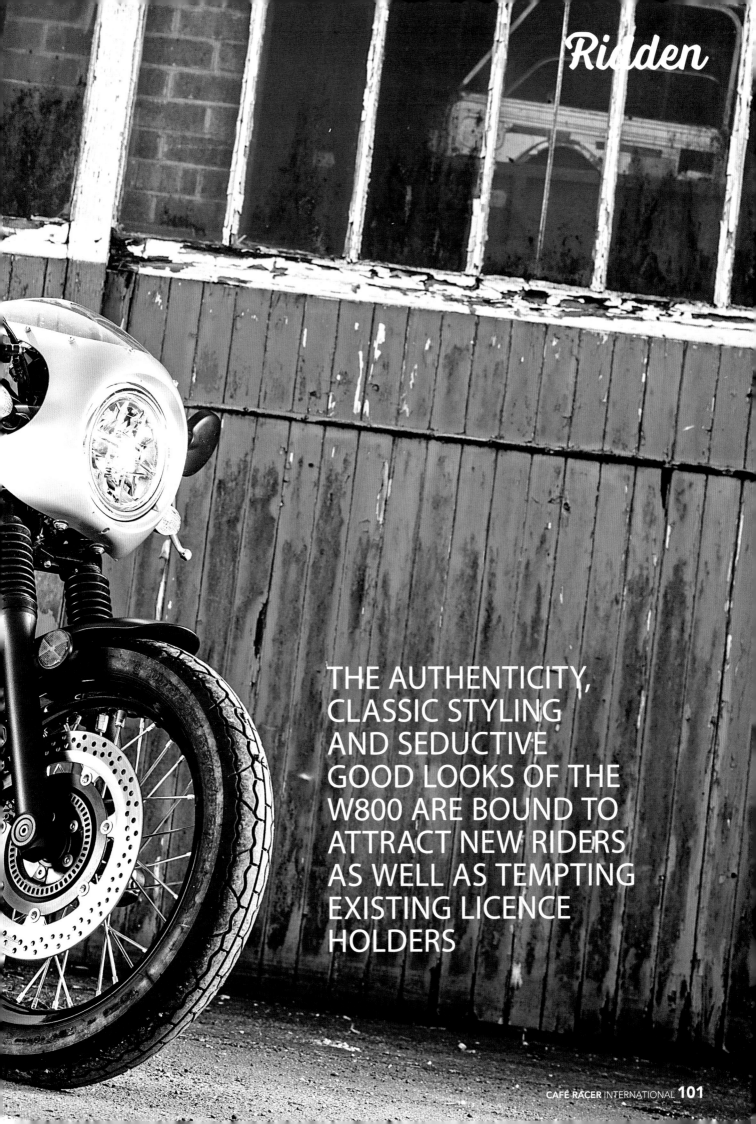

THE AUTHENTICITY, CLASSIC STYLING AND SEDUCTIVE GOOD LOOKS OF THE W800 ARE BOUND TO ATTRACT NEW RIDERS AS WELL AS TEMPTING EXISTING LICENCE HOLDERS

Second opinion

Simply starting up the W800 takes one back to, dare I say, the late 1960s when my Triumph Bonneville sounded remarkably similar – oh, so very British in sound and looks is this 773cc vertical twin. The big difference is going to be that the W800 will stay in one piece and hopefully run forever, no matter how hard pushed.

Sitting on the bike, immediately two things become obvious: firstly I can get both feet flat on the floor, a big plus for me, and secondly those handlebars are reminiscent of the ones I fitted to my 1967 Velocette Venom – already the retro side of the bike is kicking in. By modern standards, the tyres look skinny, but once on the move are more than adequate for the type of riding likely to be undertaken. Just five gears on this sleek gearbox had me double-checking for that sixth gear; not a problem though, as the top three gears are moderately high ratioed. I would like to see the footrest at least two inches further back, and please Mr Kawasaki fit a centre-stand. Starting the bike up and the engine idles at around 2000rpm whilst warming up, then settles to around 1200rpm at tickover. The most annoying part of the bike is the vibes that are felt through the footrests and handlebars at revs between 2.8k and 4.5k, something that editor Michael also picked up on.

Unfortunately, in top gear 60mph equates to 3.5k revs and 70mph to 4k revs. Ride the bike briskly through the gears and all is okay once over 4.5k revs. Overall, the W800 is a good-looking and superbly finished bike that is spoilt by those mid-range vibes.

Roger Jones

emissions that comfortably clear Euro4 regulations. The addition of an Assist & Slipper Clutch offers a much lighter feel, as well as a back-torque limiting function that helps prevent rear-wheel hop when downshifting.

Taking the bike into town after dusk, visibility is clearly enhanced by the large LED headlamp, with position lamps in the six high-beam chambers (four for low-beam, two for high-beam) ensuring the whole lamp appears lit, akin to a retro-style bulb headlamp. The compact switchgear also has been designed to add a vintage touch, giving the handlebars a light, uncluttered appearance.

As to the double-cradle frame, looks can be deceptive. It may look familiar and unchanged, but the required rigidity of each and every piece was re-evaluated, so while keeping the pipe outer diameters unchanged, the pipe thicknesses were adjusted as necessary. Round tubes with a smooth finish and minimum welds and gussets contribute to the quality appearance. Dual rear shocks, adjustable for spring preload, offer a smooth ride and clean look, whilst stronger stopping power comes care of a larger diameter 320mm front disc paired with a 270mm rear disc, the latter having been previously a drum-type brake. Also, ABS is standard equipment.

Traditional instrumentation includes individual speedometer and tachometer with classic display. The multi-function LCD screen incorporates an odometer, tripmeter and clock. A full range of indicator lamps includes an FI warning lamp, dual turn signal indicators, low fuel level indicator, high beam indicator, neutral indicator, and oil pressure warning lamp. Key styling elements include the sleek curves of the fuel tank, its larger volume – increased from 14 to 15 litres – giving it more presence, and the café racer styled front cowl contributing to the racy looks.

Of course, aside from all those sweeping, detailed, but subtle modern internals beneath the retro-style exterior, you are pretty much guaranteed a bike that will perform reliably, and one with both a planted feel and sharp handling. That handling particularly comes into its own in mid-turn, when it felt securely planted, although I did find the suspension a bit soft. Having mentioned that, it was particularly welcome on some of the patchier road surfaces I travelled.

The W800 garnered attention at most of the stops I made along the way. It's a fun, great-looking bike, comfy enough for a weekend ride.

I am not sure I would recommend it for touring, although it was not as punishing as some of the sports bikes I have ridden.

Of course, the Kawasaki W800 Café does not stand alone in the retro-styling stakes. It certainly looks the part, but then add to the equation contemporaries such as the Ducati Scrambler Café Racer, BMW R nineT Racer, Triumph Street Cup, Triumph Thruxton RS, Honda CB1000R+ Neo Sports Café, Vitpilen 701, or Royal Enfield's Continental GT 650. All stunning bikes, all satisfying styling requirements, all manufacturers vying for your attention on showroom floors, all at varying price points in this rapidly expanding market. The choice is mind-boggling, and it will only get worse. In the meantime, these are all beautiful bikes, with their own characteristics, all wearing their badges of honour with pride.

I guess you could say originality never goes out of style. I guess you could also say there is a lot to like about café racers, despite them not being built for long rides. They are cool and eye-catching, they ooze attitude and style, they kick into touch plenty of wannabes. And just to add to the confusion, Kawasaki offers the inline four Z900 RS Café. Oh dear, it brings to mind the expression, 'You'll never hang yourself.' Why? Because you can never make a decision. Best of luck in this minefield. CRI

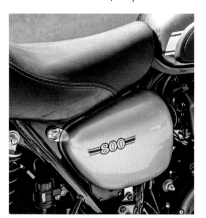

KICKING AGAINST THE MAINSTREAM

ROYAL ENFIELD CONTINENTAL GT 650 TWIN

IMAGES: GARY D CHAPMAN

THE WHIMSICAL GT MAKES YOU GO AND PLAY, BECAUSE YOU WANT TO

Technology exists for the creative common good, or so we have convinced ourselves. The internet and social media app gods are content to leave us drifting in a cyberspace bereft of human contact, as we remain consumed by daily advances from the digital kingdom. We have stood as willing bystanders while the corporate fatcats have continued to manipulate the tectonic shift in our daily lives and habits. Slowly but surely, we have become a part of the techno apparatchik, failing to lift our heads from our smartphones and Apple watches, for fear of missing the next text message. It is seemingly impossible to stop the advance of technology, even when it trips over itself. So, a question. How often do you put your computer into sleep mode after a working day, then continue to react to the pinging of emails on your cell phone? I thought so.

Time for a reality check. The British come out tops as the worst offenders for spending extended hours at their desks. It would seem that enjoying free time is somewhat of a guilty pleasure. Sickness, depression, crippling back pain, heart ailments and mental health problems are all associated with overwork. The forecast, if you did not already know it, is Burnout.

My daughter sleeps with her cell phone on her pillow. Snapchat, Facebook and text alerts are her nightly companions from hell. It has become a daily occurrence to witness people stalking Britain's high streets with heads down, coffee in one hand, texting with the other, oblivious to their surroundings. They ignore pedestrian crossings, walk in front of oncoming traffic, and then offer two fingers to any motorcyclist who has nearly ploughed into them. As long as you did not miss that last text. That is all right then. But no, it is not.

No question about it, technology has taken over our lives, and it is also on the cusp of taking over our minds and our freedom of spirit. But we still have the power to switch off the phone and walk away, if we are brave enough. So here is the rub. I challenge you to do exactly that. After leaving work on a Friday switch off your mobile, or, if you are not strong-willed enough to do that, at least switch it to silent mode, then ignore those incoming emails until Monday morning looms large once again. Unthinkable, I know. During your 48-hour weekend stretch, make time for yourself and your bike. Plan a micro adventure. It does not have to be far from home. Breathe in the fresh air, and if it happens to be raining, sod it, don the waterproofs and brave the elements anyway. You will feel a whole lot better for the experience, believe me.

But what steed, you ask? Technology, somewhat insidiously, has infiltrated our biking world, with modern iterations overwhelming us with gizmos: leaning ABS, linked braking systems, electronic quickshifters, heated hand grips, crash apps… the list goes on. It begs the question: how much do we need, and how much do we actually use?

Ridden ROYAL ENFIELD CONTINENTAL GT 650 TWIN

This literary preamble brings me nicely to Royal Enfield, who have kicked against the mainstream with the Continental GT, keeping things nice and simple and uncomplicated. Modern technology? To hell with that. With the Continental you get Bosch dual-channel ABS, and that's it. Seriously. Time to play, and you know exactly what you are playing with. The bike is retro and cool and uber familiar and, of course, boasts a significant heritage, proudly taking a step back from the real world. Instead it leads us into a world of whimsy. Climb aboard and away you go. It's something you just do because you want to. So, is this bike out of

between the Busy Bee in Watford and the Ace Cafe in Stonebridge. A hallowed fraternity. No badge of honour, just a feeling of satisfaction, and a certain level of smugness.

I never dreamt that it would happen again, but the Continental brought back the hooligan in me. Feet planted on the rear-set foot pegs, canted over the sculpted tank and hands gripping the clip-ons, with the beautiful sound of the exhaust rumbling away, and suddenly the nerves had gone and I found myself carving bends before powering away from following traffic, spitting gravel with a joie de vivre. A rough-neck rider enjoying raw emotion.

step with the real world? Who cares. Doubters would be missing a trick because this is a bike for the carefree and impulsive.

The Continental is a partition of a whole into two parts. It is old school, yet it is brand new. It carries RE's most powerful twin-cylinder engine to date, the new air-cooled 650 parallel twin, driven by a six-speed gearbox. That's a first for the brand, too. With the exhaust offering a familiar note straight from the 60s, the bike oozes the nostalgic café racer silhouette of the period, yet packs in its steel tubular frame a raft of refined modern engineering. You can expect 80 per cent of the torque arriving before 2500rpm, and it will rev all the way to the redline when pushed, maxing out at a ton.

Ah, that magical figure, the go-to speed for leather-clad café racers of old who would carve up the Tarmac from one café to the next with the aim of becoming a member of the exclusive 'Ton-Up Boys'. Forget the frills, it was a simple case of thrills on a quick burst

Being A2-licence friendly, there's only 47bhp on offer, but that's fine. The advantage of the six-speed means I could drop a couple of gears for overtakes, before opening the throttle to the next bend, when the slip-assist clutch would come into play, mitigating the effects of engine braking on fast deceleration. Back on a straight, I wind it up, and wind it up some more, and the needle heads upwards, and goodness me this is exhilarating.

I find my confidence surprisingly boosted by the Pirelli Phantom Sportcomp tyres, which offer excellent grip and control on entry into bends. The finely tuned suspension also comes in as edgy and impulsive, but still with a comfortable feel, and it all adds to the dynamic ride.

Mentioning comfort, that might be questionable for some because this bike is a café racer by its very nature. It has a low (790mm) seat, which favours those that like to plant two feet on the ground, and if your preference is for sliding back in the seat and leaning forward towards those retro clocks, whilst taking a firm grip on the clip-on handlebars, you will be in your element, even though you may find that the back of your neck is somewhat creaky if you spend overly long in the saddle.

In a nutshell, it's a 21st century café crème and, quite literally, a ton of fun and ideal for biker meets and Sunday bursts. It also about passes muster as a commuter, if you are happy to carry your lunchbox in a knapsack. But then that kind of spoils the overall look, if you get my drift. And yes, of course you can opt for something roughly similar in styling, that may knock the socks off the Continental when it comes down to power and performance, with added bells and whistles and accessories. But then it begs the question of whether you simply yearn for a café racer with stripped-back refinement. The heftier the price, the more the fun suddenly starts to trickle away along with your cash.

So often I have reached the trailhead and turned left when the arrow indicated right. A path less travelled indeed. Not knowing what is round the next corner is all part of the attraction, for then you take nothing for granted. To quote Mark Twain: 'Twenty years from now you will be more disappointed by the things you didn't do than by the ones you did do. So throw off the bowlines, sail away from the safe harbour. Catch the trade winds in your sails. Explore. Dream. Discover.' And Twain didn't give Huck Finn a smartphone when he floated down the Mississippi on a makeshift raft with the runaway slave. **CRI**

Specification

ROYAL ENFIELD CONTINENTAL GT 650 TWIN | FROM £5699 OTR

ENGINE: PARALLEL TWIN, 648CC FOUR-STROKE, SOHC, AIR-OIL COOLED | **POWER:** 47BHP (35KW) @ 7250RPM | **TORQUE:** 38.4 LB-FT/52NM @ 5250RPM | **GEARBOX:** SIX SPEED | **FRAME:** STEEL TUBULAR, DOUBLE CRADLE | **SUSPENSION:** (F) 41MM, 110MM TRAVEL (R) TWIN COIL-OVER SHOCKS, 88MM TRAVEL, FIVE-STAGE PRELOAD ADJUSTMENT | **WEIGHT:** 198KG DRY | **BRAKES:** (F) 320MM SINGLE DISC (R) 240MM SINGLE DISC | **WHEELS/TYRES:** 18-INCH ALLOY-RIMMED WHEELS. (R) PIRELLI PHANTOM SPORTCOMP 100/90 18 (L) 100/70 18 | **SEAT HEIGHT:** 790MM | **FUEL CAPACITY:** 12.5 LITRES | **CONTACT:** WWW.ROYALENFIELD.COM

JIM ALONZE'S 350CC DUCATI SINGLE

BESPOKE ENGINEERING: Bridging the gap between traditional race-inspired café racer and trophy cabinet-filling, detail-obsessed show queen, is Jim Alonze's impeccable 350cc Ducati single. The race-developed powerplant has the pedigree that a café racer deserves, yet Jim has also applied some sideways thinking and impeccable attention to detail in each and every part of this truly astounding machine. The level of bespoke engineering – from tip to tail – belies the machine's diminutive size and capacity, with the end result being a giant amongst the breed. – *Dave Manning* **CRI**

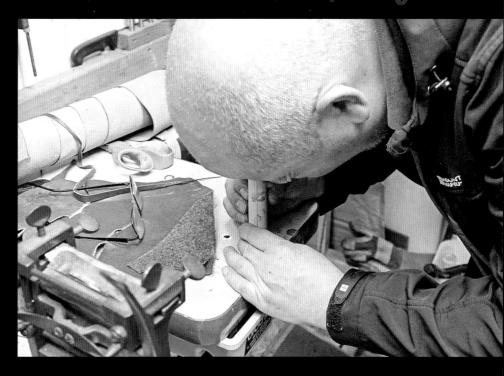

A STITCH IN TIME

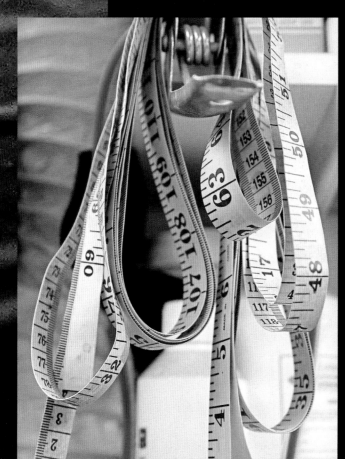

RIPS, SCUFFS, ABRASIONS, ALTERATIONS AND PANEL REPLACEMENTS. IF YOU HAVE A PROBLEM WITH YOUR LEATHERS, LINCS REPAIR IS THE GO-TO WORKSHOP FOR MANY A BIKER

LINCS REPAIR
TELEPHONE: **01522 697407**
MOBILE: **0771 9620 830**
LINCSREPAIR@TALKTALK.NET
WWW.LINCSREPAIR.CO.UK

"WHILST I HAVE A LARGE NUMBER OF CUSTOMERS FROM LINCOLNSHIRE, BIKERS COME FROM ALL OVER THE COUNTRY"

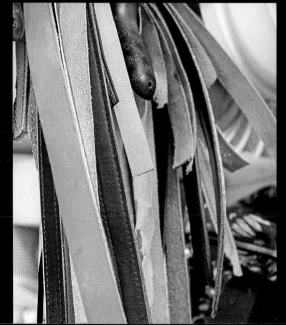

When a couple walk into a store, the wife heads one way and her husband seeks out ladies' handbags, what is one to think? Smile inwardly and ignore, or is one's curiosity piqued? Is he some kind of leather fetishist, or is he on the look-out for a present? As it happens, Al Lui is the former, and happy to admit to it.

His name is known to the motorcycle fraternity nationwide. As the owner of Lincs Repair, Al carries out leather alterations and repairs to an extremely high standard. Rips, scuffs, abrasions, alterations and panel replacements... should you have happened to slide along the Tarmac at any stage, then he is the go-to repairer, with bikers travelling the length and breadth of the country seeking his expertise.

When I popped into his small workshop, he had just cleared his rack of customers' gear, having replaced crash-damaged panels and carried out general repairs and alterations. Al can also perform ozone treatment on motorcycle clothing, a hygiene and odour elimination process. I know, I've been there. I first met Al when I acquired an RST one-piece race suit. Whilst fairly new and in great condition, it had been in a smokey environment, and also had a 'saggy' bottom. Al took two inches out of the bottom panel, reduced the amount of material on the thighs, and then put the suit into the ozone chamber to give it a thorough refresh. The results were amazing.

I guess the business name gives it away, but Al is based in Lincoln. I ask him how he got into the industry. "It began as a hobby. I used to carve with a swivel knife, outlining and cutting designs into the surface of leather as an initial stage to tooling the leather with decorations, and it progressed from there. I worked for a number of different businesses, including charities and in the care sector, repairing as much as possible including furniture, so I trained in upholstery to the stage where I was repairing everything and anything."

Al then trained in SMART repairs, a small and medium area repair technique, which uses the latest paint technology, alloy wheel refurbishment and specialised dent removal processes to restore vehicles to showroom condition. However, spending hours kneeling by the exterior of a car was simply a step too far, so eventually he gave up on that and instead pursued his main interest of all things leather.

"In the beginning my late wife Sally used to moan at me, saying she was a leather widow. We would go shopping in large department stores and I would disappear looking at leather furniture, picking up handbags, opening them and looking inside to see how well they had been put together and what with. She loved telling people that her husband had more handbags in his man cave than she had! I have been very lucky, having worked for a couple of companies within the leather industry where I learnt some extremely useful techniques and methods, saving me years of trial and error.

"Sally started working with me and we picked up a few contracts for handbag repair companies, which provided very interesting and often very challenging work. We examined everything in detail as I was interested in how they were made, what they were using, the types of stitching involved, etcetera. We condensed in six months what should have taken us six years to learn. Even today, many years later, I am still coming across things that are new, as techniques and products are constantly evolving, so I am always learning."

Al does not deal in exotic leathers. He won't buy in crocodile or alligator skins because he does not like the way the animals are farmed. He does, however, deal with kangaroo leather, although again he does not buy it in. "Quite simply, I do deal with all the leathers when they come in, but I won't buy certain leathers or hides to replace them."

As a long-time biker, Al was keen to get into motorbike leathers as a new skill-set. "I started off scrambling round the woods, stripping down C50s and everything else, and then became interested in how the clothing was put together. I knew manufacturers wouldn't use any old leather to do that. Fortunately, I was able to get in with a company who taught me quite a lot and I developed from there.

"In terms of the leather business, I have worked on everything from private jets to Lamborghinis and Ferraris, to your normal everyday cars, jackets and bags. I was even involved in the set up of an international company that makes travel gadgets. I handled the preparation of the aeroplane seats, which was part of an aeroplane mock-up made for a television commercial.

"I certainly couldn't survive if all I did was repair motorbike leathers, because sometimes they can take hours to do and then I don't actually earn anything, but it's a challenge and most of the time I enjoy it.

"Whilst I have a large number of customers from here in Lincolnshire, bikers come from all over the country. It's nice when I go out on two wheels and see other bikers wearing product that I have repaired or altered, because I know they are going to be safe wearing it. What I mean by that is there are people out there who use sewing machines both domestically and professionally to work on motorcycle leathers. Most are good at what they do, but some are not, especially when you ask them about more technical details such as on leather suit construction, when they will fall pretty short, and that is when problems can arise, such as when they are sewing a leather suit up or replacing a zip, which isn't really good enough for the job, or the techniques they adopt to do it."

A number of safety areas are brought into play when putting a suit together, the basic one being the stitch lines, whereby two pieces of leather are sewn together with a sewn seam (line); it is that thread that is holding the two pieces together, so the strength of that piece is all down to how strong the thread is, irrespective of how good the leather is.

"That most definitely is not what you would want on a motorcycle suit because you are completely relying on whatever thread has been used to keep it together," says Al. "As a minimum there should be at least two stitch lines on each seam. One seam often used, which has two stitch lines, is a flat felled seam, i.e., two pieces of leather sewn together. One side is then folded over and another stitch is laid along the length of the seam next to the first, but above it, so you have one stitch line that can be seen on top of the leather (it looks like decorative stitch) and a hidden stitch line, which is shielded between the leathers. So if you have an accident and start sliding, and you grind through that top layer of leather and stitching, you still have the one underneath as a fall back.

"If you wanted to go one step further, there would be another hidden stitch line underneath there so you have three to go through, so in essence you have to grind through all that leather and three layers of stitching before it pops open, reducing the chances of it opening and exposing your skin to the road surface. I have seen suits made with only one stitch line and I have seen the outcome of a lot of people who have been in that situation, and it worries me.

"Sometimes minor accidents can incur nasty injuries because bikers are wearing cheap leathers, or perhaps they haven't looked after them. Leather is tanned so it does not rot, but it can degrade. The fibres of the leather can start to degrade because of everything that soaks through them and then around the fibres, which weakens the strength between fibres, which holds leather together."

Previously, any hard armour had to be CE tested and the rest of the suit could be made out of any leather the maker saw fit. That was until April 2018 when it became law that any motorcycle clothing is PPE and all aspects of the newly made clothing has to be tested. (All motorcycle clothing first placed on the market from April 21, 2018 is required to conform to PPE regulations 2016/425). "I have personally seen a suit that was bought off the web and they had even used split leathers to make the suit; any accident in that would have been catastrophic for the rider," says Al.

"For example, bovine leather (cow hide) can be up to 10 or 15mm thick in some parts (motorcycle leathers are on average about 1.4mm thick), so you could potentially get a lot of slices out of one leather hide. The tanning house will skive the leather by cutting the top layer off, and that is your premium cut of leather. The fibre structure at the top of the leather hide (epidermal layer) is much more tightly knitted together and is, therefore, the strongest part of the leather. Every slice of leather under the top cut is called a split leather. Closer to the bottom of the hide the fibre structure becomes far looser, and right at the bottom of the leather hide the strength of the fibre structure is equivalent to toilet paper, so split leathers are absolutely no good for motorcycle PPE leathers whatsoever.

"Often the grain pattern you see on leather isn't the original; we call this corrected grain, where it has been artificially embossed to give a uniform grain pattern, along with being refinished with a colour coat and protective layer."

Whilst I was chatting with Al on the Sunday morning, who should pop in but Rob Child, well known as a sidecar passenger in the Isle of Man TT and Spa races. Rob had brought in his partner Jane Morris's race suit, also a sidecar passenger, but with a different team. A slider panel had been put in the wrong place when her sponsor had had the suit made, and Al was charged with sorting it out.

"I have people turning up at some really strange hours," Al tells me, "even evenings up to about 9pm after they finish work. I don't mind as long as I know they are coming and not just rocking up, as I like to get out on my bike as much as I can."

Interestingly, as a man who works daily with leather, Al prefers to wear textiles when on two wheels. "My whole life is leather, but I mostly don't wear it, partly because I get hot when riding. Leather is the best medium you have got for protecting yourself against abrasion, but there is no thermal protection in the material or impact protection, other than what is added to it. Leather also is super-absorbent, even though it has coatings on the surface to reduce the amount that goes on and soaks in. You have no protection on the underside of it, the skin side, so that makes it even more absorbent. We perspire, and when we are really concentrating on something we get really hot and that's why if you don't wear base layers, when you try and take a one-piece off you are dislocating shoulders! Textiles don't quite have the same abrasion property as leather. I had a slide recently, having lost it on a bend, and I slid across the road, ending up in the grass verge. The textiles suffered a few scuffs, so they do what they say they do. A lot of the Cordura material is like a 600 denier, so it's generally tough stuff."

We then turned our focus to caring for leathers. "People tend not to look after their leathers, even after they have been to me and had repairs or alterations made," says Al. "Being absorbent, leather will suck in all sorts of things when you are on your bike. You have a clear protective coat on the top to help protect it, it is tough, but it is very thin. Just think how many times you have ridden with your visor up; it is painful when things hit you, such as a fly. Think about grit, dust and bits of tar flicking up from the road and hitting the leather. In time it abrades it, wearing away the protective layer and attacking the all-important epidermal strength layer. Then people might chuck it in the garage, which is the worst place you can put leather. You have got all this moisture

from being outside, and the inside of the leather is full of body oils and germs. The leather is warm and you place it in a cold, damp garage, and that's where you leave it for the next week or more. That's when you find you have white mould patches when you return to it, and it starts to smell very funky. Leather doesn't rot, but think about all that body oil soaked into and surrounding each fibre. Body oil can rot; when it does it will split the leather's fibres apart and then you lose its protective strength.

"Often I have leathers brought to me to be cleaned. Fortunately I have an ozone chamber, which helps eradicate a lot of the nasties. Whilst it is difficult for people to clean the inside of leathers without appropriate cleaning and sanitising products, generally what everybody needs to do for the outside on a regular basis is buy a dedicated cleaner that has been specifically made for motorcycle leathers. I have always been against trying to name specific products because there are so many about and they change. If your suit is caked up with flies, my advice is to take a hot cloth in a bowl with the tiniest amount of washing-up liquid and simply lay it over the worst areas for a few minutes where the flies are, to soften them up before wiping them off. Grab another cloth and your cleaner and a leather protector. It's not particularly difficult, but just by giving your leathers a general clean every few rides, you are giving them far more chance of being able to carry on doing what they are supposed to do. Always allow them to dry naturally in a warm, ventilated room. Using an artificial heat source to try and dry your leathers can cause them to harden and even shrivel up. And never use anything abrasive like baby wipes!

"People buy all sorts of aroma sprays and under-sink remedies, which simply mask the smell. It's like spilling milk in the back of a car. You can try and mask the smell with sprays, but what people use is not actually getting rid of what is causing the problem, so that needs to be sorted first."

At Lincs Repair the leathers are cleaned by hand, using appropriate leather-specific, water-based cleaning products designed for the safe deep cleaning of leathers. For the inside, specialist antimicrobial products are used which are effective for political micro control of A/H1N1 swine, P.aeruginosa, E.coli, S.aureus, enterococcus hirae, bacillus subtilis, MRSA, C.difficile, aspergillus niger, listeria, salmonella and legionella pneumophila. "Unfortunately, as some odours can still stick to leather, for that I use the ozone chamber," explains Al.

"Ozone is created with super high electricity charges passing through the air molecules and it explodes them, and one part that comes off is an ozone molecule. That molecule attracts mould spores and odours, and they stick to it. Because it is very volatile, it doesn't last very long. It kills itself and takes the spores and odours with it. It then goes back to being oxygen. Ozone imparts its own kind of fragrance afterwards, which has been likened to chlorine or that smell after a violent thunderstorm, but this doesn't usually last very long."

Sadly, Al's wife Sally passed away four years ago. Now approaching his mid-50s and working alone, he is clearly still passionate about what he does. "Sometimes I don't actually earn anything by doing motorcycle leather repairs, but I enjoy a challenge. You have something tangible to deal with. You know what you started with and you know what you have got at the end of it. It's all about being as safe as you can possibly be as a rider."

Such is Al's popularity with bikers, that word of mouth, biker forums, a Facebook page and a dedicated website are his lines to the outside world. But he seems happiest inside his cramped workshop, surrounded by work benches, an eclectic assortment of machinery and looms and roll upon roll of leather, amongst which he can often be found beavering away well past midnight, by which time even the family cat has got fed with him chatting away and has slunk off into the night. CRI

"PEOPLE TEND NOT TO LOOK AFTER THEIR LEATHERS, EVEN AFTER THEY HAVE BEEN TO ME AND HAD REPAIRS OR ALTERATIONS MADE"

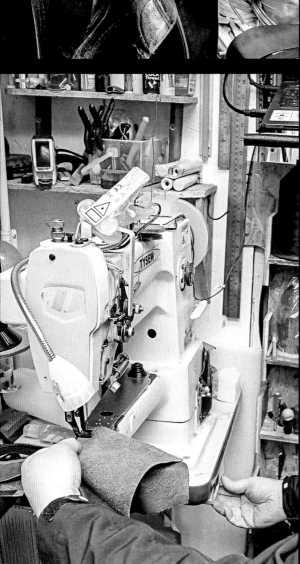

EWAN MacDONALD'S GT550

HEAD-TURNER: Despite the fact that many café racers of the Sixties were built around two-stroke engines (Ariel Leaders and Arrows, particularly), the common misconception is that motive power has to be supplied by a four-stroke engine, of either single or twin cylinder configuration. Ewan MacDonald knew differently and not only went for Suzuki two-stroke power, but also for a triple cylinder, namely a GT550! Handling of the Seventies stroker was improved by the addition of GSX-R forks, wheels and brakes, and a Harris Performance swinging arm, while the banshee wail of the two-stroke triple is set free by the Higgspeed expansion chambers. With the rust and patina of the steel fuel tank replicated on the plastic tail unit and front mudguard, and the 'MHD' family MacDonald logo on the tank, this is a bike that turns heads and confuses memories. – *Dave Manning* **CRI**

STYLE COUNCIL

ADD A TOUCH OF CLASS TO YOUR RIDES ALONG THE HIGHWAYS, BYWAYS AND BOULEVARDS WITH CRI'S SELECTION OF SOME OF THE LATEST GEAR TO TEMPT YOUR POCKET. GO ON, YOU KNOW YOU CAN'T RESIST...

SHARK S-DRAK 2 TRIPP IN KOO

£309.99 | NEVIS.UK.COM

Well, that name is a bit of a mouthful, but there is no getting away from the fact that this is a hellishly stylish helmet. Just check out the sharp-edge look of the mask and that terrific, streamlined profile, specifically designed to fit the skull shape as closely as possible. With its premium finishes, this neo-retro jet helmet simply oozes charisma and will certainly get you noticed which is, I guess, what you want when riding a motorcycle. The shell is made of multiaxial glassfibre, and incorporates a micro lock ratchet buckle system and a retractable and lightly tinted internal visor with an anti-fog deflector. It also boasts a quick visor release system. In suede lining fabric with a 'peach skin' feel, the interior is removable and is suitable for machine washing (make sure you max out at 30° centigrade). I wear both contact lenses and spectacles, so it is good to note that the S-Drak 2 has an 'EasyFit' system, offering optimal comfort for those that wear glasses. There is also a convenient slot reserved for the Sharktooth intercom. The total vision visor is anti-scratch and anti-fog, and the latter coating can be re-activated. Just a minor point, but for me, the uppermost, inner part of the nose piece could do with a spot of padding. What I find striking is the premium 'gun metal' outer finish, complete with some neat phrases, such as 'Every day is a good day for a ride', and 'The Freedom Instinct'. Neat.

Verdict: No limits, no excuses, if you hanker after neo-retro, and want a helmet that is strikingly handsome, go for it as you will not be disappointed.

NITRO NG-70 GLOVES

£39.99 | NITRORIDER.COM

Well, it just goes to show that you do not have to spend a fortune to acquire a good pair of leather gloves. The modestly priced Nitro NG-70s are part of the latest Nitro collection and I have found them to be ideal for summer riding. Short in stature, the vented construction of these urban styled gloves combines leather and 3D mesh panels for ventilation, with protection in the form of hard TPU knuckles, reinforced panels to critical areas such as the palm and fingers, and soft cushioning on the scaphoid. Touchscreen compatible on the index finger and thumb, they feature a neoprene panel on the inside of the wrist, accordion flex on the back of the hand, twin stitched panels which increases strength and durability, and a large Velcro closure to the wrist. Sizing is S-XXXL.

Verdict: Sports-styled summer riding glove packed with features at a crazy price. Grab a pair now.

ULTIMATE SQUIDGY PLUGS

SRP: £65 | ULTIMATEEAR.COM

I have suffered from tinnitus for more years than I care to remember, brought on, I believe, after years of playing bass next to drummers. All that crashing of cymbals royally screwed my higher frequencies, and as a consequence I live with a constant hiss. With one in 10 Brits suffering from the condition, no doubt there will be a considerable number of bikers in the mix. As a result, I admit to being over-sensitive, if not a little paranoid, about the condition, and therefore am extremely conscious about how to protect what hearing I have left from further damage as a result of riding a bike. So, I have been trying various different types of ear protection of late, not having been entirely happy with the cheap, disposable sort, which I found difficult both to keep in place and not particularly effective. While at last year's Motorcycle Live show, I decided to opt for a pair of custom-made Squidgy Plugs from Ultimate, which are especially engineered for riders. With moulds taken from my ears, thereby guaranteeing a perfect fit, the plugs duly arrived a few weeks later. Hygienic and hypoallergenic, the bespoke ear defenders are made from a soft squidgy material, and are easy to place in position. If 'fit and forget' is your go-to mantra, then do not trouble yourself to look any further. I have found them comfortable on long rides, and work effectively by utilising an integrated advanced precision filter developed to help block wind noise, whilst still allowing the rider to pick up on those all-important sounds without causing muffled hearing – think emergency vehicle sirens, horns, sounds from approaching vehicles and conversations. The plugs arrived in a soft, zip closure case, and included a tube of lubricant for ease of insertion.

Verdict: Hypoallergenic, easy to clean defenders constructed of a blend of soft, flexible, medical grade silicone which are durable, reliable and very comfortable.

RST ISLE OF MAN TT GRANDSTAND LEATHER 1PC SUIT

SRP: £449.99 | RST-MOTO.COM

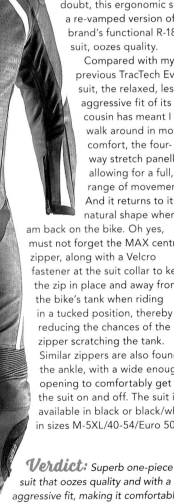

The intention never was to try and ride like a TT racer, but merely to wear a one-piece suit that offered excellent protection and day-long comfort… and I found it in this latest offering from RST.

What particularly drew me to the suit was the fact that it offered a less aggressive stance than RST's TracTech Evo suit (I recently sold mine), thereby allowing the wearer to adopt a more upright stance. That said, unless I plan for any track days in the near future, the limited edition TT knee sliders will no doubt remain pristine as I can see little point in getting one's knee down scraping Britain's roads unless I am planning on showing off… or have the bike slide from under me, for that matter. Heaven forbid if I do, but the suit, which is part of the RST IOM TT Collection, is CE Certified to Level A, and comes with CE Level 1 back protector, shoulder, elbow and knee armour, plus pocket-only hip armour and TPU shoulder cups. Oh yes, and should I be dumped unceremoniously on the bitumen having accidentally fallen on my backside, the seat area comprises double layered cowhide leather protection. The main outer four-way stretch material is constructed of leather, with soft neoprene race collar and cuffs, and a fixed comfort inner mesh lining allows for a welcoming flow of air within the suit, definitely improving the comfort factor, something I noted on some of the particularly hot days that we enjoyed this past summer.

Other notable features are triple stitching, and two useful large inner pockets. Without doubt, this ergonomic suit, a re-vamped version of the brand's functional R-18 suit, oozes quality. Compared with my previous TracTech Evo suit, the relaxed, less aggressive fit of its cousin has meant I can walk around in more comfort, the four-way stretch panelling allowing for a full, free range of movement. And it returns to its natural shape when I am back on the bike. Oh yes, must not forget the MAX central zipper, along with a Velcro fastener at the suit collar to keep the zip in place and away from the bike's tank when riding in a tucked position, thereby reducing the chances of the zipper scratching the tank. Similar zippers are also found at the ankle, with a wide enough opening to comfortably get the suit on and off. The suit is available in black or black/white, in sizes M-5XL/40-54/Euro 50-64.

Verdict: Superb one-piece suit that oozes quality and with a less aggressive fit, making it comfortable both on and off the bike.

Kit

TCX DISTRICT BOOTS

SRP: £179.99 | TCXBOOTS.COM

My go-to boots for everyday riding, come rain or shine, have been a pair of Rev'it Marshalls. These water-resistant, waxed urban-vintage style boots, constructed of full-grain cowhide leather, have served me well, although I do recall they took a good deal of breaking in before I felt comfortable in them. Not so the TCX District boots that I have been enjoying recently. Comfortable straight from the box, compared with the Marshalls, they are

like putting on a pair of favourite slippers, I kid you not. The attractive, urban styling is only half the secret, however.

The outer layer consists of ultra-lightweight, yet robust, high tenacity fabric with microfibre. Sitting underneath is a waterproof and breathable membrane, so the wearer is assured of dry, comfortable feet. The boots have a reinforced rand in the heel counter and toe, plus gear change area, which clearly helps when you are constantly shifting up. The Ortholite footbed offers excellent cushioning and a high level of breathability, so you can wear them all day, with comfort guaranteed, thanks also to the wear-resistant, anti-slip thermoplastic polyurethane sole. I take a size 44, so that is what I requested, and the fit was perfect. With a typical British foot requiring a slightly wider toe bed, I was certainly not disappointed. Lacing is simple, with the added security of a Velcro fastening cover to stop the laces getting caught in any part of the bike's controls. To complete the picture, they boast ankle reinforcements, and additional padding at the back. Size range is EU 38-48.

Verdict: *Extremely versatile, comfortable, stylish boots. With the added versatility of being waterproof, the casually styled Districts with moto-specific protection add up to one awesome pair of urban wear. Highly recommended. Just don't forget that they are not actually slippers, so don't wear them to bed.*

TUCANO URBANO STEVE GLOVES

£69.70 | NITRORIDER.COM

With a supple, yet strong, goatskin outer, the Steve glove is spot on for mid-season riding. Lying underneath the leather is a Hydroscud fully waterproof and breathable membrane backed up by a soft and comfortable microfibre lining. The adjustable tab on the cuff has two press stud options for a best fit, and the glove also features a stretch fabric inner cuff, aiding comfort. It has soft knuckle protection underneath the outer layer. The three-season Steve is also touchscreen compatible. I normally opt for a size Large in gloves, but I have found these very tight to get on, so I would advise either going for one size up if ordering on the 'net, or trying before buying. Sizes are S-XXL.

Verdict: *Lovely, soft feel, durable, three-season glove. Make sure you try before you buy.*

TUCANO URBANO POL-ICE JACKET

£ 209.99 | TUCANOURBANO.COM

No doubt many of us have in our biker wardrobe a winter jacket, one for summer use, a leather offering, waterproofs… in fact, a general assortment. So how about one that covers all four seasons? Tucano Urbano has come up with a nice solution with the Pol-ice. An odd name, undoubtedly, but in a way it makes sense, because Tucano has taken its best-selling summer jacket, the Pol, and created a versatile, attractive, short-cut jacket constructed from a tough Oxford polyamide outer shell with a waterproof, breathable membrane underneath. There is soft CE Level 1 impact absorbing armour on the shoulders and elbows, plus a pocket for an optional back protector. The removable padded thermal jacket has full-length sleeves and a soft elastic windproof inner cuff. I used the Pol-ice a lot through last winter, and I was hugely impressed with its warmth-to-weight ratio. As the seasons progressed (barring lockdown) I removed the thermal liner and enjoyed the outer on sunny days, opening the taped zips above the chest pockets, which reveal mesh vents that offer welcome airflow. Features include elasticated windproof wrist cuffs, adjustable waist, belt-connecting loop, taped seams, plus two zipped handwarmer and two popper closure chest pockets. There are also two internal popper closure pockets.

Verdict: *Highly recommended, stylish four-season, short-cut jacket with excellent water column resistant inner membrane with the benefit of a removable inner that can be worn as a separate garment.*

RICHA DAYTONA 2 JACKET

£279.99 | RICHA.EU

It goes without saying – but I will mention it anyway – that riders are spoilt for choice when it comes to choosing a leather jacket. It is a subjective matter, with style posing as much a problem as substance and safety. With different leathers, different cuts, pockets, and with or without removable inner linings, you could find yourself going through a whole store rack before deciding on one that suits you in all departments.

So let me help. I have been wearing the Daytona 2 jacket for a while, and I really like it. Yes, I have others in my wardrobe, but for a casual, lean look, the Daytona is hard to beat. Constructed of premium buffalo leather with 100% polyester lining, it offers natural abrasion resistance and is backed up by safety stitching in the shoulders and elbows, while a full complement of D3O armour is included as standard at the elbows, shoulders and back. It features two handwarmer and two chest pockets, and the detachable zip-in thermal liner with padding has a Velcro closure phone pocket and another zipped Napoleon pocket. So, what you have here is a three-season jacket that can cope with most weather conditions. Other features include a soft neoprene collar and mesh liner, specifically designed with rider comfort in mind, central zipper fastening with popper fastened closure, and adjustable sleeve zips. It also has a short zipper at the back, should you want to attach the jacket to a pair of Richa jeans.

Verdict: *An updated version of the popular Daytona 1 jacket, this classically styled, timeless, functional jacket comes with D30 protection. What more could you ask for!*

NITRO N2300 UNO SATIN BLACK HELMET

£79.99 | NITRORIDER.COM

Similar to the Nitro BG-20 gloves reviewed in these pages, once again Nitro has come up trumps with the N2300 full face helmet at a remarkable price for a quality product. I have been wearing a whole range of helmets of late, some extremely pricey, so it is funny how the Nitro has become my go-to helmet when I am popping out. I will tell you why. The custom designed multi-poly tech constructed shell features twin integrated front air vents with large contact points being particularly beneficial for ease of operation with gloved hands, and triple rear exhaust ports so you are guaranteed ultimate heat dissipation. The comfort lining is removable and washable, and I like the micrometric buckle which offers easy adjustability. The quick-release visor comes pinlock ready, and is compatible with Nitro's anti-fog pinlock insert. You also get a spring-loaded sun visor system with a side-mounted switch for ease of use.

Verdict: *If you are on a budget – or then again, even if you are not – then the N2300 is well worth a look. Bags for your buck, as they say.*

Kit

BELL CRUISER ELIMINATOR
£349.99 | BELLHELMETS.COM

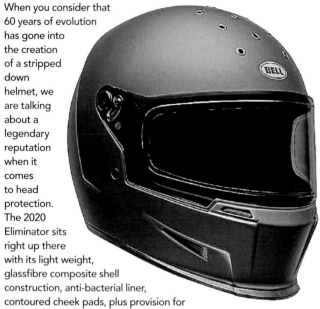

When you consider that 60 years of evolution has gone into the creation of a stripped down helmet, we are talking about a legendary reputation when it comes to head protection. The 2020 Eliminator sits right up there with its light weight, glassfibre composite shell construction, anti-bacterial liner, contoured cheek pads, plus provision for an anti-fog shield with Class 1 optics. The first thing of note are the nine circular vents that have been drilled into the top of the helmet, allowing air to pass through the shell and EPS liner. With nothing to impede the venting, they work effectively enough, as do the four smaller vents in a metal grid in the chin bar. With all those air vents, you might be thinking that this is going to be one noisy helmet. Well, there are two sides to that thought. At modest speeds it is fine, but hit the motorway and wind the power on, and you will notice the difference – but if you are anything like me and wear ear defenders, then you should be fine. I do not possess one, but as there is no way of closing the vents, I understand that Bell offers a clip-on external vent cover so you can block those top holes if you need to. Costing around £15, the smoke-tinted piece slots into place on top of the Eliminator's signature riveted vents and can be easily fitted and removed. It is also available in three size variations. My advice would be if you are buying the Eliminator, then buy one of these too, just in case. I found replacing the face shield for a darker one a bit of a faff, not having to hand immediately a 6mm allen/hex key. Should you also want to adjust the tightness of the opening/closure, you will also need a 2.5mm key. To the left side of the visor, a pin and hole lock secures the visor in place once you are on the move.

Another thing of note is the 'double glazing' groove around the inside of the visor, Bell's ProVision anti-fog system, which is neat as there are no pins involved. With it being suited to oval head shapes, you will need to check the fit before purchasing, which is obvious really, but I know some riders do buy before they try. My head size accommodates a Medium (57-58cm) helmet, and it fitted perfectly. With the retro styling comes a range of neat colour options. I really like the vanish matt blue/yellow. Usefully, the Eliminator will take a Sena 10C Evo camera and comms system. I have not fitted one yet, but imagine I would need to use a sticky mount as opposed to a clamp mount due to the thickness of the helmet's edge. I can also comfortably slide my glasses on when I have the helmet in place.

Verdict: *A stylish, retro helmet, but not that easy to live with. Suitable for the cruiser fraternity, it does come with compromises, such as the requirement of hex keys for swapping/ adjusting the visor, and the need to purchase a clip-on external vent cover unless you are a dry weather rider. If you like the looks and are happy to live with the quirkiness, then consider it.*

SENA OUTSTAR
£179 | SENA.COM

A star is born. Actually, to be more precise, an Outstar is born. The jet-style helmet comes fully equipped with a Bluetooth communication system, and like the Savage is ready for use straight out of the box. The ECE-rated Outstar was only recently made available to the European market, and is the latest addition to Sena's innovative line of smart helmets. A boom mic, speakers and control unit are neatly integrated into the helmet design, offering a communication range of up to a mile. Weighing in at 1530 grams, the jet helmet is constructed of a lightweight ECE-rated thermoplastic shell featuring a multi-layer EPS, and comes with an all-season, scratch-resistant full face visor with two inlet and one outlet port, plus a drop-down sun visor. It has a quick-release ratchet fastener chin strap, and the breathable interior is both removable and washable. Traditionally I have worn full face helmets, but I admit to really enjoying wearing the Outstar. It is extremely comfortable, and the comms system is excellent. The full face visor is easy to open and close, and the drop-down sun visor is a definite benefit. Available in Matt Black or Gloss White in sizes S-XL, if you get bored communicating with friends, you can always tune in to your favourite radio station.

Verdict: *Road-ready bluetooth integration in a quality helmet at an excellent price point. Highly recommended.*

SENA 10C EVO BLUETOOTH CAMERA 4K ABD COMMUNICATION SYSTEM

£390 | SENA.COM

I have read a number of arguments of late about the safety of riding while being able to listen to music, the radio, receive phone calls, and hear turn-by-turn GPS directions... but at the end of the day it is down to the individual and how much they see the need for such modern technology.

The ability to take real-time video recodings of one's journey is a benefit which prompted me to check out the Sena system, with the other opportunities for communication being an added bonus. The fact that the 10C Evo bluetooth communications platform comes with an integrated camera able to capture video quality at 4K/30FPS, all wrapped in a sleek, compact, aerodynamic design, sold it for me. Offering four-way bluetooth intercom up to a mile is another major plus point, particularly, on a personal note, as my daughter recently passed her CBT and is now able to ride with me and we can communicate whilst on the move.

The audio experience is excellent, with little wind resistance or noise, and with up to 20 hours of talk time and 1.5 hours of video recording, you can grab all those great moments of a ride and watch them later. Pop in a MicroSD card up to 128GB, and as well as being able to capture video in 4K at 30 frames per second, you can also take photographs in still shot, burst (eight pictures per second) or time-lapse mode (single shot every one, two, five or 10 seconds). All it takes is simple one-touch recording, as audio cues keep the rider updated on the camera's progress. The 10C Evo also includes video tagging, so any important events can be saved from a continuous loop of video recording. If you want to be really clever, Smart Audio Mix allows you to add voices to a video, courtesy of the the camera's integrated communication system, which mixes audio from the intercom and music from your smartphone into your video, on the fly. Essentially, with Smart Audio Mix, you are able to narrate your footage in real time through the intercom and capture the authenticity of the moment, while reducing the need for follow-up audio editing.

Verdict: *One truly smart piece of kit with multiple options for recording, listening and communication. Record your journey on video, and enjoy a movie night with friends...*

NEED TO KNOW

FIELD OF VIEW: 125°
APERTURE: f/2.4
LENS ROTATION: 30°
TALK TIME: Up to 20 hours
CHARGING TIME: 2.5 hours
BATTERY: Built-in 1200 mAh Lithium polymer
MEMORY: 10 preset radio stations
LISTENING IN: HD Voice enabled for high-quality phone call audio

FOR VIDEO GEEKS:

2160p: 30fps (Ultra HD)
1440p: 30fps (Quad HD)
1080p: 60fps (Full HD)
1080p: 30fps (Full HD)
VIDEO RECORDING TIME: 1.5 hours
VIDEO FILE FORMAT: MP4 (H.264)
MAX VIDEO BIT RATE: 60 Mb/s (4K)

SENA SAVAGE SMART OPEN FACE HELMET

£289.99 | SENA.COM

The Savage was the first open face helmet to arrive on the market with an integral Bluetooth 4.1 comms unit. It features a composite glassfibre and removable lining, which is very comfortable, considering it comprises integrated electronics, and securing the helmet is via a double D-ring. You will find the micro USB charging port on the left-hand strap. To the outer left of the helmet is the rotating jog dial control and a smaller push button behind it.

I appreciate that many riders wear sunglasses, but as an open face helmet, one thing the Savage lacks is a rear strap with which to secure goggles. Should you prefer clean, simple lines, however, then you will like this helmet, which comes supplied with two glass black plastic peaks – a short one and a longer Enduro-styled peak – with standard popper spacing. Most importantly, it is both DOT and ECE rated. My Medium-sized helmet hit the scales at 1100 grams, and is very comfortable on the move. As a fully integrated bluetooth unit, there is no boom mic to worry about, as it is cleverly concealed within the upper rim, works perfectly effectively, and as a result I had no problem with communication. The system also supports intercom conversation with three other people. Should you find that communication is difficult, Sena systems do come with audio boost, which can be enabled via the Device Manager on a computer or the smartphone app.

I always wear ear defenders, and have had no problem in hearing either music or callers, with wind noise restricted by Advanced Noise Control. Should you be out with other bikers, then communication is good up to a mile. Plus you can listen to or share music, take and make calls, or hear GPS directions. Generally I ride naked bikes, where sound quality is not so much affected by buffeting generated either by screens or fairings. There is a compromise 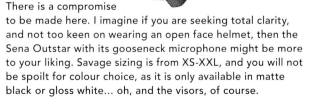 to be made here. I imagine if you are seeking total clarity, and not too keen on wearing an open face helmet, then the Sena Outstar with its gooseneck microphone might be more to your liking. Savage sizing is from XS-XXL, and you will not be spoilt for colour choice, as it is only available in matte black or gloss white... oh, and the visors, of course.

Verdict: *This excellent helmet is ready to go right out of the box, and with no hiding of wires or microphones to worry about, you can simply hit the jog dial and go. Style and comfort in one hit.*